Claire Saffitz

What's for Dessert

Simple Recipes for Dessert People

Photographs by Jenny Huang

Clarkson Potter / Publishers
New York

For Harris, my love.

Thank you for feeding me.

Contents

Chilled & Frozen Desserts   36

Stovetop Desserts   85

*Puddings, Crepes, Fried
& Flambéed Things & More*

Easy Cakes   130

Bars, Cookies & Candied Things   180

Recipe Matrix

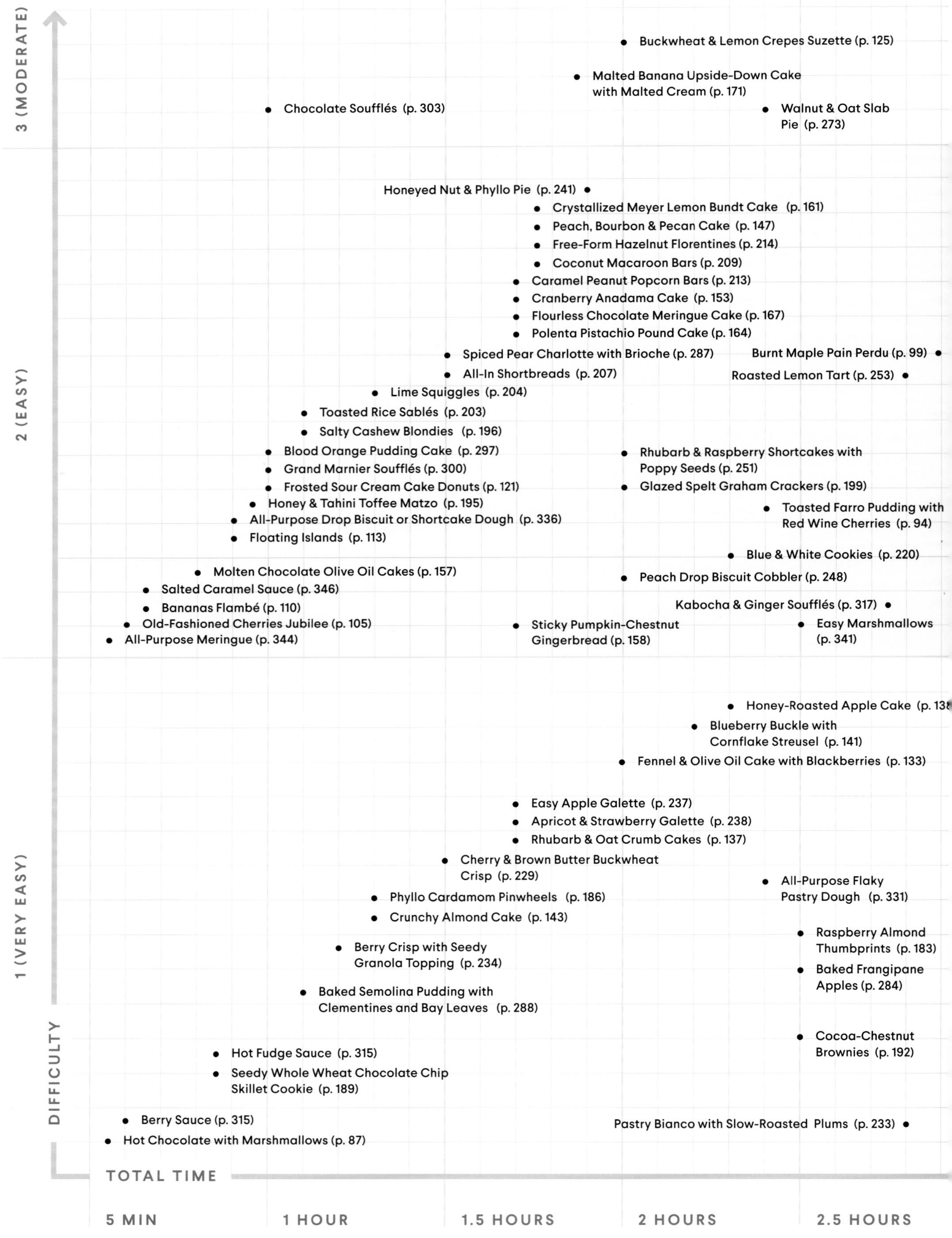

Difficulty axis (vertical):
- 3 (MODERATE)
- 2 (EASY)
- 1 (VERY EASY)

DIFFICULTY

Total Time axis (horizontal):
TOTAL TIME — 5 MIN · 1 HOUR · 1.5 HOURS · 2 HOURS · 2.5 HOURS

Plotted recipes:

- Buckwheat & Lemon Crepes Suzette (p. 125)
- Malted Banana Upside-Down Cake with Malted Cream (p. 171)
- Chocolate Soufflés (p. 303)
- Walnut & Oat Slab Pie (p. 273)
- Honeyed Nut & Phyllo Pie (p. 241)
- Crystallized Meyer Lemon Bundt Cake (p. 161)
- Peach, Bourbon & Pecan Cake (p. 147)
- Free-Form Hazelnut Florentines (p. 214)
- Coconut Macaroon Bars (p. 209)
- Caramel Peanut Popcorn Bars (p. 213)
- Cranberry Anadama Cake (p. 153)
- Flourless Chocolate Meringue Cake (p. 167)
- Polenta Pistachio Pound Cake (p. 164)
- Spiced Pear Charlotte with Brioche (p. 287)
- Burnt Maple Pain Perdu (p. 99)
- All-In Shortbreads (p. 207)
- Roasted Lemon Tart (p. 253)
- Lime Squiggles (p. 204)
- Toasted Rice Sablés (p. 203)
- Salty Cashew Blondies (p. 196)
- Blood Orange Pudding Cake (p. 297)
- Rhubarb & Raspberry Shortcakes with Poppy Seeds (p. 251)
- Grand Marnier Soufflés (p. 300)
- Glazed Spelt Graham Crackers (p. 199)
- Frosted Sour Cream Cake Donuts (p. 121)
- Honey & Tahini Toffee Matzo (p. 195)
- Toasted Farro Pudding with Red Wine Cherries (p. 94)
- All-Purpose Drop Biscuit or Shortcake Dough (p. 336)
- Floating Islands (p. 113)
- Blue & White Cookies (p. 220)
- Molten Chocolate Olive Oil Cakes (p. 157)
- Peach Drop Biscuit Cobbler (p. 248)
- Salted Caramel Sauce (p. 346)
- Bananas Flambé (p. 110)
- Kabocha & Ginger Soufflés (p. 317)
- Old-Fashioned Cherries Jubilee (p. 105)
- Easy Marshmallows (p. 341)
- All-Purpose Meringue (p. 344)
- Sticky Pumpkin-Chestnut Gingerbread (p. 158)
- Honey-Roasted Apple Cake (p. 138)
- Blueberry Buckle with Cornflake Streusel (p. 141)
- Fennel & Olive Oil Cake with Blackberries (p. 133)
- Easy Apple Galette (p. 237)
- Apricot & Strawberry Galette (p. 238)
- Rhubarb & Oat Crumb Cakes (p. 137)
- Cherry & Brown Butter Buckwheat Crisp (p. 229)
- All-Purpose Flaky Pastry Dough (p. 331)
- Phyllo Cardamom Pinwheels (p. 186)
- Crunchy Almond Cake (p. 143)
- Raspberry Almond Thumbprints (p. 183)
- Berry Crisp with Seedy Granola Topping (p. 234)
- Baked Frangipane Apples (p. 284)
- Baked Semolina Pudding with Clementines and Bay Leaves (p. 288)
- Cocoa-Chestnut Brownies (p. 192)
- Hot Fudge Sauce (p. 315)
- Seedy Whole Wheat Chocolate Chip Skillet Cookie (p. 189)
- Berry Sauce (p. 315)
- Pastry Bianco with Slow-Roasted Plums (p. 233)
- Hot Chocolate with Marshmallows (p. 87)

Whipped Cream Tres Leches Cake with Hazelnuts (p. 173)

Cinnamon-&-Sugar Apple Pie (p. 267)

Pillowy Beignets (p. 127)

Marbled Mint Chocolate Mousse (p. 77)

Mango-Yogurt Mousse (p. 83)

Fried Sour Cherry Pies (p. 271)

Coffee Stracciatella Semifreddo (p. 80)

Prune & Almond Rugelach (p. 223)

Marbled Sheet Cake (p. 176)

Souffléed Lemon Bread Pudding (p. 325)

Banoffee Pudding (p. 97)

Sweet Cheese Blintzes with Lemony Apricot Compote (p. 115)

Quince & Pineapple Jam Tart (p. 265)

Rye Bread Pudding with Rye Whiskey Caramel Sauce (p. 307)

Inverted Affogatos (p. 294)

Tiramisu-y Icebox Cake (p. 63)

No-Bake Grapefruit Bars (p. 75)

Malted & Salted Caramel Pudding (p. 119)

Crème Anglaise (p. 348)

No-Bake Lime-Coconut Custards with Coconut Crumble (p. 61)

S'mores Tart (p. 257)

Eton Mess Two Ways (p. 319)

Cherry Pavlova with Hibiscus (p. 309)

Grape Semifreddo (p. 71)

Morning Glorious Loaf Cake (p. 151)

Tapioca Pudding with Saffron and Pomegranate (p. 90)

No-Bake (18 HOURS) → Strawberry Ricotta Cheesecake (p. 67)

Black Sesame Merveilleux (p. 323)

Profiterole Bar with Berry, Hot Fudge, and Salted Caramel Sauces (p. 312)

Choose-Your-Own-Ending Custards: Crème Brûlée or Crème Caramel (p. 291)

Sugar Cookies (p. 217)

Chocolate Coupes (p. 103)

Caramelized Pear Turnover with Sage (p. 261)

Banana-Sesame Cream Tart (p. 245)

Coconut–Jasmine Rice Pudding with Lychee (p. 89)

Persimmon Panna Cotta (p. 51)

Goat Milk Panna Cotta with Guava Sauce (p. 52)

Roasted Red Plum & Biscoff Icebox Cake (p. 39)

French 75 Jelly with Grapefruit (p. 42)

Creamy Rice Pudding with Candied Kumquats (p. 93)

Melon Parfaits (p. 47)

Salty Brownie Ice Cream Sandwiches (p. 57)

Pineapple & Coconut-Rum Sundaes (p. 45)

Classic Sundae Bombe (p. 55)

Cajeta Pots de Crème (p. 279)

3 HOURS   3.5 HOURS   4 HOURS   6 HOURS   12 HOURS +

Introduction

"What's for dessert?"

It's a nightly refrain in our house. Without fail, as soon as dinner is done and before the plates are cleared, I turn and ask my husband, Harris, this question with a mix of eagerness and excitement. When I'm deep in recipe-testing mode, there's a certain tongue-in-cheekiness to the question, since we might already have a cake or pastry sitting on the countertop. But on other nights, the answer is open-ended. Dessert could be a piece of cookie dough pulled from the freezer and baked, or a spoonful of hot fudge or caramel sauce scooped from a jar in the fridge. Absent any of these options, we get creative. Harris might schmear a little chocolate-hazelnut spread over a graham cracker or whip up a glass of chocolate milk. Or, we simply dip out to our corner bodega for an ice cream bar. Whatever dessert is, I have to have it, and savoring it is a ritual Harris and I always look forward to sharing.

Asking "what's for dessert?" is more than a nightly routine, it's a personal exercise. It prompts me to imagine all the ways I can bestow myself and those around me with (edible) pleasures and comforts. Conceiving an answer and bringing it to life are acts of self-care and care for others. During the pandemic, when many of our normal sources of enjoyment disappeared, the question took on new import. I found myself at home thinking of new and creative ways I could add a little sweetness to daily life—literally.

Historically, dessert to me has always meant something baked, but this book expands that definition. Here I embrace a wide variety of desserts, from those cooked on the stovetop to those chilled in the freezer or refrigerator, as well as those served large-format and individually, free-form and composed. Whether you're into flambés, soufflés, or simple loaf cakes, there's a happiness-inducing dessert here for everyone. In celebrating this vast and beautiful spectrum, this book offers over 100 different answers to that all-important question: What's for dessert?

I hope that the breadth of recipes in this book inspires you to discover new ways of being a dessert person (or to become one, if you're not already), but I know this won't happen unless you actually want to prepare the recipes at home in your own kitchen. With that in mind, I take into account home bakers' time, space, and budget limitations in an effort to make each recipe as approachable as possible. None requires a stand mixer and only about half require a hand mixer, meaning a great number are makeable entirely by hand.

Like many people, I experienced a degree of burnout in the kitchen after preparing so many meals at home in the early months of the pandemic. This diminished ambition became an asset while I was developing the recipes for this book. It drove me to employ store-bought ingredients both thoughtfully and strategically, and to focus on simple, make-ahead recipes with wide margins of error—what Harris calls "cook's desserts." Not only can every person find a dessert here to suit their tastes, they can find one to match the time and energy they want to invest as well (see Recipe Matrix on pages 8–9).

Though none of the recipes in this book rises to the occasion of a project, they range in difficulty level from 1 (Very Easy) to 3 (Moderate). The very easy ones, like my **Honey-Roasted Apple Cake** (page 138) and **French 75 Jelly with Grapefruit** (page 42), don't require a lot of time, focus, or technique and could be made while also putting dinner on the table, doing laundry, or emptying the dishwasher (believe me, I've done all). The moderate ones, like the **Souffléed Lemon Bread Pudding** (page 325) and **Walnut & Oat Slab Pie** (page 273), are a bit more involved but provide learning and entertainment in the kitchen without being all-day affairs. No matter the difficulty level or time commitment, each recipe is streamlined so it comes together as efficiently as possible. (See About the Recipes, page 15, for more on this approach and a more detailed breakdown of the difficulty ratings.) If you're a beginner, rest assured: No dessert in this book is out of your reach.

> I developed each and every recipe with approachability in mind, taking into account home bakers' time, space, and budget limitations. None of the recipes requires a stand mixer, about half require a hand mixer, and a great number are makeable entirely by hand.

For inspiration and to broaden my dessert horizons, I turned to cookbooks by lauded pastry chefs and authors such as Claudia Fleming, Gale Gand, Gina DePalma, Emily Luchetti, Karen DeMasco, Dorie Greenspan, and Flo Braker. These works helped me get to know the canons of classic American and European desserts and planted the seeds that became many of the retro-leaning recipes here, like **Banana-Sesame Cream Tart** (page 245) and **Marbled Sheet Cake** (page 176). I also explored the charming and homespun world of community cookbooks, including ones my mom has had on her shelf for years, to learn more about the history of home desserts (these spiral-bound recipe collections, written and compiled by local organizations like church groups and rotary clubs, are gems—look for them in used bookstores and on eBay and Etsy). These sources inspired me to create recipes that feel at times humble and homey and at other times a little fancy, but always fun, joyful, and a touch whimsical.

While this book features many different kinds of desserts, there's a timeless quality to how a great number of them look and taste. In many cases, I don't mess with beloved classics that need no updating, so I provide faithful versions of **Crème Brûlée** (page 291) and **Eton Mess** (page 319). In other cases, I tweak the flavor, format, or scale of an old favorite, as I do in **Old-Fashioned Cherries Jubilee** (page 105) and **Tiramisu-y Icebox Cake** (page 63). And sometimes I incorporate familiar elements into more original creations, like **Roasted Lemon Tart** (page 253) and **Phyllo Cardamom Pinwheels** (page 186). No matter the specific recipe, you'll find the clear imprint of my style throughout: lots of fruit, no fussy decoration, clear flavors, and multiple textures.

This collection of desserts feels classic to me. That sense is a reflection of my family history, my childhood growing up in the Midwest, my culinary education in Paris, and my time living in New York City. Though what constitutes a "classic" differs for everyone according to age, geography, and life experience, I think you'll find desserts in these chapters that give you a taste of the comforting and familiar, too.

I've organized the recipes into chapters according to where and how they come together: inside the oven, on the stovetop, or in the refrigerator and freezer. The idea is to provide a certain user-friendliness. If, say, you're a college student living in a dorm, you can make no-oven-needed **Persimmon Panna Cotta** (page 51) from the Chilled & Frozen Desserts chapter, or **Malted & Salted Caramel Pudding** (page 119) from the Stovetop Desserts chapter. Or, if it's cold outside and you're in the mood to bake, select something cozy-sounding from one of the oven-focused chapters, like the **Cranberry Anadama Cake** (page 153) in Easy Cakes.

Thinking about dessert along these lines revealed fascinating patterns. About half of the recipes in the book—the ones that fall into the chapters titled Easy Cakes; Bars, Cookies & Candied Things; and Pies, Tarts, Cobblers & Crisps—get their structure from flour. The other half—the ones falling into Chilled & Frozen Desserts, Stovetop Desserts, and More Desserts from the Oven—get their structure from eggs. The wide variety of custards, puddings, and other egg-based desserts in the book means that gluten-free options abound. You'll also find a couple of vegan recipes.

While the categories indicate something essential about the recipes, they're also somewhat subjective. **Fried Sour Cherry Pies** (page 271) could be classified in both the Stovetop Desserts chapter and the Pies, Tarts, Cobblers & Crisps chapter, but, because I think of them as pies first and foremost, I decided to put them in the latter. **Blood Orange Pudding Cake** (page 297), though cakelike, is made much like a custard or soufflé, so I filed it in the More Desserts from the Oven chapter. This fluidity between categories demonstrates that, really, all desserts are related!

I've been practicing the baking and pastry arts long enough to know instinctively when to stop whipping cream for soft peaks or when curd is about to thicken. At the same time, I remember the uncertainty I felt toward these and other techniques as I was learning in the kitchen. That's why the final chapter, Essential Recipes & Techniques, focuses on the preparations and processes—both major and minor—that form the foundations of dessert, from **All-Purpose Meringue** (page 344) to Cutting Citrus (page 357). You'll find step-by-step photos and detailed instructions to guide and reassure you at every turn.

This book is my love letter to dessert. Writing it taught me more than I imagined possible about the fascinating and delicious realm of sweet flavors and deepened my appreciation and admiration for the process of creating them. Though I originally embarked on writing this cookbook to expand my own horizons and become a more well-rounded dessert person, it quickly became a vehicle for providing my fellow dessert people with a wide variety of approachable recipes. As dessert people, we share the recognition that food is about pleasure rather than guilt, sociability rather than snobbery, and inclusivity rather than exclusivity. Whether you're a fruit dessert person or a chocolate dessert person, a frozen dessert person or a baked dessert person, this book answers your burning question: What's for dessert?

About the Recipes

RECIPE PRINCIPLES

I wanted the recipes in this book to feel approachable and accessible, but I didn't want to have to follow a set of hard-and-fast rules that might restrict me. Instead, I built the following set of guiding principles that would allow me the flexibility to include recipes that ranged from quick and easy to more complex (yet still streamlined) and would simultaneously make even the more intricate recipes achievable. Here are those principles:

Ask your ingredients (and components) to work overtime. I like my ingredients to pull double-duty if they can, so if I'm using lemon juice in a recipe, I'll add the zest, too, to boost flavor. Likewise, if I'm putting yogurt in a cake batter, I'll whisk some into the glaze that goes on top. The same is true of the components in a recipe. A curd, for instance, will be folded into a mousse *and* spooned on top as a garnish. The result is recipes with shorter ingredient lists and maximum impact.

Lean on store-bought ingredients. Homemade is not always best, so I use high-quality store-bought ingredients to add flavor and texture to recipes while saving time. I rely on various jams to bring fruitiness, color, and sweetness to batters and fillings, as well as cookies such as Oreos, Famous Chocolate Wafers, and Biscoff to deliver crunch. For serving, I frequently call for store-bought ice cream, since nothing I make at home will be better than Häagen-Dazs. Used thoughtfully, these items elevate a recipe.

When it comes to fruit, use fresh or frozen. I am a fruit dessert person and usually prefer to work with what's in season, but this can be limiting, depending on geography and the time of year. Whenever you can successfully substitute frozen fruit—which is most of the time—the recipes will give you the option.

Streamline the order of operations. Even when a recipe combines multiple components—like the **Coffee Stracciatella Semifreddo** (page 80), which involves folding together a coffee base, whipped cream, and beaten egg whites—it's broken up into manageable steps which are carefully ordered to ensure a smooth flow from one phase to the next. I make sure to alert you to anything that's time- or temperature-sensitive and let you know when you can perform steps concurrently to save time.

Call upon an electric only when needed. When I call for a piece of electric equipment like a hand mixer or blender, it's because the task it performs is burdensome—or at times impossible—to do by hand. If one is helpful but not essential, I give you the option to skip it.

Keep any technique central to the recipe. A recipe might ask you to do something technical like cook a caramel or brown butter, but if it does, that technique is primary to the recipe itself. For example, if you're going to take the time to make a stiff, glossy meringue, it will be for a dessert that shows off and celebrates what's great about meringue: the crispy and marshmallow-y texture. You will always get out what you put in.

Don't skip the steps that matter. I will not compromise the outcome of a recipe just to eliminate a step, especially when the step is minor and makes a big impact. For example, I bake a graham cracker crust even when it's topped with a no-bake filling, because I want a crispy, not-soggy base, and it takes all of 15 minutes or less in the oven. If a step is included in the recipe, know it's worth doing.

Emphasize doneness, not timing. I include time ranges for most steps so you can generally gauge how long a recipe will take, but know that these ranges are suggestions, and because of differences in appliances, climate, ingredients, and equipment, they might not hold true in your kitchen. Much more important than the times are the doneness indicators, so I let you know how to determine when a recipe or component is done using sight, smell, and touch. If you focus on the indicators and not the time, you'll be more likely to succeed.

RECIPE ANATOMY

Before you begin a recipe, take a minute to read through—or at the very least, skim—the text from start to finish and note the following bits of information arranged alongside and interspersed throughout the recipe body:

Servings: Most cakes, pies, and tarts serve 8 or more, while some recipes cooked on the stovetop or baked individually serve 4 or 6 (yields are dictated by cookware and bakeware sizes). To see if you can double or halve a recipe, check the section called Can I . . . (explained below) for instructions to scale up or down.

Difficulty Rating: Recipes are assigned a difficulty rating of 1, 2, or 3 and are organized within the chapters in ascending order of difficulty. Here's what the numbers mean:

1. **Very Easy:** A nontechnical, beginner-friendly recipe with a wide margin of error.

2. **Easy:** A recipe that requires some technique but won't challenge beginners.

3. **Moderate:** A recipe that requires more than one technique, simultaneous operations, and some attention to timing, but doable for any careful home baker.

Can I . . . : This section addresses some of the most common questions I field from home bakers. It's not exhaustive, but if you have a question about making the recipe ahead of time, substituting ingredients, or scaling it up or down, you'll find the answer here.

Caramel Peanut Po

My grandma kept two very specific treats in my family visited. The first was coffee-flavore in my teeth, and the second was Poppycock popcorn and nuts that forever cemented my "bars," which are basically sliced, cube-shap take on homemade caramel popcorn. Bakin not sticky coating, while pressing the mixtur give it form. Use another nut besides peanut syrup—it's a relatively small amount and hel

Melted butter for the pan

1⅓ cups sugar (9.4 oz / 267g)

6 tablespoons unsalted butter (3 oz / 85g), cut into pieces

¼ cup light corn syrup (3 oz / 85g)

1 teaspoon Diamond Crystal kosher salt or ½ teaspoon Morton kosher salt

¾ teaspoon baking soda

10 cups unseasoned popped popcorn (2.6 oz / 75g), from about 6 tablespoons (2.6 oz / 75g) kernels

1 cup salted roasted peanuts (4 oz / 113g)

PREPARE
preferab
and two
overhang
butter a s
the mixtu

PREHEAT
preheat t

MAKE TH
and set i
corn syru
flexible s
sugar is
the mixtu
steps 3 t
remove t
soda (the

Pote
will

ADD THE
to the Du
liquid ca
and there
oven and
thorough
sure to se

PRESS TH
from the
prepared
buttered
the botto
pan and
flat, ever
to cool c

SLICE TH
popcorn
knife, slic

Can I . . .

Make it ahead? Yes. The bars, stored in an airtight container at room temperature, will keep for up to 4 days. The caramel will attract moisture from the air and become soft and sticky over time, so make sure the container is truly airtight.

Skip pressing these into the pan? Yes. While the caramel popcorn and peanut mixture is still warm from the oven, use buttered hands to form it into freeform balls. Or, spread the warm mixture out onto a parchment-lined sheet pan in a single layer and let it cool completely, then break it up into clusters.

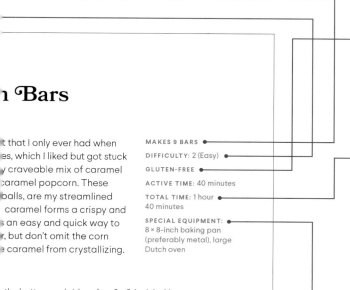

n Bars

t that I only ever had when
es, which I liked but got stuck
y craveable mix of caramel
caramel popcorn. These
balls, are my streamlined
caramel forms a crispy and
s an easy and quick way to
r, but don't omit the corn
e caramel from crystallizing.

MAKES 9 BARS

DIFFICULTY: 2 (Easy)

GLUTEN-FREE

ACTIVE TIME: 40 minutes

**TOTAL TIME: 1 hour
40 minutes**

SPECIAL EQUIPMENT:
8 × 8-inch baking pan
(preferably metal), large
Dutch oven

the bottom and sides of an 8 × 8-inch baking pan,
thin layer of melted butter, then line the bottom
with a piece of parchment paper, leaving a bit of
the parchment paper and set the pan aside. Lightly
e of parchment paper, which you will use to press
and set aside.

ange an oven rack in the center position and
°F.

a glass with water, place a pastry brush inside,
ve. In a large Dutch oven, combine the sugar, butter,
oz / 113g) water and stir gently with a heatproof
dium-high heat just until the butter is melted, the
he mixture comes to a boil, about 4 minutes. Cook
caramel (like the color of medium honey), following
king a Wet Caramel (page 346), then immediately
rom the heat. Thoroughly stir in the salt and baking
am).

t cook the caramel beyond medium golden because it
n the oven, and a deep caramel will burn.

NUTS AND BAKE: Add the popcorn and peanuts
ld, thoroughly scraping the bottom and lifting the
er the popcorn and nuts, until they're evenly coated
ooling at the bottom. Transfer the Dutch oven to the
caramel has turned deep amber, 30 to 35 minutes,
ixture every 10 minutes with the spatula and making
n of the pot where the caramel is darkening.

KTURE INTO THE PAN: Remove the Dutch oven
diately scrape half of the popcorn mixture into the
ved hand and the piece of buttered parchment,
rmly press the mixture against the sides and into
of the pan. Scrape the rest of the mixture into the
d parchment again to press it and compact it into a
fill the entire pan right to the top. Set the pan aside
bottom should not feel warm to the touch).

parchment overhang to lift the block of caramel
nd transfer it to a cutting board. Using a serrated
a 3-by-3 grid, forming 9 squares.

Bars, Cookies & Candied Things   213

Dietary Profile and/or "Serve with" Suggestion:
If a recipe is dairy-free, gluten-free, or vegan, it's
labeled as such. Additionally, if I feel the dessert
might benefit from the added flavor or texture
of a cookie or a sauce, I suggest one here (strictly
as a bonus).

Active and Total Times: These are the actual
times logged by my testers, not by me. I make sure
to factor in ingredient prep, since that's time-
consuming (flour doesn't measure itself!). Note
that when a recipe calls for an essential recipe
from the final chapter, like flaky pastry dough
or crème anglaise, that recipe's prep time is not
included.

Special Equipment: Here I list any baking,
cooking, and/or serving vessels you'll need, plus
any required electric equipment, like a hand
mixer or blender, and/or specialized tools, like a
potato masher.

Direction Headers: Keep an eye on the bolded
headers at the beginning of each step in the
directions and use them as a sort of road map. They
will walk you through the basic order of operations.

Potential Pitfall or Optional Upgrade: Within the
body of a recipe, I alert you to particularly sensitive
moments where something could go wrong so you
know to pay a little extra attention. Don't skip over
these notes—they're meant to help keep your head
in the action. Additionally, in a handful of recipes
I suggest an extra and totally optional flourish or
step to further refine or embellish the finished dish.

How to Bake with Less Anxiety . . .

I spent a significant portion of my career testing recipes written by other chefs, recipe developers, and food editors. Even as a professional, I might look at a recipe and be put off by a long ingredient list, an unfamiliar technique or process, or multiple components and moving parts. Recipes can be intimidating, especially when they ask us to venture into unknown territory—and take our time, money, and energy along for the ride.

The natural response to something that feels daunting is fear of failure, but it would be a shame if we let that fear dissuade us from taking a risk and trying something new. I still feel a twinge of anxiety or apprehension at times in the kitchen, but I've learned that if I can mentally break down a recipe into smaller parts, it feels more doable. Here are a few of my time-tested strategies—mostly practical, but also psychological—for quieting my anxiety and leading with confidence in the kitchen.

Visualize the process. Read through the recipe steps, noting all of the headers, and try to visualize the process from start to finish. For example, after reviewing the steps in a fruit crisp recipe, you might think to yourself, "Okay, first I mix the crisp topping, then I mix the fruit filling, then I assemble them in a baking dish and bake." You can even imagine yourself in the kitchen going through the motions (literally). This will help the individual words on the page recede, making them less overwhelming, and bring the general order of operations into focus.

Take baby steps before you begin. Take out any cookware or bakeware you'll need, as well as any servingware. Make room in the fridge or freezer if necessary. Grab a few ingredients and place them on the counter. Completing any of these tasks in advance clears tiny but meaningful hurdles and effectively "breaks the seal" on the recipe so it feels easier to begin.

Read and make notes on the recipe. Underline important steps so you see them coming, circle doneness indicators as reminders, and check off the ingredients as you measure them out. If you hate the idea of marking up the pages in a cookbook, let me persuade you otherwise. It helps you to engage more fully with a recipe, plus, recording what worked, what didn't, and how long the steps took in your oven or on your stove will help ensure success the next time. I've come to cherish the marginalia (my own and others') in many of the cookbooks in my collection.

Believe in yourself. Attention to detail and organizational skills can more than compensate for lack of experience in the kitchen, so have confidence in your basic competency. Though tricky at times, baking and pastry aren't rocket science, and know that you are wholly capable of making a recipe even if it seems intimidating or unfamiliar (and when you do, it's pretty empowering). In my experience, believing that you *will* achieve success can turn into a self-fulfilling prophecy.

Try to reframe your expectations. If you attempt a soufflé recipe for the first time with an attitude that goes something like, "I will only be happy if my soufflés look exactly like the photo in the book," you will probably be less than satisfied. If, however, you keep an open mind and value the process as much as the result, you stand a much better chance of feeling good about yourself *and* achieving taller, lighter soufflés next time. Becoming proficient in the kitchen is a long game, and you'll fare best if you can take hiccups in stride (and remember that most less-than-perfect desserts still taste delicious!). With this in mind, you might even come to perceive "flaws" in a recipe positively, seeing and appreciating the beauty and value in a leaky galette or a sunken cake, for example.

... AND LESS WASTE

Being a professional recipe tester and cookbook author means that behind the scenes, a big part of my job is managing (and minimizing) waste. Over the last few years I've slowly replaced single-use kitchen items like aluminum foil, parchment paper, plastic bags, and plastic wrap with reusable products. My goal is not to be perfect—I still use foil, plastic, and parchment on occasion (when I do, I wash and reuse them as many times as possible). Rather, I continually try to make more mindful decisions in the kitchen.

Below is a list of products that have helped me bake and cook more sustainably, and I've actually found that many of them work better than the single-use item they replaced (I have no relationship with any of the brands below; I just use and like their products). Some are pricey, but they're good one-time investments that'll help you save over the long term.

Silicone baking mats and cake pan liners: I use silicone baking mats sized for half-sheet pans made by the French brand Silpat, but there are many brands available. They're quite slippery, so nothing sticks, though sometimes they can cause cookies, biscuits, and shortcakes to spread more than desired (so I use parchment for these items). I also have 8- and 9-inch round Silpat cake pan liners, which are super convenient and make unmolding cakes easy.

Silicone bowl covers: I have a couple of sets of flexible silicone bowl covers in a range of sizes that can be stretched tightly over most mixing bowls (except very large ones). They're airtight and clear just like plastic.

Resealable silicone bags: These food storage bags, which come in many shapes and sizes, are a great replacement for zip-top plastic bags. I have several by the brand Stasher, which are pricey but durable, heatproof, dishwasher-safe, and tight-sealing.

Half-sheet pan covers: I use rigid plastic covers by the brand Winco designed to fit half-sheet pans. They snap into place over the rims and leave a couple of inches of headspace, which is useful if you have rising dough underneath. I especially like that they make it possible to stack pans.

Proofing bags: These are large, clear, heavy-duty plastic sleeves that seal in humidity, creating an ideal environment for proofing yeasted doughs (you just slide the sheet pan right inside the sleeve). I use them more generally when I need an airtight cover over a sheet pan or large bowl since I can fold the plastic around the sides. Proofing bags are more of a professional tool and can be found on baking supply websites.

Waxed food wrap: I use beeswax wrap, which is moldable and self-adhesive, to cover doughs that need to be tightly wrapped, like pie dough. The pieces don't last forever but can be gently washed and rinsed in cool water to extend their life. I have several pieces in various sizes from the brand Abeego that are breathable and compostable.

MORE TIPS FOR REDUCING WASTE

Compost if you can. I started composting at home because I was generating large quantities of food scraps like fruit peels and cores from my recipe tests. If composting at home isn't feasible for you, check if there's a local composting initiative in your community that will take drop-off scraps (store scraps in your freezer to manage smells in between drop-offs).

Never throw anything away. Maybe I get it from my grandma, who never threw away a tube of lipstick even when it had been used down to the metal nub, but I do not throw away food unless it smells bad or has something growing on it. I have lots of different sizes of containers so I can store any amount of a leftover ingredient, even if it's just a couple of tablespoons of something. Without fail, I end up using it down the line in another recipe, at which point I congratulate myself for saving it!

Get creative. It might feel like plastic wrap is your only option in the kitchen when you want to cover something, but there are other solutions at your fingertips. Use a dinner plate, saucepan lid, or a sheet pan to cover a bowl. To cover a sheet pan, place a damp kitchen towel or another sheet pan upside-down over the top. Reuse plastic bags and food packaging before recycling them.

Equipment

STAND MIXERS AND HAND MIXERS

I use both a stand and hand mixer at home, but because accessibility was top of mind for me as I conceived this book, I decided at the outset to call for the more affordable hand mixer. That said, each has distinct advantages and disadvantages. A stand mixer has superior power and will whip cream and egg whites quickly and efficiently with no effort required on your part, but the bowl is tall and narrow, which makes it less than ideal for folding mixtures, and it needs frequent scraping to ensure uniform mixing. A hand mixer takes some effort to operate and is less powerful, but it can be moved around easily to multiple bowls, including shallower ones, and its mobility means there are no mixing "dead zones."

If you'd like to use a stand mixer instead of a hand mixer to make any of the recipes in this book, here are some general rules for adapting the instructions:

- Use the paddle attachment when creaming butter and sugar and assembling most cake batters and cookie doughs.

- Use the whisk attachment when beating egg whites or whipping cream, or otherwise trying to work air into a mixture.

- Frequently stop the stand mixer to scrape down and around the sides and bottom of the bowl with a flexible spatula, as the attachments can't reach these areas.

- Mix on the given speed(s), but because a stand mixer will always be more efficient than a hand mixer, pay attention to the visual indicators (e.g., "light and fluffy" or "stiff peaks") and know that you'll hit the endpoint before (or at the shorter end) of the given time range.

DON'T HAVE A MIXER?

Don't have a mixer? That's okay. When a recipe calls for one, you may still be able to make it by hand. I personally wouldn't attempt to whip meringue to stiff peaks or thoroughly cream butter and sugar by hand, but, with a whisk and some extra effort, it's very possible to whip a cup of cream or beat a couple of egg whites to medium peaks.

THE IMPORTANCE OF BAKEWARE

Imagine that you follow a cake recipe to a T, preheating the oven well in advance, creaming the butter and sugar until light and fluffy, gently but thoroughly mixing in the dry ingredients, and smoothing the batter into a well-greased pan. Then, you bake it just until a cake tester comes out clean and let it cool, only to find the sides and bottom are burnt and the interior is dry. You didn't do anything wrong—the issue was likely your pan.

The type of bakeware you use has a tremendous impact on the outcome of a recipe. Whenever possible, choose heavy-duty, light-colored metal baking pans, preferably made from uncoated anodized aluminum, which is nonreactive. These heat and cool quickly and evenly, so cakes and brownies bake consistently. You can find anodized aluminum pans at well-stocked kitchen stores and on professional websites (I like the brand Fat Daddio's). Look for ones with 2-inch sides, which are the most versatile.

Darker pans, especially nonstick ones, absorb heat quickly, so cake batter will set rapidly around the sides. This leads to pronounced doming across the surface of a cake, which leads to subsequent overcooking and even burning along the sides and bottom by the time the center is done. Similarly, cookies baked on nonstick sheet pans often burn on the bottoms. On top of all that, nonstick coatings can flake off with repeated use. These pitfalls, plus the fact that you can grease and line any other kind of baking pan or sheet to prevent sticking, mean I stay away from nonstick bakeware.

Glass bakeware faces similar issues. Because glass is a poor conductor, it heats *and* cools down very slowly. When a cake finishes baking in a glass pan and you remove it from the oven, the pan stays hot and the subsequent carryover baking dries out the cake. As with nonstick, glass is not the ideal material for cakes and custards where even, consistent baking is the goal. (In some cases where overbaking isn't an issue, like a fruit pie, glass is actually your friend—it allows you to monitor the browning of the crust, and a little extra cooking around the bottom and sides is a good thing.) I also dislike the rounded corners of glass baking dishes, which result in wonky, curved slices.

I understand that glass and nonstick bakewares are less expensive than anodized aluminum and widely available at most grocery stores. If that's what you have to work with, there are a few steps you can take to improve your results: Always bake in the center of the oven, reduce the oven temperature called for in the recipe by 25°F to help mitigate overbaking, and monitor for doneness closely.

HOW TO STOCK YOUR KITCHEN

To make the recipes in this book (and really any baking or pastry recipe), you'll need a minimum set of basic tools and equipment for which there really are no substitutes. I list these under Level 1 Kitchen. It's not exactly a short list, but most items are low-cost and multipurpose. Then, if you want to make your life a little more efficient and convenient, you can add the items listed under Level 2 Kitchen, which are useful but less frequently needed, like a hand mixer. Last, for the dedicated home cook and baker, there's the Level 3 Kitchen, which lists major electrics like a stand mixer and food processor and some specialized tools you might want or need

on occasion. Stocking any kitchen is a process, so following this breakdown will help you prioritize and decide what you really need and when you might want to add to your collection.

LEVEL 1 KITCHEN

Basic Bakeware: Be sure to read The Importance of Bakeware (page 23).

- **Metal loaf pan, 4½ × 8½ inches** (measured across the top)
- **8 × 8-inch baking pan,** preferably metal
- **9-inch pie plate,** preferably glass
- **9-inch removable-bottom tart pan**
- **9-inch metal cake pan**
- **2-quart shallow baking dish,** preferably ceramic
- **13 × 9-inch pan,** preferably metal

Basic Cookware: Using heavy-bottomed stainless steel cookware will help ensure that caramel, custards, and puddings cook evenly without burning or curdling around the sides. For maximum versatility, select cookware that's ovenproof to at least 500°F, so you can go from the stovetop to the oven. The following pieces are included in most sets and provide the most mileage:

- **Small, medium, and large saucepans**
- **10- and 12-inch skillets,** preferably ovenproof

Basic Tools and Equipment

- **Bench scraper and bowl scraper:** A bench scraper is a rigid, straight-edged piece of metal used to loosen dough from a work surface and to portion and lift it (it's required to make the **All-Purpose Flaky Pastry Dough** on page 331). A bowl scraper is a curved, flexible piece of plastic uniquely suited to scraping sticky dough off the sides of a bowl.
- **Fine rasp-style grater and box grater:** A Microplane or other fine rasp-style grater is for finely grating citrus zest and fresh ginger, and a basic box grater is for grating apples, carrots, and frozen butter (to make flaky pastry).

- **Heatproof flexible spatulas:** A heatproof medium spatula is necessary for stirring compotes, jams, and other thick mixtures as they cook to prevent sticking and scorching, while a large one is necessary for folding batters, mousses, and other mixtures.

- **Kitchen scale:** I always recommend weighing ingredients for accuracy, but I know that many bakers are more accustomed to measuring in cups, which is fine—I give both volume measurements and weights for many ingredients. Regardless, you should have a scale for weighing ingredients like chocolate and fruit. I like ones by the brand Escali, which cost around $20 to $30.

- **Liquid and dry measuring cups:** Though it may sound obvious, it's worth mentioning that to ensure accurate measuring, use dry measuring cups for dry ingredients (preferably straight-sided ones so you can also use them to press crumb crusts into pans and baking dishes) and liquid measuring cups for liquids. A set of 1-, 2-, and 4-cup Pyrex measuring cups is essential, as you'll also use them to check the volumes of hot liquids as they reduce on the stovetop.

- **Mesh sieve:** You'll need one of these for draining, sifting, rinsing, and straining various ingredients.

- **Metal mixing bowls:** Have at least 1 small, 1 medium, and 1 large metal bowl, but the more the better. I use an inexpensive set by the restaurant supply brand Winco, which I like because they're wide and make folding mixtures easy. Metal bowls conduct heat and therefore work well over double boilers and inside ice baths, so they're more versatile than either glass mixing bowls, which heat up and cool down slowly, or plastic bowls, which retain grease residue and prevent egg whites from whipping.

- **Natural bristle pastry brush:** A 1- to 2-inch-wide brush is necessary for coating a pan with a thin layer of butter or oil, dusting flour off a work surface, painting egg wash on dough, and/or glazing a cake or tart. Wash it thoroughly after dipping in egg wash, or the bristles will fuse and harden.

- **Sheet pans:** Standard half-sheet pans, which measure 18 × 13 inches, are durable, inexpensive, spacious, and fit inside all but the narrowest ovens. Look for aluminum ones with a rolled edge. Unless otherwise specified, you can use a 15 × 10-inch cookie sheet or jelly-roll pan, but you might have to bake cookies in multiple batches. It's also a good idea to have a quarter-sheet pan (13 × 9 inches) for small tasks like toasting seeds and nuts (as well as making the **Walnut & Oat Slab Pie**, page 273).

- **Rolling pin:** You need a sturdy rolling pin to roll out dough (yes, you can use a wine bottle, but it's much harder to control) as well as to bash nuts and pulverize graham crackers or wafer cookies into crumbs. I like a straight dowel-style wooden pin, but if a handled or tapered French-style pin feels more comfortable, use it.

- **Ruler:** Keep one in a kitchen drawer and use it to help you roll out, trim, and portion dough to the size given in the recipe.

- **Servingware:** Many of the recipes in this book are assembled and/or served individually, so you'll need a set of 8 shallow bowls, small plates, and/or glasses.

- **Silicone baking mats and/or parchment paper:** I use reusable silicone baking mats by the brand Silpat to line sheet pans, unless I am baking cookies, biscuits, or shortcakes, as these will spread excessively on silicone. For these items, I use precut sheets of unbleached parchment, which are much more convenient than cutting from a roll, always lie flat, and fit sheet pans perfectly.

- **Small offset spatula:** This is, without a doubt, my favorite kitchen tool because it's endlessly versatile. It's essential for smoothing and spreading batters, frostings, icings, and fillings, lifting cookies from sheet pans, and cutting around the sides of pans to loosen cakes.

- **Wheel cutter:** This slices through dough quickly and cleanly and easily maneuvers around curves.

- **Whisks:** A small and medium whisk are crucial for cooking smooth curds and custards and preventing lumps in batters, while a large whisk enables you to whip cream and beat egg whites by hand. Look for heavy-duty stainless steel whisks.

LEVEL 2 KITCHEN

Bakeware

- **9- and 10-inch springform pans**
- **12-cup Bundt pan**
- **Standard 12-cup muffin pan**

Cookware

- **8- and 10-inch nonstick skillets**
- **Dutch oven (for deep-frying)**
- **Roasting pan (for baking in a water bath)**

Tools and Equipment

- **Apple corer:** For making baked apples and creating cored apple rounds for the **Honey-Roasted Apple Cake** (page 138).

- **Blender (handheld or standard):** When it comes to baking, I prefer a handheld blender over a standard blender because it allows me to blend mixtures directly in a bowl or saucepan, which means fewer dishes, but any blender is fine.

- **Cake tester:** I slide this thin metal stick with a plastic handle into cakes to test for doneness and into poached and roasted fruit to check for tenderness.

- **Deep-fry or candy thermometer:** This clips to the sides of saucepans and has an easy-to-read face with helpful graduated markings so you can monitor your oil temperature while deep-frying.

- **Dried beans or rice (for pie weights):** Dried beans or rice (or a mix) are required to weight a pie crust during parbaking so it doesn't puff, slump, and/or shrink. For a 9-inch pie, 4 cups is plenty. They can be used over and over again.

- **Hand mixer:** I've used many hand mixers from the cheapest models to the top-of-the-line ones. Generally, you get what you pay for, so more expensive ones will have a stronger motor and more speeds (I like the one by Breville, which is powerful and has a light and a timer). Some hand mixers come with multiple attachments, but the beaters are all you need.

- **Potato masher:** I mash fresh, frozen, and dried fruits into all varieties of compotes, fillings, and jams, typically inside a saucepan as they're cooking down. A potato masher, which

is wielded vertically, is the best tool for this. A large fork works but is less effective.

- **Ramekins and custard cups:** 6-ounce ramekins and glass custard cups are inexpensive and allow you to make individual baked desserts like crème brûlée, plus they're great for holding ingredients as you measure them out.

- **Reusable pastry bag:** A 1-gallon resealable plastic bag can work as a pastry bag, but the weak seams make it prone to bursting. Instead, I opt for a plastic-coated cloth pastry bag (by the brand Ateco), which is durable, reusable, and easy to clean. They come in different materials, but pick one that's around 18 inches long so it can hold a generous amount of batter or dough.

- **Spring-loaded scoops:** 1-, 1½-, and 2-ounce scoops are great for portioning cookie dough and drop biscuits, dividing batter among the cups of a muffin pan, and cleanly filling serving glasses with puddings and creams. Look for stainless steel ones with no plastic parts, as they'll last the longest.

LEVEL 3 KITCHEN

Other Tools and Equipment

- **Digital instant-read thermometer:** You don't need a digital thermometer to make any of the recipes in this book, but having one that gives instantaneous temperature readings helps take the guesswork out of cooking curds and stirred custards. I recommend the Thermapen by ThermoWorks.

- **Food processor:** While only two recipes in this book require a food processor, I use one in general for grinding nuts into meal, pulverizing graham crackers into crumbs for crusts, assembling some doughs and batters, and smoothing out lumpy mixtures. Look for one with an 11-cup bowl and extra disks for shredding and slicing.

- **Kitchen torch:** I rarely use my torch, but it's the only tool that can toast meringue and marshmallow and caramelize the sugar on top of a crème brûlée. Most broilers don't get the job done.

- **Pastry tips:** Having just a few different sizes of star and round pastry tips means you can pipe decorative frosting and butter cookies. You might also consider a coupler, which is a plastic connector that attaches the tip to the pastry bag and lets you easily switch out different tips.

- **Stand mixer:** These days I tend to use my 5-quart KitchenAid stand mixer only when mixing very wet or sticky doughs, but it's a powerful, hands-off piece of equipment that makes quick work of whipping cream, beating eggs or egg whites, creaming butter and sugar, and blending batters. It's a sound investment for the dedicated home baker. See Stand Mixers and Hand Mixers, page 23, for a note on using a stand mixer when the recipe calls for a hand mixer.

Ingredients

I stock a wide variety of pantry, fridge, and freezer staples at all times, as these are the building blocks of any recipe. Keeping them on hand means I am able to make many desserts without a trip to the store and need only to pick up a fresh or specialty ingredient when a recipe calls for it.

Chemical leaveners: Keep **baking powder** and **baking soda** sealed airtight at room temperature and replace them if older than a year, as both can lose their potency over time. Look for baking powder that's aluminum-free.

Chocolate: I generally prefer bulk or bar chocolate to chips because they don't contain stabilizers (meaning when melted, bulk and bar chocolates are smooth and fluid). Plus, I like chopping chocolate because it creates pieces of various shapes and sizes, which produce different textures in baked goods. I also buy chocolate disks or "feves" for easy melting. My go-to brands are Callebaut and Guittard. Store chocolate at room temperature, and don't worry if it acquires a streaky whitish coating—it's called "bloom," and it's just a bit of cocoa butter or sugar that has migrated to the surface, usually due to temperature fluctuations. It doesn't affect the taste, and you can use it normally. I keep these items in my pantry:

- **Unsweetened cocoa powder:** Cocoa powder comes in two styles—raw and Dutch process. The latter is alkalized, which neutralizes some of the acid and gives the cocoa a rounder flavor, while the former retains more of its natural fruitiness (to check if the cocoa is Dutch process, look for anything that mentions "alkali" in the ingredients or on the label). The difference in pH between the two styles can affect certain recipes, but you can use either one in any of the recipes here. It's your preference.

- **Semisweet chocolate (64%-70% cacao):** The percentage you see on chocolate packaging indicates how much of the actual cacao bean is present—the lower the number, the more sugar (and, in the case of milk chocolate, milk) has been added. Chocolate containing over 70% cacao is a little strong for my taste, and it will sometimes "break" when heated, meaning the cocoa butter will separate and ooze from the solids. I find any chocolate between 64% and 70% provides good intensity without being overwhelming.

Coconut products: I keep stabilizer-free cans of **coconut milk** (my preferred brands: Aroy-D and Trader Joe's Organic) in my pantry and store both **dried unsweetened shredded coconut** and **dried unsweetened coconut flakes** in the freezer to prevent rancidity.

Cornstarchs: Cornstarch is widely available and my thickener of choice for pie fillings and puddings.

Dairys: I try to buy organic dairy, but local dairy, even if it's not USDA-certified organic, is worth seeking out and purchasing. These are the essentials:

- **Butters:** I buy average-quality butter for most recipe tests and spring for European or European-style butter (which has a higher fat content and is usually richer and more buttery) for butter-based recipes like sugar cookies. I call for unsalted butter throughout because I like to control the amount of salt in the recipe myself, and the saltiness of salted butter varies from brand to brand.

- **Cultured dairy:** I am a dairy person, so I have **buttermilk, cream cheese, plain whole-milk yogurt,** and **sour cream** in my fridge most of the time. Because they're cultured, they last a long time, and I know I will cook or bake with them before they spoil. The brand doesn't matter much, as their fat contents are standardized.

- **Heavy cream:** Most commercial heavy cream is "UHT" (meaning "ultra heat treated"), which essentially renders it inert. UHT cream lasts a very long time, even months, in the refrigerator, so there's no reason not to have it on hand for baking or making whipped cream.

- **Whole milk:** I must have whole milk in my coffee every morning, so I splurge on milk from local dairies for its rich, creamy taste, commitment to animal welfare, and smaller environmental impact. If you can, try to do the same.

Eggs: I always call for large eggs, which weigh about 50g each (about 35g of white, and 15g of yolk). Extra-large eggs can be up to 25 percent larger, so don't substitute them 1:1. When buying eggs, most labels like "natural" or "cage-free" don't mean much, but if you see organic ones with the Certified Humane seal, you can be pretty sure the eggs are high-quality and the hens are cared for adequately. You can spot a fresh, healthy egg if the shell is thick and hard, the white is clear and bulbous, and the yolk is bright orange.

Extracts and alcohols: Extracts and alcohols are aged products that add depth to sweet recipes (think of them like miso paste or soy sauce in savory cooking). I keep **pure vanilla,** almond, and peppermint extracts on hand, as well as several types of distilled liquor, including dark rum and bourbon. If I had to choose one all-purpose alcohol to keep on hand, it would be **dark rum,** which is made from sugarcane and works flavor-wise in any recipe. You don't need to buy an expensive brand, but try to use something you wouldn't mind sipping. When it comes to vanilla (both for extract and whole beans), do try to seek out a fair trade brand.

Flour: Flour attracts tiny insects, so always store bags, even if they're unopened, in a sealed, airtight container. I transfer open flour out of a 5-pound bag and into a plastic bin with a tight-fitting lid and keep a big scoop inside for measuring. Weighing flour will always be the most accurate way of measuring it, but if you want to use cups, follow this method: Fluff the flour a bit (especially if you keep it in the original bag), spoon it into the measuring cup, and level. This should give you a

cup that weighs about 135g, which is the standard conversion I use in my recipes. Scooping the flour directly with the measuring cup will compact it, so you end up adding more to the recipe than intended, which can lead to dryness.

- **All-purpose:** I buy King Arthur all-purpose flour, which is high-quality, consistent, and nationally available. Feel free to use another brand, but make sure it's unbleached and unbromated.

- **Whole wheat:** If you can, buy a brand labeled "high extraction," which means it contains more parts of the whole grain and will be more flavorful. The presence of the oily germ in whole wheat flour can cause it to turn rancid relatively quickly, so store it in the freezer.

Jam: Jam is super useful in baking because it adds concentrated fruit flavor and sweetness without adding moisture, which can throw off a recipe. I have on average a half dozen different jars in my fridge at any time, but always apricot and raspberry for glazing tarts. The high sugar content means jam almost never grows mold or bacteria. I like Bonne Maman, but use any brand that lists only fruit and sugar as ingredients.

Liquid sweeteners: I keep all of my liquid sweeteners, like **maple syrup, honey,** and **light agave syrup,** in capped squeeze bottles for clean and easy dispensing. Store maple syrup in the refrigerator to prevent mold growth. For baking, you certainly don't need to use an expensive single-origin honey, but at the least buy pure honey so you know it hasn't been cut with corn syrup. Fun fact: Honey will never spoil!

STORAGE TIP

Once I open a bag or container, I'll usually transfer the contents to a plastic pint or quart container and slap a piece of tape on it labeled with the name and date (it's not the most attractive system, but it works). Keep a roll of masking tape and a permanent marker in a kitchen drawer for easy labeling, and follow the "FIFO" rule, which means "first in, first out," so ingredients don't languish and grow old, moldy, or stale.

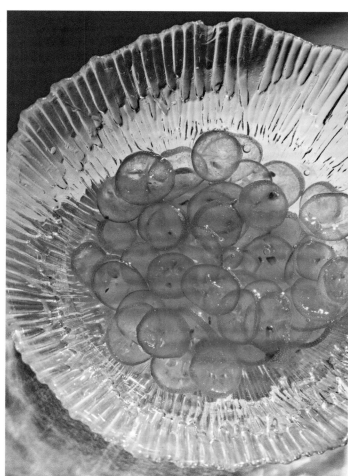

Nuts and seeds: The nuts I used most often are raw **walnuts, pecans, pistachios,** and **sliced almonds,** plus **almond flour.** I also stock **pumpkin, sunflower, sesame, flax,** and **poppy seeds.** Because nuts and seeds are high in fat, I store all of them in my freezer in airtight containers to prevent rancidity.

Rolled oats: Make sure you buy old-fashioned oats, which retain some of their chewy texture, and not quick-cooking oats, which almost completely break down when cooked. Store oats in an airtight container at room temperature.

Salt: Always keep **kosher salt** on hand (see A Note on Salt, at right, which explains the differences between Diamond Crystal kosher salt and Morton, the two major brands) and consider buying a **flaky sea salt** such as Maldon for finishing chocolate desserts, cookies, and brownies.

Spices: I keep a wide variety of clearly labeled whole and ground spices inside a drawer away from light and heat. Ground spices in particular will diminish in flavor and fragrance over time, so replace any that are more than a year old.

Sugars: Granulated sugar is a baking workhorse and the sugar you'll reach for when making cakes, cookies, meringue, and caramel. To make measuring easier, I transfer bags to a large container with a tight-fitting lid (the same one I use for storing flour). You'll want to store **light** and **dark brown sugars** in airtight containers to prevent them from drying out and hardening. I keep **demerara sugar,** which is less refined and has large crunchy crystals, on hand for topping cakes, pastry, and cookies. **Confectioners' sugar** (aka 10X or powdered sugar) is another one you'll need for making glazes and finishing some desserts.

Unflavored gelatin powder: Buy unflavored gelatin powder in any grocery store (look for the Knox brand in a little cardboard box in the baking aisle). It's not as easy to use or as dependable as sheet or leaf gelatin, which most pastry chefs prefer, but it's much easier to find.

A NOTE ON SALT

Salt, I believe, is a deeply misunderstood ingredient, both in cooking and in baking, and I want to set the record straight here: Salt is a flavor enhancer. When used properly, it makes a recipe taste like the best version of itself rather than noticeably salty. Most home cooks probably use it too timidly, and unless you need to restrict your salt intake for health reasons, try throwing a few extra pinches in your next recipe and see if you can taste a difference. You cannot build or develop flavor without salt.

When it comes to baking, salt works alongside another flavor enhancer, sugar. Much of the work I do during the testing process is balancing the quantities of salt and sugar so that each recipe tastes vibrant and focused, but not salty or overly sweet (unless, of course, I want something intentionally salty, like caramel sauce). This is why when you reduce either one, you risk muting the flavors of the finished dish. Always use the full amount of salt called for in the recipe.

DIAMOND CRYSTAL VS MORTON: Be aware of the type and brand of salt you're using. I call for kosher salt in my recipes because it's less refined and more neutral-tasting than table salt—which, because it's often iodized, I find can have a bitter, tinny flavor (most chefs and recipe developers agree). The two major brands of kosher salt available in the United States are Diamond Crystal and Morton. The crystals in Diamond Crystal kosher salt are light and flaky, while the crystals in Morton are larger and denser. This means that 1 teaspoon of Morton (which has more compact grains) will deliver almost twice as much salt to a recipe as 1 teaspoon of Diamond (the precise ratio is more like 1¾:1 but for the sake of ease, I round up to 2:1). I prefer Diamond only because the crystals dissolve more easily, but you can use either brand—just note you should always use half as much Morton as given the amount of Diamond Crystal.

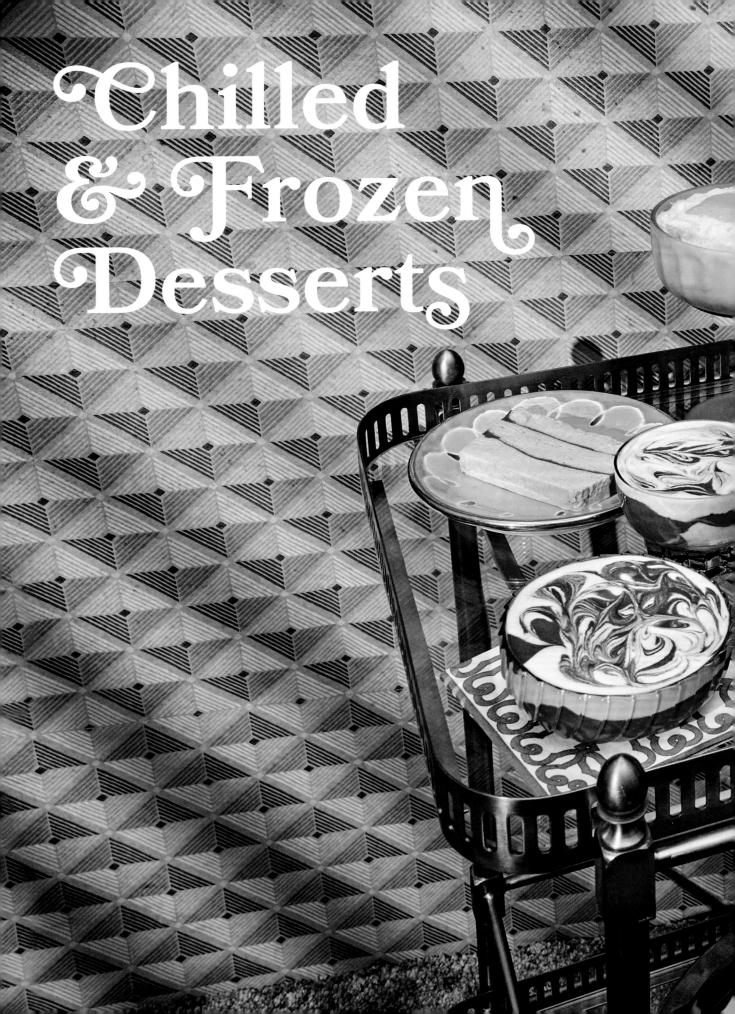

Chilled & Frozen Desserts

While the mousses, icebox cakes, panna cottas, and other chilled and frozen desserts in this chapter range from simple stir-together creations, like **Classic Sundae Bombe** (page 55) and **Roasted Red Plum & Biscoff Icebox Cake** (page 39), to more involved preparations that require a few bowls and steps, like **Marbled Mint Chocolate Mousse** (page 77), all must be made ahead to allow for thorough chilling. This means no last-minute assembly stress, and even the more elaborate desserts feel effortless when you pull them out of the refrigerator or freezer ready to serve. While there are desserts elsewhere in this book that are served cold or that include a chilled or frozen component such as ice cream, the recipes in this chapter must be chilled or frozen to ensure their integrity. Many are layered, meaning they combine multiple flavors and textures, and most depend on gelatin and/or the miraculous properties of eggs and cream to achieve airiness, creaminess, and scoopability. Coffee appears often because, in my mind, a cold coffee dessert represents the epitome of the genre, but fruit—either of the fresh, seasonal variety or the kind you can buy in a bag in the freezer aisle—gets its due, too. To me, these are the kind of joyful, nostalgia-tinged, crowd-pleasing desserts that make any occasion a party.

Roasted Red Plum & Biscoff
Icebox Cake

I sometimes have a hard time relaxing a long-held but narrow opinion that dessert should be something baked and, more specifically, something made of pastry or cake. The clever and convenient thing about icebox cake, then, is that it mimics the texture of cake with zero baking involved. It's made by layering store-bought cookies with whipped cream and other flavors, then chilling the assemblage until the cookies have absorbed some of the moisture and softened to a cakey texture. This particular icebox cake uses one of my favorite store-bought cookies, Biscoff (a brand of Belgian spice cookie), and pairs their warm, spicy flavor with tart roasted plums. The elements combine into a light, fruity, cakey confection that is definitely dessert but requires very, very little effort.

SERVES 8

DIFFICULTY: 1 (Very Easy)

ACTIVE TIME: 40 minutes

TOTAL TIME: 2 hours 45 minutes, plus at least 12 hours to chill

SPECIAL EQUIPMENT: Metal loaf pan (4½ × 8½ inches, measured across the top), hand mixer

5 medium ripe red plums (12 oz / 340g), halved and pitted, plus 1 medium plum for assembly

1 cinnamon stick or whole star anise

¼ cup demerara sugar (1.8 oz / 50g)

2 cups heavy cream (16 oz / 480g), chilled

¼ cup confectioners' sugar (1 oz / 28g)

1 teaspoon vanilla extract

Pinch of kosher salt

1 (8.8 oz / 250g) package Biscoff cookies (32 cookies)

PREHEAT THE OVEN: Arrange an oven rack in the center position and preheat the oven to 350°F.

ROAST THE PLUMS: Arrange the plum halves cut-sides up in the bottom of a 4½ × 8½-inch loaf pan (it's okay if they overlap). Pour 2 tablespoons (1 oz / 28g) water over the plums and toss in the cinnamon stick. Sprinkle the demerara sugar over the plums and transfer the pan to the oven. Roast, shaking the pan once or twice, until the halves are nearly collapsed, the flesh is mushy, and the edges are lightly browned, 45 to 60 minutes. Set the pan aside to cool completely.

MAKE THE PUREE: Remove the cinnamon stick and transfer the plums and accumulated juices to a fine-mesh sieve set over a medium bowl. Use a flexible spatula to press the plum pulp through the sieve into the bowl below, pressing on the skins to release all of the flesh and juices (discard the skins). Refrigerate the puree until it's cold, at least 1 hour. To speed up this process, you can chill the puree in an ice bath (see Chilling in an Ice Bath, page 358).

PREPARE THE PAN: Clean the loaf pan but don't fully dry it, as some water on the surface will help the plastic stick. Line the pan with plastic wrap, pressing it into the bottom and corners and leaving an inch or two of overhang on all sides. Cut the remaining plum in half and pull out the pit, then thinly slice the halves crosswise into half-moons. Arrange the slices across the bottom of the pan in an overlapping pattern. Set the pan aside.

WHIP THE CREAM: In a large bowl, with a hand mixer, beat the cream on low speed to start and gradually increase the speed to medium-high as it thickens, until you have a softly whipped cream that forms droopy peaks (see Whipping Cream, page 355). Reduce the speed to low and add the confectioners' sugar, vanilla, and salt and beat until combined, then increase the speed to medium-high and beat until you have a firmly whipped cream that holds a stiff peak.

MAKE THE PLUM FILLING: Scrape the chilled plum puree into the bowl with the whipped cream and fold with a large flexible spatula until mostly combined but still streaky (for more on the proper technique, see Folding a Mixture, page 351).

→

Can I . . .

Make it ahead? Yes. The icebox cake, covered and refrigerated, will keep for up to 3 days but is best served by the second day. After 3 days, the cookies will lose their texture and become mushy.

Use a different fruit and/or cookie? Yes. Use an equal weight of another stone fruit such as peaches or apricots, but try to pick smaller fruits that are less juicy. You want a thick puree that won't add too much moisture to the cream. Light and crispy cookies such as graham crackers and wafer-style gingersnaps work well in place of the Biscoffs.

ASSEMBLE THE CAKE: Add ½ cup (2.6 oz / 74g) of the whipped cream mixture to the prepared pan and carefully smooth it into a thin, even layer over the plum slices, working it all the way to the corners and sides. Arrange as many cookies as will fit in the pan on top of the cream in a single layer, cutting the cookies as necessary with a serrated knife so they're flush. Add 1 level cup (5.1 oz / 145g) of the cream mixture to the pan, then smooth it over the cookies in an even layer. Repeat the layering process with more cookies, cutting them to fit as needed, and additional cups of whipped cream mixture, until you have 4 layers of cookies separated by 3 layers of cream. Scrape the remaining cream (you will have about ½ cup leftover) over the final layer of cookies, then wrap the plastic up and over the filling and press directly onto the surface. Refrigerate the cake until the cookies are softened, at least 12 hours.

SERVE: Remove the pan from the refrigerator and peel back the plastic from the surface. Tug gently on the ends of the plastic to help loosen the icebox cake from the pan. Place a plate or serving platter upside down over the pan, making sure the ends of the plastic are out of the way, then invert the plate and pan together. Remove the pan, pulling downward on the plastic to help release it if needed. Carefully peel away the plastic, then slice and serve.

French 75 Jelly

with Grapefruit

People have lots of different associations with jelly desserts. Some might recall retro molded desserts one's great aunt would make for special occasions (I personally had one such aunt who never cooked but was famous in the 1970s for her elaborate Jell-O molds), or fancy fine dining desserts with *gelées* (which in French just means "jellies"), or perhaps Asian desserts, where sweet jellies are found in many forms and flavors. Regardless of your association, I encourage you to embrace jellied desserts. This recipe, inspired by my favorite cocktail, the gin and champagne-based French 75, is a particularly elegant spin on the category, and, with the addition of fresh grapefruit segments, it proves a satisfying and light end to a meal. If a more fitting New Year's Eve dessert exists, I have yet to find it.

SERVES 8

DIFFICULTY: 1 (Very Easy)

GLUTEN-FREE

ACTIVE TIME: 25 minutes

TOTAL TIME: 4 hours 30 minutes (includes 4 hours for chilling)

SPECIAL EQUIPMENT: 8 × 8-inch baking pan (or 9-inch pie plate), 8 serving glasses

4 teaspoons unflavored gelatin powder

⅓ cup sugar (2.4 oz / 67g)

½ cup gin (4 oz / 113g)

Pinch of kosher salt

3 tablespoons fresh lemon juice

2½ cups dry sparkling rosé wine, prosecco, or champagne if you're feeling fancy (20 oz / 567g), chilled

4 large Oro Blanco and/or red grapefruits (about 4 lb / 1.8kg)

SOFTEN THE GELATIN: Place ¼ cup (2 oz / 57g) cold tap water in a small shallow bowl and sprinkle the gelatin evenly over the top (do not stir). Set the bowl aside to allow the gelatin to soften, 5 to 10 minutes (for more information, see Softening Gelatin, page 341).

MEANWHILE, MAKE THE GIN SYRUP: In a small saucepan, combine the sugar, gin, and salt and bring to a boil over medium-high heat, stirring to dissolve the sugar. Reduce the heat to medium and vigorously simmer, swirling the saucepan frequently, until the mixture is syrupy and reduced to ⅓ cup (3.5 oz / 100g), about 5 minutes (pour it into a heatproof liquid measuring cup to check the volume, then return to the saucepan and continue to reduce if it's not there yet). Transfer the syrup to a heatproof measuring cup and set aside to cool. Reserve the saucepan.

MELT THE GELATIN: Scrape the softened gelatin, which will have solidified, into the reserved saucepan and warm over low heat, swirling the saucepan, until the gelatin is completely melted and translucent with no visible sign of granules, about 1 minute. Pour the gelatin mixture into the measuring cup with the gin syrup, scraping in every last drop, then add the lemon juice and stir to combine. Set the mixture aside to cool until warm but not hot.

Potential Pitfall: If the gelatin isn't fully melted, the jelly will not completely set (and, because alcohol interferes generally with the setting properties of gelatin, the final set of the champagne-based jelly will already be soft). Make sure you examine the melted gelatin mixture closely while it's still in the saucepan to make sure it's free of granules. Don't let it boil, either, as this could destroy its setting power.

Can I . . .

Make it ahead? Yes. The jelly can be made up to 1 day ahead. Keep covered and refrigerated until you're ready to assemble and serve.

Halve the recipe? Yes. Halve all of the above ingredient quantities, except for the ⅓ cup sugar, which doesn't divide easily. Instead, use 2 tablespoons plus 2 teaspoons sugar. Follow the recipe as written, reducing the gin syrup to 3 tablespoons and chilling the jelly in a loaf pan. Divide the jelly and grapefruit among four serving glasses.

MAKE THE JELLY: Gently pour the sparkling wine into a shallow 8 × 8-inch baking dish to maintain the bubbles. Slowly pour the gin/gelatin mixture into the pan and stir gently to combine. Cover and refrigerate until the jelly is set, at least 4 hours.

CUT THE GRAPEFRUIT: Up to 3 hours before serving, cut the grapefruits into segments according to the step-by-step instructions for Cutting Citrus on page 357. Place the segments in an airtight container and refrigerate.

SERVE: Divide the chilled grapefruit segments evenly among eight serving glasses or cups, leaving behind any juices that have accumulated. Remove the jelly from the refrigerator, uncover, and use a small spoon to scoop the jelly into the serving glasses, dividing evenly. Serve immediately.

Pineapple & Coconut-Rum Sundaes

The inspiration for this sundae is a drink that is basically already a dessert: the piña colada, queen of all tiki drinks (and maybe the queen of all drinks everywhere)! I usually treat myself to a piña colada only when I'm on vacation, but after enduring a global pandemic, I see no reason not to enjoy the supreme combination of coconut, rum, and pineapple whenever and wherever the mood strikes. These sundaes bring a little bit of tropical joy to winter, when pineapples are in season, and just happen to be vegan and gluten-free. Even though I make every effort not to call for extra equipment throughout the book, this is one of the few places where a food processor is necessary, since it produces a creamy, scoopable no-churn sorbet.

SERVES 8

DIFFICULTY: 1 (Very Easy)

GLUTEN-FREE, VEGAN

ACTIVE TIME: 1 hour 20 minutes

TOTAL TIME: 6 hours (includes several hours for freezing)

SPECIAL EQUIPMENT: 13 × 9-inch pan (preferably metal), food processor

2 (13.5 oz / 400ml) cans unsweetened full-fat coconut milk (not light coconut milk)

1 cup mashed ripe banana (8 oz / 227g), from 2 large or 3 small bananas

⅔ cup sweetened cream of coconut, such as Coco López (5.3 oz / 150g)

¼ cup dark rum (2 oz / 57g)

Pinch of kosher salt

2 teaspoons vanilla extract

1 medium pineapple (about 4.2 lb / 1.9kg)

¼ cup packed light brown sugar (1.8 oz / 50g)

1 tablespoon coconut oil, melted to liquefy

½ cup dried unsweetened coconut flakes (1.2 oz / 35g)

Maraschino cherries, for serving

COOK THE SORBET BASE: In a large saucepan, combine the coconut milk, banana, cream of coconut, rum, and salt and bring to a boil over medium-high heat, whisking frequently to melt any coconut fat and dissolve the cream of coconut. Reduce the heat to maintain a vigorous simmer and continue to cook, whisking often, until the mixture is reduced to about 4 cups, 25 to 30 minutes (carefully pour the hot mixture into a heatproof liquid measuring cup to check the volume and return to the saucepan and continue to reduce if it's not there yet). The mixture will look lumpy and possibly separated (depending on the brand of coconut milk), which is okay. Remove it from the heat, stir in the vanilla, and set aside.

Potential Pitfall: Keep an eye on the coconut mixture, as it will boil over quickly and make a mess. Once it boils, take a minute to regulate the heat and find the level where the mixture is simmering vigorously but not boiling. If it does start to boil over, immediately remove the saucepan from the heat and blow on the surface to make it subside.

FREEZE THE SORBET BASE: Line a 13 × 9-inch pan, preferably metal, with plastic wrap, leaving just a bit of overhang. Pour the hot sorbet base into the pan and freeze uncovered until completely solid, at least 3 hours.

CUT THE FROZEN BASE INTO PIECES: Remove the pan from the freezer, turn over, and rinse the bottom for just a few seconds under warm tap water to help release the frozen base. Tug on the plastic to pop the base out of the pan, then peel off the plastic (discard) and place the frozen block on a cutting board. Reserve the pan. Working quickly, use a chef's knife to cut the base into rough 1-inch pieces.

PROCESS THE SORBET: Transfer about one-third of the pieces to a food processor, then return the remaining pieces to the reserved pan and place back in the freezer. Pulse the food processor to break up the pieces, then process, periodically stopping and scraping down the sides and folding the mixture, until you have a very thick, completely smooth consistency with no hard frozen bits. Scrape the mixture into a 1-quart lidded container, cover, and freeze. Repeat, processing the remaining frozen base in two batches and transferring the smooth sorbet to the same lidded container. Freeze for at least 1 hour. The texture is optimal after a couple of hours of freezing, but even if frozen solid it will remain somewhat scoopable.

PREHEAT THE OVEN: Arrange an oven rack in the center position and preheat the oven to 400°F.

→

SLICE THE PINEAPPLE: Working on a cutting board and using a chef's knife, place the pineapple on its side and cut crosswise at each end to remove the leaves and base (discard). Stand the pineapple upright. Slice off the thick skin by cutting down and around the sides, following the contours of the fruit and rotating it as you go. Be generous as you cut, fully removing the knobby exterior (go back with a paring knife if necessary to remove any "eyes"). Cut the pineapple lengthwise into quarters, lay the quarters flat on their sides, then, working one piece at a time, slice lengthwise along the fibrous inner cores to remove them. Cut the pineapple quarters crosswise into ¼-inch-thick slices.

ROAST THE PINEAPPLE: Transfer the sliced pineapple to the (rinsed and dried) 13 × 9-inch pan and add the brown sugar, coconut oil, and a pinch of salt. Toss to combine, then roast the pineapple, shaking the pan every 15 minutes to encourage even caramelization, until the pineapple is golden brown, translucent, and tender, 45 minutes to 1 hour. Remove from the oven and set aside to cool completely.

TOAST THE COCONUT: Place the coconut on a small sheet pan and toast until golden brown, 5 to 7 minutes, tossing halfway through. Set the pan aside to cool completely.

SERVE: Place the roasted pineapple, toasted coconut, and maraschino cherries in separate serving bowls. Remove the sorbet from the freezer, uncover, and put it out with a scoop for a DIY sundae bar.

Can I . . .

Make it ahead? Yes. The processed sorbet will keep for up to 1 month in the freezer. Let it soften at room temperature for several minutes before scooping. The pineapple can be roasted up to 1 day ahead. Cover and refrigerate, then let come to room temperature before serving.

Melon Parfaits

My favorite way to eat juicy, ripe watermelon will always be plain. My second-favorite way is topped with cottage cheese. It's a combination I have enjoyed since childhood, and anyone who's tried a salad of watermelon and a salty, creamy cheese like feta knows it's a winning match. A parfait is a layered, chilled dessert, and this one alternates layers of a refreshing melon granita (watermelon, cantaloupe, or honeydew all work), a whipped, lightly sweetened mixture of cottage cheese and mascarpone, and fresh cubes of melon. It's a light treat, but unlike some other "light" desserts, it doesn't leave me wanting a scoop of something richer. This might go without saying, but the success of the dessert is wholly dependent on the quality of the melon, so try to pick a good one. A ripe watermelon will sound hollow when tapped, have an orangey patch (where it rested against the ground), and feel heavy for its size.

SERVES 8

DIFFICULTY: 1 (Very Easy)

GLUTEN-FREE

SERVE WITH: Lime Squiggles (page 204)

ACTIVE TIME: 20 minutes

TOTAL TIME: 3 hours 40 minutes (includes 3 hours for freezing)

SPECIAL EQUIPMENT: Blender (handheld or standard), 8 × 8-inch baking pan, pastry bag (or 1-gallon resealable plastic bag), 8 serving glasses

MELON GRANITA

1 pound (454g) ripe seedless watermelon, honeydew, or cantaloupe flesh, coarsely chopped (about 4 cups)

2 tablespoons fresh lime juice

2 tablespoons light agave nectar

Pinch of kosher salt

COTTAGE CHEESE MIXTURE

2 cups full-fat cottage cheese (15.9 oz / 450g), chilled

1 cup mascarpone cheese (8.5 oz / 240g), chilled

⅓ cup confectioners' sugar (1.3 oz / 37g)

ASSEMBLY

12 ounces (340g) ripe seedless watermelon, honeydew, or cantaloupe flesh, scooped with a melon baller or cut into small cubes (about 2½ cups)

1 lime, for serving

Can I . . .

Make it ahead? Partially, yes. The granita, frozen in an airtight container, will keep for up to 1 week. The cottage cheese mixture can be prepared several hours ahead and kept refrigerated in the pastry bag. Assemble the parfaits just before serving.

Halve the recipe? Yes. Halve all the above ingredient quantities and follow the recipe as written, but freeze the granita in a loaf pan and divide the components among four serving glasses.

MAKE THE MELON GRANITA: In a medium bowl, combine the coarsely chopped melon, lime juice, agave, and salt and blend using a handheld blender until smooth (or mostly smooth; some pieces are okay). (Alternatively, combine the ingredients in a standard blender and blend on medium-low until smooth.) Pour the mixture into an 8 × 8-inch baking pan and freeze solid, at least 3 hours. Using a fork, scrape the surface of the frozen watermelon mixture in all directions, until you've turned all of it into an icy snow. Transfer the granita to a lidded container and keep frozen until serving.

MAKE THE COTTAGE CHEESE MIXTURE: In a medium bowl, combine the cottage cheese, mascarpone, and confectioners' sugar and use a handheld blender to blend the mixture until it's light, thick, and completely smooth, about 1 minute. (Alternatively, blend the mixture in a standard blender on medium-high until smooth.) Scrape the mixture into a pastry bag or gallon-sized resealable plastic bag, press out any air, and seal (see Filling a Pastry Bag, page 342). Refrigerate until it's time to serve.

ASSEMBLE: Remove the pastry bag with the cottage cheese mixture from the refrigerator and snip a 1-inch opening at the tip or corner. Dividing evenly, pipe about half of the cottage cheese mixture into the bottoms of eight serving glasses. Divide half of the melon balls or cubes evenly among the glasses, then remove the granita from the freezer and generously spoon a couple of tablespoons into each of the glasses. Dividing evenly, pipe the remaining cottage cheese mixture over the granita. Repeat the layering with the remaining melon and more granita (no need to use it all—freeze any remaining granita, which will keep for a week). Use a fine rasp-style grater to shave lime zest over the top of the parfaits, then cut the lime into wedges and serve immediately alongside the parfaits.

Persimmon Panna Cotta

The mild, sweet flavor of persimmons has grown on me over the past few years, as both Fuyus and Hachiyas, the two most common varieties, have become more widely available during their fall season. Hachiya persimmons, the tapered, acorn-shaped variety, are inedibly tannic when unripe, so you must let them sit on your counter until the flesh has ripened to a squishy, translucent, jelly-like consistency. Ripe Hachiya flesh is blended into the buttermilk base of this panna cotta, while slices of Fuyu persimmons, which are firmer, are macerated in lemon juice and sugar and served on top. It's a subtle dessert for persimmon enthusiasts who appreciate their delicate flavor.

SERVES 8

DIFFICULTY: 1 (Very Easy)

GLUTEN-FREE

ACTIVE TIME: 30 minutes

TOTAL TIME: 4 hours
30 minutes (includes 4 hours
for chilling)

SPECIAL EQUIPMENT:
Loaf pan (4½ × 8½ inches,
measured across the top),
blender (handheld or
standard)

2 teaspoons unflavored gelatin powder

Neutral oil for the pan

1¼ cups buttermilk (10.6 oz / 300g)

1 cup ripe Hachiya persimmon flesh (8.5 oz / 240g), scooped from about 2 medium persimmons

1 tablespoon finely grated lemon zest

1 teaspoon vanilla extract

1¼ cups heavy cream (10.6 oz / 300g)

Pinch of kosher salt

⅓ cup plus 1 tablespoon sugar (2.8 oz / 79g)

2 medium Fuyu persimmons (about 10 oz / 284g)

2 tablespoons fresh lemon juice

SOFTEN THE GELATIN: Place 3 tablespoons (1.5 oz / 42g) cold tap water in a small shallow bowl and sprinkle the gelatin evenly over the top (do not stir). Set the bowl aside to allow the gelatin to soften, 5 to 10 minutes (for more information, see Softening Gelatin, page 341).

MEANWHILE, PREPARE THE PAN: Brush the bottom and sides of a 4½ × 8½-inch loaf pan with a very thin layer of oil, then set aside.

MAKE THE BASE: In a large bowl, combine the buttermilk, Hachiya flesh, lemon zest, and vanilla and set aside. In a small saucepan, combine the heavy cream, salt, and ⅓ cup (2.3 oz / 65g) sugar and heat the mixture over medium-low heat, stirring often with a flexible spatula, just until the mixture is steaming and the sugar is dissolved, about 5 minutes. Pour the mixture into the bowl with the buttermilk mixture. Reserve the saucepan.

MELT THE GELATIN: Scrape the softened gelatin, which will have solidified, into the reserved saucepan (no need to wash it first) and warm over low heat, swirling until it's melted and translucent with no visible granules, about 30 seconds. Remove from the heat and scrape into the bowl with the buttermilk mixture.

> *Potential Pitfall:* If the gelatin isn't fully melted, the panna cotta will not set, so be very sure the mixture is free of granules. Don't let it boil.

BLEND AND CHILL THE BASE: Use a handheld blender to blend the buttermilk mixture until smooth. (Alternatively, blend the mixture in a standard blender on medium speed until smooth.) Pour the base into the prepared pan and cover. Refrigerate until the panna cotta is set, at least 4 hours.

MACERATE THE FUYU PERSIMMONS: About 30 minutes before serving, slice the Fuyu persimmons horizontally into thin rounds (discard the very bottom and the leafy stem end). In a small bowl, toss the slices with the lemon juice and remaining 1 tablespoon sugar until coated. Let the slices sit, gently tossing once or twice, until they're softened and have released their juices, about 20 minutes. (For more information on this process, see Macerating Fruit, page 355.)

SERVE: Just before serving, fill a large bowl with a few inches of hot tap water. Remove the pan from the refrigerator, uncover, and lower the bottom and sides into the water for several seconds. Run a knife around the sides of the panna cotta, pressing the knife firmly against the pan, then invert the pan onto a serving platter. Tap the platter on the counter to release the panna cotta (it might take several seconds), then remove the pan. Top the panna cotta with some of the sliced persimmons and their juices. Serve slices of panna cotta with the remaining persimmons on the side.

Can I . . .

Make it ahead? Yes. The panna cotta, covered and refrigerated, will keep for up to 3 days, but is best served within the first 2 days.

Halve the recipe? Yes. Halve all of the above ingredient quantities and follow the recipe as written. You will have a thinner panna cotta that serves four.

Goat Milk Panna Cotta

with Guava Sauce

Panna cotta is known as a "cook's dessert" because it's quick and easy to make: All you do is chill a mixture of sweetened, flavored dairy and gelatin until set. I'm a huge lover of Cuban pastelitos de guayaba, which are flaky guava and cream cheese pastries, as well as other Latin American desserts that combine guava and cheese, so I pair similar flavors here, contrasting the sweet-tart fruitiness of guava paste against the mild creaminess of goat milk. This recipe calls for a can of shelf-stable evaporated goat milk (the brand Meyenberg is available in most big grocery stores), which delivers a concentrated goat flavor, or, to use fresh goat milk, which is milder, see Can I . . . , below. The guava paste, which you can find in Latin American grocery stores, is thinned with water to make a sauce that's floated atop the delicate base. It's an unimpeachable dessert that will deceive your guests into thinking it's much more complicated than it is.

SERVES 8

DIFFICULTY: 1 (Very Easy)

GLUTEN-FREE

SERVE WITH: Salty Cashew Blondies (page 196)

ACTIVE TIME: 25 minutes

TOTAL TIME: 4 hours 30 minutes (includes 4 hours for chilling)

SPECIAL EQUIPMENT: 8 serving cups or glasses

1 (0.25 oz / 7g) envelope unflavored gelatin powder (about 2¼ teaspoons)

1 (12 oz / 340g) can evaporated goat milk

1 teaspoon vanilla extract

2 cups heavy cream (16 oz / 480g), chilled, divided

⅓ cup sugar (2.4 oz / 67g)

Pinch of kosher salt

6 ounces (170g) guava paste, cut into ¼-inch pieces (about 1 cup)

Can I . . .

Make it ahead? Yes. The panna cottas, covered and refrigerated, will keep for up to 3 days, but they're best served within the first 2 days. The guava sauce, covered and refrigerated, will keep for up to 1 week. Top the panna cottas with the guava sauce just before serving.

Halve the recipe? Yes. Halve all of the above ingredient quantities, except for the ⅓ cup sugar, which does not divide easily. Instead, use 2 tablespoons plus 2 teaspoons sugar. Follow the recipe as written, dividing the panna cotta mixture among four glasses.

Make the panna cotta with fresh cow milk or fresh goat milk? Yes. Substitute 2 cups (16 oz / 480g) fresh cow or goat milk for the can of evaporated goat milk.

SOFTEN THE GELATIN: Place ¼ cup (2 oz / 57g) cold tap water in a small shallow bowl and sprinkle the gelatin evenly over the top (do not stir). Set the bowl aside to allow the gelatin to soften, 5 to 10 minutes (for more information, see Softening Gelatin, page 341).

MEANWHILE, MAKE THE GOAT MILK BASE: Pour the goat milk into a medium bowl, then add ¼ cup (2 oz / 57g) water to the can and swirl it around to "deglaze" and dissolve any solids that are stuck on the bottom. Add the liquid to the bowl along with the vanilla and 1 cup (8.5 oz / 240g) of the heavy cream.

HEAT THE CREAM AND SUGAR MIXTURE: In a small saucepan, combine the remaining 1 cup (8.5 oz / 240g) heavy cream, the sugar, and salt. Heat the mixture over medium-low, stirring often, just until it's steaming and the sugar is dissolved, about 5 minutes. Pour the mixture into the medium bowl with the goat milk base. Reserve the saucepan.

MELT THE GELATIN: Scrape the softened gelatin, which will have solidified, into the reserved saucepan (no need to wash it first) and warm over low heat, swirling until it's melted and translucent with no visible granules, about 30 seconds. Remove from the heat and scrape into the bowl with the goat milk mixture.

> **Potential Pitfall:** If the gelatin isn't fully melted, the panna cotta will not set, so be completely sure the mixture is completely free of granules. Don't let it boil.

CHILL THE BASE: Stir the goat milk mixture thoroughly to combine. Divide the base evenly among eight serving cups or glasses. Cover the glasses and refrigerate until the panna cottas are set, at least 4 hours.

MAKE THE GUAVA SAUCE: In a small saucepan, combine the guava paste and ⅔ cup (5.3 oz / 150g) water. Warm over medium heat, whisking constantly, until the guava paste is completely dissolved and you have a smooth but thick sauce (it might look a little grainy, which is okay). Remove the saucepan from the heat and let the mixture cool completely. You should have about 1 cup—if you have less, add more water to get there.

ASSEMBLE AND SERVE: Remove the panna cottas from the refrigerator, uncover, top each with about 2 tablespoons of guava sauce, and serve.

Classic Sundae Bombe

This recipe for a bombe—a type of molded ice cream dessert—combines all of the elements of a classic ice cream sundae, allowing you to serve sundaes to a crowd in one fell swoop without an assembly line. It's more of a craft project than a recipe, as it mixes and layers store-bought ingredients and involves no cooking or technique (other than toasting nuts and making ganache). I hope that doesn't sound disparaging, because it's not—as much as I love to cook and bake, I appreciate an easy recipe where all the effort goes into the looks. As long as you buy good-quality ice cream, you know the bombe will be delicious. I normally find maraschino cherries sickeningly sweet and artificial, but, when frozen inside the bombe, they become mellower and instantly evoke memories of childhood ice cream sundaes. Omit them if you must, but I think they do something special here.

SERVES 10

DIFFICULTY: 1 (Very Easy)

SERVE WITH: Hot Fudge Sauce (page 315)

ACTIVE TIME: 45 minutes

TOTAL TIME: 5 hours 15 minutes (includes several hours for freezing)

SPECIAL EQUIPMENT: 2-quart bowl (preferably metal)

⅔ cup slivered almonds (2.6 oz / 74g)

1 (9 oz / 255g) package Nabisco Famous Chocolate Wafers

1 pint best-quality chocolate ice cream

2 pints best-quality vanilla ice cream

¾ cup maraschino cherries (4.5 oz / 128g), drained, rinsed, and patted dry

2 ounces (57g) semisweet chocolate (64%-70% cacao), chopped

1¼ cups heavy cream (10.6 oz / 300g), chilled, divided

Sprinkles, for serving

PREPARE THE MOLD: Pick out a bowl to use as the mold for the bombe. It should have a 2-quart capacity (pour 8 cups of water into the bowl to make sure) and ideally be made of metal and have a rounded bottom. Line the bowl with two crisscrossed pieces of aluminum foil, pressing the pieces into the bottom and up the curved sides and smoothing the folds and wrinkles thoroughly. The foil should extend to the rim of the bowl (fold over any excess). Pour 7 cups of water into the lined bowl and mark the water line with a permanent marker or piece of tape. Dump out the water, dry the foil, and transfer the lined bowl to the freezer.

TOAST THE ALMONDS: Arrange an oven rack in the center position and preheat the oven to 350°F. Place the almonds on a sheet pan and toast until they're golden brown and fragrant, 5 to 8 minutes, tossing halfway through. Transfer the almonds to a cutting board and let cool, then coarsely chop and set aside. Turn the oven off.

CRUSH THE WAFERS: Place the chocolate wafers in a resealable bag, press out the air, and seal. Set the bag on the work surface and use a rolling pin or the bottom of a heavy saucepan to break the wafers into small pieces. Continue to crush the wafers, occasionally shaking the bag so the larger pieces settle to one side, until you have some fine crumbs and some coarse crumbs and a few large pieces. Transfer the crumbs to a separate large bowl.

MAKE THE CHOCOLATE LAYER: Remove the chocolate ice cream from the freezer. Take the lid off and slice lengthwise down through the carton with a chef's knife to cut it in half. Peel away the carton and discard, then cut the ice cream pieces in half again and transfer to the bowl with the crumbs. (If the carton isn't made of paper, just scoop the ice cream into the bowl.) Working quickly to prevent melting, use a flexible spatula to work the ice cream against the sides of the bowl, mixing in the crumbs, until the ice cream is spreadable and the crumbs are evenly distributed.

MOLD THE CHOCOLATE LAYER: Remove the mold from the freezer and scrape in about three-quarters of the chocolate ice cream mixture. Scrape the remaining chocolate ice cream mixture into a smaller bowl, cover, and transfer to the freezer for later. Use the back of a spoon to spread the mixture into the bottom and up the sides of the lined bowl in an even layer, working it up to the line you previously marked all the way around. Return the bowl to the freezer and freeze until solid, at least 1 hour.

MAKE THE VANILLA LAYER: Remove the vanilla ice cream from the freezer. Take the lids off and slice open both cartons just as you did for the chocolate, then cut the ice cream into pieces. Transfer the ice cream to a large, clean bowl and work with a flexible spatula until it's slightly softened and spreadable. Add the cherries and toasted almonds and fold to combine. Remove the mold from the freezer and scrape in the vanilla ice cream mixture. Use the spatula to press it into the cavity inside the chocolate layer, doing your best to eliminate air pockets, and smooth the surface. It should come to just below the top of the chocolate layer. Return the bowl to the freezer and freeze until the vanilla layer is firm, at least 2 hours.

TOP WITH THE REMAINING CHOCOLATE MIXTURE AND FREEZE: Remove the small bowl filled with the remaining chocolate ice cream mixture from the freezer and stir with a flexible spatula until spreadable. Remove the bombe from the freezer and spread the remaining chocolate mixture evenly over the vanilla layer all the way to the sides. Return the bombe to the freezer and freeze until completely solid, at least 1 hour. Place a serving plate for the bombe in the freezer.

MAKE THE GANACHE: Place the chopped chocolate in a small heatproof bowl. In a small saucepan, heat ¼ cup (2.1 oz / 60g) of the cream over medium heat just until it's steaming and bubbling around the sides. Pour the hot cream over the chocolate and let the mixture sit until the chocolate is fully melted, about 3 minutes. Whisk the ganache gently until it's completely smooth.

FINISH THE BOMBE: Remove the frozen plate and the bombe from the freezer. Place the plate upside down over the bowl, then invert the plate and bowl together. Lift off the bowl and carefully peel away the foil. Pour the ganache over the bombe, pouring onto the highest part of the dome and letting it cascade down the sides in big drips. Before the ganache hardens, shower sprinkles over the top. Return the bombe to the freezer and freeze until the ganache is hardened, about 30 minutes.

WHIP THE CREAM AND SERVE: In a medium bowl, with a whisk or hand mixer, whip the remaining 1 cup (8.5 oz / 240g) cream on low speed to start and gradually increase the speed to medium-high as it thickens, until you have a softly whipped cream that forms droopy peaks (see Whipping Cream, page 355). Remove the bombe from the freezer, slice into wedges with a hot knife, and serve with dollops of whipped cream.

Can I . . .

Make it ahead? Yes. The frozen bombe, without the ganache coating, can be covered tightly and frozen for up to 1 month. Any leftover coated bombe can be covered and frozen for up to 2 weeks.

Use other ice cream flavors? Yes! The recipe keeps it classic with chocolate and vanilla, but you can use any combination of two flavors as long as there's a color contrast (for example, strawberry and pistachio). You can also use another type of cookie such as vanilla wafers.

Salty Brownie
Ice Cream Sandwiches

I love the idea of a homemade ice cream sandwich, but what I'm looking for, and so often missing, is an exterior that actually yields to the ice cream and isn't impossible to eat. My goal was to create an ice cream sandwich that brings to mind a Good Humor bar, so I turned to a fudgy brownie base, since brownies become chewy and don't fully harden when frozen. The brownie batter is baked in two thin sheets, then layered with store-bought vanilla ice cream studded with Oreos for extra texture, flavor, and nostalgia. It's a salty-sweet, easy-to-eat, make-ahead treat that will have you humming to the tune of your local ice cream truck.

MAKES 8 ICE CREAM SANDWICHES

DIFFICULTY: 2 (Easy)

ACTIVE TIME: 1 hour

TOTAL TIME: 3 hours 30 minutes

SPECIAL EQUIPMENT: 8 × 8-inch baking pan (preferably metal)

Neutral oil for the pan

4 ounces (113g) semisweet chocolate (64%-70% cacao), coarsely chopped

5 tablespoons unsalted butter (2.5 oz / 71g), cut into ½-inch pieces

2 tablespoons neutral oil, such as grapeseed or avocado

¼ cup sugar (1.8 oz / 50g)

2 large eggs (3.5 oz / 100g)

1 teaspoon vanilla extract

½ cup all-purpose flour (2.3 oz / 65g)

1 teaspoon Diamond Crystal kosher salt or ½ teaspoon Morton kosher salt

Flaky sea salt for topping

2 pints best-quality vanilla ice cream

4 ounces (113g) Oreo cookies (about 10), lightly crushed

PREHEAT THE OVEN AND PREPARE THE PAN: Arrange an oven rack in the center position and preheat the oven to 325°F. Line a metal 8 × 8-inch baking pan, preferably metal, with foil, working the foil carefully into the corners and pressing it firmly against the sides, smoothing to flatten any creases. Brush the bottom of the foil with a thin layer of oil and set the pan aside.

MELT THE CHOCOLATE MIXTURE: Fill a medium saucepan with about 1 inch of water and bring to a simmer over medium heat, then reduce the heat to maintain a gentle simmer. In a large heatproof bowl, combine the chocolate, butter, and oil and set it over the saucepan, making sure the bottom of the bowl doesn't touch the water (this is called a double boiler—for more information, see Setting Up a Double Boiler, page 341). Heat the mixture, whisking occasionally, until the chocolate and butter are melted and the mixture is smooth. Remove the bowl from the heat and set aside.

MAKE THE BROWNIE BATTER: In a separate medium bowl, vigorously whisk together the sugar, eggs, and vanilla until foamy and slightly thickened, about 1 minute. Pour the egg mixture into the chocolate mixture and whisk thoroughly to combine. Add the flour and kosher salt and whisk until the last trace of flour disappears and the batter is thick, smooth, and glossy.

BAKE THE FIRST BROWNIE LAYER: Scrape half of the batter into the prepared pan and smooth it all the way to the corners and sides in a thin, even layer. Sprinkle the surface with flaky salt, then bake until the surface is shiny and puffed in places but firm and dry to the touch, 8 to 10 minutes. Remove the pan from the oven and set it aside to cool until the brownie layer is warm but not hot (it will flatten as it cools). Leave the oven on.

UNMOLD THE BROWNIE LAYER: Use the edges of the foil to carefully lift the brownie layer out of the pan and place it on the work surface. Gently slide an offset spatula between the foil and the brownie, taking care not to tear either one—the brownie is especially delicate while still warm—then carefully slide the brownie off the foil and onto a cutting board to cool completely. Reserve the foil for baking the second layer.

BAKE THE SECOND BROWNIE LAYER: Press the reserved foil back into the pan, brush with more oil, and pour in the remaining brownie batter. Smooth it into an even layer and bake just as you did the first layer, but this time omit the flaky salt. Remove from the oven and let the second layer cool completely in the pan, then transfer the pan to the freezer and chill until the brownie is frozen solid, 15 to 20 minutes.

→

Optional Upgrade: For the most aesthetically pleasing sandwiches with glossy brownie on both sides, remove the second cooled brownie layer from the pan before freezing, loosen from the foil just as you did the first layer, and transfer it to a plate or cutting board. Press the foil back into the pan, then invert the brownie layer into the pan so it's shiny-side down before freezing solid.

MAKE THE ICE CREAM FILLING: Place a large bowl, preferably metal, in the freezer for about 5 minutes. Remove the ice cream from the freezer. Remove the lids and slice lengthwise down through the cartons with a chef's knife, cutting each pint in half. Peel away the cartons and discard, then cut the ice cream pieces in half again and transfer to the chilled bowl (if the cartons aren't made of paper, just scoop the ice cream into the bowl). Working quickly to prevent melting, use a flexible spatula to work the ice cream against the sides of the bowl just until it's slightly softened and spreadable. Fold in the crushed Oreos until combined. Remove the pan from the freezer, scrape in the ice cream mixture, and use an offset spatula to smooth it into a flat, even layer all the way to the sides. Freeze until solid, at least 45 minutes.

ASSEMBLE: When the ice cream is firm, remove the pan from the freezer and slide the first brownie layer into the pan salted-side up, centering it and pressing gently so it lies flat and has full contact with the ice cream layer. Place the pan back in the freezer and freeze until completely solid, at least 1 hour.

CUT THE ICE CREAM SANDWICHES: Remove the pan from the freezer, use the edges of the foil to help you lift the entire slab out of the pan, and transfer it to a cutting board. Peel away the foil and discard. Using a chef's knife and working quickly to prevent melting, create clean cut sides by shaving off a thin border of ice cream from around all four sides of the slab (snack on the scraps). Cut the square in half, then cut each half crosswise into 4 equal rectangles to make 8 ice cream sandwiches. Serve immediately or place in a resealable bag or lidded container and freeze.

Can I . . .

Make them ahead? Yes. The ice cream sandwiches, stored airtight in the freezer, will keep for up to 1 month.

Make them gluten-free? Yes. Use an equal amount of your favorite gluten-free flour blend in place of the all-purpose flour. Omit the Oreos.

Use a different ice cream or cookie for the filling? Yes! Use any ice cream flavor you prefer, and omit the Oreos or include a different cookie. You can also use two different flavors of ice cream, 1 pint each, and swirl them together.

No-Bake Lime-Coconut Custards

with Coconut Crumble

These no-bake custards taste like a tropical Key lime pie and have an ultradelicate set, courtesy of an ingenious technique borrowed from the old-timey English dessert known as posset. Citrus juice is added to a reduced sweetened cream mixture, and the acid in the citrus curdles the proteins in the cream, causing it to set. But because the fat in the cream blocks the formation of curds, the texture stays smooth and luxurious instead of lumpy. Here I use coconut milk in addition to cream and lime juice as the acid, then I top the custard with a crunchy coconut-graham crumble and softly whipped cream. Technically they're not custards because they contain no eggs, but the texture is so smooth and silky that the name fits.

SERVES 8

DIFFICULTY: 2 (Easy)

ACTIVE TIME: 1 hour

TOTAL TIME: 7 hours (includes 6 hours for chilling)

SPECIAL EQUIPMENT: Blender (handheld or standard), 8 serving glasses

1 (13.5 oz / 400ml) can unsweetened full-fat coconut milk (not light coconut milk)

3½ cups heavy cream (29.6 oz / 840g), chilled, divided

½ cup plus 2 tablespoons light agave syrup (6.9 oz / 195g)

Several pinches of kosher salt

2 teaspoons finely grated lime zest, from about 2 limes

½ cup fresh lime juice (4 oz / 113g), from about 5 limes

5 ounces (142g) graham crackers (about 9 sheets)

¼ cup dried unsweetened shredded coconut (0.8 oz / 23g)

⅓ cup virgin coconut oil (2.6 oz / 75g), melted and cooled

1 lime, for serving

REDUCE THE CREAM AND COCONUT MILK MIXTURE: In a large saucepan, whisk together the coconut milk, 2 cups (16 oz / 480g) of the cream, ½ cup (5.5 oz / 156g) of the agave, and a generous pinch of salt. Bring to a boil over medium-high heat, then reduce the heat to maintain a simmer and continue to cook the coconut milk mixture, whisking occasionally, until it's thickened and reduced to 3 cups, 15 to 20 minutes (carefully pour the hot mixture into a heatproof liquid measuring cup to check the volume and return it to the saucepan and continue to reduce if it's not there yet). Remove the saucepan from the heat.

Potential Pitfall: Keep an eye on the coconut milk mixture, as it will boil over quickly and make a mess. Once it boils, take a minute to regulate the heat and find the level where the mixture is simmering vigorously but not boiling. If it does start to boil over, immediately remove the saucepan from the heat and blow on the surface to make it subside.

ADD THE LIME JUICE AND BLEND: Add the lime zest and lime juice to the saucepan and use a handheld blender to blend the hot mixture directly in the saucepan on high speed until it's completely smooth—this will bring it back together if it separated during cooking and reduce the size of the fat particles in the coconut milk, making for a smoother set. (Alternatively, pour the mixture into a standard blender and blend on high.) Pour the mixture into eight serving glasses, dividing evenly. Cover the glasses and refrigerate the custards until they're set, at least 6 hours.

MAKE THE CRUMBLE: Place the graham crackers in a medium bowl, breaking them up with your fingers into smaller pieces. Use the bottom of a sturdy glass to crush the pieces until you have mostly fine crumbs with a few larger pieces. Add the shredded coconut and a generous pinch of salt and toss to combine. Drizzle the coconut oil and remaining 2 tablespoons agave over the mixture and stir with a fork to thoroughly combine. Switch to your hands and rub the mixture between your fingertips until it looks like wet sand. Cover the bowl and refrigerate until the crumble is cold, at least 30 minutes.

→

Can I . . .

Make them ahead? Yes. The custards (without the crumble and cream), covered and refrigerated, will keep for up to 4 days. Store the crumble in an airtight container (refrigerated if unbaked and at room temperature if baked) for up to 4 days.

Halve the recipe? Yes. Halve all the ingredient quantities, except for the ⅓ cup coconut oil, which doesn't divide easily. Instead, use 2 tablespoons plus 2 teaspoons coconut oil for the crumble. Follow the recipe as written, reducing the cream and coconut milk mixture to 1½ cups in a small saucepan and dividing the custard, crumble, and whipped cream among four serving glasses.

Make it gluten-free? Yes. Use a brand of gluten-free graham-style crackers for the crumble.

Optional Upgrade: The chilled crumble has a soft crunch and pleasant chew from the coconut, but for a toastier flavor and more crunch, you can bake it. Arrange an oven rack in the center position and preheat the oven to 350°F. Spread the chilled crumble on a sheet pan in a single layer and bake, stirring halfway through, until the crumble is toasty-smelling and deep golden brown, 10 to 12 minutes. Let cool completely on the pan, then store in an airtight container until you're ready to assemble the custards.

WHIP THE CREAM: In a large bowl, with a whisk or hand mixer, whip the remaining 1½ cups (12.7 oz / 360g) cream on low speed to start and gradually increase the speed to medium-high as it thickens, until you have a softly whipped cream that forms droopy peaks (see Whipping Cream, page 355).

ASSEMBLE AND SERVE: Just before serving, remove the chilled custards from the refrigerator and uncover. Divide the crumble evenly among the glasses, then do the same with the whipped cream. Use a rasp-style grater to shave the zest of the whole lime over each glass and serve immediately.

Tiramisu-y Icebox Cake

I used to think I didn't like tiramisu, but when I really pondered it, I couldn't make sense of not liking a coffee-flavored dessert—it seemed physically impossible. Having never made homemade tiramisu myself, I reasoned that maybe I'd only ever eaten versions that were too boozy, too cold, or too sweet (or all three), and the desire to make my own hit hard. I take lots of liberties here, molding it into a loaf-shaped icebox cake, using Kahlúa as the booze, covering the whole thing in whipped cream, and serving it in slices. The first taste was a light, coffee-flavored revelation, and now I count this tiramisu-y icebox cake as one of my favorite recipes in the book.

SERVES 8

DIFFICULTY: 2 (Easy)

ACTIVE TIME: 1 hour

TOTAL TIME: 13 hours (includes 12 hours for chilling)

SPECIAL EQUIPMENT: Metal loaf pan (4½ × 8½ inches, measured across the top), hand mixer

¾ cup strong brewed coffee (6 oz / 170g)

¼ cup Kahlúa (2.3 oz / 65g)

3 large egg yolks (1.6 oz / 45g), at room temperature

¼ cup sugar (1.8 oz / 50g)

2 teaspoons instant coffee granules

1 teaspoon vanilla extract

½ teaspoon Diamond Crystal kosher salt or ¼ teaspoon Morton kosher salt

1 cup mascarpone cheese (8.5 oz / 240g), chilled

1½ cups heavy cream (12.7 oz / 360g), chilled, divided

1 (7 oz / 200g) package ladyfingers or savoiardi

Unsweetened cocoa powder, for sprinkling

LINE THE PAN: Line a 4½ × 8½-inch loaf pan with two crisscrossed pieces of plastic wrap, pressing them into the corners and allowing a few inches to hang over the sides (to get the plastic to stick, wet the pan lightly), then set aside.

MAKE THE SOAK: In a shallow bowl, combine the brewed coffee and Kahlúa and set aside.

WHIP THE EGG YOLKS: Place the yolks in a medium bowl and set aside. Have a hand mixer at the ready. In a small saucepan, combine the sugar, instant coffee, vanilla, salt, and ¼ cup (2 oz / 57g) water and bring to a boil over medium heat, stirring with a heatproof flexible spatula to dissolve the sugar and coffee granules. When the mixture comes to a boil, remove the saucepan from the heat and slowly stream the syrup into the yolks, beating constantly with the hand mixer on medium speed (the hot syrup will pasteurize the yolks; add it slowly so you don't scramble them). Once you've added all the syrup, increase the speed to medium-high and continue to beat until the yolk mixture is very light, thick, and mousse-y and has cooled to room temperature, about 3 minutes. Set the bowl aside.

MAKE THE FILLING: In a large bowl, combine the mascarpone and ½ cup (4.2 oz / 120g) of the heavy cream and beat with the hand mixer (no need to wash it first) on low speed to start and gradually increase the speed to medium-high as it thickens until the mixture holds a stiff peak, about 1 minute. Stop the mixer and scrape in the yolk mixture. Mix on low to combine, then increase the speed to medium-high and beat until it holds stiff peaks again, 1 to 2 minutes longer. Set the bowl aside.

ASSEMBLE: Trim the ends off 6 or 7 ladyfingers (they need to fit crosswise along the bottom of the loaf pan in a tight-fitting row) and set the ladyfingers aside. Scrape a level ½ cup (2.5 oz / 70g) of the filling into the lined loaf pan and use the back of a spoon to spread it across the bottom all the way to the sides and corners in an even layer. Quickly dunk the trimmed ladyfingers, one at a time, into the coffee-Kahlúa mixture, then place them crosswise in a row in the pan. Scrape a level 1 cup (4.9 oz / 140g) of the filling over the ladyfingers in the pan, spreading it in an even layer. Repeat the trimming, dipping, and arranging process for a second layer of ladyfingers and top with another 1 cup of the filling, spreading it evenly. Add a third crosswise layer of dipped ladyfingers, noting that you won't have to trim them this time because the top of the pan is wider than the base. Scrape the remaining filling on top and smooth it all the way to the sides and into the corners.

$\rightarrow$

Can I...

Make it ahead? Yes. Prior to being covered in whipped cream, the icebox cake can be kept covered and refrigerated in the pan for up to 2 days, but it's best served within 24 hours to prevent the ladyfingers from becoming too soggy. The finished cake can be covered with whipped cream, loosely covered, and refrigerated for up to 4 hours. Dust with cocoa powder just before serving. Any leftovers can be stored in an airtight container and refrigerated for up to 24 hours.

Use a stand mixer instead of a hand mixer? Yes, but . . . For recipes like this one that require you to whip multiple components separately before combining them, a hand mixer is the better tool because you can easily move it around to different bowls. If a stand mixer is your only option, place the yolks in the stand mixer and drizzle in the hot syrup, beating with the whisk attachment. Scrape the cooled whipped yolk mixture into a separate bowl, then use the stand mixer to beat the cream and mascarpone and make the filling. Note that the components will whip faster in the stand mixer, so pay attention to the doneness indicators.

CHILL: Wrap the plastic up and over the top of the pan and press it gently onto the surface of the filling. Refrigerate until the filling is set and the ladyfingers are completely softened, at least 12 hours.

WHIP THE CREAM: Just before serving, in a medium bowl, with a whisk or the hand mixer, whip the remaining 1 cup (8.5 oz / 240g) cream on medium-low speed to start and gradually increase the speed to medium-high as it thickens, until you have medium peaks (see Whipping Cream, page 355).

TOP WITH CREAM AND SERVE: Remove the loaf pan from the refrigerator and peel back the plastic from the surface. Tug gently on the overhang of the plastic to help loosen the icebox cake from the pan. Place a plate or serving platter upside down over the pan, making sure the ends of the plastic are out of the way, then invert the plate and pan together. Remove the pan, pulling downward on the plastic to help release it if needed, then carefully peel away the plastic. Scrape the whipped cream over the icebox cake and spread it across the top and down the sides. Sprinkle the icebox cake lightly with cocoa powder, then cut crosswise into slices and serve.

No-Bake Strawberry Ricotta Cheesecake

Coeur à la crème is exactly the kind of dessert I want to eat in summertime with fresh berries. It's a lightly sweetened mixture of heavy cream and cream cheese (though sometimes crème fraîche, ricotta, or farmer cheese) that's whipped, spread into a heart-shaped mold lined with cheesecloth, and drained overnight in the fridge until it's creamy and thick. The filling for this no-bake cheesecake is a spin on coeur à la crème, made with ricotta and brightened with lemon juice. Chilled in a graham cracker crust and covered with a set strawberry topping, it becomes a light, fresh, no-bake cheesecake (actually, the crust is baked, so it's not technically a no-bake recipe, but let's not split hairs).

SERVES 8

DIFFICULTY: 2 (Easy)

ACTIVE TIME: 1 hour 30 minutes

TOTAL TIME: 18 hours (mostly for straining the filling)

SPECIAL EQUIPMENT: Blender (handheld or standard), hand mixer, cheesecloth, 9-inch springform pan

FILLING

1¼ cups whole-milk ricotta cheese (10.6 oz / 300g)

½ cup confectioners' sugar (1.9 oz / 55g)

2 tablespoons fresh lemon juice

2 teaspoons vanilla extract

1 teaspoon finely grated lemon zest

¾ teaspoon Diamond Crystal kosher salt or ¼ teaspoon Morton kosher salt

8 ounces (225g) cream cheese, cut into 1-inch pieces, chilled

¾ cup heavy cream (6.3 oz / 180g), chilled

CRUST

6 ounces (170g) graham crackers (about 11 sheets)

4 tablespoons unsalted butter (2 oz / 57g), melted and cooled

3 tablespoons granulated sugar

1 large egg yolk (0.5 oz / 15g)

Pinch of kosher salt

STRAWBERRY TOPPING

10 ounces (283g) strawberries, hulled and thinly sliced lengthwise

⅓ cup granulated sugar (2.4 oz / 67g)

1 teaspoon unflavored gelatin powder

BLEND THE RICOTTA MIXTURE: In a medium bowl, combine the ricotta, confectioners' sugar, lemon juice, vanilla, zest, and salt and stir with a flexible spatula to incorporate the confectioners' sugar, then blend the mixture on high using a handheld blender until it's completely smooth without a speck of graininess. (Alternatively, combine the ingredients in a standard blender and blend on high speed until completely smooth, then scrape into a medium bowl.) Set the bowl aside and reserve the blender.

MAKE THE FILLING: In a separate medium bowl, combine the cream cheese and heavy cream and blend with the handheld blender until the mixture is smooth, lump-free, and thick. (Alternatively, combine them in a standard blender and blend on medium-high, then scrape into a separate medium bowl.) Using a hand mixer, beat the cream cheese mixture on medium-low and gradually add the ricotta mixture, mixing until incorporated, then increase the speed to medium-high and beat until you have a light, thick mixture that holds its shape, about 30 seconds longer.

DRAIN THE FILLING: Line a mesh sieve with a double layer of cheesecloth, leaving several inches of overhang, and set it over a medium bowl. Scrape the filling into the sieve, fold the cheesecloth up and over the filling, and place a small plate on top. Place two 15-ounce cans on top of the plate, then refrigerate until the filling has released a couple of tablespoons of water and has thickened to the consistency of whipped cream cheese, 12 to 18 hours.

PREHEAT THE OVEN: Arrange an oven rack in the center position and preheat the oven to 350°F.

MAKE THE CRUST: Place the graham crackers in a resealable bag, press out the air, and seal. Use a rolling pin or heavy-bottomed saucepan to crush the crackers, periodically shaking the bag so the larger pieces settle to one side, and continue to crush until you have very fine, uniform crumbs. (You can also pulse them in a food processor until finely ground, but it's very doable by hand.) Transfer the crumbs to a medium bowl and add the melted butter, granulated sugar, yolk, and salt. Toss with a fork until the mixture is well combined, then rub the mixture with your fingertips until it looks like wet sand.

$\rightarrow$

PRESS IN THE CRUST AND BAKE: Transfer half the mixture to a 9-inch springform pan and scatter the crumbs evenly around the perimeter. Use a straight-sided glass or 1-cup dry measure to very firmly press the crumbs 1¾ inches up the sides, then scatter the remaining crumbs across the bottom of the pan and use the bottom of the glass or measuring cup to flatten the mixture into an even layer. Place the springform pan on a sheet pan and bake until the crust is fragrant, firm to the touch, and dark brown around the edges, 13 to 18 minutes. Remove from the oven and let cool completely.

FILL THE CRUST: Remove the filling from the refrigerator, uncover, and gently turn it out of the cheesecloth into the prepared crust (discard any liquid it released into the bowl; you can wash and reuse the cheesecloth). Use the back of a spoon or a spatula to smooth the filling into a flat, even layer all the way to the sides. Loosely cover the pan and refrigerate while you make the strawberry topping.

MACERATE THE STRAWBERRIES: Fill a small saucepan with about 1 inch of water and bring to a simmer over medium heat, then reduce the heat to low to maintain a bare simmer. In a heatproof medium bowl, combine the strawberries and granulated sugar and toss gently to combine. Cover the bowl tightly with plastic or a silicone bowl cover and set it over the saucepan, making sure the bottom of the bowl isn't touching the water (this is called a double boiler—for more information, see Setting Up a Double Boiler, page 341). Allow the berries to macerate, swirling the bowl several times to help dissolve the sugar, until they're softened and swimming in a translucent red liquid, 15 to 20 minutes. Remove the bowl from the saucepan and set aside. Empty the saucepan and reserve.

MAKE THE STRAWBERRY TOPPING: Place 2 tablespoons cold tap water in a small shallow bowl and sprinkle the gelatin evenly over the top (do not stir). Set the mixture aside to allow the gelatin to soften, 5 to 10 minutes (for more information, see Softening Gelatin, page 341). Scrape the softened gelatin, which will have solidified, into the reserved saucepan and warm over low heat, swirling until it's completely melted and translucent with no visible granules, about 30 seconds. Remove from the heat and scrape the melted gelatin into the bowl with the macerated strawberries and stir gently to combine. Refrigerate the strawberry topping, stirring it every 10 minutes or so, until the liquid has thickened but not fully set, 30 to 40 minutes.

TOP THE CHEESECAKE AND CHILL: Remove the springform pan from the refrigerator, uncover, and gently spoon the warm strawberry mixture evenly over the surface, distributing the slices all around and drizzling any juices over the top. Loosely cover again and refrigerate until both the filling and topping are completely set, at least 4 hours.

Can I . . .

Make it ahead? Yes. The cheesecake, covered loosely and refrigerated, will keep for up to 2 days but is best served within 24 hours to prevent the crust from becoming soggy.

Make it gluten-free? Yes. Use a brand of gluten-free graham-style crackers for the crust.

Use a stand mixer instead of a hand mixer? Yes. To make the filling, place the blended cream cheese mixture in a stand mixer fitted with the whisk attachment and proceed with the recipe as written.

A WORD ON CURD

Curd is perhaps my favorite pastry preparation and one of the first things I taught myself how to make when I began baking. While it can be served on its own, topped with berries and whipped cream, curd is most commonly used as a component in other desserts like mousses, trifles, tarts, and pavlovas. I consider curd an essential recipe, but I don't feature it in the Essential Recipes & Techniques chapter because I use several variations throughout this book, each with a different fruit as its base (and therefore, a slightly different approach). So I'll take a moment here, then, to share some of its finer points.

Curd is a type of stirred custard ("stirred" indicating that it's cooked on the stovetop) that's citrus-based rather than dairy-based—though it does have butter in it—and that gets its thick texture from egg yolks and no added starch. Traditional curd enriches lemon juice with eggs, butter, and sugar and transforms it from a puckeringly sour liquid into a thick, silky, delicious, sweet-tart mixture.

The eggs in curd need acid to set. Lemon and lime are typical, but you can substitute juice from other acidic fruits such as pomegranate, passion fruit, and cranberries, too. You can also incorporate sweeter fruits as long as you bolster them with sufficient acid from lemon or lime juice. Whether you're making Concord grape curd for **Grape Semifreddo** (see opposite), mango curd for **Mango-Yogurt Mousse** (page 83), passion fruit curd for **Eton Mess** (page 319), or lemon curd for **Souffléed Lemon Bread Pudding** (page 325), follow these tips for a thick, smooth consistency:

Use a heavy saucepan. To prevent the eggs from curdling as the mixture cooks, use a saucepan with thick walls and a heavy bottom, which heats evenly. A thinner, lighter saucepan could overcook and scorch the mixture around the sides. If that's the only type of saucepan you have, consider cooking

the curd instead in a double boiler (see Setting Up a Double Boiler, page 341). The gentler heat of a double boiler will cook the eggs slowly and evenly.

Stir constantly and watch for signs of thickening. Curd must be stirred or whisked constantly over low to medium heat until the eggs thicken (never let it boil, as this will overcook it). The change that occurs at this point can be subtle, so here are the signs that it's done cooking:

- Any foam on the surface (a result of constantly agitating the mixture) will dissipate.

- It will go from translucent to opaque.

- It will be thick enough to coat the back of a spoon (see above).

- If you have an instant-read thermometer, it will register 170°F.

Store curd in a nonreactive container. I've made the mistake of refrigerating curd overnight in a metal bowl only to find the next day that it's taken on a metallic flavor. This is because the acid in curd reacts with metal (including stainless steel), so store it in a glass or plastic container and cover tightly.

Grape Semifreddo

Manischewitz wine, grape jelly, and Dimetapp (yes, the cough syrup) all pretty much put me off Concord grapes for decades. But real, ripe, in-season Concord grapes are one of the most fragrant and flavorful fruits, and I am now obsessed with extracting their unique character in a way that also avoids their annoying seeds and tough skins. Grape curd, I've found, is a particularly delicious application, and here I use it as a base to create a light, creamy semifreddo. The weather is usually still warm at the height of Concord season, so enjoy this before the cooler weather sets in and the grapes disappear.

SERVES 8

DIFFICULTY: 2 (Easy)

SERVE WITH: Glazed Spelt Graham Crackers (page 199)

ACTIVE TIME: 1 hour

TOTAL TIME: 8 hours (includes several hours for chilling and freezing)

SPECIAL EQUIPMENT: Potato masher, metal loaf pan (4½ × 8½ inches, measured across the top), hand mixer

2 cups Concord grapes (10.4 oz / 296g), picked from the stem and rinsed

2 teaspoons finely grated lemon zest

⅓ cup fresh lemon juice (2.7 oz / 77g), from about 2 lemons

½ teaspoon Diamond Crystal kosher salt or ¼ teaspoon Morton kosher salt, plus a pinch

4 large egg yolks (2.1 oz / 60g)

¾ cup sugar (5.3 oz / 150g), divided

1 stick unsalted butter (4 oz / 113g), cut into ½-inch pieces, chilled

1 teaspoon vanilla extract

1½ cups heavy cream (12.7 oz / 360g), chilled

2 large egg whites (2.5 oz / 70g), at room temperature

COOK DOWN THE GRAPES: In a small saucepan, combine the grapes and ¼ cup (2 oz / 57g) water and bring to a boil over medium-high heat. Reduce the heat to medium and cook, mashing the grapes often with a potato masher until they're broken down and the skins and seeds are swimming in liquid, about 4 minutes. Switch to a heatproof flexible spatula and continue to cook, stirring the mixture often, until it's thickened and reduced to about ¾ cup, another 8 to 12 minutes (pour it into a heatproof liquid measuring cup to check the volume, then return to the saucepan and continue to reduce if it's not there yet).

COOK THE GRAPE CURD: Remove the saucepan from the heat and stir in the lemon zest, lemon juice, and ½ teaspoon salt, then set aside. In a medium bowl, whisk the yolks and ½ cup (3.5 oz / 100g) of the sugar until combined, then whisk vigorously until the mixture is light, thick, and pale, about 30 seconds. Whisking constantly, slowly stream the grape mixture into the yolk mixture. Return the entire mixture to the saucepan and cook it over medium-low heat, whisking constantly, until the foam subsides, the curd barely holds the marks of the whisk, and it's thick enough to coat the back of a spoon, about 3 minutes (see A Word on Curd, opposite, for a photo of curd coating a spoon—if you want a more precise endpoint, it will register 170°F on an instant-read thermometer). Immediately remove the saucepan from the heat.

WHISK IN THE BUTTER AND VANILLA: Whisk in the butter a piece or two at a time, waiting for the pieces to disappear before adding more, until all the butter is incorporated and the mixture is smooth. Whisk in the vanilla.

CHILL THE CURD: Pass the curd through a fine-mesh sieve into a medium glass or plastic bowl or container and press on the solids with a flexible spatula (discard the solids). Press a piece of plastic wrap directly onto the surface of the curd (this will prevent a skin from forming). Refrigerate until the curd is cold and set, at least 3 hours. To speed up this process, you can chill the curd in an ice bath (see Chilling in an Ice Bath, page 358).

PREPARE THE PAN: Line a 4½ × 8½-inch metal loaf pan with plastic wrap, leaving a couple inches of overhang along the sides (to get the plastic to stick, wet the pan lightly). Place the pan in the freezer.

$\rightarrow$

BEAT THE EGG WHITES AND SUGAR: In a clean medium, nonplastic bowl, with a hand mixer, beat the egg whites and a pinch of salt on medium-low speed until the whites are broken up and frothy, about 20 seconds. Increase the speed to medium-high and continue to beat until the whites are foamy and opaque, about 30 seconds, then gradually add the remaining ¼ cup (1.8 oz / 50g) sugar in a slow, steady stream, beating constantly. Once all the sugar is added, continue to beat just until you have dense, glossy egg whites that hold a medium peak (see page 339 for what this stage looks like). Try not to overbeat or the whites will take on a dry, grainy texture and be difficult to incorporate. Set the bowl aside.

WHIP THE CREAM: In a large bowl, with the hand mixer, beat the cream on low speed to start and gradually increase the speed to medium-high as it thickens, until you have a firmly whipped cream that holds a stiff peak (see Whipping Cream, page 355).

MAKE THE SEMIFREDDO MIXTURE: Remove the curd from the refrigerator and scrape all but about ½ cup (3.8 oz / 109g) into the bowl with the cream and whisk to combine. Scrape the egg whites into the bowl and fold the mixture gently with a large flexible spatula until no streaks remain (for more on the proper technique, see Folding a Mixture, page 351).

ASSEMBLE AND FREEZE: Remove the loaf pan from the freezer and scrape about one-third of the semifreddo mixture into the pan and smooth it into a single layer all the way to the corners. Dollop about half of the remaining curd across the surface and spread it around with the back of a spoon into an even layer. Scrape half of the remaining semifreddo mixture on top and smooth, then top with dollops of the remaining curd and spread with the back of a spoon. Scrape the remaining semifreddo mixture on top and smooth the surface. Fold the overhang of plastic up and over the filling to cover, then freeze the semifreddo until solid, at least 4 hours.

SERVE: Remove the loaf pan from the freezer and dip the bottom and sides into a bowl of warm tap water for just a few seconds. Peel the plastic away from the surface of the semifreddo, then place a plate or serving platter upside down over the pan, making sure the ends of the plastic are out of the way. Invert the plate and pan together. Remove the pan, pulling downward on the plastic to help release the semifreddo if needed. Carefully peel away the plastic, then slice crosswise and serve immediately.

Can I . . .

Make it ahead? Yes. The semifreddo, well wrapped and frozen, will keep for up to 2 weeks.

Use a stand mixer instead of a hand mixer? Yes, but . . . For recipes like this one that require you to whip multiple components separately before combining them, a hand mixer is the better tool because you can easily move it around to different bowls. If a stand mixer is your only option, whip the egg whites and cream separately in a stand mixer fitted with the whisk attachment, transferring each to a separate bowl as it's done (note that recipe steps will take less time in a stand mixer because it has more power than a hand mixer). Proceed with the recipe as written.

No-Bake Grapefruit Bars

Because I adore the piercing, floral, and tart-bitter flavor of grapefruit, I was on a mission to develop a dessert that would show it off. Lots of testing taught me that if it's baked or cooked in any way, grapefruit becomes flat and bitter, so to incorporate it into a dessert, I knew that I had to keep it fresh. These bars have a whipped, creamy, no-bake filling that allows the flavor of grapefruit to come through. (Because I insist on baking the crust to keep it crispy, I can't *technically* call the entire recipe no-bake, but it's a worthwhile step.) To make sure the point isn't lost, juicy, fresh segments of grapefruit top each bar.

MAKES 12 BARS

DIFFICULTY: 2 (Easy)

ACTIVE TIME: 45 minutes

TOTAL TIME: 4 hours 45 minutes (includes 4 hours for chilling)

SPECIAL EQUIPMENT: 8 × 8-inch baking pan (preferably metal), hand mixer

Melted butter for the pan

6 ounces (170g) graham crackers (about 11 sheets)

5 tablespoons unsalted butter (2.5 oz / 71g), melted and cooled

2 tablespoons plus ½ cup sugar (4.4 oz / 125g)

Several pinches of kosher salt

1⅔ cups heavy cream (14.1 oz / 400g)

1 tablespoon finely grated grapefruit zest

½ cup fresh red grapefruit juice (4 oz / 113g), from about 1 medium grapefruit

3 tablespoons fresh lemon juice, from about 1 medium lemon

1½ teaspoons vanilla extract

8 ounces (227g) cream cheese, chilled

1 medium red grapefruit, for serving

PREHEAT THE OVEN AND PREPARE THE PAN: Arrange an oven rack in the center position and preheat the oven to 350°F. Line an 8 × 8-inch baking pan, preferably metal, with foil, working the foil carefully into the corners, pressing it firmly against the sides to eliminate air pockets, and smoothing any creases. Brush the bottom of the foil with a thin layer of melted butter. If you're using a glass pan, note that those tend to have narrower bases and rounder sides, so your bars will be taller and a little less square.

MAKE THE CRUST: Place the graham crackers in a resealable bag, press out the air, and seal. Use a rolling pin or heavy-bottomed saucepan to crush the crackers, periodically shaking the bag so the larger pieces settle to one side, until you have very fine, uniform crumbs. (You can also pulse them in a food processor until finely ground, but it's very doable by hand.) Transfer the crumbs to a medium bowl and add the melted butter, 2 tablespoons of the sugar, and a pinch of salt. Toss with a fork until the mixture is well combined, then rub it between your fingertips until it looks like wet sand.

PRESS IN THE CRUST AND BAKE: Transfer the mixture to the prepared pan and use the bottom of a 1-cup dry measure or glass to flatten it into an even, compact layer. Place the pan on a sheet pan and bake until the crust is fragrant, firm to the touch, and dark brown around the edges, 13 to 18 minutes. Remove from the oven and let cool completely.

REDUCE THE CREAM: In a large saucepan, combine the cream, remaining ½ cup (3.5 oz / 100g) sugar, and a pinch of salt and bring to a boil over medium-high heat, stirring to dissolve the sugar. Reduce the heat to maintain a lively simmer and continue to cook, whisking occasionally, until the mixture is reduced to 1¼ cups, 10 to 15 minutes (pour it into a heatproof liquid measuring cup to check the volume, then return to the saucepan and continue to reduce if it's not there yet).

Potential Pitfall: Keep an eye on the cream mixture, as it will boil over quickly and make a mess. Once it boils, take a minute to regulate the heat and find the level where the mixture is simmering vigorously but not boiling. If it does start to boil over, immediately remove the saucepan from the heat and blow on the surface to make it subside.

CHILL THE CREAM MIXTURE: Remove the saucepan from the heat and set aside. Fill a large bowl about a quarter of the way with ice water and place the saucepan inside, making sure that the water level hits below the top of the saucepan. Let it sit, whisking occasionally, until the mixture is cold, 5 to 10 minutes (see Chilling in an Ice Bath, page 358).

→

MAKE THE FILLING: Remove the saucepan from the ice water and stir in the grapefruit zest, grapefruit juice, lemon juice, and vanilla, then set aside. Empty the bowl of ice water, dry it, add the cream cheese, and beat with a hand mixer on medium speed until the cream cheese is smooth. Add a couple tablespoons of the cold cream mixture and beat on medium to incorporate, then continue to beat the cream cheese, gradually adding the cream mixture, until you have a smooth mixture. Increase the speed to medium-high and beat until you have a very thick, whipped filling, about 3 minutes.

> *Potential Pitfall:* If, despite adding the cream mixture slowly and beating constantly, your filling has lumps of cream cheese, use a blender to smooth it out. If you find that your filling isn't whipping, it might not be cold enough, so refrigerate it until cold.

FILL THE CRUST: Scrape the filling into the cooled crust and use a spatula to work it all the way to the sides and into the corners, taking care not to form any air pockets, then smooth the surface. Cover and refrigerate until the filling is set, at least 4 hours.

TOP WITH FRESH GRAPEFRUIT AND SERVE: Use a sharp knife to cut away the peel from the whole grapefruit (discard) and slice the grapefruit crosswise into ½-inch-thick rounds, following the instructions in Cutting Citrus on page 357. Then, using your fingertips and working one round at a time, gently separate the individual fan-shaped pieces of grapefruit from the membranes (discard the membranes). Remove the pan from the refrigerator, uncover, and use the edges of the foil to lift the bars out of the pan and transfer to a cutting board. Slice the slab into a 3-by-4 grid, forming 12 bars. Dividing evenly, top the bars with the pieces of fresh grapefruit and serve.

ℭan I . . .

Make them ahead? Yes. The unsliced bars can be covered and refrigerated in the pan for up to 5 days but are best served by the third day to prevent the crust from becoming soggy. To store leftover bars, remove the pieces of fresh grapefruit, transfer the bars to an airtight container, and refrigerate for up to 3 days.

Make it gluten-free? Yes. Use a brand of gluten-free graham-style crackers for the crust.

Use a stand mixer instead of a hand mixer? Yes. To make the filling, beat the cream cheese in a stand mixer fitted with the paddle attachment on medium speed until smooth, then switch to the whisk attachment. Very gradually stream in the cold cream mixture, beating constantly, and proceed with the recipe as written.

Marbled Mint Chocolate Mousse

Chocolate mousse has always felt a bit intimidating to me and easy to mess up. While good chocolate mousse is excellent, a bad chocolate mousse is not something I want to eat (as opposed to bad versions of some other desserts, like cheesecake or yellow cake, which I'll happily eat). I am very pleased that I tackled mousse here and learned in the process that it's not something to fear. For this recipe, you actually make two different kinds of mousse—one dark chocolate, one white chocolate and peppermint—and swirl them together. It requires four separate bowls, two large ones for whipping cream and beating egg whites separately, and two heatproof ones for melting the two chocolates. All the spooning and layering and swirling can get a little messy, but the reward is a delicious, light, dissolve-on-your-tongue mousse that looks grand.

SERVES 8

DIFFICULTY: 3 (Moderate)

GLUTEN-FREE

ACTIVE TIME: 45 minutes

TOTAL TIME: 4 hours 45 minutes (includes 4 hours for chilling)

SPECIAL EQUIPMENT: Hand mixer, 8 serving glasses

4 ounces (113g) white chocolate, coarsely chopped

4 ounces (113g) bittersweet chocolate (70%-72% cacao), coarsely chopped

4 tablespoons unsalted butter (2 oz / 57g), cut into pieces

1 cup heavy cream (8.5 oz / 240g), chilled

4 large eggs (7 oz / 200g), whites and yolks separated, at room temperature

¼ teaspoon peppermint extract

½ teaspoon Diamond Crystal kosher salt or ¼ teaspoon Morton kosher salt

⅓ cup sugar (2.4 oz / 67g)

MELT THE CHOCOLATES SEPARATELY: Fill a medium saucepan with about 1 inch of water and bring to a simmer over medium heat, then reduce the heat to low. Place the white chocolate in a heatproof medium bowl and set over the saucepan, making sure the bottom of the bowl is not touching the water (this is called a double boiler—for more information, see Setting Up a Double Boiler, page 341). Stir the white chocolate occasionally with a heatproof flexible spatula until it's completely melted, then carefully remove the bowl from the saucepan and set aside. Combine the bittersweet chocolate and butter in a separate heatproof medium bowl and place it over the saucepan. Stir the mixture occasionally until the chocolate and butter are melted and the mixture is smooth, then remove the bowl and set it next to the white chocolate. Allow both to cool to room temperature.

MEANWHILE, WHIP THE CREAM: In a large bowl, with a hand mixer, beat the cream on low speed to start and gradually increase the speed to medium-high as it thickens, until you have a softly whipped cream that holds droopy peaks (see Whipping Cream, page 355). Transfer the bowl of whipped cream to the refrigerator. Clean the beaters well for the egg whites.

Potential Pitfall: A firmly whipped cream will be difficult to fold into the mousse, so try not to beat past the point of soft peaks. If you think you've gone too far, see page 355 for how to loosen cream that's been overwhipped.

WHISK THE YOLKS INTO THE CHOCOLATES: Whisk 2 of the egg yolks into the cooled white chocolate, then add 1 tablespoon (0.5 oz / 14g) cold tap water and the peppermint extract and whisk until the mixture is smooth (incorporating the egg yolks will make the chocolate grainy, but the water will bring it back together). Set the bowl aside. Whisk the remaining 2 yolks into the cooled bittersweet chocolate mixture, then whisk in 2 tablespoons (1 oz / 28g) cold tap water until the mixture is thick, smooth, and glossy. Set the bowl aside.

BEAT THE EGG WHITES AND SUGAR: In a separate clean, large, nonplastic bowl and using the hand mixer fitted with clean beaters, beat the egg whites and salt on medium-low speed until the whites are broken up and frothy, about 20 seconds. Increase the speed to medium-high and continue to beat until the whites are foamy and opaque, about 30 seconds, then add the sugar in a slow, steady stream, beating constantly. Once all the sugar

Can I...

Make it ahead? Yes. The mousse, covered and refrigerated in the serving glasses, will keep for up to 5 days.

Halve the recipe? Yes, but . . . This recipe requires several steps and is easier to make in the given quantities. Halve all of the ingredient quantities, except for the ⅓ cup sugar, which doesn't divide easily. Instead, use 2 tablespoons plus 2 teaspoons sugar. Follow the recipe as written. Note that the times for whipping smaller quantities of cream and egg whites will be shorter. Divide the two mousses among four serving glasses as directed.

Make a version that's chocolate-only? Yes. Omit the white chocolate and peppermint extract, then melt 8 ounces (227g) coarsely chopped semisweet chocolate (64%–70% cacao) and 6 tablespoons (3 oz / 85g) unsalted butter in a large heatproof bowl over the double boiler. Proceed with the recipe as written, whisking all 4 yolks and 3 tablespoons cold water (1.5 oz / 42g) into the chocolate mixture and folding in all the whipped cream and beaten egg whites.

Use a stand mixer instead of a hand mixer? Yes. Whip the cream in a stand mixer fitted with the whisk attachment as written. Scrape the whipped cream into a separate bowl, thoroughly wash and dry the stand mixer bowl and whisk, then proceed to beat the egg whites as written. Note that these steps will take less time in a stand mixer because it's more powerful than a hand mixer.

is added, continue to beat just until you have dense, glossy egg whites that hold a medium peak (see page 339 for what this stage looks like). Try not to overbeat, or the whites will take on a dry, grainy texture and be difficult to incorporate. Set the bowl aside.

MAKE THE MOUSSE: Have your serving glasses ready. Remove the whipped cream from the refrigerator and scrape half into the bowl of dark chocolate mixture and half into the bowl of white chocolate mixture. Fold each with a flexible spatula to incorporate the cream and lighten the two mixtures (it's helpful to have two flexible spatulas so you can designate one per chocolate). Scrape about one-quarter of the beaten egg whites into each bowl and fold gently until a few streaks remain (for more on the proper technique, see Folding a Mixture, page 351). Scrape the remaining egg whites into the bowls, dividing evenly, and then fold each mixture gently until just a few streaks remain. The white chocolate mousse will have a loose, almost pourable consistency, while the chocolae mousse will be thicker.

SPOON INTO SERVING GLASSES AND SWIRL: Dividing as evenly as possible, use two large spoons to scoop the two mousses into 8 serving glasses, alternating spoonfuls and letting the two mousses layer on top of each other inside the glasses. Drag a skewer or paring knife through each glass in a figure-eight pattern to swirl the two flavors together, then wipe down the sides of the glasses to clean, if necessary.

CHILL: Cover the glasses with plastic or reusable food wrap and refrigerate until the mousse is cold and set, at least 4 hours.

Coffee Stracciatella Semifreddo

I have a cooking and baking philosophy that goes like this: If the store-bought version is better than my homemade version, I buy it rather than make it. That's why I rarely make ice cream at home, since the limitations of home machines mean that a high-end brand will always be smoother and creamier. Semifreddo, though, is not ice cream. While scoopable, it's a frozen style of mousse that has a lighter, airier texture than ice cream, and it doesn't require spinning or churning. This particular semifreddo is coffee flavored—because coffee frozen desserts are the best frozen desserts—with the addition of melted chocolate that's drizzled in stracciatella-style so it forms fine chips that melt in your mouth. It's not ice cream, but it satisfies in the same way. Keep in mind that it contains raw eggs.

SERVES 8

DIFFICULTY: 3 (Moderate)

GLUTEN-FREE

SERVE WITH: Free-Form Hazelnut Florentines (page 214)

ACTIVE TIME: 40 minutes

TOTAL TIME: 4 hours 40 minutes (includes 4 hours for freezing)

SPECIAL EQUIPMENT: Metal loaf pan (4½ × 8½ inches, measured across the top), hand mixer

2 cups heavy cream (16 oz / 480g), chilled

2 ounces (57g) semisweet chocolate (64%-70% cacao), melted and cooled

2 large eggs (3.5 oz / 100g), whites and yolks separated, at room temperature

1 tablespoon instant espresso powder

1 teaspoon vanilla extract

½ teaspoon Diamond Crystal kosher salt or ¼ teaspoon Morton kosher salt

¼ cup plus 3 tablespoons sugar (3.1 oz / 88g)

PREPARE THE PAN: Line a 4½ × 8½-inch metal loaf pan with plastic wrap, leaving a couple inches of overhang along the sides. Place the pan in the freezer.

WHIP THE CREAM AND DRIZZLE THE CHOCOLATE: In a large bowl, with a hand mixer, beat the cream on low speed to start and gradually increase the speed to medium-high as it thickens, until you have a firmly whipped cream that holds a stiff peak (see Whipping Cream, page 355). Drizzle the melted chocolate over the cream in a thin stream, making a random crisscross pattern, then transfer the bowl to the refrigerator.

WHIP THE YOLK MIXTURE: In a medium bowl, combine the egg yolks, espresso powder, vanilla, salt, and ¼ cup (1.8 oz / 50g) of the sugar and beat with the hand mixer (no need to wash the beaters after whipping the cream) on medium speed until combined. Increase the speed to medium-high and continue to beat the mixture until it's extremely light and thick and forms a slowly dissolving ribbon as it falls off the beaters, about 5 minutes (for a visual of "ribbony" egg yolks, see Blanching and Tempering Eggs, page 348). Set the mixture aside and clean the beaters well for the egg whites.

BEAT THE EGG WHITES AND SUGAR: Place the egg whites in a separate clean, medium, nonplastic bowl. Beat on medium-low speed with the hand mixer until the whites are broken up and frothy, about 20 seconds. Increase the speed to medium-high and continue to beat until the whites are foamy and opaque, about 30 seconds, then gradually add the remaining 3 tablespoons sugar in a slow, steady stream, beating constantly. Once all the sugar is added, continue to beat just until the egg whites are dense and glossy and form a medium peak (see page 339 for what this stage looks like). Try not to overbeat or the whites will take on a dry, grainy texture and be difficult to incorporate. Set the bowl aside.

Can I . . .

Make it ahead? Yes. The semifreddo, well wrapped and frozen, will keep for up to 1 week.

Use a stand mixer instead of a hand mixer? Yes, but . . . For recipes like this one that require you to whip multiple components individually before combining them, a hand mixer is the better tool because you can easily move it around to different bowls. If a stand mixer is your only option, separately whip the cream, yolk mixture, and egg whites in a stand mixer fitted with the whisk attachment, transferring each to a separate bowl as it's done (note that recipe steps will take less time in a stand mixer because it has more power than a hand mixer). Make sure to thoroughly wash and dry the stand mixer bowl and whisk before whipping the egg whites. Proceed with the recipe as written.

ASSEMBLE THE SEMIFREDDO AND FREEZE: Remove the bowl of whipped cream from the refrigerator and scrape in the yolk mixture. Beat with the hand mixer on medium-high until incorporated, then increase the speed to high and beat until the mixture holds a stiff peak and the chocolate is broken up into fine pieces, about 1 minute. Scrape in the egg whites and fold gently to combine (for more on the proper technique, see Folding a Mixture, page 351). Scrape the mixture into the prepared pan and smooth the surface. Cover with the overhanging plastic, pressing it directly onto the surface of the semifreddo, and transfer to the freezer. Chill until the mixture is frozen solid, at least 4 hours.

SERVE: Uncover the pan and scoop the semifreddo into bowls. Serve immediately.

Mango-Yogurt Mousse

Every time I drink a mango lassi, I am convinced that it's the tastiest, most addictive, and most refreshing thing in the world. This mousse is my attempt to translate all the flavors of lassi—sweet mango, tart yogurt, and floral cardamom—into dessert form. It requires a few steps to make the curd base, but using frozen mango simplifies the process. Not only is it a light and intensely flavored fruit dessert, but it's also gluten-free.

SERVES 8

DIFFICULTY: 3 (Moderate)

GLUTEN-FREE

SERVE WITH: Toasted Rice Sablés (page 203)

ACTIVE TIME: 45 minutes

TOTAL TIME: 4 hours 45 minutes (includes 4 hours for chilling)

SPECIAL EQUIPMENT: Blender (handheld or standard), hand mixer, 8 serving glasses

2 teaspoons unflavored gelatin powder

4 large egg yolks (2.1 oz / 60g)

¾ cup sugar (5.3 oz / 150g)

½ cup fresh orange juice (4 oz / 113g), from about 1 large orange

3 tablespoons fresh lemon juice

½ teaspoon ground cardamom

½ teaspoon Diamond Crystal kosher salt or ¼ teaspoon Morton kosher salt

1 pound (454g) frozen mango chunks (about 4 cups)

½ cup plain whole-milk Greek yogurt (4.2 oz / 120g)

2 cups heavy cream (16 oz / 480g), chilled

Can I . . .

Make it ahead? Yes. The mousse can be covered and refrigerated for up to 3 days.

Halve the recipe? Yes. Halve all of the above ingredient quantities and follow the recipe as written. Keep in mind that because you will only be making half as much curd, it will cook more quickly in the saucepan. Divide the mousse and curd among four serving glasses.

Use a stand mixer instead of a hand mixer? Yes. Whip the cream in a stand mixer fitted with the whisk attachment and proceed with the recipe as written.

SOFTEN THE GELATIN: Place 3 tablespoons (1.5 oz / 43g) cold tap water in a small shallow bowl and sprinkle the gelatin evenly over the top (do not stir). Set the bowl aside to allow the gelatin to soften, 5 to 10 minutes (for more information, see Softening Gelatin, page 341).

MEANWHILE, ASSEMBLE THE CURD: In a small saucepan, combine the yolks and sugar and whisk vigorously, making sure no unincorporated sugar is trapped around the sides, until the mixture is pale and thick, about 2 minutes. Stream in the orange and lemon juices, whisking constantly and scraping around the sides, until the mixture is smooth. Whisk in the cardamom and salt.

COOK THE CURD: Place the saucepan over medium-low heat and cook, whisking constantly, until the foam has subsided and the curd barely holds the marks of the whisk and is thick enough to coat the back of a spoon, about 5 minutes (see A Word on Curd, page 70, for a photo of curd coating a spoon—if you want a more precise endpoint, it will read 170°F on an instant-read thermometer). Immediately remove the saucepan from the heat and scrape in the softened gelatin, which will have solidified. Whisk briskly for about 30 seconds to dissolve the gelatin.

ADD THE MANGO AND BLEND: Add the frozen mango directly to the saucepan with the curd and stir to combine. Set the saucepan aside until the mango is mostly thawed and the curd is cold, about 5 minutes. Use a handheld blender to blend the mixture until it's completely smooth. (Alternatively, transfer the mixture to a standard blender and blend on high.) Measure out 1 cup of the mango curd and set it aside at room temperature.

WHISK IN THE YOGURT: Whisk the yogurt into the remaining curd in the saucepan until smooth. Set the saucepan aside.

WHIP THE CREAM: In a large bowl, with a hand mixer, beat the cream on low speed to start and gradually increase the speed to medium-high as it thickens, until you have a firmly whipped cream that holds a stiff peak (see Whipping Cream, page 355).

MAKE THE MOUSSE: Scrape the curd/yogurt mixture into the bowl with the whipped cream and fold gently with a flexible spatula until combined and just a few streaks remain (for more on the proper technique, see Folding a Mixture, page 351).

PORTION AND CHILL: Dividing evenly, spoon the mixture into eight serving glasses. Tap the glasses gently on the counter to help the mousse settle, then top each with about 2 tablespoons of the reserved curd. Cover the glasses and refrigerate until the mousse is cold and set, at least 4 hours.

Stovetop Desserts

Puddings, Crepes, Fried & Flambéed Things & More

As much as I love baking—and in particular, that magical, alchemical moment when something emerges from the oven completely transformed—sometimes when I'm feeling lazy or impatient, or when it's hot outside, I don't want to turn on my oven. That's when I look to stovetop desserts. There's an ease to them, and because the heat from a burner is much more targeted and direct than the heat from an oven, they often come together faster than their baked counterparts. Additionally, I get great satisfaction from observing the cooking of a stovetop dessert from start to finish and witnessing exciting moments during the process, like when a piece of pale dough puffs into a golden, light donut in hot oil, or when caramelized crepes, doused with Cognac in a hot skillet, ignite in flames.

The fried and flambéed recipes in this chapter, such as **Old-Fashioned Cherries Jubilee** (page 105) and **Pillowy Beignets** (page 127), should be made à la minute and served right away. They therefore double as dessert *and* entertainment for friends and guests. In contrast, the many puddings can and should be made ahead, eliminating performance anxiety and setting you up for success. And since many of the recipes in this chapter involve no flour at all, gluten-free options abound. The direct heat of the stove means that egg-based desserts, which have particular points of doneness, could overcook easily, like the poached meringues in **Floating Islands** (page 113) or the pudding in **Chocolate Coupes** (page 103). It's therefore important to observe the size of the saucepan or skillet specified in the recipes and to keep an eye on your heat level at every step. You'll notice that making a dessert on the stovetop is no different than any other type of cooking, and all the same principles apply, so for all you cooks out there who don't want to bother with the oven, these desserts are for you.

Hot Chocolate
with Marshmallows

I tend to dislike intensely chocolaty desserts, except when it comes to hot chocolate, one of my favorite cold-weather treats. This hot chocolate is modeled after a thick and markedly unsweet version I had at a popular café in Paris near the Sorbonne called Pâtisserie Viennoise. I use unsweetened chocolate and balance out the bitterness with sweetened condensed milk for extra creaminess. For something customized to your tastes, feel free to swap in a different base, sweetener, or chocolate (see Can I . . . , below, for additional options). Because this version is intense, I serve ½-cup portions, leaving space for my **Easy Marshmallows** (page 341), which partially melt from the heat and add a little extra sweetness to the drink.

SERVES 8

DIFFICULTY: 1 (Very Easy)

GLUTEN-FREE

ACTIVE TIME: 10 minutes (does not include making the marshmallows)

TOTAL TIME: 10 minutes

3 cups whole milk (25.4 oz / 720g)

3 ounces (85g) unsweetened chocolate, chopped

⅓ cup sweetened condensed milk (3.5 oz / 100g)

Generous pinch of kosher salt

¼ teaspoon vanilla extract

Optional flavoring: ¼ teaspoon ground cinnamon, ½ teaspoon instant espresso powder, or ⅛ teaspoon peppermint extract

Easy Marshmallows (optional; page 341)

MAKE THE HOT CHOCOLATE: In a small saucepan, combine the milk, chocolate, sweetened condensed milk, salt, and ¼ cup water (2 oz / 57g) and warm over medium-low heat, whisking frequently, until the chocolate is melted and the mixture is smooth and steaming, 5 to 8 minutes (for a frothy consistency, whisk the mixture vigorously as it warms). Do not let it boil.

ADD THE VANILLA AND ANY OPTIONAL FLAVORING: Remove the saucepan from the heat and whisk in the vanilla. If desired, add your choice of flavoring and whisk to combine.

SERVE: Pour the hot chocolate into mugs, portioning about ½ cup (4.2 oz / 120g) per person. If desired, top with marshmallows.

Can I . . .

Make it ahead? Yes. The hot chocolate, stored airtight and refrigerated, will keep for a week or longer, depending on the freshness of your milk. It will separate as it sits, so rewarm in a small saucepan over medium-low heat, whisking until it's smooth and steaming.

Halve the recipe? Yes. Halve all the above ingredient quantities, except the ⅓ cup sweetened condensed milk, which doesn't divide easily. Instead, use 3 tablespoons sweetened condensed milk. Proceed with the recipe as written.

Choose a different base, chocolate, and/or sweetener? Yes. Use a base of half-and-half to make it richer, water to thin it out, or oat or almond milk to make it dairy-free. Use bittersweet chocolate, milk chocolate, or straight cocoa powder, then sweeten to taste with agave, maple syrup, or demerara sugar.

Substitute store-bought marshmallows? Of course! You can also opt for sweetened whipped cream.

Coconut–Jasmine Rice Pudding

with Lychee

I didn't realize until I had made this recipe a couple of times that it's a true pantry recipe, requiring not one item from the fridge, which is rare for a dessert. That wasn't my intent; I just wanted to create a vegan rice pudding that incorporated the delicate aroma of jasmine tea. The recipe starts by emulsifying canned coconut milk, which, if stabilizer-free, will separate into coconut water and fatty solids at colder temperatures (for the best result, use a good-quality, pure-tasting brand such as Aroy-D or Trader Joe's Organic). Blending breaks the coconut fat into smaller particles so that the chilled rice pudding is smooth and luscious and free of bits of hardened fat. Other than that, it's quick and simple to make; just be sure to allow time for the jasmine tea to infuse the pudding.

SERVES 6

DIFFICULTY: 1 (Very Easy)

DAIRY-FREE, GLUTEN-FREE, VEGAN

ACTIVE TIME: 1 hour

TOTAL TIME: 9 hours (includes 8 hours for chilling)

SPECIAL EQUIPMENT: Blender (handheld or standard), 6 serving bowls

2 (13.5 oz / 400ml) cans unsweetened full-fat coconut milk (not light coconut milk)

1 cup jasmine rice (6.8 oz / 193g)

2 cups unsweetened plain rice milk (16 oz / 480g)

½ cup sugar (3.5 oz / 100g)

1½ teaspoons Diamond Crystal kosher salt or ¾ teaspoon Morton kosher salt

1 teaspoon vanilla extract

4 jasmine green tea bags

1¼ cups (10 oz / 284g) boiling water

1 (15 oz / 425g) can lychees in syrup

½ cup unsweetened toasted coconut chips (1.2 oz / 35g), for serving

Can I . . .

Make it ahead? Yes. The rice pudding will keep, covered and refrigerated, for up to 1 week. The halved lychees in the steeped syrup can be refrigerated in an airtight container for several weeks.

Halve the recipe? Yes. Halve all the quantities in the ingredient list and follow the recipe as written, but cook the rice pudding in a small saucepan. Divide among three serving glasses.

EMULSIFY THE COCONUT MILK: Combine the cans of coconut milk in a large saucepan. If the liquid has separated from the solids, heat the coconut milk over medium heat, whisking frequently, until you have a smooth liquid, then remove the saucepan from the heat (if the coconut milk has not separated, skip this step). Use a handheld blender to blend the coconut milk directly in the saucepan on high speed for 1 minute—this is to break the fat particles into smaller pieces so the final pudding is smooth. (Alternatively, transfer the coconut milk to a standard blender and blend on high speed for about 30 seconds, then return to the saucepan.) Set aside.

RINSE THE RICE: Place the rice in a mesh sieve and rinse with cool water, tossing the rice gently with your hand, until the water goes from cloudy to clear. Shake to remove any excess water, then set the sieve aside.

MAKE THE RICE PUDDING: Add the rice milk, sugar, and salt to the saucepan and bring the mixture to a simmer over medium-high heat, stirring with a heatproof flexible spatula or wooden spoon to dissolve the sugar. Add the rice, stirring to prevent the grains from sticking together, and bring back to a simmer. Reduce the heat to maintain a gentle simmer and cook the rice, stirring frequently, until the mixture is thick and the rice is translucent and tender, 30 to 35 minutes. Remove the saucepan from the heat, then stir in the vanilla. Transfer the rice pudding to a large bowl and set aside.

MAKE THE TEA AND INFUSE THE RICE PUDDING: In a small heatproof bowl, steep 3 of the tea bags in the boiling water for 5 minutes, then remove the tea bags and set aside but do not discard. Stir the tea into the rice pudding (it will look liquidy but will thicken up), then submerge the 3 tea bags in the pudding, placing the strings over the side of the bowl. Cover the bowl and refrigerate until the rice pudding is cold, set, and infused with tea flavor, 8 to 12 hours.

INFUSE THE LYCHEES: Pour the can of lychees into a mesh sieve set over a small saucepan, letting the syrup drain into the saucepan. Slice the lychees in half lengthwise, transfer to a medium bowl, and set aside. Bring the syrup to a simmer over medium heat, then remove from the heat and add the remaining tea bag to the saucepan. Let the tea steep in the syrup for 5 minutes, then remove the tea bag and pour the syrup over the lychees.

SERVE: Stir the rice pudding to even out the consistency (discard the tea bags), then divide among six serving bowls. Top with the lychees and a drizzle of the jasmine-infused syrup. Sprinkle with the toasted coconut chips and serve.

Tapioca Pudding

with Saffron & Pomegranate

I am hooked on the chewy texture of the tapioca pearls in Taiwanese bubble tea, so it wasn't a big surprise to learn that I also have a liking for American-style tapioca pudding, which I'd only had once or twice before testing recipes for this chapter. An old-fashioned dessert of small tapioca pearls cooked in sweetened milk, tapioca pudding has a satisfying texture and neutral, creamy flavor, so here I add just enough saffron and cardamom, two assertive flavors that work harmoniously together, to complement the creaminess. To play on the shape and size of the tapioca pearls, I top the pudding with pomegranate arils, which provide a contrasting burst of tart flavor. For how easy it is to make, the final dish is especially pretty, flavorful, and fun to eat. Though Kraft Minute tapioca is a common quick-cooking brand, I prefer the texture of small pearl tapioca (available in Asian grocers and packaged by Bob's Red Mill), which requires soaking before cooking.

SERVES 8

DIFFICULTY: 2 (Easy)

GLUTEN-FREE

ACTIVE TIME: 35 minutes

TOTAL TIME: 5 hours 35 minutes (includes 4 hours for chilling)

SPECIAL EQUIPMENT: 8 serving glasses

4 cups whole milk (32 oz / 960g)

⅓ cup plus 1 tablespoon small pearl tapioca (2.4 oz / 67g), not instant or quick-cooking

⅛ teaspoon finely crumbled saffron threads

1 cup boiling water (8 oz / 227g)

1 teaspoon Diamond Crystal kosher salt or ½ teaspoon Morton kosher salt

¼ teaspoon ground cardamom

⅓ cup plus 2 tablespoons sugar (3 oz / 92g)

2 large egg yolks (1.1 oz / 30g)

1 cup fresh pomegranate arils (6.1 oz / 174g), divided

Can I . . .

Make it ahead? Yes. The tapioca pudding will keep, covered and refrigerated, for up to 1 week.

Buy pomegranate arils, or should I seed a pomegranate myself? Either. You can usually find packaged pomegranate arils in the refrigerated produce section of the grocery store. Or, to seed one yourself, cut a pomegranate in half horizontally and, holding one half over a large bowl of water to catch the arils, hit the uncut side forcefully with a wooden spoon to release the arils. Repeat with the other half, then drain and pat the arils dry.

SOAK THE TAPIOCA: In a medium saucepan, combine the milk and tapioca and stir to make sure the pearls don't clump together. Set aside and let the tapioca soak for 1 hour.

STEEP THE SAFFRON: Place the saffron in a heatproof liquid measuring cup, then pour in the boiling water. Allow the saffron to steep, stirring once or twice, until the water is a vibrant golden yellow, about 5 minutes. Pour the water and saffron into the saucepan with the milk and tapioca.

COOK THE TAPIOCA: Add the salt, cardamom, and ⅓ cup (2.4 oz / 67g) of the sugar to the saucepan. Bring the mixture to a boil over medium-high heat, stirring with a heatproof flexible spatula to dissolve the sugar, then immediately turn the heat down to maintain a gentle simmer. Cook, stirring frequently and scraping the bottom and sides of the pan to prevent the pearls from clumping, until the tapioca is tender but still chewy and has turned translucent except for a tiny speck of white in the center, 12 to 18 minutes. Remove the saucepan from the heat.

BLANCH AND TEMPER THE YOLKS: In a medium bowl, vigorously whisk the yolks and remaining 2 tablespoons sugar until pale and thick, about 1 minute. Whisking constantly, slowly pour about 1 cup of the tapioca mixture into the bowl with the yolk mixture to temper it (for more information, see Blanching and Tempering Eggs, page 348).

BRING THE TAPIOCA PUDDING BACK TO A SIMMER: Whisk the egg yolk mixture into the saucepan and set it over medium-low heat. Stir constantly with the heatproof flexible spatula just until it comes to a simmer (to check for a simmer, stop stirring for a few seconds—you should see slow bubbling beneath the surface). Remove the saucepan from the heat.

CHILL THE PUDDING: Scrape the pudding into a large lidded container or bowl (it will look very liquidy, but will set up quite a bit as it cools). Cover and refrigerate until the pudding is cold and set, about 4 hours.

SERVE: Uncover and stir the cold pudding thoroughly to loosen and even out the consistency. Divide the pudding among eight serving glasses, then top each with 2 tablespoons of the pomegranate arils and serve.

Creamy Rice Pudding

with Candied Kumquats

Rice pudding is like pizza for me. Even when it's not so good, I still think it's pretty good, and I'll gladly eat most versions. My personal preference, though, is a creamy, vanilla-flecked rice pudding with a thick but not gloopy texture and tender but not mushy grains. This recipe achieves all that. To enhance creaminess and add a bit of tang, I fold crème fraîche through the cooked rice mixture before serving. That tanginess plays well against the tart, floral flavor of candied kumquats, which I serve on top. Kumquats are a tiny citrus fruit that are entirely edible, including the seeds. There's a brightness as well as a comforting richness to this dessert, and both components can be done days in advance.

SERVES 8

DIFFICULTY: 1 (Very Easy)

GLUTEN-FREE

ACTIVE TIME: 1 hour 20 minutes

TOTAL TIME: 5 hours 20 minutes (includes 4 hours for chilling)

1 cup Arborio or Carnaroli rice (5.3 oz / 150g)

6½ cups whole milk (55 oz / 1.6kg)

1½ teaspoons Diamond Crystal kosher salt or ¾ teaspoon Morton kosher salt

Seeds scraped from 1 vanilla bean (pod reserved) or 2 teaspoons vanilla extract

1 cup sugar (7 oz / 200g), divided

5 ounces (142g) kumquats, thinly sliced crosswise (about 1 cup)

1 tablespoon fresh lemon juice

8 ounces (227g) crème fraîche or sour cream

1 tablespoon finely grated lemon zest

Can I . . .

Make it ahead? Yes. The rice pudding will keep, covered and refrigerated, for up to 5 days. Wait to fold in the crème fraîche and lemon zest until just before serving. The candied kumquats, covered and refrigerated, will keep for up to 3 months.

Halve the recipe? Yes. Halve all the quantities in the ingredient list and follow the recipe as written, but cook the rice pudding in a small saucepan. Divide among four serving bowls.

RINSE THE RICE: Place the rice in a mesh sieve and rinse with cool water, tossing the rice gently with your hand, until the water goes from cloudy to clear. Shake to remove any excess water, then set the sieve aside.

MAKE THE RICE PUDDING: In a large saucepan, combine the milk, salt, vanilla seeds and pod (if using extract, set it aside for later), and ½ cup (3.5 oz / 100g) of the sugar and bring to a simmer over medium-high heat, stirring to dissolve the sugar with a heatproof flexible spatula or wooden spoon. Stir in the rice, bring the mixture back to a simmer, then reduce the heat to maintain a gentle simmer and cook the rice, stirring frequently, until the mixture is very thick and the rice is translucent and tender, 30 to 35 minutes. Remove the saucepan from the heat. If using vanilla extract, stir it in.

CHILL THE RICE PUDDING: Transfer the rice pudding to a large lidded container or bowl, cover, and refrigerate until the mixture is cold, at least 4 hours. Leave the vanilla pod in the mixture to allow it to infuse the rice pudding.

MEANWHILE, MAKE THE CANDIED KUMQUATS: Place the kumquats in a small saucepan and add water to barely cover them. Bring to a boil over medium-high heat and cook for 1 minute, then drain the kumquats in a mesh sieve and rinse with cool water. Return the kumquats to the same saucepan and add ½ cup (4 oz / 113g) water and the remaining ½ cup (3.5 oz / 100g) sugar. Bring the mixture to a simmer over medium heat, stirring to dissolve the sugar. Reduce the heat to maintain a bare simmer and continue to cook, swirling the saucepan occasionally, until the kumquats are completely translucent and very tender, 30 to 35 minutes. Remove the saucepan from the heat and stir in the lemon juice. Transfer the kumquats and syrup to a lidded container and refrigerate until cold, at least 1 hour.

SERVE: Uncover and stir the cold rice pudding several times with a flexible spatula to loosen the consistency. Add the crème fraîche and lemon zest and fold the mixture several times until evenly mixed. Divide the rice pudding among eight serving bowls and top each with about 1 tablespoon of the candied kumquats and syrup. Serve the remaining kumquats and syrup on the side.

Toasted Farro Pudding

with Red Wine Cherries

My forays into bread baking over the past several years have given me a great appreciation for the multidimensional flavors of whole grains. As with **Rye Bread Pudding** (page 307), this is a dessert whose main flavor is grain itself, specifically, farro. An ancient Italian grain related to wheat, farro has a nutty flavor and toothsome texture. Like rice, it releases starch as it cooks, so farro makes a flavorful substitute for white rice in rice pudding (if you've heard of *farroto*, aka "farro risotto," think of this as the sweet version). I toast the farro in butter to coax maximum flavor from the grains and top the pudding with dried cherries plumped in red wine, but you could garnish it instead with fresh berries or a dollop of jam.

SERVES 6

DIFFICULTY: 2 (Easy)

ACTIVE TIME: 1 hour 30 minutes

TOTAL TIME: 2 hours 30 minutes

SPECIAL EQUIPMENT: 6 serving glasses or bowls

2 tablespoons unsalted butter

1 cup semi-pearled farro (6.2 oz / 175g)

4 cups whole milk (32 oz / 960g)

2 tablespoons honey

1 teaspoon Diamond Crystal kosher salt or ½ teaspoon Morton kosher salt

1 cinnamon stick

6 tablespoons demerara sugar (2.6 oz / 75g), divided

2 large egg yolks (1 oz / 30g)

1 tablespoon finely grated lemon zest, from 1 medium lemon

1 teaspoon vanilla extract

½ cup dried sweet cherries (3.4 oz / 95g)

½ cup red wine (4 oz / 113g)

Can I . . .

Make it ahead? Yes. The farro pudding, stored in an airtight container and refrigerated, will keep for up to 1 week. The red wine cherries, stored in an airtight container and refrigerated, will keep for up to 2 weeks. If making the pudding ahead, wait to stir in the lemon zest and vanilla. Before serving, reheat the pudding in a medium saucepan over medium-low heat, stirring often, just until it's warm, then stir in the lemon zest and vanilla. Let the red wine cherries come to room temperature before serving.

Halve the recipe? Yes. Halve all the quantities in the ingredient list and follow the recipe as written, but cook the farro pudding in a small saucepan. Divide the pudding and red wine cherries among three serving glasses.

TOAST THE FARRO: In a medium saucepan, melt the butter over medium-high heat until it's foaming, then add the farro and cook, stirring constantly with a heatproof flexible spatula, until the grains have darkened slightly and smell nutty and the butter is golden brown, about 4 minutes. Remove the saucepan from the heat.

COOK THE FARRO PUDDING: Add 1 cup (8 oz / 227g) water to the saucepan (it's hot, so beware of sputtering), then add the milk, honey, salt, cinnamon stick, and 2 tablespoons of the demerara sugar. Bring the mixture to a boil over medium-high heat, stirring to dissolve the honey and sugar, then reduce the heat to maintain a gentle simmer. Cook the farro, stirring occasionally and scraping the bottom and sides of the saucepan, until the grains have split and are tender and the milk is thickened to the consistency of heavy cream, 1 hour to 1 hour 20 minutes. Remove the saucepan from the heat.

BLANCH AND TEMPER THE YOLKS: In a medium bowl, combine the yolks and 2 tablespoons of the demerara sugar and whisk vigorously until the mixture is pale and thick, about 1 minute. Whisking constantly, slowly pour about 1 cup of the hot farro mixture into the bowl with the yolk mixture to temper it (for more information, see Blanching and Tempering Eggs, page 348).

FINISH THE PUDDING AND COOL: Whisk the warmed egg yolk mixture into the saucepan and set it over medium-low heat. Stir constantly with the heatproof flexible spatula just until it comes back to a simmer (to check for a simmer, stop stirring for a few seconds—you should see slow bubbling beneath the surface). Remove the saucepan from the heat, remove the cinnamon stick, and stir in the lemon zest and vanilla. Let the pudding sit at room temperature, stirring occasionally, until it's warm but not hot, 45 minutes to 1 hour.

MEANWHILE, MAKE THE RED WINE CHERRIES: In a small saucepan, combine the cherries, red wine, ¼ cup (2 oz / 57g) water, and remaining 2 tablespoons demerara sugar. Bring to a simmer over medium heat, swirling the saucepan to dissolve the sugar. Reduce the heat to maintain a gentle simmer and cook, swirling the saucepan occasionally, until the cherries are plump and the liquid is syrupy, 6 to 9 minutes. Remove the saucepan from the heat and let cool to room temperature.

SERVE: Divide the warm pudding among six serving glasses or bowls and top with the red wine cherries, dividing evenly.

Banoffee Pudding

"Pudding," in the UK, as I understand, is a generic term that can refer to any number of desserts. In a bit of wordplay, this recipe translates the British pudding banoffee pie, a tart filled with sliced bananas, dulce de leche, and whipped cream, into an American custard-style pudding. Banana and dulce de leche are cooked into a silky, smooth custard and then layered with whipped sour cream, digestive biscuits (though you could use graham crackers), and more dulce de leche. To give the dessert a shareable quality, I assemble it large-format. Any glass serving dish or bowl with a 2-quart capacity works, but assembling it in individual glasses is an option, too.

SERVES 8

DIFFICULTY: 2 (Easy)

ACTIVE TIME: 1 hour

TOTAL TIME: 9 hours (includes 8 hours for chilling)

SPECIAL EQUIPMENT: Blender (handheld or standard), hand mixer, 2-quart glass dish or serving bowl

PUDDING

6 tablespoons unsalted butter (3 oz / 85g), divided

1 large overripe banana (8.8 oz / 250g), peeled and cut into 1-inch pieces

2¼ cups whole milk (19 oz / 540g)

⅔ cup dulce de leche (7.4 oz / 210g)

1½ teaspoons Diamond Crystal kosher salt or ¾ teaspoon Morton kosher salt

¼ cup cornstarch (1.1 oz / 32g)

2 tablespoons sugar

4 large egg yolks (2.1 oz / 60g), at room temperature

1 large egg (1.8 oz / 50g), at room temperature

2 teaspoons vanilla extract

ASSEMBLY

1½ cups heavy cream (12.7 oz / 360g), chilled

½ cup sour cream (4.2 oz / 120g), chilled

6 ounces (170g) digestive biscuits (about 12 cookies) or graham crackers (about 11 sheets)

4 tablespoons dulce de leche (2.8 oz / 79g), divided

CARAMELIZE THE BANANA FOR THE PUDDING: In a heavy-bottomed medium saucepan, heat 2 tablespoons of the butter over medium heat. (Refrigerate the remaining butter for whisking into the finished pudding.) When the butter is foaming, add the banana and cook, occasionally stirring and mashing the pieces with the back of a heatproof flexible spatula or wooden spoon, until the banana is browned in spots and very soft and mushy, 5 to 7 minutes. Remove the saucepan from the heat.

BLEND AND HEAT THE MILK MIXTURE: Add the milk, dulce de leche, and salt to the saucepan and blend with a handheld blender on high until the mixture is completely smooth. (Alternatively, scrape the banana mixture into a standard blender, add the milk, dulce de leche, and salt and blend until smooth, then return to the saucepan.) Heat the milk mixture over medium heat, whisking occasionally, until it's steaming and just starting to ripple beneath the surface, about 5 minutes. Remove the saucepan from the heat.

BLANCH AND TEMPER THE EGGS: In a medium bowl, combine the cornstarch and sugar and whisk until combined and free of lumps. Add the yolks and whole egg and whisk to combine, then whisk vigorously until the mixture is slightly pale, thickened, and light, about 2 minutes. Whisking the egg mixture constantly, slowly pour about two-thirds of the hot milk mixture into the bowl, to temper the egg mixture, then whisk the warmed contents of the bowl back into the saucepan with the remaining milk mixture (for more information, see Blanching and Tempering Eggs, page 348).

COOK THE PUDDING: Have a clean medium bowl nearby for transferring the hot pudding. Set the saucepan back over medium heat and cook the mixture, whisking constantly and scraping around the sides and bottom of the saucepan, until the pudding is thickened, the foam on the surface has subsided, and it holds the marks of the whisk, about 4 minutes. Stop whisking for a few seconds and check for slow bubbling beneath the surface, indicating the mixture is at a boil, then continue to whisk vigorously for another 15 seconds. Immediately remove the saucepan from the heat and pour the pudding into the reserved medium bowl.

Potential Pitfall: When transferring the pudding, don't scrape the bottom of the saucepan where you might have a bit of curdling, since it will mar the smooth texture. If some curdled pudding gets into the bowl, it's okay—you're going to whisk in the butter, which will help to smooth it out.

→

Make it ahead? Yes. The assembled dish, covered and refrigerated, will keep for up to 3 days (the biscuits will continue to soften as they sit). The pudding, stored covered or in an airtight container in the refrigerator, will keep for up to 1 week.

Halve the recipe? Yes and no. Making the full amount of pudding is recommended, as decreasing the quantities will increase the likelihood of overcooking and curdling, but feel free to halve the quantities of cream, sour cream, digestive biscuits, and dulce de leche and layer everything in a 1-quart vessel, using half of the pudding to serve 4.

Use a stand mixer instead of a hand mixer? Yes. Combine the heavy cream and sour cream in a stand mixer fitted with the whisk attachment and follow the recipe as written, taking care not to overwhip the cream (see page 355 for what to do if this happens).

WHISK IN THE COLD BUTTER AND VANILLA, THEN CHILL: Cut the reserved 4 tablespoons (2 oz / 57g) chilled butter into ½-inch pieces, then whisk the butter into the pudding a few pieces at a time, waiting for the pieces to disappear before adding more, until all the butter is incorporated and the mixture is smooth. Whisk in the vanilla. Press a piece of plastic wrap directly onto the surface of the pudding and refrigerate until it's cold and set, at least 4 hours.

WHIP THE SOUR CREAM: In a large bowl, with a hand mixer, whip the heavy cream and sour cream on low speed to start and gradually increase the speed to medium-high as the mixture thickens, until you have a firmly whipped cream that holds a stiff peak (see Whipping Cream, page 355).

ASSEMBLE: Remove the pudding from the refrigerator and stir to loosen the consistency. Spread about one-quarter of the pudding in an even layer in the bottom of the 2-quart glass dish or serving bowl, then spread about one-quarter of the whipped sour cream over the top. Top with one-third of the digestive biscuits, breaking them into pieces as needed to fit in an even layer, and drizzle with 1 tablespoon of the dulce de leche. Repeat the layering process two more times with the same quantities of pudding, cream, biscuits, and dulce de leche (you'll use all the biscuits but have more of the pudding, whipped sour cream, and dulce de leche). Spread the remaining pudding over the final layer of biscuits, then scrape the remaining cream mixture on top and smooth almost to the edges. Drizzle the remaining 1 tablespoon of dulce de leche over the top, then use the back of a spoon to swirl the dulce de leche into the cream. Loosely cover the dish and refrigerate for at least 4 hours to allow the biscuits to soften before scooping into bowls and serving.

Burnt Maple Pain Perdu

Pain perdu is a simple dessert that's similar to French toast except it's richer, custardier, and all-around way better. Here, slices of toasted brioche are soaked in an eggy custard and then caramelized in a skillet in maple syrup and butter, which crisps the surface and lends some texture to an otherwise soft dish. The oven does come into play here, both to toast the bread (which must be thoroughly dried before it's soaked, otherwise it falls apart) and to keep the slices warm as you cook multiple batches, but all the action happens on the stovetop. Caramelizing the pain perdu in front of guests just before serving doubles as a great party trick, just plan ahead to allow the bread slices to soak for a couple of hours.

SERVES 8

DIFFICULTY: 2 (Easy)

ACTIVE TIME: 45 minutes

TOTAL TIME: 2 hours 45 minutes

SPECIAL EQUIPMENT: Hand mixer, 10- or 12-inch nonstick skillet

1 loaf brioche bread (about 1.3 lb / 454g)

¼ cup plus 3 tablespoons maple syrup (5.2 oz / 148g), plus more for drizzling

2⅔ cups half-and-half (22.6 oz / 640g), at room temperature

Seeds scraped from ½ vanilla bean (pod reserved)

½ teaspoon Diamond Crystal kosher salt or ¼ teaspoon Morton kosher salt

4 large egg yolks (2.1 oz / 60g), at room temperature

2 large eggs (3.5 oz / 100g), at room temperature

¼ cup demerara sugar (1.8 oz / 50g)

1½ cups heavy cream (12.7 oz / 360g), chilled

3 tablespoons unsalted butter, cut into pieces, divided

PREHEAT THE OVEN: Arrange an oven rack in the center position and preheat the oven to 325°F.

SLICE AND TOAST THE BRIOCHE: Use a serrated knife to slice the bread crosswise into eight generous 1-inch-thick slices. Depending on the size and shape of your loaf, you may have smaller slices and some bread leftover, which is fine (save any remaining brioche for another use). Arrange the slices on a sheet pan, spacing evenly, and bake, turning once or twice, until they're dry and browned all over, 20 to 25 minutes. Set the pan aside and allow the bread to cool. Turn the oven off.

REDUCE THE MAPLE AND HEAT THE HALF-AND-HALF: In a small saucepan, bring ¼ cup (3 oz / 85g) of the maple syrup to a boil over medium heat. Cook, swirling the saucepan occasionally, until the syrup has darkened in color, is reduced, and smells nutty, and the bubbles are large, glassy, and slow to pop, about 3 minutes. Remove the saucepan from the heat and slowly whisk in the half-and-half (it will sputter a bit). Add the vanilla seeds and pod and salt. Heat again over medium heat, whisking occasionally, until the mixture is steaming and just starting to ripple beneath the surface, about 5 minutes. Remove the saucepan from the heat and set aside.

BLANCH AND TEMPER THE EGGS: In a medium bowl, combine the egg yolks, whole eggs, and demerara sugar and whisk vigorously until the mixture is frothy and slightly thickened, about 1 minute. Whisking the egg mixture constantly, slowly pour the hot half-and-half mixture into the bowl to temper the egg mixture, then continue to whisk the custard until the sugar is completely dissolved, about 30 seconds (for more information, see Blanching and Tempering Eggs, page 348).

SOAK THE BREAD: Slowly pour the custard (including the vanilla pod) over the bread slices on the pan. Let them sit for a minute, then carefully turn the slices. Cover the pan and let it sit at room temperature, tilting the pan occasionally to redistribute the custard, until the bread has absorbed all (or nearly all) of the custard, 1 to 2 hours.

MEANWHILE, WHIP THE CREAM: In a large bowl, with a hand mixer, whip the cream on low speed to start and gradually increase the speed to medium-high as it thickens, until you have medium peaks (see Whipping Cream, page 355). Cover the bowl and refrigerate until serving.

PREHEAT THE OVEN: Arrange an oven rack in the center position and preheat the oven to 150°F. Line a large sheet pan with a silicone baking mat or parchment paper and place inside the oven.

COOK THE FIRST BATCH: Heat a 10- or 12-inch nonstick skillet over medium-high heat. Add ½ tablespoon of the butter and 1 tablespoon of the remaining maple syrup and cook, stirring with a heatproof flexible spatula, until the mixture is thick and bubbling all over, about 30 seconds. Uncover the pan and use a broad, flat spatula to carefully transfer 3 of the soaked bread slices to the skillet, turning them so that the side that was facing upward in the pan is now downward (the soaked slices are delicate). Reduce the heat to medium, then gently shake the skillet to move the slices around so they pick up all the caramelized maple/butter mixture. Continue to cook the slices, gently shaking the skillet here and there but leaving them mostly undisturbed, until they're slightly puffed across the surface and the bottoms are deep golden brown, about 3 minutes. Turn them gently, add another ½ tablespoon of the butter to the skillet, and swirl. Continue to cook the slices until they're springy to the touch in the centers, another 2 minutes. Transfer the slices to the prepared sheet pan inside the oven.

COOK THE REMAINING BATCHES: Cook the 5 remaining slices in two more batches in the same skillet with the remaining 2 tablespoons butter and 2 tablespoons maple syrup, just as you did the first batch. Transfer the slices to the sheet pan as they finish cooking.

SERVE: Remove the sheet pan from the oven and transfer the slices to serving plates. Remove the whipped cream from the refrigerator—if it has deflated a bit, beat it vigorously with a whisk until it forms medium peaks again. Serve the pain perdu topped with a dollop of whipped cream and an extra drizzle of maple syrup.

Can I . . .

Make this ahead? No. Pain perdu should be eaten right after it's cooked.

Halve the recipe? Yes. Halve all the ingredient quantities and follow the recipe as written, but toast and soak the bread in an 8 × 8-inch baking pan. Cook the pain perdu in two batches, using 1 tablespoon of maple syrup and 1 tablespoon of butter for each batch.

❦Chocolate Coupes

Drinking out of—or even just holding—a coupe glass makes me feel ritzy and Gatsby-esque, so I love that a coupe isn't just for gimlets or champagne; it's also a category of dessert (often involving ice cream and fruit, but just as often not—it's a little vague). I knew this book needed a homey, straightforward chocolate pudding that was delicious enough to be served all on its own, but I felt like dressing it up into a fancier, celebration-worthy dessert, so I layer it with cookies and cream in coupe glasses. Intermingled with the pudding, the chocolate wafers and whipped cream (which, together, recall the classic "refrigerator roll" on the box of Nabisco Famous Chocolate Wafers—a dessert I love) make a texturally varied and balanced dessert. The coupe glasses make it a party!

SERVES 6

DIFFICULTY: 2 (Easy)

ACTIVE TIME: 45 minutes

TOTAL TIME: 5 hours 15 minutes (includes 4 hours for chilling)

SPECIAL EQUIPMENT: Hand mixer, six 8-ounce coupe or serving glasses

⅔ cup packed light brown sugar (5.2 oz / 147g)

¼ cup unsweetened cocoa powder (0.7 oz / 21g)

3 tablespoons cornstarch

½ teaspoon instant coffee granules (optional)

2¾ cups whole milk (23.3 oz / 660g)

1½ teaspoons Diamond Crystal kosher salt or ¾ teaspoon Morton kosher salt

4 large egg yolks (2.1 oz / 60g), at room temperature

1 large egg (1.8 oz / 50g), at room temperature

4 ounces (113g) semisweet chocolate (64%-70% cacao), coarsely chopped

4 tablespoons unsalted butter (2 oz / 57g), cut into ½-inch pieces, chilled

2 teaspoons vanilla extract

5 ounces (142g) Nabisco Famous Chocolate Wafers (about 23 wafers)

1⅔ cups heavy cream (14.1 oz / 400g), chilled

MAKE THE SUGAR AND STARCH MIXTURE: In a medium bowl, combine the brown sugar, cocoa powder, cornstarch, and instant coffee granules (if using) and whisk to combine, then use your fingertips to break up any lumps of brown sugar and whisk again until you have an even mixture. Set the bowl aside.

HEAT THE MILK: In a heavy-bottomed medium saucepan, combine the milk and salt and heat over medium heat until the mixture is steaming and just starting to ripple beneath the surface, about 5 minutes. Remove the saucepan from the heat.

BLANCH AND TEMPER THE EGGS: Add the egg yolks and whole egg to the bowl with the sugar mixture and whisk until combined, then whisk more vigorously until the mixture is several shades paler and voluminous and it falls off the whisk in a slowly dissolving ribbon, about 2 minutes. Whisking the egg mixture constantly, slowly pour about two-thirds of the hot milk mixture into the bowl to temper the eggs, then whisk the warmed contents of the bowl into the saucepan with the remaining milk mixture (for more information, see Blanching and Tempering Eggs, page 348).

COOK THE PUDDING: In a large heatproof bowl, combine the chopped chocolate and butter and set aside. Return the saucepan to medium heat and cook, whisking constantly and scraping around the sides and bottom of the saucepan, until the pudding is thickened, the foam on the surface has subsided, and it holds the marks of the whisk, about 4 minutes. Stop whisking for a few seconds and check for slow bubbling beneath the surface, indicating the mixture is at a boil, then continue to whisk vigorously for another 15 seconds. Immediately remove the saucepan from the heat and pour the pudding into the bowl with the chocolate and butter.

> *Potential Pitfall:* When transferring the pudding, don't scrape the bottom of the saucepan where you might have a bit of curdling, since it will mar the smooth texture. If some curdled pudding gets into the bowl, it's okay—you're going to whisk in the chocolate and butter, which will help to smooth it out.

FINISH THE PUDDING AND CHILL: Let the pudding sit for a minute or two to melt the chocolate and butter, then whisk until the chocolate is incorporated and you have a smooth, glossy pudding. Whisk in the vanilla. Press a piece of plastic wrap directly onto the surface of the pudding and refrigerate until it's cold and set, at least 4 hours.

→

Can I . . .

Make it ahead? Yes. The coupes can be assembled, covered, and refrigerated for up to 12 hours before serving (the cookie crumbs will continue to soften as they sit). The pudding, stored covered or in an airtight container in the refrigerator, will keep for up to 1 week.

Halve the recipe? Yes and no. Making the full amount of pudding is recommended, as decreasing the quantities will increase the likelihood of overcooking and curdling, but feel free to halve the quantities of cream and chocolate wafer cookies and assemble three rather than six coupes using half the quantity of pudding.

Use a stand mixer instead of a hand mixer? Yes. Whip the cream in a stand mixer fitted with the whisk attachment, taking care not to overwhip it (if you think you've gone too far, see page 355 for how to loosen cream that's been overwhipped).

CRUSH THE COOKIES: Place the cookies in a resealable bag and seal, pressing out the air. Use a rolling pin, mallet, or heavy-bottomed saucepan to crush the wafers, breaking them into coarse crumbs with some larger pieces. Set the bag aside.

WHIP THE CREAM: In a bowl, with a hand mixer, whip the cream on low speed to start and gradually increase the speed to medium-high as it thickens, until you have a light, softly textured whipped cream that holds a droopy peak (see Whipping Cream, page 355).

ASSEMBLE THE COUPES: Stir the cold pudding to loosen the consistency, then spoon about half of the pudding into the bottoms of six coupe glasses, dividing evenly (it will be about ⅓ cup per glass). Spoon about half of the whipped cream into the glasses, dividing evenly, then sprinkle half of the cookie crumbs over the whipped cream. Repeat the layering with the remaining pudding, whipped cream, and cookie crumbs. Cover the glasses loosely and refrigerate them for at least 30 minutes to allow the cookies to soften slightly before serving.

Old-Fashioned Cherries Jubilee

I dub this recipe for cherries jubilee "old-fashioned" not because it's a classic (it is), but because it incorporates the flavors of an old-fashioned cocktail, which is made with orange and bourbon and garnished with a cherry. The key to the recipe's success is first reducing the liquid components to a very thick syrup—thicker than you think it should be—before adding the cherries and bourbon and igniting everything (yes, you actually light it on fire!). This is because the cherries themselves release a bit of additional liquid, and you won't achieve a dramatic flame if the skillet is too full. That's why I use jarred sour cherries in syrup, as they retain their shape and texture and aren't excessively juicy, unlike fresh cherries. There's also a convenience factor (no need to pit anything), so the recipe is done from start to finish in about 15 minutes, making it one of the quickest in the book.

SERVES 6

DIFFICULTY: 2 (Easy)

GLUTEN-FREE

ACTIVE TIME: 15 minutes

TOTAL TIME: 15 minutes

SPECIAL EQUIPMENT:
10-inch skillet, stick lighter or long match, 6 serving bowls

1 (24 oz / 680g) jar pitted sour cherries in light syrup

½ cup fresh orange juice (4 oz / 113g), strained

3 tablespoons demerara sugar

1 tablespoon Angostura bitters

Pinch of kosher salt

3 tablespoons bourbon

1 teaspoon vanilla extract

1½ pints best-quality vanilla ice cream, for serving

6 store-bought ladyfingers, for serving (optional)

Can I . . .

Make it ahead? Partially, yes. It's best to flambé the cherries just before serving (do it in front of guests—it's theater!), but the orange juice, demerara sugar, bitters, salt, and cherry syrup can be combined in the skillet and reduced several hours ahead of time. Set the skillet aside, then bring the syrup back to a boil over medium-high heat before proceeding with the recipe. Any leftover cherries jubilee will keep, refrigerated in a jar or airtight container, for several weeks. Rewarm it in a small saucepan over medium-low.

DRAIN THE CHERRIES AND RESERVE SOME SYRUP: Empty the jar of cherries into a mesh sieve set over a medium bowl. Shake the sieve to release any liquid, then set the cherries aside. Measure out 1 cup (8.8 oz / 250g) of the syrup and discard the rest (or reserve it for cocktails).

REDUCE THE LIQUID COMPONENTS AND SKIM: In a 10-inch skillet, combine the orange juice, demerara sugar, bitters, salt, and reserved cherry syrup. Bring the mixture to a lively boil over high heat, whisking to dissolve the sugar, then stop whisking and use a spoon to skim off and remove the orangey foam collecting in the center of the skillet (this will help make the final syrup translucent rather than cloudy). Reduce the heat to medium-high and continue to boil, whisking often, until you have just a thin layer of syrup in the skillet that's teeming with high-rising bubbles, about 3 minutes. The mixture should be very reduced, otherwise the bourbon will not ignite as dramatically, so err on the side of more reduced rather than less (the cherries and bourbon will add more liquid).

ADD THE CHERRIES: With the heat still on medium-high, add the drained cherries to the skillet and stir with a wooden spoon or heatproof flexible spatula to coat them in the syrup, also scraping around the sides. Heat the mixture, swirling the skillet often, just until the cherries are hot and the syrup is bubbling vigorously around the sides, about 1 minute.

FLAMBÉ: Have the lighter or match ready, then add the bourbon to the skillet all at once and, holding your head back, quickly ignite it. Shake the skillet with a gloved hand until the flames subside (the flames might appear modest at first, but shaking will increase their intensity). Turn off the heat, stir in the vanilla, and slide the skillet to a cool burner to cool for a few minutes.

SERVE: Let the ice cream soften for a few minutes at room temperature, then scoop it into six serving bowls and spoon the warm cherries and syrup over top, dividing evenly. If desired, garnish each bowl with a ladyfinger. Serve immediately.

FLAMBÉING AND DEEP-FRYING AT HOME

Nothing feels dicier in the kitchen than setting something on fire (intentionally, of course) or heating multiple cups of oil to burning-hot temperatures. I'll admit that my heart beats just a tiny bit faster when I do either. When deep-frying or flambéing at home, the first rule to remember is to be organized. Have all of your ingredients measured out and your equipment ready to go. You do not want to have to go digging in a drawer for a spider right when donuts finish cooking, nor go searching for a lighter at the moment alcohol hits a hot skillet. In both cases, the action happens fast, and you don't want a window of opportunity to close on you. While neither flambéing nor deep-frying should be feared, below are some best practices and safety tips to guarantee all goes smoothly.

FOR FLAMBÉING

Measure your alcohol. Never pour alcohol straight from the bottle. Instead, measure out the precise quantity called for in the recipe and keep it covered in a small container until you're ready to flambé. (Tip: For alcohol to ignite, it must be at least 80 proof, so keep that in mind if you're going to make any substitutions.)

Make sure you have ample space. Work on a stovetop with plenty of airspace to accommodate the flames. The height they'll reach depends on how much alcohol you add, the size of the skillet, and what's already inside. Generally speaking, to achieve tall, dramatic flames, you need a very hot skillet with very little liquid inside (which is why fruits that release a lot of juice are not ideal for flambéing; dry ones like bananas work great). Anticipate that your flames will rise at least a foot in the air and maybe two, so it's not advised to flambé on a stove covered by a low-hanging microwave-hood combo or cabinetry.

Give people a heads-up. When I was in culinary school in France, my classmates and I were taught that one should always shout, "*Je flambe!*" before setting anything alight in the kitchen to alert the other cooks. If anyone is around you, let them know to keep their heads, bodies, and arms back and away from the skillet before you add the alcohol.

Ask a helper to talk you through the steps. Both **Bananas Flambé** (page 110) and **Old-Fashioned Cherries Jubilee** (page 105) are cooked quickly over high heat. If you're making either, you might want to enlist a helper to read you the recipe instructions aloud so you can keep uninterrupted focus on what's happening on the stovetop.

FOR DEEP-FRYING

Use the right vessel. If you're frying just a few pieces of something, a high-sided skillet or medium saucepan will work just fine, but for frying in batches, you'll need a large, heavy saucepan or Dutch oven, which will heat the oil evenly. A wide Dutch oven lets you easily see what's inside and gives the food some room to move around, but make sure it's tall enough that a couple of inches of oil will fill it no more than halfway (you need the additional depth to account for oil displacement when you add the food and any active bubbling that occurs). Make sure you can safely lift or slide the saucepan or Dutch oven even when there's oil inside in case you need to remove it from the heat.

Watch your oil, and keep extra room temperature oil on hand. To prevent big temperature drops and spikes, keep an eye on the thermometer and continually adjust the heat so the oil temperature stays as consistent as possible. Remember that adding food to the oil will cause the temperature to fall, so you'll need to increase the heat; reduce it again when the oil returns to the desired temperature. If the oil temperature accidentally spikes, kill the heat and add more room temperature oil to cool it down quickly.

Have kosher salt and a lid nearby as a safety precaution. If any oil spills over onto the stovetop and ignites (this is somewhat unlikely by the way), turn off the heat and pour salt over the flames to extinguish them. Water and hot oil do not mix, so never use water to extinguish a grease fire. If water or anything wet inadvertently gets into the oil, causing it to splatter all over the place, cover the saucepan or Dutch oven with a lid or sheet pan and wait until the popping and hissing stop.

Reuse oil, then dispose of it responsibly. Cooking oil can be reused, though the number of times depends on what and how much you're frying at one time. Hold on to the bottle(s) the oil came in, then to reuse the oil, let it cool completely and pour through a fine-mesh sieve and then a funnel back into the original bottle(s). Store away from light and heat. The oil will break down with repeated use, so stop using it when it starts to smell acrid and has turned a few shades darker than its original color (food will also foam rather than bubble in old oil). Used cooking oil is hazardous to the environment and plumbing systems, so never pour it down a drain. To dispose of used oil, let it cool completely, then transfer it back into the original bottle(s) and seal. Either discard it in your trash or, better yet, find a local restaurant or recycling center that accepts used cooking oil.

Bananas Flambé

When my sisters and I were kids, my dad, a great lover of New Orleans cuisine, would make us bananas Foster, a dish of bananas flambéed in rum immortalized at Brennan's restaurant. When developing this recipe, I asked him for tips for making the dish. His response: "Add a lot of booze and stand back!" Although this recipe includes the rum and banana liqueur traditionally used in bananas Foster, it's a saucier version of the classic and uses cream at the end to bring the mixture together into a boozy, butterscotch-y sauce. I serve it over whipped mascarpone, but feel free to use vanilla ice cream instead. It's a quick recipe that takes just 20 minutes from start to finish, though pay close attention to your heat throughout, which will help ensure the bananas caramelize without falling apart. Have both your wits and ingredients about you, because the action happens fast.

SERVES 6

DIFFICULTY: 2 (Easy)

GLUTEN-FREE

ACTIVE TIME: 20 minutes

TOTAL TIME: 20 minutes

SPECIAL EQUIPMENT: Hand mixer, 10-inch skillet, stick lighter or long match

¾ cup mascarpone cheese (6.2 oz / 175g), chilled

1¼ cups heavy cream (10.6 oz / 300g), chilled, divided

A pinch plus ½ teaspoon Diamond Crystal kosher salt or ¼ teaspoon Morton kosher salt

¼ cup packed light brown sugar (1.9 oz / 55g)

3 tablespoons unsalted butter, cut into 1-tablespoon pieces

3 tablespoons banana liqueur

¼ teaspoon ground cinnamon

⅛ teaspoon ground nutmeg

3 large ripe but firm bananas (1.5 lb / 680g), peeled, halved crosswise and lengthwise

3 tablespoons dark rum

½ cup salted roasted macadamia nuts (2.5 oz / 70g), very coarsely chopped

WHIP THE MASCARPONE: In a large bowl, combine the mascarpone, 1 cup (8.5 oz / 240g) of the heavy cream, and a pinch of salt and whip with a hand mixer on low speed to start and gradually increase the speed to medium-high as the mixture thickens, until you have stiff peaks (see Whipping Cream, page 355). Cover the bowl and refrigerate until serving.

PREP THE REMAINING INGREDIENTS: Set aside the remaining ¼ cup (2.1 oz / 60g) of cream and let it come to room temperature. Make sure you have all the remaining ingredients and a lighter or match at the ready.

CARAMELIZE THE BANANAS: In a 10-inch skillet, combine the brown sugar, butter, banana liqueur, cinnamon, nutmeg, and ½ teaspoon salt. Stir the mixture over medium heat until the butter is melted and the sugar is dissolved, then let the mixture come to a boil and continue to cook, stirring often, until the mixture is dark brown, thick, and bubbling all over, 2 to 3 minutes. Add the bananas cut-sides down, fitting them tightly in the skillet and ensuring they're all lying flat. Increase the heat to high and cook, shaking the skillet occasionally, until the bananas are browned in spots on the cut sides, about 3 minutes (the sugar mixture pooling around the sides of the skillet might start to look separated and darkened in spots, but that's okay—it will come back together when you add the cream later).

FLAMBÉ: Reduce the heat to low and turn the bananas carefully so the cut sides are up. Have the lighter or match ready, then add the rum to the skillet all at once and, holding your head back, quickly ignite it—be careful, the flames will reach about 2 feet high! Shake the skillet with a gloved hand until the flames subside. Turn off the heat and slide the skillet to a cool burner.

ADD THE CREAM: Drizzle the room temperature cream around the bananas, shaking and swirling the skillet until the cream mingles with the brown sugar mixture and forms a smooth sauce. Set the skillet aside.

SERVE: Dividing evenly, dollop the whipped mascarpone onto six plates. Place 2 pieces of banana on each plate, arranging them cut-sides up. Dividing evenly, drizzle the remaining sauce over the bananas. Top with a sprinkle of macadamia nuts and serve immediately.

Can I ...

Make it ahead? No. The bananas flambé must be cooked from start to finish right before serving.

Substitute a different alcohol? Yes. Instead of rum, you can use an equal quantity of bourbon, rye, or Cognac (really, any alcohol that's at least 80 proof). You can also omit the banana liqueur if you don't want to invest in an entire bottle, instead adding 2 tablespoons (1 oz / 28g) water.

Floating Islands

I have described many desserts in this book as "not too sweet," which I generally mean as a selling point. This, however, is a decidedly sweet dessert, and that's not a bad thing at all. Floating island (known as *îles flottantes* or *oeufs à la neige* in French) is a dish of poached meringues served on a pool of crème anglaise topped with caramel and toasted almonds (I do use the oven here to toast the almonds, but you could use a toaster oven). The main components are sweet, but the contrasting temperatures and textures also make it interesting. Poaching is not a technique you often see applied to meringue, but it quickly sets the egg whites into a firm yet tender cloud. (Warning: This is quite an eggy dessert, so if you don't like egg flavor, it's not for you.) While traditionally the meringue "islands" are rounded between two spoons into egglike shapes before being poached, I take a more free-form approach, so don't expect beautifully smooth results. I encourage you to lean into both the sweetness and the, shall we say, "unique" look of the meringues, because the end result is still sophisticated and delicious.

SERVES 6

DIFFICULTY: 2 (Easy)

GLUTEN-FREE

ACTIVE TIME: 50 minutes (does not include making the crème anglaise)

TOTAL TIME: 50 minutes

SPECIAL EQUIPMENT: 10-inch skillet, hand mixer

½ cup sliced almonds (2 oz / 57g)

1 cup sugar (7 oz / 200g), divided

2 cups whole milk (16 oz / 480g)

½ teaspoon Diamond Crystal kosher salt or ¼ teaspoon Morton kosher salt, plus a pinch

5 large egg whites (6.2 oz / 175g), at room temperature

Crème Anglaise (page 348), chilled, for serving

TOAST THE ALMONDS: Arrange an oven rack in the center position and preheat the oven to 350°F. Line a sheet pan with a silicone baking mat or parchment paper and scatter the almonds across the surface. Toast until the almonds are golden brown and fragrant, 7 to 10 minutes, tossing halfway through. Set the sheet pan next to the stove and let the almonds cool while you make the caramel. Turn the oven off.

MAKE THE CARAMEL: Fill a glass with water, place a pastry brush inside, and set it next to the stove. In a small saucepan, combine 3 tablespoons (1.5 oz / 43g) water and ½ cup (3.5 oz / 100g) of the sugar and stir gently with a heatproof flexible spatula over medium-high heat just until the sugar dissolves to form a clear syrup and the mixture comes to a boil, about 3 minutes. Cook the mixture to an amber caramel following steps 3 through 5 in Cooking a Wet Caramel (page 346), then immediately remove the saucepan from the heat and proceed to the next step.

DRIZZLE THE CARAMEL OVER THE ALMONDS: Working quickly, drizzle the hot caramel evenly over the almonds on the sheet pan (you won't necessarily cover them fully). Set the pan aside at room temperature to allow the caramel to cool and harden, then break the caramel and almonds into small pieces with your fingertips. Set aside.

> *Potential Pitfall:* If it's humid in your kitchen, the caramel will quickly become sticky. If that's the case, transfer the cooled toasted almond and caramel mixture to an airtight container and store at room temperature until serving.

PREPARE THE POACHING LIQUID: In a 10-inch skillet, combine the milk, ½ teaspoon salt, ¼ cup (1.8 oz / 50g) of the sugar, and 2 cups (16 oz / 454g) water. Bring the mixture to a boil over high heat, stirring with a heatproof flexible spatula or wooden spoon to dissolve the sugar (keep an eye on it, since milk will boil over quickly!). When it comes to a boil, skim and discard any foam that has collected on the surface, then reduce the heat so the mixture is steaming and rippling just below the surface but not actively bubbling (you want it just below a simmer). If needed, continue to adjust the heat to find this point while you make the meringue.

→

BEAT THE EGG WHITES AND SUGAR: In a clean, large, nonplastic bowl, combine the egg whites and a pinch of salt and beat on medium-low speed using a hand mixer until the whites are broken up and frothy, about 20 seconds. Increase the speed to medium-high and continue to beat until the whites are foamy and opaque, about 30 seconds, then gradually add the remaining ¼ cup (1.8 oz / 50g) sugar in a slow, steady stream, beating constantly. Once all the sugar is added, continue to beat just until the egg whites are glossy and form a stiff peak (see page 339 for what this stage looks like). Try not to overbeat or the whites will take on a dry, grainy texture.

POACH THE FIRST BATCH OF MERINGUES: Set a towel-lined plate next to the stove. Use a flexible spatula to fold the meringue several times to smooth and even out the consistency, then, using the spatula and tilting the bowl just over the skillet, scrape a large dollop of meringue about the size of a medium lemon (ideally, about one-sixth of the meringue, though it's tough to eyeball) into the skillet. Fold the meringue again and scrape another dollop into the skillet about the same size as the first, then repeat again so you have 3 free-form meringues floating in the skillet. Poach them undisturbed until the meringues have expanded noticeably in size and the surface is firm to the touch, about 2 minutes, then use the spatula and a large slotted spoon to very carefully and gently turn the meringues and poach for another 2 minutes on the second side. Use the slotted spoon to transfer the meringues to the towel-lined plate and set aside uncovered.

> *Potential Pitfall:* Overcooking the meringues will cause them to deflate and take on a spongy texture. Pay close attention to them as they cook, and if you see the surface start to crater ever so slightly, remove them from the poaching liquid.

POACH THE REMAINING MERINGUES: Skim the surface of the poaching liquid to remove any foam or bits of cooked meringue, then repeat the folding and scraping process with the remaining meringue, forming 3 approximately equal-size blobs and poaching them just as you did the first batch. Transfer the second batch of meringues to the towel-lined plate with the slotted spoon. If desired, run a damp finger around each of the 6 meringues to remove any particularly knobby, rough areas (they'll never be perfectly smooth). Set the plate aside.

SERVE: Pour ⅓ cup (2.5 oz / 70g) of the chilled crème anglaise into each of six shallow serving bowls (you will have some crème anglaise leftover; save for another use). Gently place a meringue in the center of each bowl, then top each meringue with a sprinkle of the toasted almonds and caramel. Serve immediately.

Can I...

Make it ahead? No. The meringues don't hold well, so serve them as soon as possible after poaching. Stored airtight at room temperature, the toasted almond and caramel mixture will keep for up to 2 days.

Use a stand mixer instead of a hand mixer? Yes. To make the meringue, combine the egg whites and a pinch of salt in a stand mixer fitted with the whisk attachment and proceed with the recipe as written, but note that the meringue will whip faster in the stand mixer, so be careful not to overbeat.

Reduce the sweetness? Yes. You can omit the caramel and/or scatter a tart fruit such as raspberries or blackberries around the meringues to counteract some of the sweetness. However, it's not recommended to reduce the amount of sugar in the crème anglaise or the meringue, as it's critical to achieving the correct texture.

Sweet Cheese Blintzes

with Lemony Apricot Compote

Although I consider making blintzes my birthright, I had never actually made—or even eaten!—a blintz until I worked on this book. Blintzes, for the uninitiated, are a Jewish dessert made of an eggy crepe-like pancake that's filled with a sweetened mixture of cream cheese and farmer cheese and pan-fried until the pancake is golden brown. My mom used to help her mother, my Nanny, make blintzes when she was a child. Nanny would stand at the stove manning two skillets, cooking the pancakes two at a time. She'd bang them out onto the counter, which was lined with brown paper bags, fill and fold them up, and then pack the blintzes into a shoebox lined with wax paper and freeze them. Nanny didn't use a recipe, so when I started testing blintzes for the book, my mom provided the taste memory and guidance to make sure I wasn't far off. It was a fun project, and I learned that Nanny's blintzes are mildly sweet and therefore perfect for breakfast or dessert served with any kind of jam or preserves (a fruit topping or sauce is traditional). That said, I like them with this lemony apricot compote and a drizzle of honey.

SERVES 8

DIFFICULTY: 2 (Easy)

ACTIVE TIME: 2 hours

TOTAL TIME: 3 hours

SPECIAL EQUIPMENT: Blender (handheld or standard), 8-inch nonstick skillet, 10-inch skillet

LEMONY APRICOT COMPOTE

8 ounces (227g) dried apricots, coarsely chopped (about 1¾ cups)

2 tablespoons honey

Pinch of kosher salt

1 medium lemon

PANCAKE BATTER

1 cup plus 2 tablespoons all-purpose flour (5.4 oz / 152g)

4 large eggs (7 oz / 200g), at room temperature

1 cup whole milk (8.5 oz / 240g), at room temperature

5 tablespoons unsalted butter (2.5 oz / 71g), melted and cooled

1 tablespoon sugar

1 teaspoon Diamond Crystal kosher salt or ½ teaspoon Morton kosher salt

FILLING AND ASSEMBLY

16 ounces (454g) farmer cheese, chilled

8 ounces (227g) cream cheese, cut into ½-inch pieces, chilled

1 large egg (1.8 oz / 50g)

3 tablespoons sugar

½ teaspoon vanilla extract

Pinch of kosher salt

6 tablespoons unsalted butter (3 oz / 85g), melted and cooled

Honey, for serving

MAKE THE COMPOTE: In a small saucepan, combine the apricots, honey, salt, and 2 cups (16 oz / 454g) water and bring to a simmer over medium heat, then reduce the heat to maintain a gentle simmer and cook, mashing the apricots often with the back of a spoon or flexible spatula, until the apricots have broken down, the liquid has reduced, and the mixture looks like a loose, chunky applesauce, 25 to 30 minutes. Remove the saucepan from the heat and set aside to cool slightly. Meanwhile, finely grate 1 tablespoon zest from the lemon and set it aside for the filling. Cut the lemon in half and squeeze to get 2 tablespoons juice and stir it into the saucepan. Transfer the compote to a lidded container and refrigerate until serving.

MAKE THE PANCAKE BATTER: In a medium bowl, combine the flour, eggs, milk, melted butter, sugar, and salt and blend using a handheld blender, pausing to scrape the bottom and sides of the bowl with a flexible spatula, until the mixture is completely smooth. (Alternatively, combine the ingredients in a standard blender and blend on medium-low speed until smooth.) Cover the batter and set aside to rest at room temperature for at least 1 hour.

MAKE THE FILLING: In a separate medium bowl, combine the farmer cheese, cream cheese, egg, sugar, vanilla, salt, and reserved lemon zest and blend using a handheld blender until the mixture is light and smooth—it will have a bit of graininess from the farmer cheese, but that's normal. (Alternatively, combine the ingredients in a standard blender and blend on medium until smooth.) Cover and refrigerate the filling until you're ready to fill the blintzes.

COOK THE PANCAKES: Place the melted butter in a small bowl next to the stovetop. Also place a sheet pan lined with a clean kitchen towel next to the stovetop for holding the cooked pancakes. Heat an 8-inch nonstick skillet over medium heat. Use a pastry brush to brush the skillet with a thin layer of the melted butter, then tilt the skillet and add a scant ¼ cup (1.5 oz / 42g) batter and swirl slowly until the batter coats the entire surface in an even layer. Let the pancake cook undisturbed until the surface is matte, the edges are dry and beginning to curl, and the bottom is lightly

→

Can I . . .

Make them ahead? Mostly, yes. The blintzes are best eaten right after they're pan-fried, but the pancakes can be cooked and filled up to 1 hour ahead. Keep the uncooked blintzes covered on the plate. The uncooked blintzes can also be packed into an airtight container and stacked in layers separated by sheets of parchment or wax paper and frozen for up to 2 months (like Nanny did). To cook frozen blintzes, fry them from frozen as directed in the recipe, but start them on low heat and cook covered for 5 to 8 minutes to thaw them before uncovering and increasing the heat to medium and browning them.

Halve the recipe? Yes. To make 8 blintzes, which will serve 4, divide the ingredient quantities for the pancake batter and filling and assembly in half and follow the recipe as written, using just the yolk of an egg for the filling. You will be able to fry the blintzes in a single batch.

Make it gluten-free? Not advised. The pancakes benefit from having a bit of elasticity, courtesy of the gluten in flour, so they can wrap around the filling without tearing. So it's best not to substitute a gluten-free flour or blend.

browned in spots, about 1 minute. Invert the skillet and turn the pancake out onto the towel-lined sheet pan (you only cook the pancake on one side; the other side will be fried later). Repeat the cooking process with the remaining batter and melted butter, turning out the pancakes one at a time onto the lined sheet pan and overlapping and stacking as necessary. You should get about 16 pancakes total. Once they're all cooked, cover the sheet pan with a second kitchen towel to prevent the pancakes from drying out. Reserve the remaining butter for frying (you should have around 4 tablespoons left, but if you don't, melt more to yield that amount).

FILL THE PANCAKES: Remove the filling from the refrigerator. Place one of the pancakes on the work surface browned-side up, then scoop a scant ¼ cup (1.7 oz / 48g) of filling and scrape it into the center of the pancake. Use the back of a spoon to work the filling into a thick 4-inch-long line running left to right, then wrap the pancake around the filling like a burrito, folding the bottom up and over the filling, folding in the left and right sides, then rolling it up. Transfer the blintz to a plate seam side down and cover with a clean kitchen towel. Repeat until you've used all the filling and filled all the pancakes, and all the blintzes are covered on the plate.

PAN-FRY THE BLINTZES: Heat a 10-inch skillet over medium heat. Add half of the remaining melted butter (or 2 tablespoons) and swirl the skillet to coat. Gently transfer half of the blintzes to the skillet and cook, shaking the skillet occasionally, until the undersides are golden brown all over, about 5 minutes. Turn the blintzes over and shake the skillet to coat them in butter, then cook until the second sides are browned, about 2 minutes longer. Transfer the blintzes to a serving platter and repeat the cooking process with the remaining 2 tablespoons of butter and blintzes. Serve them warm, 2 per serving, with the lemony apricot compote and more honey for drizzling over top.

Malted & Salted Caramel Pudding

If I had to choose one dessert flavor to eat for the rest of my life, it would be, without hesitation, caramel. Even though I'm tempted to add caramel to basically any sweet recipe, swapping it in wherever sugar is called for, I know it's best only to deploy its bittersweet intensity when it can play a leading role. A silky, dense pudding is an ideal vehicle for caramel's star power. Here, malted milk powder, an old-fashioned ingredient found in conventional grocery stores, plays a supporting yet key role, enhancing both the creaminess of the pudding and the toasty-ness of the caramel.

SERVES 8

DIFFICULTY: 2 (Easy)

ACTIVE TIME: 30 minutes

TOTAL TIME: 4 hours 40 minutes (includes 4 hours for chilling)

SPECIAL EQUIPMENT: 8 serving glasses or small serving cups

3 cups heavy cream (25.4 oz / 720g), chilled, divided

1¼ cups sugar (8.8 oz / 250g), divided

3 cups whole milk (25.4 oz / 720g), at room temperature

Seeds scraped from 1 vanilla bean (pod reserved) or 2 teaspoons vanilla paste or extract

¼ cup cornstarch (1.1 oz / 31g)

3 tablespoons malted milk powder

1½ teaspoons Diamond Crystal kosher salt or ¾ teaspoon Morton kosher salt, plus more to taste

4 large egg yolks (2.1 oz / 60g), at room temperature

2 large eggs (3.5 oz / 100g), at room temperature

1.8 ounces (50g) Biscoff or gingersnap cookies (about 6), lightly crushed, for serving

WARM SOME OF THE CREAM: In a small saucepan, heat 2 cups (16.9 oz / 480g) of the cream over medium heat, whisking once or twice, just until it's steaming, then remove it from the heat. (Alternatively, microwave the cream in a heatproof liquid measuring cup in 30-second bursts until it's hot, then set aside.)

MAKE THE CARAMEL: Fill a glass with water, place a pastry brush inside, and set it next to the stove. In a large saucepan, combine ¼ cup (2 oz / 57g) water and 1 cup (7 oz / 200g) of the sugar and stir gently with a heatproof flexible spatula over medium-high heat just until the sugar dissolves to form a clear syrup and the mixture comes to a boil, about 3 minutes. Cook the mixture to a deep amber caramel following steps 3 through 5 in Cooking a Wet Caramel (page 346), then immediately remove the saucepan from the heat and proceed to the next step.

STREAM IN THE CREAM: Slowly stream the warm cream into the caramel to halt the cooking, stirring gently with the spatula (take care, it will sputter at first). Once all the cream is added and you have a smooth, liquid caramel, pour in the milk, followed by the vanilla seeds and pod or vanilla paste (if using vanilla extract, set it aside to add later). Return the saucepan to medium heat and heat until the mixture is steaming and just starting to ripple beneath the surface, about 5 minutes. Remove the saucepan from the heat.

Potential Pitfall: If your cream was cool, or if you added it a bit too quickly, the caramel may have hardened in places, which is okay. If this happens, whisk the mixture over the heat until the caramel dissolves.

BLANCH AND TEMPER THE EGGS: In a medium bowl, whisk the cornstarch, malted milk powder, salt, and remaining ¼ cup (1.8 oz / 50g) sugar until combined and lump-free. Add the yolks and whole eggs and whisk to combine, then whisk vigorously until the mixture is pale and thick, about 2 minutes. Whisking the egg mixture constantly, slowly pour or ladle about half of the hot caramel mixture into the egg mixture to temper it, then pour the warmed egg mixture into the saucepan (for more information, see Blanching and Tempering Eggs, page 348).

COOK THE PUDDING: Have a separate medium bowl at the ready for transferring the cooked pudding. Set the saucepan back over medium heat and cook, whisking constantly and scraping around the sides and bottom of the saucepan, until the pudding is thickened, the foam on the surface has subsided, and it holds the marks of the whisk, about 4 minutes. Stop whisking for a few seconds and check for slow bubbling beneath the

Can I . . .

Make it ahead? Yes. The pudding, covered and refrigerated, will keep for up to 1 week. Whip the cream just before serving.

Halve the recipe? Yes. Halve all the quantities in the ingredient list and follow the recipe as written, but cook the pudding in a small saucepan. Divide among four serving glasses.

Make a low-fat substitute for the cream? No. A lower-fat dairy, such as milk or light cream, will likely curdle when you add it to the hot caramel, ruining your pudding. You need the high fat content for a smooth, luscious caramel.

surface, indicating the mixture is at a boil, then continue to whisk vigorously for another 15 seconds. Immediately remove the saucepan from the heat and pour the pudding into the reserved bowl.

> *Potential Pitfall:* Don't scrape the bottom of the saucepan where you might have a bit of curdling, since it will mar the smooth texture of the pudding.

CHILL THE PUDDING: If using vanilla extract, whisk it in now. Press a piece of plastic wrap directly onto the surface of the pudding and refrigerate until the pudding is cold and set, at least 4 hours.

WHIP THE CREAM: In a medium bowl, with a whisk or a hand mixer, whip the remaining 1 cup (8.5 oz / 240g) cream on low speed to start and gradually increase the speed to medium-high as it thickens, until you have a softly whipped cream that holds a droopy peak (see Whipping Cream, page 355).

SERVE: Whisk the cold pudding to even out the consistency, then taste it and add more salt if desired. Dividing evenly, spoon the pudding into serving bowls or glasses. Top with a dollop of the whipped cream and a sprinkling of the crumbled cookies.

Frosted Sour Cream Cake Donuts

Cake donuts fall into a category of pastry, along with scones and croissants, that must be eaten fresh. Sitting around does them no favors, so the best, fluffiest, lightest cake donuts are actually the ones you make at home. Fortunately, it's easy and fun, and deep-frying is not nearly as scary or messy as it may seem (see Flambéing and Deep-Frying at Home, page 108, for my frying safety tips). To avoid rolling out a soft, sticky dough with excess flour and then re-rolling scraps, which can result in tough donuts, I pipe rings of dough onto squares of parchment paper, which allows for a seamless transfer to the hot oil and eliminates dough waste. The chocolate, strawberry, and vanilla frostings (see **Donut Frostings,** page 122) are inspired by the paintings of Wayne Thiebaud, one of my favorite artists, who, at the time I was writing this, had just passed away at the age of 101. To simplify things though, you can finish the donuts with just a dusting of confectioners' sugar.

MAKES ABOUT 12 DONUTS

DIFFICULTY: 2 (Easy)

ACTIVE TIME: 1 hour

TOTAL TIME: 1 hour, plus time to cool and set

SPECIAL EQUIPMENT: Pastry bag (or 1-gallon resealable plastic bag), deep-fry thermometer, medium Dutch oven (or large heavy-bottomed saucepan)

DONUT DOUGH

2⅓ cups cake flour (10.3 oz / 293g)

2 teaspoons baking powder

1½ teaspoons Diamond Crystal kosher salt or ¾ teaspoon Morton kosher salt, plus a pinch

½ teaspoon baking soda

¼ teaspoon ground nutmeg

3 large egg yolks (1.6 oz / 45g), at room temperature

½ cup sugar (3.5 oz / 100g)

4 tablespoons unsalted butter (2 oz / 57g), melted and cooled

¾ cup sour cream (6.3 oz / 180g), at room temperature

2 teaspoons vanilla extract

FRYING AND ASSEMBLY

6 cups neutral oil (2.9 lb / 1.3kg), such as peanut, for frying

Chocolate, **Strawberry**, or **Vanilla Donut Frosting** (page 122)

Sprinkles, for topping (optional)

MIX THE DRY INGREDIENTS: In a medium bowl, whisk together the cake flour, baking powder, 1½ teaspoons salt, baking soda, and nutmeg until thoroughly combined.

MAKE THE DOUGH: In a large bowl, whisk the egg yolks and sugar until combined (it will be very thick at first), then whisk vigorously until the mixture is pale and light, about 2 minutes. Whisking constantly, slowly stream in the melted butter and continue to whisk until the mixture is satiny and smooth. Add about half of the dry ingredients and whisk just until the last trace of flour disappears, then add the sour cream and vanilla and whisk until the mixture is smooth. Add the remaining dry ingredients and fold with a flexible spatula, scraping the bottom and sides, just until you have a soft, sticky, evenly mixed dough with no dry spots. Transfer the dough to a pastry bag or a 1-gallon resealable plastic bag, press out the air, and seal (see Filling a Pastry Bag, page 342). Set the bag aside.

PIPE THE BATTER: Use scissors to cut twelve 4-inch squares of parchment paper. Arrange the squares inside a large sheet pan so they're side by side but not overlapping (if necessary, use a second pan). Snip a 1¼-inch opening in the tip or corner of the bag and, working on a single square of parchment, pipe a ring of dough measuring about 3 inches across with a 1-inch-wide hole in the center, overlapping the dough slightly where the ends meet. Repeat with the remaining squares until you've used all the batter (you might get one more or less than 12 rings, depending on how thickly you piped them). Use a wet finger to pat down the dough at the seams and smooth any rough areas. Cover the pan loosely and let sit at room temperature while you heat the oil.

HEAT THE OIL: Clip a deep-fry thermometer to the side of a medium Dutch oven or large heavy-bottomed saucepan and pour in the oil until it reaches between one-third and halfway up the sides, but no higher (if you have any remaining oil, save it for another use). Heat the oil over medium-high heat until it reaches 325°F. Reduce the heat to medium and continue to heat the oil until it registers 350°F on the thermometer. While it's heating, line a large sheet pan with paper towels and set a wire rack on top, then place it next to the stovetop.

→

FRY THE DONUTS: When the oil is at 350°F, slide a thin metal spatula underneath a square of parchment paper and lift and lower the ring of dough carefully into the oil, parchment and all. After a second or two, the donut should bob to the surface, then use a pair of tongs to gently slide the parchment out from underneath the donut and remove it from the oil. Repeat with 2 or 3 more donuts, adding only as many as can comfortably fit in the Dutch oven or saucepan with some room to swim around. Fry the donuts until the side that's submerged in the oil is deep golden brown, about 2 minutes, then turn gently with a spider and fry until the second side is deep golden brown, another 2 minutes or so. Transfer the donuts as they finish frying to the wire rack, then repeat the frying process with the remaining donuts, working in two or three more batches and transferring them to the wire rack as they're done. Let the donuts cool until they're warm but not hot.

Potential Pitfall: Pay attention to the oil temperature throughout the process— adding the rings of dough will cause the temperature to drop, so increase the heat until it reaches 350°F again, and then adjust as needed to maintain that temperature (or thereabouts). Donuts fried at too low a temperature will absorb more oil and be greasy and heavy, so try not to let it dip below 340°F.

FROST THE DONUTS: Uncover the frosting of your choice and whisk if needed to smooth it out. Gently grasp a warm donut around the sides and dip it into the frosting so it's partially submerged, then wiggle it gently for a few seconds to encourage all the nooks and crannies on the surface to pick up the frosting. Lift the donut out and let any excess frosting drip back into the bowl for a moment, then turn it frosting-side up and place back on the wire rack. Repeat until all the donuts are frosted. Shower the sprinkles (if using) over the frosting. Let the donuts sit just until the frosting is set, about 5 minutes, then serve immediately.

Can I . . .

Make them ahead? No. The donuts should be fried and eaten right away. Do not let the rings of dough sit on the covered sheet pan for more than 30 minutes before frying or the donuts will not be as light.

DONUT FROSTINGS

CHOCOLATE FROSTING: In a medium bowl, whisk together 1 cup confectioners' sugar (3.9 oz / 110g), ⅓ cup unsweetened cocoa powder (0.9 oz / 25g), and a pinch of kosher salt. Add ⅓ cup room temperature sour cream (2.8 oz / 80g) and 1 teaspoon vanilla extract and stir slowly until combined, then whisk vigorously until you have a thick, smooth frosting. Cover the bowl and set it aside until you're ready to frost the donuts.

STRAWBERRY FROSTING: Place ½ cup freeze-dried strawberries (0.3 oz / 9g) in a resealable bag and close the bag, pressing out the air. Use a rolling pin or the bottom of a saucepan to crush the strawberries into a fine powder. Transfer the pulverized strawberries to a mesh sieve and shake over a medium bowl, letting the fine particles fall through (save the larger pieces inside the sieve for eating over oatmeal, ice cream, or

EACH MAKES ENOUGH TO FROST 12 DONUTS

yogurt). Add 1½ cups confectioners' sugar (5.8 oz / 65g), sifted if lumpy, to the bowl with the strawberry dust and whisk to combine. Add ¼ cup room temperature sour cream (2.1 oz / 60g), 1 teaspoon fresh lemon juice, and a pinch of salt and stir slowly until combined, then whisk vigorously until you have a thick, smooth frosting. Cover the bowl and set it aside until you're ready to frost the donuts.

VANILLA FROSTING: In a medium bowl, whisk together ¼ cup room temperature sour cream (2.1 oz / 60g), 1½ teaspoons vanilla extract, 1 teaspoon fresh lemon juice, and a pinch of salt until smooth. Whisking slowly, gradually add 2 cups confectioners' sugar (7.8 oz / 220g), sifted if lumpy, then whisk vigorously until you have a thick, smooth frosting. Cover the bowl and set it aside until you're ready to frost the donuts.

Buckwheat & Lemon Crepes Suzette

Crêpes Suzette, a dish of folded crepes caramelized and set aflame in a mixture of butter, sugar, and orange zest and juice, is one of my favorite French desserts. Here, I bring to it the distinct flavor of another favorite French food of mine, a savory buckwheat crepe called a galette (often it's filled with ham, cheese, and a fried egg, called a galette complète). The minerally-ness of buckwheat adds another dimension of flavor to the dish, and to give it some brightness and zip, I replace orange with lemon. While I wouldn't call this an easy recipe—you must be precise with your heat, and the process of cooking and caramelizing the crepes individually takes a bit of time—you can break up the steps and do much of it in advance.

SERVES 4

DIFFICULTY: 3 (Moderate)

ACTIVE TIME: 1 hour 30 minutes

TOTAL TIME: 2 hours

SPECIAL EQUIPMENT: 8-inch nonstick skillet (or crepe pan), 10-inch skillet, stick lighter or long match

CREPES

6 tablespoons unsalted butter (3 oz / 85g), at room temperature, divided

½ cup all-purpose flour (2.4 oz / 67g)

½ cup buckwheat flour (2.1 oz / 60g)

3 tablespoons sugar

½ teaspoon Diamond Crystal kosher salt or ¼ teaspoon Morton kosher salt

2 large eggs (3.5 oz / 100g), beaten, at room temperature

1¼ cups whole milk (10.6 oz / 300g), at room temperature

LEMON "BEURRE SUZETTE" AND ASSEMBLY

2 medium lemons

½ cup sugar (3.5 oz / 100g)

Pinch of kosher salt

5 tablespoons unsalted butter (2.5 oz / 71g), at room temperature

3 tablespoons Cognac or Grand Marnier

1 pint vanilla ice cream, for serving

BROWN THE BUTTER FOR THE CREPES: In a small saucepan, melt 4 tablespoons (2 oz / 57g) of the butter over medium heat. Let the butter come to a boil and cook, stirring constantly with a heatproof flexible spatula and scraping the bottom and sides, until the sputtering subsides, the butter starts to foam, and you see tiny golden brown specks floating around, about 4 minutes (for a visual guide to the process, see Browning Butter, page 353). Remove the saucepan from the heat and scrape the browned butter plus all the golden bits into a small heatproof bowl. Set the bowl aside and let the browned butter cool. Melt the remaining 2 tablespoons butter and reserve for cooking the crepes.

MAKE THE CREPE BATTER: In a large bowl, whisk together the all-purpose flour, buckwheat flour, sugar, and salt. Make a well in the center of the bowl and add the beaten eggs. Whisking constantly in the center of the bowl, slowly stream in the milk and continue to whisk, gradually working in the flour mixture from around the sides of the bowl, until you have a smooth, thin batter that's the consistency of cold heavy cream. Stream in the browned butter, whisking constantly. Cover the batter and set aside to rest at room temperature for 30 minutes.

SLICE AND BLANCH THE LEMON ZEST: Use a vegetable peeler to remove the zest from 1 of the lemons in long, lengthwise strips (just the yellow part, not the white pith, which is bitter), then use a knife to very thinly slice the strips lengthwise. Place the sliced lemon zest in the bottom of a small saucepan and add water just to cover the zest (you can use the same saucepan you used to brown the butter, no need to wash). Bring the water to a boil over medium-high heat, then remove the saucepan from the heat and drain the zest, discarding the water. Transfer the zest to a small bowl and let cool, then cover and set aside.

MAKE THE LEMON "BEURRE SUZETTE": Working over a medium bowl, finely grate the zest of the remaining lemon with a rasp-style grater until you have about 1 tablespoon, then set the bowl aside. Halve the lemon and juice the halves into a glass measuring cup until you have ¼ cup (2 oz / 57g). Set the juice aside. To the bowl with the grated zest, add the sugar and salt and massage the mixture with your fingertips until it's fragrant and looks like wet sand. Add the butter and work the mixture with a flexible spatula until smooth, then add 2 tablespoons of the lemon juice and stir with the spatula until combined (the mixture might look a bit separated, which is fine). Cover the bowl and set aside.

$\rightarrow$

COOK THE CREPES: Place a dinner plate and clean towel next to the stove as a landing pad for the cooked crepes and stir the crepe batter to recombine. Heat an 8-inch nonstick skillet or crepe pan over medium heat. Use a pastry brush to brush the skillet with a thin layer of the reserved melted butter, then tilt the skillet and add ¼ cup (2.3 oz / 65g) of the batter and slowly swirl the skillet until the batter coats the entire surface in an even layer. Cook the crepe undisturbed until the edges are golden and starting to curl and the surface is matte and covered with tiny beads of moisture, about 2 minutes. Slide a heatproof flexible spatula underneath the crepe and flip it—the first side should be browned in spots. Cook the second side just until it's set, another 30 seconds, then transfer the crepe to the plate and cover loosely with the towel. Repeat the cooking process with the remaining melted butter and batter, transferring the crepes one at a time to the plate, stacking them and keeping the plate covered as you work. You'll have around 9 crepes total, but will only need 8 for the finished dish, so if you have an extra, feel free to snack on it.

CARAMELIZE AND FOLD THE CREPES: Line a small sheet pan with parchment and place near the stove for transferring the folded and caramelized crepes. Heat a 10-inch skillet over medium heat. Set aside about ¼ cup (1 oz / 29g) of the lemon beurre Suzette for the final sauce, then add a scant tablespoon of the remaining beurre Suzette to the skillet and swirl to melt. Add one of the crepes browned-side down to the skillet. Scrape a hazelnut-sized knob of the beurre Suzette into the center of the crepe and cook, shaking the skillet often, until the underside is covered in a golden brown caramel, about 2 minutes. Use a heatproof flexible spatula to fold the crepe in half and then in half again, forming a fan shape, and transfer it carefully to the prepared sheet pan. Repeat the caramelizing and folding process with the beurre Suzette and remaining crepes one at a time (note that they'll caramelize more quickly as the skillet continues to heat), transferring each folded crepe to the sheet pan as you work (it's okay if they overlap or touch).

MAKE THE SAUCE AND FLAMBÉ THE CREPES: Add the reserved sliced lemon zest, reserved ¼ cup beurre Suzette, and the remaining 2 tablespoons lemon juice to the skillet and cook over medium heat, stirring constantly, until the mixture is combined and bubbling, about 20 seconds (the skillet will still be hot, so this happens quickly). Carefully transfer the folded, caramelized crepes to the skillet (they're hot!) in an overlapping pattern. Allow the crepes to heat through for about a minute, swirling the skillet to coat them in the sauce. Have the lighter or match ready, then add the Cognac all at once and, holding your head back, quickly ignite it. Shake the skillet with a gloved hand until the flames subside. Turn off the heat and slide the skillet to a cool burner to cool for a few minutes.

SERVE: Let the ice cream soften for a few minutes at room temperature. Transfer the hot crepes to plates or shallow bowls, 2 per serving, then spoon the sliced lemon zest and any saucy caramel left in the skillet on top, dividing it evenly. Scoop the ice cream on top of the warm crepes and serve immediately.

Can I . . .

Make it ahead? Partially, yes. The crepes should be caramelized and flambéed just before serving, but the batter can be covered and refrigerated for up to 1 day. Let it come to room temperature before cooking. The cooked crepes can be covered tightly and refrigerated for up to 1 day.

Make it gluten-free? Not advised. While some buckwheat crepes are made with 100 percent buckwheat, which is gluten-free, they have a very intense flavor and are fragile, making them unsuitable here. This recipe calls for all-purpose flour in equal proportion to buckwheat because the gluten lends needed elasticity to the crepes and mellows the buckwheat flavor.

Just make the crepes and skip the flambéing? Yes! The buckwheat crepes are delicious for breakfast, lightly buttered and/or served with jam. You can also fill them with a fried egg, cheese, and thinly sliced ham.

Pillowy Beignets

It's faith-restoring when a food item (or anything, for that matter) lives up to the great hype surrounding it, so it was an affirming experience when I had my first beignets at Café Du Monde in New Orleans several years ago. Beignets are squares of fried dough similar to donuts, and even with high expectations, I found the chewiness and lightness of the ones at Café Du Monde miraculous. I have wanted to re-create something similar ever since, and this is my attempt. Though it's the only yeasted recipe in the book, these beignets are straightforward to make and, deep-frying aside, hard to mess up because they shouldn't look too uniform or neat. Like the ones at Café Du Monde, my beignets start with a wet dough (one of the keys to the large interior holes) and emerge from the fryer as airy pillows. When I say to generously coat them in confectioners' sugar, I mean *generously,* and serve with a cup of strong coffee.

MAKES 35 TO 40 BEIGNETS

DIFFICULTY: 3 (Moderate)

ACTIVE TIME: 1 hour 10 minutes

TOTAL TIME: 6 hours 10 minutes (depending on the rise time)

SPECIAL EQUIPMENT: Bowl scraper (optional but recommended), deep-fry thermometer, medium Dutch oven (or large heavy-bottomed saucepan), wheel cutter

3¾ cups all-purpose flour (17.8 oz / 506g), preferably a high-protein brand such as King Arthur, plus more for rolling

¼ cup rye or whole wheat flour (1.2 oz / 34g)

½ cup granulated sugar (3.5 oz / 100g)

2¾ teaspoons Diamond Crystal kosher salt or 1½ teaspoons Morton kosher salt

1 teaspoon baking powder

1 teaspoon active dry yeast

½ cup whole milk (4.2 oz / 120g), at room temperature

2 large eggs (3.5 oz / 100g), beaten, at room temperature

6 cups neutral oil (2.9 lb / 1.3kg), such as peanut, for deep-frying

Confectioners' sugar, for serving

MIX THE DRY INGREDIENTS: In a large bowl, whisk together the all-purpose flour, rye flour, granulated sugar, salt, and baking powder to combine. Set aside.

DISSOLVE THE YEAST, THEN MIX THE WET INGREDIENTS: In a medium bowl, combine the yeast and ¾ cup plus 2 tablespoons (7 oz / 200g) lukewarm water and whisk thoroughly to dissolve the yeast. Add the milk and eggs and whisk thoroughly until smooth.

Potential Pitfall: I generally skip the step of "proofing" yeast, or waiting for it to foam to prove it's alive, as I'm confident the active dry yeast I keep at home is fresh. However, if your yeast is old or from an opened package, proof it by whisking a pinch of sugar into the water and yeast mixture and letting it sit undisturbed until you see foamy patches across the surface, 5 to 10 minutes. Whisk in the milk and eggs and proceed.

MIX THE DOUGH: Make a well in the center of the dry ingredients, then pour in the wet ingredients. Use a bowl scraper or a large flexible spatula to mix until all of the flour is hydrated and you have a very wet, evenly mixed dough that almost looks like a thick batter. Use the scraper or spatula to scrape down the sides, making sure there's no unincorporated flour in the bottom of the bowl, then clean off the scraper and set it aside.

KNEAD THE DOUGH: Hold the bowl steady with one hand and use the other to grasp a handful of dough from along the side of the bowl, then stretch it upward and fold it into the center. Rotate the bowl slightly, then repeat this motion, lifting a portion of the dough and pressing it back into the center. It will be very loose and sticky but will gradually firm up and start to hold its shape as you work. Continue to knead, pausing occasionally and using the bowl scraper or spatula to clean the dough from your hand and scrape down the sides of the bowl, until the dough is elastic and puts up some resistance as you lift it, 10 to 12 minutes (it will still be very sticky, though less sticky than before). Scrape down the sides of the bowl one more time and gather the dough into a single mass in the bottom.

LET THE DOUGH RISE, THEN CHILL IT: Cover the bowl and let the dough sit at room temperature until it's doubled in size and bubbly across the surface, 1 to 1½ hours. Transfer the covered bowl to the refrigerator and chill until the dough is cold, at least 4 hours (this will help develop the flavor of the beignets and make the dough easier to handle).

→

HEAT THE OIL: Clip a deep-fry thermometer to the side of a medium Dutch oven or large heavy-bottomed saucepan. Pour in the oil until it reaches between one-third and halfway up the sides, but no higher (if you have any remaining oil, save it for another use). Heat the oil over medium-high heat until it reaches 325°F. Reduce the heat to medium and continue to heat the oil until it registers 375°F on the thermometer. While it's heating, line a large sheet pan with paper towels and set a wire rack on top, then place it next to the stovetop.

MEANWHILE, ROLL OUT AND CUT THE BEIGNETS: *Very* generously flour an 18 × 13-inch area of work surface, then remove the dough from the refrigerator and scrape it out onto the floured surface. Generously flour the surface of the dough, then pat it down with your palms into a rectangular slab measuring about ⅜ inch thick, 18 inches long, and 13 inches wide, adding more flour as needed to prevent sticking. Use a wheel cutter to cut the slab into 2½-inch squares. Discard any scraps from along the edges, then quickly separate the squares on the work surface and dust with more flour to prevent sticking along the cut sides. Cover the beignets with a clean towel.

FRY THE BEIGNETS: When the oil is ready, uncover the dough, pick up a square, and toss it back and forth gently between your hands to dust off excess flour, then drop it carefully into the oil. Repeat with more squares of dough, adding only as many as can comfortably fit in the Dutch oven or saucepan with some room to swim around (keep the remaining pieces covered on the work surface). Fry the beignets, turning them several times with a slotted spoon or spider, until they're puffed and deep golden brown all over, 2 to 3 minutes total. Use the spider to transfer the beignets to the wire rack, then repeat the frying process with the remaining squares of dough in additional batches, transferring the beignets to the wire rack as they're done.

> *Potential Pitfall:* Pay attention to the oil temperature throughout the process—adding the cold dough will cause the temperature to drop, so increase the heat until it comes back to 375°F and then adjust as needed to maintain that temperature (or thereabouts).

SERVE: While the beignets are still hot and resting on the wire rack, dust them very generously with confectioners' sugar. Transfer the beignets to a plate or platter and serve immediately.

Can I . . .

Make them ahead? Only the dough. The beignets should be eaten right after frying, but the dough can be kept covered and refrigerated for up to 12 hours.

Halve the recipe? Yes. Halve all of the ingredient quantities, using 1¾ cups plus 2 tablespoons all-purpose flour (8.9 oz / 253g) and 1½ teaspoons Diamond Crystal kosher salt (or ¾ teaspoon Morton kosher salt). Follow the recipe as written, patting the dough into a 9 × 13-inch slab.

Use a stand mixer to assemble the dough? Yes. Whisk together the flour, rye flour, granulated sugar, salt, and baking powder in a stand mixer fitted with the dough hook and make a well in the center. Dissolve the yeast and mix the wet ingredients in a separate bowl as directed. Pour the wet ingredients into the stand mixer and stir with a flexible spatula or wooden spoon until all of the flour is hydrated. Mix with the hook on medium-low speed, stopping the mixer to scrape down the sides of the bowl once or twice, until the dough is smooth, elastic, and somewhat gathered around the hook but still quite sticky, 15 to 20 minutes. Proceed with the recipe as written.

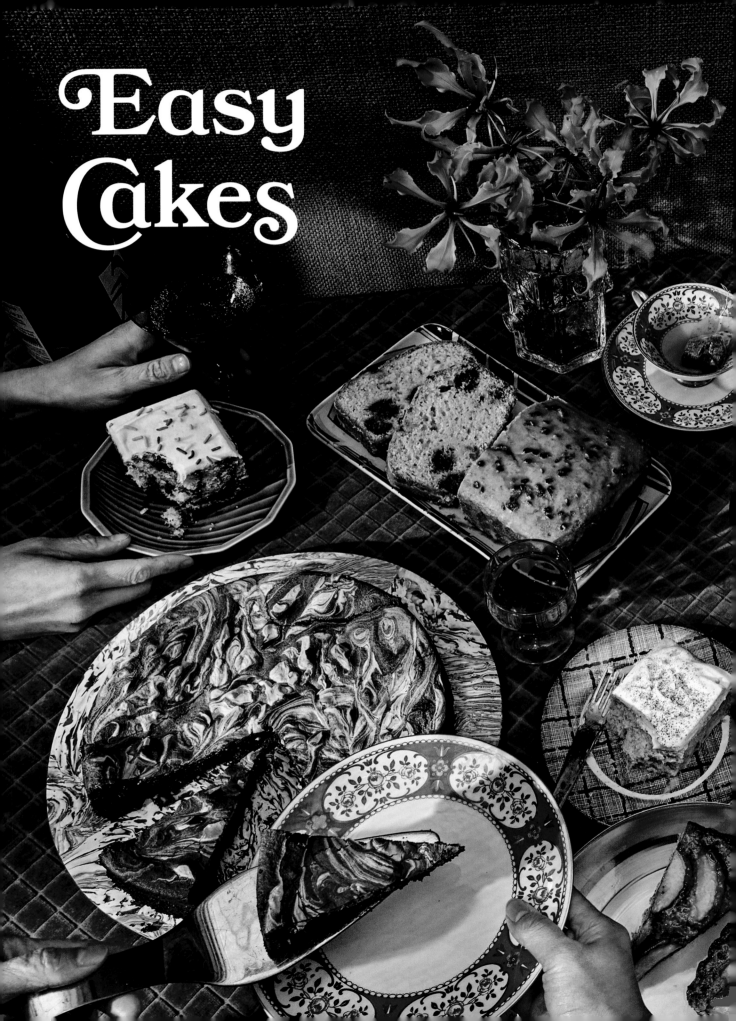

Easy Cakes

I have written this before, but it's worth repeating: Even though I love to bake, I am becoming an increasingly lazy baker. For example, I am loath to lift my stand mixer off the cart in my kitchen where I keep it tucked away and place it on my countertop. This laziness has actually become an asset, as it spurred an all-around drive toward simplicity in this book. I didn't want the lack of an expensive stand mixer to impede any person's ability to bake these recipes, so the easy cakes in this chapter require at most a hand mixer, and several can be made entirely by hand. There are snackable cakes that keep well on your counter and can be enjoyed any time of day, like **Crunchy Almond Cake** (page 143), cakes that pull double-duty as dessert and sweet breakfast, like **Rhubarb & Oat Crumb Cakes** (page 137), and cakes that are celebratory, like **Marbled Sheet Cake** (page 176). You'll find reinterpreted classics that maintain the familiar flavors of the originals while subtly enhancing them with an unexpected ingredient or texture, like **Polenta Pistachio Pound Cake** (page 164) or **Blueberry Buckle with Cornflake Streusel** (page 141). I hope one or more of these becomes a new classic in your kitchen.

Fennel & Olive Oil Cake

with Blackberries

Kalustyan's in Manhattan is one of the most fascinating and impressive spice and specialty food stores anywhere. I stop by whenever I'm in the neighborhood, often just to browse, and usually end up buying several things I never knew I needed. One item I make a point of buying there is saunf mukhwas, or Indian candy-coated fennel seeds. They're used as a palate cleanser, breath freshener, and digestive aid, but I just like nibbling on them for their heady mix of sweet, floral, and licorice-y flavors. That combination is what inspired this olive oil loaf cake. Just ¼ teaspoon chopped fennel seeds, sizzled in olive oil, perfumes the entire cake. It's interesting, which is not always a high compliment when it comes to dessert, but in this case, the brightening addition of blackberries and lemon steers it into highly snackable territory.

MAKES 1 LOAF

DIFFICULTY: 1 (Very Easy)

ACTIVE TIME: 30 minutes

TOTAL TIME: 2 hours, plus time to cool

SPECIAL EQUIPMENT: Metal loaf pan (4½ × 8½ inches, measured across the top), hand mixer

Olive oil for the pan

½ cup plus 1 teaspoon extra-virgin olive oil (4.1 oz / 117g)

¼ teaspoon fennel seeds, finely chopped

2 teaspoons finely grated lemon zest

1⅔ cups plus 1 tablespoon all-purpose flour (8.2 oz / 233g)

1¼ teaspoons baking powder

1 teaspoon Diamond Crystal kosher salt or ½ teaspoon Morton kosher salt

½ teaspoon baking soda

⅔ cup plus 1 tablespoon plain whole-milk (not Greek) yogurt (6.2 oz / 175g)

2 tablespoons plus 1 teaspoon fresh lemon juice

1 teaspoon vanilla extract

2 large eggs (3.5 oz / 100g), at room temperature

1 cup granulated sugar (7 oz / 200g)

6 ounces (170g) fresh or frozen (but not thawed) blackberries, halved crosswise if large (about 1½ cups)

¾ cup confectioners' sugar (2.9 oz / 83g), sifted if lumpy

PREHEAT THE OVEN AND PREPARE THE PAN: Arrange an oven rack in the center position and preheat the oven to 350°F. Brush the bottom and sides of a 4½ × 8½-inch metal loaf pan with a thin layer of olive oil. Line the bottom and two longer sides with a piece of parchment paper, leaving an overhang of an inch or two on each side. Oil the parchment paper, then set the pan aside.

MAKE THE FENNEL OIL: In a small saucepan, combine ½ cup (4 oz / 112g) of the olive oil and the fennel seeds and heat over medium-low heat, swirling the pan occasionally, until the seeds begin to sizzle and the mixture is fragrant, about 3 minutes. Remove the saucepan from the heat and stir in the lemon zest (it will immediately sizzle and sputter, then subside). Set the saucepan aside and let the oil infuse with the fennel and lemon as it cools.

MIX THE DRY INGREDIENTS: In a medium bowl, whisk together 1⅔ cups (7.9 oz / 225g) of the flour, the baking powder, salt, and baking soda to combine. Set aside.

MIX THE WET INGREDIENTS: In a separate medium bowl, whisk together ⅔ cup (5.6 oz / 160g) of the yogurt, 2 tablespoons of the lemon juice, and the vanilla until smooth. Set aside.

BEAT THE EGGS AND SUGAR, THEN STREAM IN THE INFUSED OIL: In a separate large bowl, with a hand mixer, beat the eggs and granulated sugar on medium-low speed until the eggs are broken up, then increase the speed to medium-high and beat until the mixture is light, thick, and mousse-y, about 3 minutes. Beating constantly, very gradually stream in the cooled infused olive oil mixture, pausing to scrape in all the seeds and zest, and continue to beat just until the mixture is smooth and emulsified.

MAKE THE BATTER: Reduce the mixer speed to low, then add about one-third of the dry ingredients and mix just until the flour disappears. Add half of the wet ingredients and mix just until combined, then add the remaining dry ingredients in two additions, alternating with the remaining wet ingredients, and mix just until the last trace of flour disappears. Switch to a flexible spatula and fold the mixture several times, thoroughly scraping the bottom and sides of the bowl, to make sure the batter is evenly mixed.

→

Can I . . .

Make it ahead? Yes. The cake, covered and stored at room temperature, will keep for up to 4 days but is best served on the first or second day while the glaze is fresh.

Use a stand mixer instead of a hand mixer? Yes. Combine the eggs and sugar in a stand mixer fitted with the whisk attachment and proceed with the recipe as written, switching to the paddle after streaming in the infused olive oil.

Bake this in a different pan? Yes. You can bake the cake in a 9-inch round cake pan lined with a silicone or parchment round and brushed with oil. Start checking for doneness around 35 minutes.

ADD THE BLACKBERRIES: Set aside 2 whole blackberries for the glaze, then toss the remaining blackberries in the remaining 1 tablespoon flour in a small bowl until evenly coated (this will help prevent the berries from sinking to the bottom of the cake). Add the coated berries to the batter and fold gently until the berries are distributed, then scrape the batter into the prepared pan and smooth the top.

BAKE: Bake the cake until the surface is golden brown, risen, and split, and a cake tester or skewer inserted into the center comes out clean, 50 to 60 minutes. Remove the cake from the oven and let cool in the pan for 20 minutes, then use a paring knife or a small offset spatula to cut down between the cake and the pan along the shorter sides. Use the parchment overhang to lift out the loaf and let it cool completely on a wire rack.

MAKE THE GLAZE: While the cake is cooling, place the 2 reserved blackberries in a medium bowl and crush them thoroughly with the back of a spoon to release their juices. Add the remaining 1 tablespoon yogurt, 1 teaspoon lemon juice, and 1 teaspoon olive oil and whisk to combine. Add the confectioners' sugar and whisk until the glaze is lump-free and fluid. Pour the glaze over the top of the cooled cake and let it sit until the glaze is set, at least 15 minutes.

Rhubarb & Oat Crumb Cakes

My mom, a great baker, has amassed an impressive collection of recipes over several decades, clipped from newspapers and magazines or copied onto notecards in her distinctive handwriting. Going through her recipe box and reading the stained, yellowed, and worn pages brings up vivid food memories from childhood. One memory is savoring her rhubarb bars from the still-warm pan. The recipe, which my aunt passed to my mom, uses a single stir-together oat crumble as both the base and the topping for the rhubarb filling. Those bars inspired these rhubarb and oat crumb cakes, which are baked individually in a muffin pan and make a moderately sweet, fruit-heavy summertime snack (and even breakfast). Like the bars, they're made from a single oat base that becomes the cake and crumb topping.

SERVES 10

DIFFICULTY: 1 (Very Easy)

ACTIVE TIME: 30 minutes

TOTAL TIME: 1 hour 40 minutes, plus time to cool

SPECIAL EQUIPMENT: Standard 12-cup muffin pan (preferably not nonstick)

2 cups all-purpose flour (9.5 oz / 270g)

¾ cup old-fashioned rolled oats (2.1 oz / 60g)

¾ cup sugar (5.3 oz / 150g)

1 teaspoon Diamond Crystal kosher salt or ½ teaspoon Morton kosher salt

¾ teaspoon ground cardamom

10 tablespoons unsalted butter (5 oz / 141g), melted and cooled, divided

1½ teaspoons baking powder

½ cup unsweetened applesauce (4.2 oz / 120g)

2 large eggs (3.5 oz / 100g), at room temperature

2 teaspoons vanilla extract

8 ounces (226g) rhubarb stalks, halved lengthwise if thick, cut crosswise into ½-inch pieces (about 1½ cups)

⅓ cup strawberry jam or preserves (3.8 oz / 107g)

PREHEAT THE OVEN AND PREPARE THE PAN: Arrange an oven rack in the center position and preheat the oven to 375°F. Line a 12-cup muffin pan with paper liners.

MAKE THE BASE AND TOPPING: In a large bowl, whisk together the flour, oats, sugar, salt, and cardamom to combine. Transfer 1 cup of the mixture to a separate medium bowl, add 4 tablespoons (2 oz / 57g) of the melted butter, and stir with a fork until no dry spots remain and the mixture holds together in large crumbs—this is your topping. Set aside.

MAKE THE BATTER: To the remaining flour mixture in the large bowl, add the baking powder and whisk to combine (this step is easy to miss—don't forget the baking powder!). Make a well in the center of the bowl. Add the remaining 6 tablespoons (3 oz / 85g) melted butter, the applesauce, eggs, and vanilla and whisk, starting in the center and working outward, until you have a smooth batter. Set aside.

MIX THE RHUBARB AND JAM: In a separate medium bowl, mix the rhubarb and strawberry jam with a flexible spatula until the rhubarb is completely coated. Set aside.

ASSEMBLE AND BAKE THE CAKES: Use a scoop or two spoons to drop the batter into the muffin cups, dividing evenly (it will be about ¼ cup / 1.9 oz / 55g of batter per cup). Spoon the rhubarb mixture over the batter, dividing evenly, then sprinkle the crumb topping over the rhubarb, also dividing evenly. Bake until the cakes are domed, the crumb topping is golden brown, and the centers are springy to the touch, 20 to 25 minutes. Remove the cakes from the oven and let them cool completely in the pan.

Can I . . .

Make them ahead? Yes. The cakes, covered and stored at room temperature, will keep for up to 3 days.

Use another fruit if I can't find rhubarb? Yes. Replace the rhubarb with an equal weight of blackberries, blueberries, or raspberries. Use any type of jam but decrease the amount to 2 tablespoons, because these fruits are sweeter than rhubarb.

Honey-Roasted Apple Cake

My entire career, I have been on a quest for the perfect Jewish apple cake. To me that means a simple, oil-based cake packed with apples and flavored with honey (in order to make it fitting for Rosh Hashanah, the Jewish New Year, when apples and honey are eaten together). My exhaustive testing determined that before they're added to the batter, the apples really must be cooked to draw out their juices and tenderize them, thereby preventing squidginess and gaps around the fruit in the baked cake. Here I drizzle 2 pounds of sliced apples with honey and a little olive oil and roast them, ensuring the many layers of apples inside the light, tender cake are soft enough to cut with a spoon. It's the apple cake of my dreams.

SERVES 8

DIFFICULTY: 1 (Very Easy)

DAIRY-FREE

ACTIVE TIME: 40 minutes

TOTAL TIME: 2 hours 20 minutes, plus time to cool

SPECIAL EQUIPMENT: 9-inch springform pan, apple corer

2 pounds (907g) firm sweet-tart apples, such as Pink Lady (about 5 medium)

4 tablespoons honey (3 oz / 84g), divided

1 tablespoon plus ½ cup extra-virgin olive oil (4.4 oz / 126g)

1⅔ cups all-purpose flour (7.9 oz / 225g)

1¾ teaspoons baking powder

1 teaspoon Diamond Crystal kosher salt or ½ teaspoon Morton kosher salt

½ teaspoon baking soda

½ teaspoon ground cinnamon

¼ teaspoon ground allspice

⅛ teaspoon ground nutmeg

4 large eggs (7 oz / 200g), at room temperature

½ cup plus 2 tablespoons demerara sugar (4.4 oz / 124g)

2 teaspoons vanilla extract

2 teaspoons apple cider vinegar

Can I . . .

Make it ahead? Yes. The cake, well wrapped and stored at room temperature, will keep for up to 4 days and is best eaten on the second day once the flavors have a chance to meld (the apple slices will keep it moist).

Bake this in a different pan? Yes. Roast the apples and bake the cake in an 8 × 8-inch baking pan, preferably metal, brushed with olive oil and lined across the bottom and two opposite sides with a piece of parchment paper. The bake time will be about the same.

PREHEAT THE OVEN AND PREPARE THE PAN: Arrange an oven rack in the center position and preheat the oven to 350°F. Press a 12-inch square of parchment paper into the bottom of a 9-inch springform pan, smoothing it up the sides and pressing down on any folds to flatten.

SLICE THE APPLES: Set the apples on a cutting board and, working one at a time, use a sharp knife to slice off a thin piece of flesh from the base and stem ends of the apples, creating two flat surfaces on each (discard or snack on the trim). Stand each apple upright and use an apple corer to cut out the cores, then use a mandoline or a sharp knife to cut them horizontally into ⅛-inch-thick slices (try to slice them evenly, but some variation in thickness is fine).

ROAST THE APPLES: Arrange about one-quarter of the apple slices in the bottom of the prepared pan and drizzle with 1 tablespoon of the honey. Layer in more apples, drizzle with another tablespoon of honey, and repeat two more times with the remaining apples and 2 tablespoons of the honey. Drizzle 1 tablespoon of the olive oil over the layers of apples and honey. Transfer to the oven and roast until the slices have released their juices and are translucent and tender (it's okay if some of them start to fall apart), 1 hour to 1 hour 15 minutes, folding the apples gently every 20 minutes with a spatula. Set the pan aside and allow the apples to cool. Leave the oven on.

MIX THE DRY INGREDIENTS: In a medium bowl, whisk together the flour, baking powder, salt, baking soda, cinnamon, allspice, and nutmeg. Set aside.

MAKE THE BATTER: In a large bowl, combine the eggs and ½ cup (3.5 oz / 100g) of the demerara sugar and whisk vigorously until the mixture is slightly thickened, about 1 minute. Slowly stream in the remaining ½ cup (4 oz / 112g) olive oil, whisking constantly, until the mixture is smooth, satiny, and thick. Whisk in the vanilla and vinegar. Add the dry ingredients and whisk just until the last trace of flour disappears and you have a smooth, evenly mixed batter.

FOLD IN THE APPLES: Set aside 10 or 11 apple slices for arranging on top of the cake, then tip the rest of the apples and the roasting juices into the bowl with the batter (leave the parchment in the pan and reserve for baking the cake). Fold the mixture with a flexible spatula, scraping the bottom and sides of the bowl, until the apples are evenly distributed and the juices have been absorbed. Don't worry if folding breaks up some of the apple slices— the softer pieces will just blend into the cake.

ASSEMBLE AND BAKE: Scrape the batter into the reserved pan and smooth into an even layer. Arrange the reserved apple slices across the surface, then sprinkle with the remaining 2 tablespoons demerara sugar. Bake until the cake is deep golden brown across the surface and a toothpick or cake tester inserted into the center comes out clean, 45 to 50 minutes. Let the cake cool completely in the pan.

Blueberry Buckle

with Cornflake Streusel

One of my favorite things about summer is spending time on Cape Cod with my family and eating my mom's blueberry buckle. It's a Martha Stewart recipe from many years ago, and it was my introduction to buckles, a category of streusel-topped cakes that incorporate lots of fruit. What I love about Martha's recipe is that it's almost more fruit than cake, featuring clusters of berries barely held together by a tender batter. I wanted to create a similar blueberry buckle that incorporated the flavors and textures of corn, since corn and blueberries are natural partners. I do this two ways: First, crushed cornflakes are mixed into the streusel topping, contributing a light and satisfying crunch, and second, cornmeal is added to the batter, providing some textural contrast against the soft berries. Serve the buckle with vanilla ice cream for dessert and then enjoy again for breakfast the next morning, which is how we eat Martha's.

SERVES 12

DIFFICULTY: 1 (Very Easy)

ACTIVE TIME: 35 minutes

TOTAL TIME: 2 hours 20 minutes, plus time to cool

SPECIAL EQUIPMENT: 10-inch springform pan, hand mixer

STREUSEL

1 cup all-purpose flour (4.8 oz / 135g)

½ cup packed light brown sugar (3.9 oz / 110g)

½ teaspoon Diamond Crystal kosher salt or ¼ teaspoon Morton kosher salt

½ teaspoon ground cinnamon

1 stick unsalted butter (4 oz / 113g), cut into ½-inch pieces, at room temperature

1 cup cornflakes (1.2 oz / 35g), lightly crushed

CAKE

Melted butter for the pan

1⅔ cups all-purpose flour (7.9 oz / 225g)

⅓ cup coarse-ground yellow cornmeal (1.8 oz / 50g)

2 teaspoons Diamond Crystal kosher salt or 1 teaspoon Morton kosher salt

1½ teaspoons baking powder

½ teaspoon baking soda

1 cup granulated sugar (7 oz / 200g)

2 teaspoons finely grated lemon zest

10 tablespoons unsalted butter (5 oz / 141g), at room temperature

2 large eggs (3.5 oz / 100g), at room temperature

½ cup buttermilk (4.2 oz / 120g), at room temperature

1 teaspoon vanilla extract

1½ pounds (680g) fresh or frozen (but not thawed) blueberries (2 dry pints / about 4 cups)

MAKE THE STREUSEL: In a medium bowl, whisk together the flour, brown sugar, salt, and cinnamon until combined. Add the butter to the bowl and mash with a fork until the pieces are blended into the dry ingredients but the mixture is still floury, then use your fingertips to work the mixture until you have moist crumbs that hold together easily when squeezed and no dry spots. Add the crushed cornflakes and toss gently to distribute them throughout the streusel. Set aside.

PREHEAT THE OVEN AND PREPARE THE PAN: Arrange an oven rack in the center position and preheat the oven to 350°F. Brush the bottom and sides of a 10-inch springform pan with melted butter. Line the bottom with a silicone or parchment round and set the pan aside.

MIX THE DRY INGREDIENTS: In a medium bowl, whisk together the flour, cornmeal, salt, baking powder, and baking soda until combined. Set aside.

CREAM THE SUGAR, ZEST, AND BUTTER: In a large bowl, combine the granulated sugar and lemon zest and massage the mixture with your fingertips until it's very fragrant and looks like wet sand. Add the butter and beat with a hand mixer on medium-low speed until combined, then increase the speed to medium-high and beat, pausing occasionally to scrape down the sides of the bowl with a flexible spatula, until the mixture is pale and fluffy, about 4 minutes (see Creaming Butter and Sugar, page 351).

BEAT IN THE EGGS: Beat in the eggs one at a time on medium-high until smooth, then continue to beat until the mixture is very light, thick, and creamy, about 2 minutes longer.

MAKE THE BATTER: Reduce the mixer speed to low and add about one-third of the dry ingredients, mixing just until incorporated, then add half of the buttermilk and mix until combined. Add the remaining dry ingredients in two additions, alternating with the remaining buttermilk and the vanilla, and mix just until the last trace of flour disappears. Switch to a flexible spatula and fold the batter several times, scraping the bottom and sides of the bowl, to make sure it's evenly mixed (it will be thick). Add the blueberries—it will seem like a lot of berries for the amount of batter, but that's right—and fold gently to incorporate, trying not to crush them. If you're using frozen

→

Can I . . .

Make it ahead? Yes. The buckle, covered and stored at room temperature, will keep for up to 3 days, but it's best served on the first or second day while the streusel is crunchy (it will soften over time).

Use a stand mixer instead of a hand mixer? Yes. Use your fingertips to massage the sugar and lemon zest in a stand mixer fitted with the paddle attachment, then add the butter and proceed with the recipe as written.

Bake this in a different pan? Yes. You can bake the cake in a 9 × 9-inch baking pan brushed with melted butter and lined across the bottom and two opposite sides with parchment paper. The bake time will be about the same.

blueberries, they'll turn the batter purplish and cause it to seize in places—don't worry, it won't affect the final cake.

ASSEMBLE AND BAKE: Scrape the batter into the prepared pan and smooth it into an even layer, taking care not to form any air pockets, then sprinkle the reserved streusel across the batter in an even layer. Bake until the surface of the cake is slightly domed, the streusel is golden brown, and a cake tester or skewer inserted into the center comes out clean, 1 hour 30 minutes to 1 hour 40 minutes for fresh berries, or 1 hour 45 minutes to 1 hour 55 miniutes for frozen. Let the cake cool completely in the pan, then use a paring knife or small offset spatula to cut down between the cake and the sides of the pan all the way around to loosen. Remove the outer ring of the pan.

Crunchy Almond Cake

Warning: This cake, which is made from almond paste, spiked with amaretto, and topped with sugared sliced almonds, is intensely almondy and should be served to true almond lovers only! It hits all the right notes for me: not too cakey, not too dense, not too sweet, filled with rich oils from the almond paste, and incredibly satisfying from the crunch of toasted almonds. You can serve it with any fruit (I suggest the **Slow-Roasted Plums**, page 233), but as an almond lover, I find it just as appealing plain.

SERVES 8

DIFFICULTY: 1 (Very Easy)

SERVE WITH: Slow-Roasted Plums (page 233)

ACTIVE TIME: 40 minutes

TOTAL TIME: 1 hour 25 minutes, plus time to cool

SPECIAL EQUIPMENT: 9-inch cake pan, hand mixer

1 cup sliced unblanched almonds (4 oz / 113g)

Melted butter for the pan

¼ cup demerara sugar (1.8 oz / 50g)

¾ cup plus 2 tablespoons all-purpose flour (4.1 oz / 118g)

1 teaspoon baking powder

¾ teaspoon Diamond Crystal kosher salt or ½ teaspoon Morton kosher salt

7 ounces (200g) almond paste

1½ sticks unsalted butter (6 oz / 170g), at room temperature

⅔ cup granulated sugar (4.7 oz / 133g)

4 large eggs (7 oz / 200g), at room temperature

¼ cup amaretto (2 oz / 57g)

2 teaspoons vanilla extract

PREHEAT THE OVEN: Arrange an oven rack in the center position and preheat the oven to 350°F.

TOAST THE ALMONDS: Scatter the sliced almonds across a sheet pan in an even layer and toast until they're golden and fragrant, 5 to 8 minutes, tossing halfway through. Set aside to cool. Leave the oven on.

PREPARE THE PAN: Brush the bottom and sides of a 9-inch cake pan with melted butter, then line the bottom with a round of parchment paper and smooth it to eliminate any air bubbles. Butter the parchment.

MAKE THE CRUNCHY LAYER: Lightly sprinkle some of the demerara sugar across the bottom of the prepared pan, then scatter a handful of the toasted almonds on top (it's fine if they're warm). Sprinkle with more demerara sugar, scatter more almonds, and continue alternating until you've used all the demerara sugar and toasted almonds and covered the bottom of the pan in an even layer. Set the pan aside.

MIX THE DRY INGREDIENTS: In a medium bowl, whisk together the flour, baking powder, and salt until combined. Set aside.

CREAM THE ALMOND PASTE, BUTTER, AND SUGAR: Crumble the almond paste into a large bowl and break up any larger pieces with your fingertips. Add the butter and granulated sugar and beat with a hand mixer on medium-low speed until the sugar and butter are incorporated. Increase the speed to medium-high and beat, pausing occasionally to scrape down the sides of the bowl with a flexible spatula, until the almond paste is broken down into tiny pieces and the mixture is pale and fluffy, about 5 minutes.

> *Optional Upgrade:* The bits of almond paste mostly disappear during baking, but for an ultrasmooth batter and a more finely textured cake—or if your almond paste is particularly dry or hard—combine the crumbled almond paste, butter, and sugar in a food processor and pulse until the mixture is completely smooth, then transfer to a large bowl and beat with the hand mixer as directed.

BEAT IN THE EGGS: Beat in the eggs one at a time on medium-high until smooth, then continue to beat until the mixture is very light, thick, and creamy, about 1 minute longer.

→

✿Can I . . .

Make it ahead? Yes. The cake, well wrapped and stored at room temperature, will keep for up to 4 days.

Make it gluten-free? Yes. Replace the all-purpose flour with an equal amount of your preferred gluten-free flour blend and bake as directed.

Use a stand mixer instead of a hand mixer? Yes. Combine the crumbled almond paste, butter, and sugar in a stand mixer fitted with the paddle attachment and proceed with the recipe as written. The stand mixer will be more efficient than the hand mixer at breaking down the almond paste, so you'll have a smoother batter.

MAKE THE BATTER: Reduce the mixer speed to low and add about half of the dry ingredients, mixing just until the flour disappears, then add the amaretto and vanilla and mix until combined. Add the remaining dry ingredients and mix just until you have a smooth batter. Switch to a flexible spatula and fold the batter several times, scraping the bottom and sides of the bowl, to make sure it's evenly mixed.

FILL THE PAN: Slowly and gently scrape the batter into the prepared pan, trying not to disturb the almonds and sugar at the bottom. Carefully work the batter to the sides of the pan with a spatula and smooth the surface.

BAKE: Bake the cake until the surface is domed and deep golden brown (it will brown more than you might expect) and a toothpick or cake tester inserted into the center comes out clean, 35 to 40 minutes. Let the cake cool in the pan for 15 minutes, then, using a small offset spatula or paring knife and keeping it pressed firmly up against the side of the pan, cut down and around the cake to loosen it. Invert the cake onto the wire rack and slowly remove the pan, then carefully peel away the parchment. Let the cake cool completely.

Potential Pitfall: Don't let the cake cool in the pan for longer than 15 or 20 minutes before turning it out, or the crunchy almond layer will start to harden and stick to the pan around the edge (despite the parchment paper).

Peach, Bourbon & Pecan Cake

Fruit tarts made with frangipane, a creamy almond filling that's commonly used in French pastry, are among my favorite desserts, and this cake—inspired by the very American Southern combination of pecans and peaches—is like an easier version. The buttery frangipane-like batter is packed with crushed toasted pecans, sweetened with brown sugar, and spiked with a little bourbon (the first taste instantly reminded me of New Orleans–style pralines, the candies made from pecans and brown sugar). Use ripe freestone peaches if you can, since they'll be much easier to pit and slice, but see Can I . . . on page 148 if you'd like to use frozen.

SERVES 8

DIFFICULTY: 2 (Easy)

ACTIVE TIME: 35 minutes

TOTAL TIME: 1 hour 45 minutes, plus time to cool

SPECIAL EQUIPMENT: 9-inch removable-bottom tart pan (or 9-inch springform pan), hand mixer

Butter and flour for the pan

1½ cups pecan halves or pieces (6 oz / 170g)

1 cup all-purpose flour (4.8 oz / 135g)

1½ teaspoons baking powder

1 stick unsalted butter (4 oz / 113g), at room temperature

⅔ cup packed dark brown sugar (5.2 oz / 147g)

1 teaspoon Diamond Crystal kosher salt or ½ teaspoon Morton kosher salt

3 large eggs (5.3 oz / 150g), at room temperature

2 tablespoons bourbon or other whiskey

2 teaspoons vanilla extract

3 ripe medium peaches (about 12 oz / 340g), halved, pitted, and cut into 1-inch-thick wedges

⅓ cup peach or apricot jam (3.8 oz / 107g)

PREHEAT THE OVEN AND PREPARE THE PAN: Arrange an oven rack in the upper third of the oven and preheat the oven to 350°F. Brush the bottom and sides of a 9-inch removable-bottom tart pan with a generous layer of room temperature butter. Dust the buttered surfaces with several pinches of flour, then shake and tilt the pan in all directions to coat. Tap out any excess flour.

TOAST AND CRUSH THE PECANS: Place the pecans on a sheet pan and toast them until golden brown and fragrant, 7 to 10 minutes, tossing halfway through. Set the pan aside and let the pecans cool completely, then transfer them to a resealable bag, press out the air, and seal. Use a rolling pin, mallet, or heavy-bottomed saucepan to pulverize the pecans into small bits (they don't need to be processed into a meal; some larger pieces are okay). Add the flour and baking powder to the bag, seal, and shake to combine. Set the bag aside.

CREAM THE BUTTER AND SUGAR: In a medium bowl, with a hand mixer, beat the butter, brown sugar, and salt on low speed until combined, then increase the speed to medium-high and beat, pausing occasionally to scrape down the sides of the bowl with a flexible spatula, until the mixture is pale and fluffy, about 4 minutes (see Creaming Butter and Sugar, page 351).

MAKE THE BATTER: Add the eggs one at a time, beating thoroughly after each addition, until you have a smooth, light, and satiny mixture. Scrape down the sides of the bowl, then beat in the bourbon and vanilla. Add the pecan mixture, thoroughly shaking out the bag so no flour or pecan pieces are left behind, and beat on low speed just until the flour disappears. Fold the mixture several times with the flexible spatula, scraping the bottom and sides of the bowl, to make sure everything is well incorporated.

ASSEMBLE THE CAKE: Scrape the batter into the prepared pan and smooth it into an even layer all the way to the sides. Arrange the peach slices on top of the batter in rows, concentric circles, or any pattern you like and press them gently into the surface. In a small saucepan, warm the jam over low heat, whisking frequently, just until it's fluid. (Alternatively, microwave it in a small bowl in 20-second bursts.) Pass the jam through a mesh sieve and into a small bowl, pressing on the solids with the back of a spoon (scrape any jam solids back into the jar). Brush a thin layer of strained jam over the peach slices, then set aside any remaining jam for glazing the finished cake.

Can I . . .

Make it ahead? Yes. The cake, covered loosely and stored at room temperature, will keep for up to 3 days, but it's best served the day it's baked.

Use frozen peaches? Yes. Frozen sliced peaches are a great substitute when you can't find fresh (just know you won't get the rosy color from the skins, since the frozen wedges come peeled). Thaw 10 ounces (283g) frozen sliced peaches at room temperature, then pat them dry before assembling the tart.

Substitute another stone fruit or nut? Yes. Try this with an equal weight of nectarines or plums, cut the same way, and substitute an equal quantity of raw walnuts or blanched hazelnuts for the pecans.

Omit the bourbon? Yes. You can substitute an equal volume of dark rum for the bourbon, or, for an alcohol-free alternative, replace it with unsweetened apple juice or milk.

BAKE: Place the pan on a sheet pan and bake until the cake is golden brown across the entire surface and browned around the edges, 40 to 45 minutes. Let the cake cool completely in the pan.

GLAZE THE CAKE: The cake will have likely pulled away from the sides of the pan as it cooled, but if not, use a paring knife to cut down between the cake and the pan all the way around the fluted edge to loosen it. Press up on the bottom of the pan to pop it out of the fluted ring and place on a serving plate. Warm the remaining strained jam, if necessary, so it's fluid, then brush it over the entire surface of the cooled cake.

FRUIT MANAGEMENT

As a fruit dessert person, I spend a lot of my time in the kitchen doing what I call "fruit management." Because most fruits either can't or shouldn't be added to a recipe raw—they're typically too firm, too seedy, and/or too juicy—fruit management consists of the various processes that soften or smooth a fruit's texture and reduce or control its moisture content so it can be successfully incorporated into a batter, filling, or dough.

Poaching, roasting, stewing, pureeing, and/or straining are all techniques used in fruit management. In some cases these steps are optional, but I almost always find it's worth the time and effort to make sure a fruit behaves optimally in a recipe. For example, I roast sliced apples for my **Honey-Roasted Apple Cake** (page 138) to tenderize them and coax out their juices before folding them into the batter. Leaving the slices raw would mean they'd release their juices into the cake and shrink during baking, making the batter squidgy and producing gaps around the slices.

And because the cake bakes for less than an hour to an internal temperature around 210°F, the apples don't have sufficient time to soften. The pre-roast is necessary to adjust the moisture level and achieve the soft texture I desire.

Understanding the characteristics of different fruits is key to deciding how to treat them. Firm, juicy fruits like pears and apples are often cooked into compotes to drive off moisture, concentrate flavors, and break down their texture. Small fruits with higher skin-to-flesh ratios like strawberries or blackberries might be sliced or crushed and then macerated with sugar to soften them (see Macerating Fruit, page 355). Citrus juice is cooked into curd to enrich, sweeten, and thicken it, while markedly nonjuicy fruits like cranberries or bananas might actually need additional liquid before they can be incorporated into a recipe. Whether it starts on the stovetop or in the oven, fruit management is key to the success of most fruit-based recipes, and you'll see it all over these pages.

Morning Glorious Loaf Cake

I tasted my first Morning Glory muffin, which was invented on Nantucket, while visiting a friend a couple of years ago on nearby Martha's Vineyard. Not being a fan of muffins, and knowing that the Morning Glory kind is considered "healthy," I had low expectations. But I was surprised—it was tender, moist, lightly spiced, and pleasantly chewy in places from coconut and grated carrots. That gave me the idea for this cake, which marries a Morning Glory muffin and carrot cake. The ingredient list is long but the method is simple, and the finished cake, which is filled and covered with a maple-sweetened cream cheese, is a great option for home bakers who like carrot cake but don't want the hassle of baking and assembling layers.

MAKES 1 LOAF

DIFFICULTY: 2 (Easy)

ACTIVE TIME: 45 minutes

TOTAL TIME: 3 hours 40 minutes

SPECIAL EQUIPMENT: Metal loaf pan (4½ × 8½ inches, measured across the top)

Melted coconut oil for the pan

1 small Granny Smith apple (5 oz / 143g), peeled and grated on the large holes of a box grater

4 ounces (114g) carrots, peeled and grated on the small holes of a box grater (about 1 cup)

¼ cup dried unsweetened shredded coconut (0.8 oz / 23g)

¼ cup salted roasted sunflower seeds (1.2 oz / 35g)

1⅔ cups all-purpose flour (7.9 oz / 225g)

2 teaspoons ground cinnamon

1 teaspoon ground ginger

1½ teaspoons baking powder

1 teaspoon Diamond Crystal kosher salt or ½ teaspoon Morton kosher salt

½ teaspoon baking soda

½ cup packed light brown sugar (3.9 oz / 110g)

2 large eggs (3.5 oz / 100g), at room temperature

½ cup unsweetened applesauce (4.2 oz / 120g)

¼ cup plus 3 tablespoons maple syrup (5.2 oz / 148g), plus more for drizzling

⅔ cup virgin coconut oil (5.3 oz / 149g), gently warmed to liquefy

8 ounces (227g) cream cheese, at room temperature

PREHEAT THE OVEN AND PREPARE THE PAN: Arrange an oven rack in the center position and preheat the oven to 350°F. Brush the bottom and sides of a 4½ × 8½-inch metal loaf pan with a thin layer of melted coconut oil. Line the bottom and two longer sides with a piece of parchment paper, leaving an inch or two of overhang on both sides. Brush the parchment paper with more oil and set aside.

COMBINE THE MIX-INS: In a medium bowl, toss together the apple, carrot, coconut, and sunflower seeds to combine. Set the mix-ins aside.

MIX THE DRY INGREDIENTS: In a large bowl, whisk together the flour, cinnamon, ginger, baking powder, salt, and baking soda until combined. Set aside.

MIX THE WET INGREDIENTS: In a separate medium bowl, whisk together the brown sugar, eggs, applesauce, and ¼ cup (3 oz / 85g) of the maple syrup until combined, then whisk vigorously until the mixture is smooth and slightly thickened, about 1 minute. Add the coconut oil and whisk until the mixture is smooth and satiny, about 20 seconds.

MAKE THE BATTER: Make a well in the center of the dry ingredients and pour in the wet ingredients. Whisk, starting at the center of the bowl and working outward, until you have a smooth, evenly mixed batter with no dry spots. Add the mix-ins and fold with a flexible spatula until everything is well combined.

FILL THE PAN AND BAKE: Scrape the batter into the prepared loaf pan and use the spatula to work it into the corners, then smooth the surface. Bake until the surface of the cake is risen and split, the center of the split looks dry, and a skewer or cake tester inserted into the tallest part of the loaf comes out clean, 50 to 60 minutes. Let the cake cool in the pan for 20 minutes, then use a paring knife or small offset spatula to cut down between the cake and the pan along the shorter sides. Use the parchment overhang to lift out the loaf and transfer it to a wire rack. Let the cake cool completely.

MAKE THE FROSTING: In a medium bowl, combine the cream cheese and the remaining 3 tablespoons maple syrup and work with a flexible spatula until the mixture is mostly smooth (a few lumps are fine). Switch to a whisk and beat vigorously until the mixture is lump-free and slightly fluffy, about 1 minute. Set the frosting aside.

→

Can I . . .

Make it ahead? Yes. The frosted cake, covered and refrigerated, will keep for up to 4 days (refrigerate the cake uncovered to set the frosting, then cover). Let it come to room temperature before serving. The baked but unsplit and unfrosted cake, well wrapped and stored at room temperature, will keep for up to 4 days. Split and frost before serving.

Make any substitutions? Yes. You can replace the coconut oil with an equal quantity of neutral oil, such as grapeseed or avocado, or olive oil. For the sunflower seeds, you can substitute an equal quantity of any other roasted seed or chopped nut, such as walnuts, pecans, or pumpkin seeds.

Bake this in a different pan? Yes. Bake the cake in an 8 × 8-inch metal baking pan brushed with oil and lined across the bottom and two opposite sides with parchment paper, or in a 9-inch round cake pan brushed with oil and lined with a silicone or parchment round. In either pan, start checking for doneness around 35 minutes. Leave the cake whole and frost just the top.

SPLIT AND FROST THE CAKE: Rest the cooled loaf on one of its longer sides on a cutting board and use a serrated knife to slice lengthwise down through the loaf, splitting it into two horizontal layers. Place the bottom layer on a plate or serving platter and spread half of the frosting over the cut surface, working it all the way to the edges. Gently place the top layer back over the bottom and spread the remaining frosting over the top of the loaf. Transfer the loaf to the refrigerator and chill just until the frosting is set, 10 to 15 minutes.

SERVE: Drizzle the loaf with more maple syrup. Cut into slices with a serrated knife and serve.

Cranberry Anadama Cake

Even though I grew up in the Midwest, my parents have lived in the Boston area for the last fifteen-plus years, and I spent my college years there, so I consider myself a partial New Englander. My attraction to the region has a lot to do with its rich culinary traditions (exemplified in iconic dishes like chowder, lobster rolls, and blueberry pie) and the many unique ingredients found there, like Concord grapes, maple syrup, and my personal favorite, cranberries. Here I bring cranberries together with another New England favorite: anadama bread. Anadama bread is a yeasted wheat bread made with cornmeal and molasses, and both of those ingredients work extremely well against the tart-bitter intensity of cranberries. All these flavors, plus a little bit of orange and ground clove, are united here in a humble-looking but delicious cake.

SERVES 8

DIFFICULTY: 2 (Easy)

ACTIVE TIME: 40 minutes

TOTAL TIME: 1 hour 40 minutes, plus time to cool

SPECIAL EQUIPMENT: 9-inch cake pan, hand mixer

Butter and flour for the pan

2 tablespoons molasses

12 ounces (340g) fresh or frozen cranberries, thawed if frozen, divided

¾ teaspoon baking soda

1½ teaspoons vanilla extract

½ cup plus 2 tablespoons whole milk (5.3 oz / 150g)

1½ cups all-purpose flour (7.2 oz / 203g)

⅔ cup coarse-ground yellow cornmeal (3.5 oz / 100g)

1¾ teaspoons baking powder

1 teaspoon Diamond Crystal kosher salt or ½ teaspoon Morton kosher salt

⅛ teaspoon ground cloves

1 medium orange

1 cup plus 2 tablespoons granulated sugar (7.9 oz / 225g)

12 tablespoons unsalted butter (6 oz / 170g), at room temperature, divided

2 large eggs (3.5 oz / 100g), at room temperature

1 cup confectioners' sugar (3.9 oz / 110g), sifted if lumpy

PREPARE THE PAN: Brush the bottom and sides of a 9-inch cake pan with room temperature butter, then line the bottom with a silicone or parchment round and brush with more butter. Dust the buttered surfaces with several pinches of flour, then shake and tilt the pan in all directions to coat. Tap out any excess flour and set the pan aside.

COOK DOWN THE CRANBERRIES AND MOLASSES: In a small saucepan, combine the molasses, 8 ounces (227g) of the cranberries, and ¼ cup (2 oz / 57g) water. Bring the mixture to a simmer over medium heat and cook, stirring frequently with a heatproof flexible spatula, until the cranberries pop and collapse and you have a thick, jammy mixture, 8 to 10 minutes. Remove the saucepan from the heat and thoroughly stir in the baking soda (it will foam and turn an unappealing gray color, which is normal!). Add the vanilla and ½ cup (4.2 oz / 120g) of the milk and stir until the mixture is smooth, then scrape it into a small bowl. Set the cranberry mixture aside and let it cool to room temperature, stirring it occasionally (to cool it down very quickly, you can stir it in an ice bath—see Chilling in an Ice Bath, page 358).

PREHEAT THE OVEN: Arrange an oven rack in the center position and preheat the oven to 350°F.

MIX THE DRY INGREDIENTS: In a medium bowl, whisk together the flour, cornmeal, baking powder, salt, and cloves to combine. Set aside.

CREAM THE ZEST, SUGAR, AND BUTTER: Use a rasp-style grater to finely grate the zest of the orange until you have 1 teaspoon (reserve the orange for finely grating more zest over the glazed cake). In a large bowl, combine the zest and 1 cup (3.5 oz / 100g) of the granulated sugar and massage the mixture with your fingertips until it's very fragrant and looks like wet sand. Add 10 tablespoons (5 oz / 142g) of the butter and beat the mixture using a hand mixer on low speed until combined. Increase the speed to medium-high and continue to beat, pausing once or twice to scrape down the sides of the bowl with a flexible spatula, until the mixture is light and fluffy, about 4 minutes (see Creaming Butter and Sugar, page 351).

BEAT IN THE EGGS: Beat in the eggs one at a time on medium-high speed until smooth, then continue to beat until the mixture is very light, thick, and creamy, about 1 minute longer.

→

Can I . . .

Make it ahead? Yes. The cake, covered and stored at room temperature, will keep for up to 3 days.

Use a stand mixer instead of a hand mixer? Yes. Use your fingertips to massage the orange zest and sugar in a stand mixer fitted with the paddle attachment, then add the butter and proceed with the recipe as written.

Bake this in a different pan? Yes. You can bake the cake in an 8 × 8-inch baking pan brushed with room temperature butter and lined across the bottom and two opposite sides with parchment paper. The bake time will be about the same.

MAKE THE BATTER: Reduce the mixer speed to low and add about one-third of the dry ingredients, mixing just until the flour disappears, then add about half of the cooled cranberry mixture (it's okay if it's slightly warm) and beat until combined. Add the remaining dry ingredients in two additions, alternating with the remaining cranberry mixture, and mix just until you have a smooth, thick batter. Switch to a flexible spatula and fold the batter several times, scraping the bottom and sides of the bowl, to make sure it's evenly mixed.

ASSEMBLE THE CAKE: Scrape the batter into the prepared pan and smooth the surface, working it all the way to the sides. Melt 1 tablespoon of the butter and toss it with the remaining 4 ounces (113g) cranberries in a small bowl. Add the remaining 2 tablespoons granulated sugar and stir with a flexible spatula until the cranberries are coated. Scatter the sugared cranberries across the surface of the batter.

BAKE: Bake the cake until the surface is browned and springy to the touch and a cake tester or toothpick inserted into the center comes out clean, 45 to 55 minutes. Let the cake cool in the pan for 20 minutes, then, using a small offset spatula or paring knife and pressing it firmly against the side of the pan, cut down and around the cake to loosen it. Invert the cake onto a plate, then remove the pan and peel away the parchment paper. Reinvert the cake onto a wire rack and let it cool completely.

MAKE THE GLAZE: Melt the remaining 1 tablespoon butter and combine in a medium bowl with the confectioners' sugar and remaining 2 tablespoons milk. Whisk the mixture until it's smooth and glossy, then drizzle the glaze over the surface of the cake and let it drip down the sides. Let the cake sit until the glaze is partially set, about 5 minutes, then top with more freshly grated orange zest from the reserved orange. Let the glaze set completely.

Can I . . .

Make it ahead? Just the batter. The cakes must be served immediately—immediately!—after they emerge from the oven, but you can prepare the batter and fill the molds ahead of time. Cover and refrigerate the filled molds for up to 24 hours, then let them sit out for several hours so they come to room temperature before baking.

Make it dairy-free? Yes. The recipe is dairy-free except for the butter coating the molds. Instead, you can use a generous amount of oil-based, nonstick baking spray with flour, such as Baker's Joy. Regular oil is not recommended, as

Halve the recipe? Yes. Halve all of the ingredient quantities and follow the recipe as written, but to halve the 3 whole eggs, combine 1 large egg with half of a whole egg that's been thoroughly beaten and measured. Start checking the cakes for doneness after 5 minutes.

Use a stand mixer instead of a hand mixer? Yes. Combine the yolks, whole eggs, sugar, and salt in a stand mixer fitted with the whisk attachment and proceed with the recipe as written, noting that the eggs will whip faster than the time noted in the recipe.

Bake these in a muffin pan? Yes. Baking the cakes in a standard 12-cup muffin pan will yield 9 slightly smaller cakes. Thoroughly butter and flour 9 muffin cups as directed in the recipe, then proceed as written, dividing the batter among the prepared cups and filling them nearly to the top. Bake the cakes for 5 to 6 minutes, checking for the doneness indicators given in the recipe, then let them rest for 1 minute. Turn the cakes out all at once by inverting the pan onto a cutting board, then transfer the cakes to plates and serve immediately.

Molten Chocolate Olive Oil Cakes

I am going to let you in on what feels like a very big secret: Molten chocolate cake, that stalwart of dessert menus from chain restaurants to fine-dining establishments, is actually a two-bowl dessert, only a half-step up from brownies, that's ready in under 45 minutes. This is a fairly standard version except for one ingredient: olive oil. Compared to butter, olive oil makes the batter slightly more fluid, enhancing the "molten" effect, and the flavor pairs especially well with chocolate. Keep a close eye on the cakes during baking, since they can overcook quickly and lose their molten centers. Serve them immediately for the most dramatic presentation.

SERVES 8

DIFFICULTY: 2 (Easy)

ACTIVE TIME: 30 minutes

TOTAL TIME: 40 minutes

SPECIAL EQUIPMENT: Eight 4-ounce fluted metal brioche molds or ramekins, hand mixer

Butter and flour for the molds

¾ cup extra-virgin olive oil (5.9 oz / 168g)

9 ounces (255g) semisweet chocolate (64%–70% cacao), chopped

6 large egg yolks (3.2 oz / 90g), at room temperature

3 large eggs (5.3 oz / 150g), at room temperature

½ cup sugar (3.5 oz / 100g)

1 teaspoon Diamond Crystal kosher salt or ½ teaspoon Morton kosher salt

2 teaspoons vanilla extract

2 tablespoons all-purpose flour

Vanilla ice cream, for serving (optional)

PREPARE THE MOLDS: Use a pastry brush to liberally brush the bottoms and sides of eight 4-ounce fluted metal brioche molds or ramekins with room temperature butter, then dust the interiors with flour and shake to coat all over. Tap out any excess flour and set the molds aside.

PREHEAT THE OVEN: Arrange an oven rack in the upper third of the oven and preheat the oven to 450°F.

MELT THE CHOCOLATE MIXTURE: Fill a medium saucepan with about 1 inch of water and bring to a simmer over medium heat, then reduce the heat to maintain a gentle simmer. In a large heatproof bowl, combine the olive oil and chocolate and set over the saucepan, taking care that the bottom of the bowl doesn't touch the water (this is called a double boiler—for more information, see Setting Up a Double Boiler, page 341). Stir the chocolate mixture occasionally with a heatproof flexible spatula until it's melted and completely smooth, then remove the bowl from the heat and set aside.

BEAT THE EGGS AND SUGAR: In a separate medium bowl, with a hand mixer, beat the egg yolks, whole eggs, sugar, and salt on medium-low speed until the eggs are broken up, then increase the speed to medium-high and continue to beat until the mixture is very pale, thick, mousse-y, and approximately doubled in volume, about 2 minutes. Beat in the vanilla and flour.

MAKE THE BATTER: Slowly pour the egg mixture into the melted chocolate mixture, beating constantly with the hand mixer on medium-low speed, until you have an evenly mixed batter. It will be thick but fluid.

FILL THE MOLDS AND BAKE: Divide the batter evenly among the prepared molds (they will be filled nearly to the top). Place the molds on a large sheet pan, spacing evenly, and bake until the surfaces of the cakes are puffed, matte (with just a touch of glossiness in the centers), and dry to the touch but still extremely soft when pressed in the centers, 6 to 8 minutes for metal molds and 7 to 9 minutes for ramekins. Remove the sheet pan from the oven immediately and set the cakes aside to rest for about 30 seconds.

UNMOLD THE CAKES AND SERVE: Working as quickly as possible (it's helpful to have an extra set of hands for this), place a small serving plate upside down over a cake, then invert the cake and plate together and lift off the mold (careful, it's hot!). Repeat with the remaining cakes and serve immediately with vanilla ice cream, if desired.

Sticky Pumpkin-Chestnut Gingerbread

This cake combines elements of three ultracomforting fall and winter baking recipes: pumpkin bread, gingerbread, and sticky toffee pudding. It tastes quintessentially of the holidays and would be an easy replacement for more labor-intensive pies on your Thanksgiving or Christmas table. It incorporates peeled roasted chestnuts—the kind you find in a jar or bag at the grocery store, usually year-round but for sure around the holidays—along with molasses, fresh ginger, and lots of warm spices. The canned pumpkin adds flavor and color, of course, but also moisture and tenderness. You could stop at just making the cake, which is very good on its own, but the toffee sauce upgrades it to a celebration-worthy centerpiece.

SERVES 12 TO 15

DIFFICULTY: 2 (Easy)

ACTIVE TIME: 40 minutes

TOTAL TIME: 1 hour 40 minutes, plus time to cool

SPECIAL EQUIPMENT: 13 × 9-inch baking pan (preferably metal), hand mixer

CAKE

Neutral oil for the pan

6 ounces (170g) peeled roasted chestnuts (1 generous cup), from a jar or bag, rinsed and patted dry

¼ cup molasses (3 oz / 85g)

½ teaspoon baking soda

1 (15 oz / 425g) can unsweetened pumpkin puree (not pumpkin pie filling)

1 tablespoon finely grated fresh ginger

1½ teaspoons vanilla extract

2½ cups all-purpose flour (11.9 oz / 338g)

2¼ teaspoons baking powder

1½ teaspoons Diamond Crystal kosher salt or ¾ teaspoon Morton kosher salt

1½ teaspoons ground cinnamon

¼ teaspoon ground nutmeg

⅛ teaspoon ground cloves

1¼ cups granulated sugar (8.8 oz / 250g)

4 large eggs (7 oz / 200g), at room temperature

⅔ cup neutral oil (5.3 oz / 150g), such as grapeseed or avocado

TOFFEE SAUCE AND SERVING

10 tablespoons unsalted butter (5 oz / 142g)

1 cup packed dark brown sugar (7.8 oz / 220g)

1 cup heavy cream (8.5 oz / 240g), at room temperature

¾ teaspoon Diamond Crystal kosher salt or ½ teaspoon Morton kosher salt

PREHEAT THE OVEN AND PREPARE THE PAN: Arrange an oven rack in the center position and preheat the oven to 350°F. Brush the bottom and sides of a 13 × 9-inch pan, preferably metal, with neutral oil. Line just the bottom of the pan with a rectangle of parchment paper, cut to fit, and smooth to eliminate air bubbles. Brush the parchment with more oil and set the pan aside.

COOK THE CHESTNUTS AND MOLASSES: In a small saucepan, combine the chestnuts, molasses, and ½ cup (4 oz / 113g) water and bring to a simmer over medium heat. Reduce the heat to maintain a very gentle simmer, cover, and cook until the chestnuts are soft and easily break apart when pressed against the side of the pan, 12 to 15 minutes. Remove from the heat, uncover, and mash the chestnuts with a fork or a potato masher to break them down into pieces no larger than a pea (don't mash into a paste, though—you want them to add texture to the cake).

MIX THE WET INGREDIENTS: To the saucepan with the chestnut mixture, add the baking soda and stir thoroughly to combine. The mixture will foam, which is normal. Scrape the mixture into a medium bowl, then stir in the pumpkin, ginger, and vanilla. Set the pumpkin mixture aside and let it cool to room temperature, stirring it occasionally (to cool it down very quickly, you can stir it in an ice bath—see Chilling in an Ice Bath, page 358).

MIX THE DRY INGREDIENTS: In a large bowl, whisk together the flour, baking powder, salt, cinnamon, nutmeg, and cloves to combine. Make a well in the center and set the bowl aside.

BEAT THE EGGS AND SUGAR, THEN STREAM IN THE OIL: In a separate large bowl, with a hand mixer, beat the sugar and eggs on medium-low speed until the eggs are broken up, then increase the speed to medium-high and continue to beat until the mixture is pale, mousse-y, and doubled in volume, about 3 minutes. Beating constantly, very gradually stream in the oil and continue to beat just until the mixture is smooth, thick, and emulsified.

MAKE THE BATTER: Add the pumpkin mixture to the bowl with the egg mixture and mix on medium-low just until blended, then scrape that mixture into the bowl of dry ingredients. Mix on medium-low, starting in the center and gradually working outward, until you have a smooth, evenly mixed batter with no traces of flour. Switch to a flexible spatula and fold the batter several times to make sure it's evenly mixed. Pour the batter into the prepared pan.

→

Can I . . .

Make it ahead? Ideally, no. The cake is best eaten slightly warm while the toffee sauce is glossy (the butter in the sauce will solidify when cool). Any leftover cake can be covered in the pan and stored at room temperature for up to 2 days. Rewarm it uncovered in a 300°F oven until the surface is glossy again, 5 to 7 minutes. Any leftover toffee sauce, stored in a lidded container in the refrigerator, will keep for up to 2 weeks. Scrape it into a small saucepan and rewarm over medium-low heat, stirring constantly, until it's glossy and fluid.

Use a stand mixer instead of a hand mixer? Yes. Combine the sugar and eggs in a stand mixer fitted with the whisk attachment and proceed with the recipe as written. After adding the pumpkin mixture, switch to the paddle attachment, reduce the mixer speed to low, and add the dry ingredients to the bowl in two additions.

BAKE: Bake until the surface of the cake is deeply browned and springy to the touch and a toothpick or cake tester inserted into the center comes out clean, 30 to 35 minutes. Set the cake aside.

MEANWHILE, MAKE THE TOFFEE SAUCE: In a medium saucepan, combine the butter, brown sugar, and ¼ cup (2 oz / 57g) water and bring to a boil over medium-high heat, stirring to melt the butter and dissolve the sugar. Continue to cook, stirring often, until the mixture is reduced and slightly thickened, about 3 minutes, then remove the saucepan from the heat and slowly add the cream (take care, it will sputter), stirring constantly until the mixture is smooth. Bring to a boil again over medium-high heat and cook, stirring occasionally, until the toffee sauce is slightly reduced and thickened, about 3 minutes longer. Stir in the salt and set the saucepan aside.

SOAK THE CAKE: Use a toothpick to poke deep holes all over the hot cake, then slowly pour 1 cup (8.2 oz / 233g) of the warm toffee sauce over the entire surface. Let the cake sit until it has absorbed some of the toffee sauce and is slightly warm. Cover the saucepan to keep the remaining toffee sauce warm.

SERVE: Cut around the sides of the cake with a small offset spatula or paring knife, then use a serrated knife to slice the cake into a 3-by-4 grid to make 12 generous portions, or into a 3-by-5 grid to make 15 slightly smaller portions. Lift the slices out of the pan and transfer to serving plates. The toffee sauce will separate as it sits, so stir to bring it back together. If the butter in the sauce has started to solidify, rewarm it over medium-low heat. Pour the toffee sauce into a small pitcher or serving vessel and serve on the side.

Crystallized Meyer Lemon Bundt Cake

One of my favorite sources for dessert inspiration is the work of several renowned pastry chefs and cookbook authors from the 1980s and '90s. One such author is Flo Braker, whose impeccable (and impeccably written) recipes are models of the craft. One of Flo's famous recipes is her Crystal Almond Pound Cake, so-called because the sugary glaze crystallizes into a crunchy shell around the cake. Here I apply Flo's glazing technique to my olive oil-based Meyer lemon Bundt cake. Because incorporating too much lemon juice into the batter can weaken the structure and throw off the leavening, I add it to the glaze for extra fresh lemon flavor. The olive oil in the glaze helps to preserve the cake and keeps it moist and delicious for an entire week.

SERVES 12

DIFFICULTY: 2 (Easy)

ACTIVE TIME: 40 minutes

TOTAL TIME: 1 hour 45 minutes, plus time to cool

SPECIAL EQUIPMENT: 12-cup metal Bundt pan, hand mixer

Butter and flour for the pan

3 cups all-purpose flour (14.2 oz / 405g)

2½ teaspoons baking powder

1 teaspoon Diamond Crystal kosher salt or ½ teaspoon Morton kosher salt

½ teaspoon baking soda

1 cup whole milk (8.5 oz / 240g), at room temperature

2 teaspoons vanilla extract

¾ cup Meyer lemon juice (6 oz / 170g), divided

1 tablespoon finely grated Meyer lemon zest, from about 2 lemons

1¾ cups plus ⅔ cup sugar (17 oz / 483g)

4 large eggs (7 oz / 200g), at room temperature

1⅓ cups plus 2 tablespoons extra-virgin olive oil (11.5 oz / 327g)

PREHEAT THE OVEN AND PREPARE THE PAN: Arrange an oven rack in the upper third of the oven and preheat the oven to 350°F. Brush the inside of a 12-cup metal Bundt pan with room temperature butter, making sure to coat every facet and crevice. Dust the inside with several pinches of flour, then shake and tilt the pan in all directions to coat the buttered surfaces completely. Tap out any excess flour and set the pan aside.

MIX THE DRY INGREDIENTS: In a medium bowl, whisk together the flour, baking powder, salt, and baking soda to combine. Set aside.

MIX THE WET INGREDIENTS: In a separate medium bowl or 2-cup liquid measuring cup, stir together the milk, vanilla, and ¼ cup (2 oz / 57g) of the Meyer lemon juice. Set aside.

BEAT THE EGGS AND SUGAR, THEN STREAM IN THE OIL: In a large bowl, combine the lemon zest and 1¾ cups (12.3 oz / 350g) of the sugar and massage the mixture with your fingertips until it's fragrant and looks like wet sand. Add the eggs and beat with a hand mixer on medium-low speed until the eggs are broken up, then increase the speed to medium-high and beat until the mixture is light, thick, and mousse-y, about 3 minutes. Beating constantly, very gradually stream in 1⅓ cups (10.5 oz / 99g) of the olive oil and continue to beat just until the mixture is smooth, thick, and emulsified.

MAKE THE BATTER: Reduce the mixer speed to low and add about one-third of the dry ingredients, mixing just until the flour disappears, then stream in half of the milk mixture and mix until combined. Add the remaining dry ingredients in two additions, alternating with the remaining milk mixture, and mix just until you have a smooth, thick batter with no traces of flour. Switch to a flexible spatula and fold the batter several times, scraping the bottom and sides of the bowl, to make sure it's evenly mixed.

BAKE: Pour the batter into the prepared Bundt pan and bake until the top is risen, split, and golden brown, and a skewer or cake tester inserted into the tallest part of the cake comes out clean, 45 to 55 minutes. Set the cake aside to cool in the pan for 15 minutes.

→

Can I . . .

Make it ahead? Yes. The cake, well wrapped and stored at room temperature, will keep for up to 1 week and will improve in flavor and texture over the first couple of days.

Make it with regular lemons? Yes. You can substitute regular lemon juice for the Meyer lemon juice but decrease the quantity to ½ cup plus 2 tablespoons (5 oz / 142g), adding 2 tablespoons to the wet ingredients and ½ cup (4 oz / 113g) to the glaze. (Note that the lemon juice will cause the milk to curdle, but this won't affect the recipe.) Use an equal quantity of regular lemon zest.

Bake this in a different pan? Not recommended (except for a tube pan). This cake needs lots of surface area where the glaze can soak in and crystallize, so a Bundt or tube pan works best.

Use a stand mixer instead of a hand mixer? Yes. Use your fingertips to massage the zest and 1¾ cups (12.3 oz / 350g) of the sugar in a stand mixer fitted with the whisk attachment, then add the eggs and proceed with the recipe as written.

MEANWHILE, MAKE THE GLAZE: In a small bowl, combine the remaining ½ cup (4 oz / 113g) Meyer lemon juice, ⅔ cup (4.7 oz / 133g) granulated sugar, and 2 tablespoons olive oil and stir vigorously with a fork or whisk to dissolve some of the sugar.

GLAZE THE CAKE: While the cake is still hot inside the pan, use a toothpick to poke holes all over the surface, then generously brush some of the glaze over the top to soak it. Use a paring knife to cut down carefully between the cake and the pan all the way around and along the inner tube to loosen it. Invert the cake onto a wire rack, lift away the Bundt pan, and set the rack on a sheet pan to catch drips. Poke more holes across the entire surface and brush with the remaining glaze. It will seem like too much liquid, but keep applying it layer by layer until you've used it all, letting the cake absorb it gradually. Use the brush to pick up drips of glaze from the sheet pan and reapply to the cake. Let it cool completely.

Polenta Pistachio Pound Cake

Polenta, corn grits, and cornmeal are all varieties of dried and ground corn. When added to a cake raw, each lends crunch and corn flavor. But polenta is also an Italian dish in which ground corn is cooked into a porridge, and it was the soft, creamy texture of that dish that I wanted to capture in a cake. Parcooking the polenta in milk introduces a high proportion of liquid to this cake, so it resists drying out, and lends a porridgy texture that feels distinct from other cornmeal and polenta cakes. Crushed pistachios coat the exterior and stud the fine, tight crumb, giving the cake color, crunch, flavor, and an Italianish edge.

MAKES 1 LOAF

DIFFICULTY: 2 (Easy)

ACTIVE TIME: 45 minutes

TOTAL TIME: 1 hour 40 minutes, plus time to cool

SPECIAL EQUIPMENT: Metal loaf pan (4½ × 8½ inches, measured across the top), hand mixer

1¼ cups whole milk (10.6 oz / 300g)

½ cup coarse-ground polenta (2.6 oz / 75g)

1 teaspoon vanilla extract

Butter for the pan

⅔ cup raw pistachios (2.8 oz / 79g)

1 tablespoon plus ¾ cup sugar (5.7 oz / 163g)

1¼ cups all-purpose flour (6 oz / 169g)

1½ teaspoons baking powder

1 teaspoon Diamond Crystal kosher salt or ½ teaspoon Morton kosher salt

1 teaspoon finely grated lemon zest

10 tablespoons unsalted butter (5 oz / 141g), at room temperature

2 large eggs (3.5 oz / 100g), at room temperature

PARCOOK THE POLENTA: In a small saucepan, bring the milk to a simmer over medium-high heat. Slowly sprinkle in the polenta, whisking constantly, then continue to whisk until the mixture is thick like porridge and holds the marks of the whisk, about 3 minutes (if you let it sit undisturbed, it should bubble). Remove the saucepan from the heat and whisk in the vanilla. Scrape the mixture into a medium bowl and set it aside uncovered to cool completely, stirring occasionally to prevent lumps.

PREPARE THE PAN: Brush the bottom and sides of a 4½ × 8½-inch metal loaf pan with room temperature butter. Line the bottom and two longer sides with a piece of parchment paper, leaving an overhang of an inch or two on each side. Butter the parchment paper, then set the pan aside.

CRUSH AND SIFT THE PISTACHIOS: Place the pistachios inside a resealable bag, press out the air, and seal. Lay the bag flat on the work surface and bash the pistachios with a rolling pin, mallet, or heavy-bottomed saucepan, occasionally lifting and shaking the bag so the larger pieces settle to one side, until the nuts are crushed and the largest pieces are about the size of a lentil. Transfer the nuts to a mesh sieve set over a medium bowl and shake the sieve, allowing the finer bits to fall into the bowl. Set aside the sieve with the larger pieces of pistachios.

SPRINKLE THE PAN WITH PISTACHIOS: Add 1 tablespoon of the sugar to the bowl with the fine pistachio bits and toss to combine. Sprinkle several generous pinches of the pistachio/sugar mixture inside the prepared pan, shaking and tilting the pan in all directions to coat. Set the pan aside and reserve any remaining pistachio/sugar mixture for sprinkling over the batter.

PREHEAT THE OVEN: Arrange an oven rack in the center position and preheat the oven to 350°F.

MIX THE DRY INGREDIENTS: In a medium bowl, whisk together the flour, baking powder, and salt to combine. Set aside.

CREAM THE ZEST, SUGAR, AND BUTTER: In a large bowl, combine the lemon zest and remaining ¾ cup (5.3 oz / 150g) sugar and massage with your fingertips until the mixture is fragrant and looks like wet sand. Add the butter and beat with a hand mixer on medium-low until combined, then increase the speed to medium-high and beat, pausing occasionally to scrape down the sides of the bowl with a flexible spatula, until the mixture is pale and fluffy, about 4 minutes (see Creaming Butter and Sugar, page 351).

→

Can I . . .

Make it ahead? Yes. The cake, well wrapped and stored at room temperature, will keep for up to 4 days.

Use a stand mixer instead of a hand mixer? Yes. Use your fingertips to massage the lemon zest and sugar in a stand mixer fitted with the paddle attachment, then add the butter and proceed with the recipe as written.

Bake this in a different pan? Yes. Bake the cake in a 9-inch cake pan brushed with room temperature butter and lined on the bottom with a silicone or parchment round. Do not coat the bottom and sides of the pan with the pistachio/sugar mixture; instead, sprinkle the entire mixture over the surface of the batter. Start checking the cake for doneness after 35 minutes.

BEAT IN THE EGGS: Beat in the eggs one at a time on medium-high speed until smooth, then continue to beat until the mixture is very light, thick, and creamy, about 2 minutes longer.

MAKE THE BATTER: Reduce the mixer speed to medium-low and add about one-third of the dry ingredients, mixing until thoroughly combined. Fold the cooled polenta mixture a few times with a flexible spatula to work out any lumps, as it will have thickened quite a bit, and add half to the bowl. Mix on medium until lump-free and combined, then add the remaining dry ingredients in two additions, alternating with the remaining polenta mixture, and mix until you have a smooth, lump-free batter. Tip the reserved larger pieces of pistachios (in the mesh sieve) into the batter, then use a flexible spatula to fold the batter several times, scraping the bottom and sides of the bowl, until the nuts are distributed and everything is evenly mixed.

FILL THE PAN AND BAKE: Scrape the batter into the prepared pan and work it into the corners. Smooth the surface, then sprinkle with the reserved pistachio/sugar mixture. Bake until the surface of the cake is risen and split, the center of the split looks dry, and a skewer or cake tester inserted into the tallest part of the loaf comes out clean, 50 to 60 minutes. Let the cake cool in the pan for 20 minutes, then use a paring knife or small offset spatula to cut down between the cake and the pan along the shorter sides. Use the parchment overhang to lift out the loaf and transfer it to a wire rack. Let it cool completely.

Flourless Chocolate Meringue Cake

Meringue is a magical mixture of egg whites and sugar that can be used in many ways, but the first time I learned it could be baked *directly on top* of a cake was a couple of years ago when I saw pastry chef Liz Prueitt's recipe for Sweet Potato Tea Cake with Meringue, which she developed for Tartine Manufactory along with then head of pastry Michelle Lee. It struck me as an exceptionally smart technique that I wanted to try, and it made sense to employ it in a cake where meringue is already a part of the recipe, like flourless chocolate cake (one of my favorite moments in baking is the swirl you get when folding meringue into a chocolate batter—see the cover!). Not only does it look appealing on top of the cake, it bakes into a light and crispy shell that yields to the rich crumb. This cake is dairy- and grain-free, making it Passover-friendly.

SERVES 10

DIFFICULTY: 2 (Easy)

DAIRY-FREE, GLUTEN-FREE

ACTIVE TIME: 30 minutes

TOTAL TIME: 1 hour 40 minutes, plus time to cool

SPECIAL EQUIPMENT: 9-inch springform pan, hand mixer

Neutral oil for the pan

10 ounces (283g) semisweet chocolate (64%-70% cacao), coarsely chopped

6 tablespoons neutral oil, such as grapeseed or avocado (3 oz / 84g)

¼ cup brewed coffee (2 oz / 57g)

1½ teaspoons Diamond Crystal kosher salt or ¾ teaspoon Morton kosher salt, plus a pinch

5 large eggs (8.8 oz / 250g), whites and yolks separated, at room temperature

2 teaspoons vanilla extract

1 cup sugar (7 oz / 200g), divided

¾ cup almond flour (2.5 oz / 70g), sifted if lumpy

PREHEAT THE OVEN AND PREPARE THE PAN: Arrange an oven rack in the center position and preheat the oven to 350°F. Brush the bottom and sides of a 9-inch springform pan with oil, making sure to coat the sides all the way to the rim. Line the bottom with a silicone or parchment round and brush with more oil, then set the pan aside.

MELT THE CHOCOLATE MIXTURE: Fill a medium saucepan with about 1 inch of water and bring to a simmer over medium heat, then reduce the heat to maintain a gentle simmer. In a large heatproof bowl, combine the chocolate, oil, coffee, and 1½ teaspoons salt and set it over the saucepan, taking care that the bottom of the bowl doesn't touch the water (this is called a double boiler—for more information, see Setting Up a Double Boiler, page 341). Stir occasionally with a heatproof flexible spatula until the chocolate is melted and the mixture is completely smooth, then remove the bowl from the heat and set aside.

WHISK IN THE YOLKS, SUGAR, AND ALMOND FLOUR: Add the egg yolks, vanilla, and ¼ cup (1.8 oz / 50g) of the sugar to the chocolate mixture and vigorously whisk to combine. Whisk in the almond flour until thoroughly combined. It will look broken and separated, which is okay! Add ¼ cup (2 oz / 57g) water and whisk vigorously until the mixture comes back together and looks smooth and glossy. Set the bowl aside.

MAKE THE MERINGUE: In a separate clean, large, nonplastic bowl, with a hand mixer, beat the egg whites and a pinch of salt on medium-low speed until the whites are broken up and frothy, about 20 seconds. Increase the speed to medium-high and continue to beat until the whites are foamy and opaque, about 30 seconds, then gradually add the remaining ¾ cup (5.3 oz / 150g) sugar in a slow, steady stream, beating constantly. Once all the sugar is added, increase the speed to high and continue to beat just until you have a dense, glossy meringue that holds a stiff peak (see page 339 for what this stage looks like). Try not to overbeat, or the whites will take on a dry, grainy texture and be difficult to incorporate.

MAKE THE BATTER: Scoop a heaping cup of the meringue and set it aside for swirling on top of the cake. Scrape about half of the remaining meringue into the bowl with the chocolate mixture and fold gently until just a few streaks remain (for more on the proper technique, see Folding a Mixture,

→

Can I . . .

Make it ahead? Yes. The cake, well wrapped and stored at room temperature, will keep for up to 4 days, but it's best eaten on the first or second day while the meringue topping is still crispy (it will soften over time).

Make this nut-free? Yes. Although it's not a common item in most grocery stores, sunflower seed flour is a good nut-free alternative to almond flour.

Use a stand mixer instead of a hand mixer? Yes. Combine the egg whites and salt in a stand mixer fitted with the whisk attachment and proceed with the recipe as written, noting that the meringue will whip faster and be easier to overbeat in the stand mixer.

page 351). Scrape in the rest of the meringue and fold just until you have a light, airy, evenly mixed batter. Scrape the batter into the prepared pan, then dollop spoonfuls of the reserved meringue across the entire surface. Use a skewer or toothpick to swirl the meringue into the batter and vice versa. Swirl a little or a lot; it's up to you.

BAKE: Bake the cake until the surface is risen and cracked, the meringue is light golden, and a skewer or cake tester inserted into the center comes out shiny but clean, 1 hour to 1 hour 10 minutes. Remove the cake from the oven and place on a wire rack, then immediately run a paring knife or small offset spatula between the very top of the cake and the rim of the pan all the way around to loosen any areas that may be stuck (this will help the cake settle evenly as it cools). Let the cake cool completely. Cut around the sides again to loosen the cake, then remove the outer ring of the pan.

Malted Banana Upside-Down Cake

with Malted Cream

While I don't usually eat bananas on their own—my acceptable window of ripeness, post-green and pre-spots, lasts about 2 hours—I do love banana desserts of all kinds, especially ones that include chocolate, nuts, and/or tangy dairy. This cake, inspired by malted banana milkshakes, is made with roasted bananas, which are highly concentrated in flavor, as well as a generous amount of malted milk powder, which adds a dose of savoriness to balance out the banana-y sweetness. The batter is assembled using a clever one-bowl mixing method called "reverse creaming," which starts with working the fat into the dry ingredients and produces a finely textured, tender crumb. Caramelizing banana halves in a skillet for the top adds a few steps, but I think it's worth it for the pretty (and tasty) upside-down effect.

SERVES 9

DIFFICULTY: 3 (Moderate)

ACTIVE TIME: 1 hour

TOTAL TIME: 1 hour 50 minutes, plus time to cool

SPECIAL EQUIPMENT: 10- or 12-inch nonstick skillet, 8 × 8-inch baking pan (preferably metal), hand mixer

CAKE

6 ripe but unspeckled medium bananas (2.25lb / 1kg), unpeeled, divided

Butter for the pan

2 tablespoons plus ½ cup granulated sugar (4.4 oz / 125g)

½ cup sour cream (4.2 oz / 120g), at room temperature

3 tablespoons dark rum

1 teaspoon vanilla extract

½ cup packed dark brown sugar (3.9 oz / 110g)

1⅓ cups all-purpose flour (6.3 oz / 180g)

½ cup malted milk powder (2.3 oz / 64g)

1 teaspoon baking powder

1 teaspoon baking soda

1 teaspoon Diamond Crystal kosher salt or ½ teaspoon Morton kosher salt

1 stick unsalted butter (4 oz / 113g), cut into 1-tablespoon pieces, at room temperature

2 large eggs (3.5 oz / 100g), beaten, at room temperature

MALTED CREAM

¾ cup heavy cream (6.3 oz / 180g), chilled

¼ cup sour cream (2.1 oz / 60g), chilled

2 tablespoons malted milk powder

1 tablespoon confectioners' sugar

PREHEAT THE OVEN: Arrange an oven rack in the center position and preheat the oven to 350°F.

ROAST THE BANANAS: Place the 3 ripest bananas of the bunch on a small sheet pan, keeping them whole and unpeeled, and roast until the skins are split and nearly blackened, the flesh is very soft, and you see some bubbling juices on the sheet pan, 20 to 25 minutes. Set the roasted bananas aside to cool.

PREPARE THE PAN: Brush the bottom and sides of an 8 × 8-inch baking pan, preferably metal, with a thin layer of room temperature butter, then line the bottom and two opposite sides with a piece of parchment paper, leaving a slight overhang. Smooth the parchment to eliminate air bubbles, then brush it with butter and set the pan aside.

CARAMELIZE THE REMAINING BANANAS: Slice the stems off of the remaining 3 bananas, then slice the bananas in half lengthwise, leaving the peels on, and set aside. Heat a 10- or 12-inch nonstick skillet over medium-high heat. Sprinkle 1 tablespoon of the granulated sugar into the skillet in three evenly spaced rows each about the length and width of the banana halves (that's 1 teaspoon of sugar per row), then place 3 of the banana halves cut-sides down over the sugar. Cook the banana halves undisturbed, gently shaking the skillet occasionally, until you see golden brown caramel bubbling around the edges, about 5 minutes. Use a small offset spatula or butter knife to turn the bananas and carefully slide them caramel-side up out of the skillet and onto a plate. Set the plate aside and caramelize the 3 remaining banana halves with another 1 tablespoon of the granulated sugar just as you did the first batch.

Potential Pitfall: Try to make sure the banana halves land caramel-side up as you transfer them to the plate, otherwise the hot caramel will stick to the plate and come away from the banana.

ARRANGE THE CARAMELIZED BANANAS IN THE PREPARED PAN: Let the caramelized banana halves sit until they're cool enough to handle, then lift up one half (the flesh is soft, so be careful not to break it) and place it caramel-side down in the prepared pan. Starting at one end, carefully lift away the peel, leaving the flesh in the pan. Arrange the remaining halves one by one in the pan in a tight row and remove the peels (if you are using large bananas, you may have to cut the halves to fit, and you may have some extra). Set the pan aside.

MASH THE ROASTED BANANAS AND MIX THE WET INGREDIENTS: Unzip the skins of the roasted bananas with a paring knife and scoop the softened flesh into a 1-cup measure, leaving behind any liquid on the sheet pan. When you have a level cup, scrape it into a medium bowl and mash with a fork to break up the flesh (a little more or less than a cup is fine, but if you have extra roasted banana, freeze it for another use, like smoothies). Add the sour cream, rum, and vanilla and whisk to combine. Set aside.

MIX THE DRY INGREDIENTS: In a large bowl, combine the brown sugar and remaining ½ cup (3.5 oz / 100g) granulated sugar and whisk to combine. Break up any lumps of brown sugar with your fingertips, then add the flour, malted milk powder, baking powder, baking soda, and salt and whisk to combine.

WORK IN THE BUTTER AND HALF OF THE WET INGREDIENTS: To the bowl with the dry ingredients, add the butter and about half of the roasted banana mixture. Beat with a hand mixer on low speed until the dry ingredients are moistened, then increase the mixer to medium-high and beat until you have a thick, smooth, glossy batter, about 1 minute.

> *Potential Pitfall:* Make sure your butter is thoroughly room temperature, as cool butter will form stubborn lumps in the batter. If this happens, set the bowl in a warm spot and let the mixture sit just until the butter is soft, then proceed.

BEAT IN THE EGGS AND REMAINING WET INGREDIENTS: Add the eggs and scrape in the remaining roasted banana mixture, then beat on medium-high speed, pausing to scrape down the sides of the bowl once or twice, until the batter is light, fluffy, and satiny smooth, about 2 minutes.

BAKE: Scrape the batter into the prepared pan and work it over the caramelized banana halves to the sides and into the corners, then smooth the surface. Bake the cake until the surface is deep golden brown, the center is springy to the touch, and a cake tester or toothpick inserted into the center comes out clean, 45 to 55 minutes. Let the cake cool in the pan for 20 minutes, then use a paring knife or small offset spatula to cut down between the cake and the pan on the unlined sides. Invert the cake onto a wire rack, then carefully lift off the pan and peel away the parchment paper. Let the cake cool completely.

WHIP THE MALTED CREAM AND SERVE: In a medium bowl, with the hand mixer, whip the heavy cream, sour cream, malted milk powder, and confectioners' sugar on medium-low speed to start and gradually increase the speed to medium-high as the mixture thickens, until you have a softly whipped cream that forms droopy peaks (see Whipping Cream, page 355). Slide the cooled cake onto a serving plate and slice into squares with a serrated knife. Serve with the malted cream on the side.

Can I . . .

Make it ahead? Yes. The cake, covered and stored at room temperature, will keep for up to 3 days, but it's best served on the first day while the caramelized banana layer is fresh.

Bake this in a different pan? Yes. Assemble and bake the cake in a 9-inch cake pan that has been brushed with room temperature butter and lined on the bottom with a buttered silicone or parchment round. The bake time will be about the same.

Use a stand mixer instead of a hand mixer? Yes. Combine the brown sugar and ½ cup (3.5 oz / 100g) of the granulated sugar in a stand mixer fitted with the paddle attachment and proceed with the recipe as written.

Skip caramelizing the bananas? Yes. You can omit this step entirely and bake the cake without the layer of bananas on the bottom (I don't recommend using raw bananas for the upside-down layer, as they'll turn gray and won't fully soften underneath the batter).

Omit the rum? Yes. You can substitute an equal volume of banana liqueur or bourbon for the rum, or, for an alcohol-free alternative, replace it with milk.

Whipped Cream Tres Leches Cake
with Hazelnuts

I am slightly embarrassed to admit that as a dessert person, and more specifically as a cake person, I hadn't spent much time getting to know tres leches cake, a beloved Latin American dessert, prior to this book. But, as tres leches is a sponge cake soaked liberally with three kinds of dairy (usually sweetened condensed and evaporated milks, and one other), I knew we'd be a good match. At the time I developed this recipe, I'd been playing around with the idea of a sponge cake lightened with whipped cream rather than egg whites. The whipped cream contributes butterfat as well as air, producing a sponge that is light but firm—absolutely perfect, as it happens, for tres leches cake, which needs sufficient structure to be able to absorb all that liquid. When I tasted my first test, the delicate flavors of cinnamon and cream called out for a toasted nut, so I added finely chopped toasted hazelnuts to the batter. The result is a slightly unusual but very special cake.

SERVES 15

DIFFICULTY: 3 (Moderate)

ACTIVE TIME: 1 hour 15 minutes

TOTAL TIME: 6 hours 15 minutes (includes 3 hours for chilling)

SPECIAL EQUIPMENT: 13 × 9-inch pan (preferably metal but not nonstick), hand mixer

WHIPPED CREAM HAZELNUT SPONGE

Neutral oil for the pan

½ cup blanched hazelnuts (2 oz / 57g)

1¼ cups heavy cream (10.6 oz / 300g), chilled

2 teaspoons vanilla extract

2 cups all-purpose flour (9.5 oz / 270g)

2 teaspoons baking powder

1 teaspoon Diamond Crystal kosher salt or ½ teaspoon Morton kosher salt

¾ teaspoon ground cinnamon

7 large eggs (12.3 oz / 350g), at room temperature

1 cup sugar (7 oz / 200g)

SOAK AND ASSEMBLY

2 cups whole milk (16 oz / 480g)

1 cup sweetened condensed milk (10.5 oz / 298g)

1 teaspoon vanilla extract

Pinch of kosher salt

4 cups heavy cream (32 oz / 960g), chilled, divided

Ground cinnamon, for sprinkling

PREPARE THE PAN: Brush the bottom of a 13 × 9-inch pan with a thin layer of oil (do not grease the sides). Line the bottom with a rectangle of parchment paper, cut to fit (don't extend it up the sides), and smooth to eliminate air bubbles. Brush the parchment with more oil and set the pan aside.

Potential Pitfall: Greasing the sides of the pan or lining them with parchment paper will make it harder for the sponge to rise, leading to a denser cake, so make sure only the bottom is lined and oiled (to allow the cake to be unmolded). This is also why it's not recommended to use a nonstick pan, as the batter needs some friction with the pan to be able to "climb" as it bakes.

PREHEAT THE OVEN: Arrange an oven rack in the center position and preheat the oven to 325°F.

TOAST AND FINELY CHOP THE HAZELNUTS: Place the hazelnuts on a small sheet pan and toast until they're golden brown and fragrant, 8 to 10 minutes, tossing halfway through. Let the hazelnuts cool completely on the sheet pan, then transfer them to a cutting board and chop as finely as possible (there will be a mix of some larger pieces and dusty bits, which is fine). If you have a food processor, you can pulse the nuts until they're finely ground, but a knife and a little patience are all you need. Reserve 2 tablespoons of the chopped hazelnuts for sprinkling over the finished cake, then set aside the remaining nuts.

WHIP THE CREAM FOR THE SPONGE: In a medium bowl, with a hand mixer, whip the cream and vanilla on medium-low speed to start and gradually increase the speed to medium-high as the cream thickens, until you have medium peaks (see Whipping Cream, page 355). Transfer the bowl to the refrigerator while you assemble the sponge.

Potential Pitfall: A firmly whipped cream will be difficult to fold into the sponge, so try not to whip beyond medium peaks. If you think you've gone too far, see page 355 for how to loosen cream that's been overwhipped.

MIX THE DRY INGREDIENTS: In a separate medium bowl, whisk together the flour, baking powder, salt, and cinnamon until combined. Set aside.

→

BEAT THE EGGS AND SUGAR FOR THE SPONGE: In a large bowl, with the hand mixer, beat the eggs and sugar on medium-low speed until the eggs are broken up, then increase the speed to high and continue to beat until the mixture is pale and mousse-y and forms a slowly dissolving ribbon as it falls off the beaters back into the bowl, about 6 minutes.

MAKE THE SPONGE BATTER: Using a fine-mesh sieve, sift about one-third of the dry ingredients over the egg mixture, then mix on low speed with the hand mixer just until it's incorporated. Sift in the remaining dry ingredients in two additions, mixing after each addition just until combined. Remove the whipped cream from the refrigerator and scrape it into the bowl with the egg mixture. Add the chopped hazelnuts (not including the 2 tablespoons you set aside for topping the cake) and fold with a flexible spatula just until the cream and nuts are incorporated and you have a thick, airy batter (for more on the proper technique, see Folding a Mixture, page 351).

BAKE: Scrape the batter into the prepared pan and gently smooth it into an even layer. Bake until the surface of the sponge is risen, golden brown, and springy to the touch, and a cake tester inserted into the center comes out clean, 30 to 35 minutes, rotating the pan front to back after 20 minutes. When the cake is done, immediately remove it from the oven and invert the pan onto a wire rack. Let the cake cool upside down (still in the pan) until the bottom of the pan is completely cool to the touch (cooling upside down prevents the sponge from sinking).

MAKE THE SOAK AND POUR OVER THE CAKE: In a medium bowl or any 5-cup vessel with a pour spout, whisk the whole milk, sweetened condensed milk, vanilla, salt, and 2 cups (16 oz / 480g) of the heavy cream until combined. Turn the pan right-side up and use a toothpick or skewer to poke dozens of holes across the cooled sponge, pressing down to the bottom of the pan. Slowly pour the soak all over the cake. If it starts to pool on the surface, stop pouring and wait for it to absorb before continuing. It will seem like an excessive amount of soak, but use it all. Cover the pan and refrigerate for at least 3 hours to allow the cake to evenly absorb the milks.

WHIP THE CREAM: Just before serving, in a large bowl, with the hand mixer, whip the remaining 2 cups (16 oz / 480g) cream on medium-low speed to start and gradually increase the speed to medium-high as it thickens, until you have a softly whipped cream that holds a droopy peak. Set it aside.

UNMOLD THE CAKE: Remove the cake from the refrigerator and use a paring knife or small offset spatula to cut around the sides of the pan to loosen the cake. Invert the cake onto a cutting board or serving platter and tap sharply on the counter to help release it from the pan—it might take a few moments to release, but gravity will eventually do its job. Carefully remove the pan and peel away the parchment paper. A bit of the soak will pool on the board or serving platter, which is normal.

ASSEMBLE THE CAKE AND SERVE: Scrape the whipped cream onto the surface of the sponge (the bottom is now the top) and spread it all the way to the edges, making large swooshes with the back of a spoon. Sprinkle the reserved 2 tablespoons of hazelnuts over the cake and dust with several pinches of cinnamon. Cut into squares and serve.

Can I . . .

Make it ahead? Yes. The assembled cake, covered and refrigerated, will keep for up to 3 days. If making it in advance, cover and refrigerate the soaked cake in the pan for up to 24 hours before topping with the whipped cream, reserved hazelnuts, and cinnamon and serving.

Use a stand mixer instead of a hand mixer? Yes. To make the sponge, whip the cream and vanilla in a stand mixer fitted with the whisk attachment as directed, then scrape the whipped cream into a separate bowl and refrigerate. Thoroughly wash and dry the stand mixer bowl and whisk before beating the eggs and sugar. Proceed with the recipe as written.

Marbled Sheet Cake

My mom always made a cake for family birthday celebrations when I was growing up, but if she was throwing a birthday party for me and my friends, she'd take me to our local grocery store, Schnucks, to order a sheet cake from the bakery. I remember flipping through laminated pages of design options, and, on at least one occasion, selecting a marbled sheet cake with white icing. Here I've created a homemade version, and to replicate the moist and tender crumb found in store-bought cakes, I use mayonnaise in the batter. Don't turn the page—it's not as weird as it sounds. Mayonnaise is, after all, a mixture of egg, oil, salt, and acid, and each of these things plays a role in cake making. I cover the cake in ermine frosting, an old-fashioned frosting that's super light and fluffy and recalls (in a good way) the artificial frosting on grocery store sheet cakes. Some of this may sound dubious, but please give it a try.

SERVES 15

DIFFICULTY: 3 (Moderate)

ACTIVE TIME: 1 hour 10 minutes

TOTAL TIME: 3 hours

SPECIAL EQUIPMENT: 13 × 9-inch baking pan (preferably metal), hand mixer

CAKE

Neutral oil for the pan

3 cups all-purpose flour (14.2 oz / 405g)

2 teaspoons baking powder

1 teaspoon baking soda

1 teaspoon Diamond Crystal kosher salt or ½ teaspoon Morton kosher salt

⅓ cup unsweetened cocoa powder (1.1 oz / 30g), sifted if lumpy

⅓ cup brewed coffee (2.7 oz / 77g), at room temperature

2 tablespoons plus 1¾ cups sugar (13.2 oz / 375g)

4 large eggs (7 oz / 200g), at room temperature

1¼ cups mayonnaise (9.7 oz / 275g), such as Hellmann's

1 tablespoon vanilla extract

1¼ cups buttermilk (10.6 oz / 300g), at room temperature

FROSTING

5 tablespoons all-purpose flour (1.5 oz / 42g)

½ teaspoon Diamond Crystal kosher salt or ¼ teaspoon Morton kosher salt

1 cup whole milk (8.5 oz / 240g)

2 teaspoons vanilla extract

1½ sticks unsalted butter (6 oz / 170g), cut into 1-tablespoon pieces, at room temperature

6 ounces (170g) cream cheese, cut into 1-tablespoon pieces, at room temperature

¾ cup sugar (5.3 oz / 150g)

Sprinkles, for serving

PREHEAT THE OVEN AND PREPARE THE PAN: Arrange an oven rack in the center position and preheat the oven to 325°F. Brush the bottom and sides of a 13 × 9-inch pan with a thin layer of oil. Line the bottom and two longer sides of the pan with a piece of parchment paper, leaving a bit of overhang and smoothing it to eliminate air bubbles.

MIX THE DRY INGREDIENTS: In a medium bowl, whisk together the flour, baking powder, baking soda, and salt to combine. Set aside.

MAKE THE COCOA MIXTURE: In a separate medium bowl, whisk together the cocoa powder, coffee, and 2 tablespoons of the sugar until smooth. Set aside.

BEAT THE EGGS AND SUGAR, THEN BEAT IN THE MAYONNAISE: In a large bowl, with a hand mixer, beat the eggs and remaining 1¾ cups (12.3 oz / 350g) sugar on medium-low speed until combined, then increase the speed to high and beat until the mixture is thick, pale, and voluminous, about 3 minutes. Gradually add the mayonnaise, a few tablespoons at a time, beating constantly, and continue to beat until the mixture is smooth and well combined, about 2 minutes. Beat in the vanilla.

MAKE THE BATTER: Reduce the mixer speed to medium-low and add about one-third of the dry ingredients, mixing just until the flour disappears. Stream in about half of the buttermilk and beat until incorporated, then add the remaining dry ingredients in two additions, alternating with the remaining buttermilk, and mix just until the last trace of flour disappears. Fold the batter several times with a flexible spatula, scraping the bottom and sides of the bowl to make sure it's evenly mixed.

MAKE THE CHOCOLATE BATTER: Pour half of the batter—about 4 cups (27.1 oz / 770g) if you want to be exact—into the bowl with the cocoa mixture and beat with the hand mixer on medium-low until the chocolate batter is streak-free.

SWIRL THE BATTER IN THE PAN: Holding a bowl with each hand, alternate pouring the vanilla and chocolate batters into the prepared pan, layering them on top of each other. Scrape in every last bit of both batters, then drag a skewer or the tip of a paring knife through the pan, making figure eights, to swirl the batters together.

→

BAKE: Bake until the surface of the cake is risen and light golden across the vanilla patches, and a cake tester or skewer inserted into the center comes out clean, 40 to 45 minutes, rotating the pan front to back after 25 minutes. Let the cake cool completely in the pan.

COOK THE FLOUR AND MILK FOR THE FROSTING: In a small saucepan, combine the flour and salt and whisk to eliminate any lumps. Stream in the milk, whisking constantly, until you have a smooth, fluid mixture, then set the saucepan over medium-high heat and cook, whisking constantly, until the mixture is bubbling and thick and has the consistency of smooth mashed potato, about 3 minutes. Remove the saucepan from the heat and whisk in the vanilla. Scrape the mixture into a small bowl and press a piece of plastic directly onto the surface to prevent a skin from forming, then set the mixture aside to cool completely.

> *Potential Pitfall:* Depending on the size of your saucepan and whisk, you could have a few lumps in your flour mixture. These lumps will persist in the frosting, so press the mixture through a mesh sieve to smooth it out before proceeding.

MAKE THE FROSTING: In a large bowl, with a hand mixer, beat the butter, cream cheese, and sugar on medium speed until smooth, then increase the speed to high and beat until the mixture is pale and light, about 3 minutes. Beating constantly, add the cooled flour mixture to the butter mixture a couple of tablespoons at a time, beating thoroughly after each addition. Once all of the flour mixture has been added, continue to beat until the sugar has completely dissolved (rub a dab between your fingers to check for any grit) and the frosting is nearly white and looks like whipped cream, about 4 minutes. If the frosting is a little bit loose and doesn't hold a stiff peak, place the bowl in the refrigerator and chill, beating briefly with the hand mixer every 10 minutes, until it holds a stiff peak (see page 354 for an illustration of stiff peaks). Set the frosting aside.

FROST THE CAKE: Use a paring knife or small offset spatula to cut between the cake and the pan along the shorter sides. Invert the cake onto a wire rack, then lift off the pan and peel away the parchment paper. Reinvert the cake onto a serving platter (or a cutting board, if you don't have a platter large enough for the cake). Scrape the frosting onto the cooled cake and spread across the surface and down the sides. Top with sprinkles.

> *Potential Pitfall:* The frosting is temperature-sensitive, so store the frosted cake away from any sources of heat to prevent it from melting.

Can I . . .

Make it ahead? Yes. The frosted cake, well wrapped and refrigerated, will keep for up to 3 days. Refrigerate it uncovered until the frosting has hardened, then cover it loosely with plastic wrap. Allow the cake to sit at room temperature for at least 1 hour before serving. If making it in advance, keep the unfrosted cake well wrapped at room temperature for up to 2 days, then frost just before serving.

Use a stand mixer instead of a hand mixer? Yes. To make the batter, combine the eggs and 1¾ cups (12.3 oz / 350g) of the sugar in a stand mixer fitted with the whisk attachment and proceed with the recipe as written, but note that the mixing times will be shorter in the stand mixer. Blend the chocolate batter in a separate bowl with a whisk. To make the frosting, beat the butter, cream cheese, and sugar in the stand mixer fitted with the whisk and proceed with the recipe as written.

Bars, Cookies & Candied Things

The focus of the cookies, bars, and candied things in this chapter is fun. They're fun to eat, featuring a variety of shapes and textures, as well as fun to make, employing approachable and streamlined methods. I try to bring maximum flavor to these small packages, for example, toasting rice flour for **Toasted Rice Sablés** (page 203) and pulverizing freeze-dried raspberries for **Raspberry Almond Thumbprints** (see opposite). I like cookies that are either tender, like **Lime Squiggles** (page 204), or chewy, like **Salty Cashew Blondies** (page 196), so most of the recipes here fall into either of those categories. More than half can be made entirely by hand since tenderness and chewiness don't depend on electric mixing.

In cookie making, the repetition of forming dozens of pieces and baking in batches can get tedious, so ease of assembly is important. That's why I generally avoid punching out cookies from rolled dough (which yields scraps), instead favoring more efficient forming techniques like slice-and-bake and drop-and-bake. The bars and candied things in this chapter are baked or set in slabs and then sliced or broken up, so they're high-yield. And when it comes to candied things, like **Caramel Peanut Popcorn Bars** (page 213) and **Honey & Tahini Toffee Matzo** (page 195), don't be intimidated—while you do have to cook some sugar, there's no candy thermometer (or candy-making know-how) required.

Raspberry Almond Thumbprints

These macaroon-like almond cookies—loosely based on ricciarelli, a cookie native to Siena, Italy—are crispy on the outside and chewy in the middle, a textural combination I prize. And because macaroons of all varieties trend sweet, this cookie is flavored with raspberry jam, which is added to the dough and spooned into the thumbprint centers, as well as pulverized freeze-dried raspberries, to add some fruity acidity. I love the crinkled look the cookies develop while baking, and I especially love that they remind me, both in flavor and in texture, of much more elaborate French macarons while requiring a fraction of the time, effort, and technical skill to make.

MAKES ABOUT 22 COOKIES

DIFFICULTY: 1 (Very Easy)

DAIRY-FREE, GLUTEN-FREE

ACTIVE TIME: 40 minutes

TOTAL TIME: 2 hours 30 minutes

SPECIAL EQUIPMENT: Hand mixer

2¼ cups almond flour (7.6 oz / 216g)

1 teaspoon baking soda

½ teaspoon Diamond Crystal kosher salt or ¼ teaspoon Morton kosher salt

1 teaspoon finely grated lemon zest

1 teaspoon vanilla extract

½ teaspoon almond extract

3 tablespoons plus ½ cup raspberry jam (7.8 oz / 220g)

2 large egg whites (2.5 oz / 70g), at room temperature

⅓ cup granulated sugar (2.3 oz / 66g)

½ cup plus ⅓ cup confectioners' sugar (3.2 oz / 92g)

1 cup freeze-dried raspberries (1 oz / 28g)

MIX THE DRY INGREDIENTS: In a medium bowl, whisk together the almond flour, baking soda, and salt to combine. Set aside.

MIX THE WET INGREDIENTS: In a small bowl, stir together the lemon zest, vanilla, almond extract, and 3 tablespoons of the raspberry jam until smooth. Set aside.

BEAT THE EGG WHITES AND SUGAR: In a clean, large, nonplastic bowl, with a hand mixer, beat the egg whites on medium-low speed until they're broken up and frothy, about 20 seconds. Increase the speed to medium-high and continue to beat until the whites are foamy and opaque, about 30 seconds, then gradually add the granulated sugar in a slow, steady stream, beating constantly. Once all the sugar is added, continue to beat just until you have dense, glossy egg whites that hold stiff peaks (see page 339 for what this stage looks like). Set the bowl aside.

MAKE AND CHILL THE DOUGH: Use a large flexible spatula to gently fold the dry ingredients into the beaten egg whites until well combined, then scrape in the jam mixture and continue to fold until you have an evenly mixed, stiff, and tacky dough (for more on the proper technique, see Folding a Mixture, page 351). The baking soda will react with the acidity in the jam and turn the batter grayish, which is normal. Cover the bowl and refrigerate the dough for at least 1 hour to let it rest.

PORTION AND FREEZE THE DOUGH: Scoop a rounded tablespoon of dough and roll it between your palms to form a smooth sphere, then transfer it to a plate. If the dough sticks to your palms, dampen your palms lightly with a drop or two of water. Repeat until you've rolled all of the dough into spheres and transferred them to the plate. You should have about 22 spheres. Transfer the plate to the freezer and chill uncovered until the spheres are cold and no longer tacky to the touch (but not frozen solid), 15 to 20 minutes.

PREHEAT THE OVEN AND PREPARE THE PAN: Arrange an oven rack in the center position and preheat the oven to 325°F. Line a large sheet pan with parchment paper and set aside.

COAT THE COOKIES: Place ½ cup (1.9 oz / 55g) of the confectioners' sugar in a small bowl. Remove the plate from the freezer and, working one piece at a time, toss the spheres in the confectioners' sugar until generously coated all over, then place on the prepared sheet pan, spacing them about 2 inches apart. You should be able to fit all the spheres (they spread just a little during baking).

$\rightarrow$

Can I . . .

Make them ahead? Yes. The thumbprints, stored in an airtight container at room temperature, will keep for up to 3 days, but they're best eaten on the day they're baked while the edges are still crispy (the jam will cause the cookies to soften over time). Stack them in layers separated by sheets of parchment or wax paper. The uncoated, unfilled cookies can be stored in an airtight container for up to 1 day. Coat in the raspberry sugar and fill with jam before serving.

Make these by hand? Yes. Follow the visual cues in the recipe, using a large whisk rather than an electric mixer to beat the egg whites and keeping in mind that it will take longer at each stage and require a bit of effort.

Use a stand mixer instead of a hand mixer? Yes. Beat the egg whites in a stand mixer fitted with the whisk attachment as directed in the recipe, keeping in mind that the egg whites will whip faster and be easier to overbeat in the stand mixer.

BAKE AND FORM THE THUMBPRINTS: Transfer the sheet pan to the oven and bake until the cookies have a crinkled surface and are golden brown around the edges, 12 to 15 minutes, rotating the pan front to back after 10 minutes. While the cookies are still hot from the oven, press the handle end of a wooden spoon straight down into the center of each cookie and wiggle slightly to make an impression, but don't press all the way through to the sheet pan. Allow the cookies to cool completely on the sheet pan, then carefully peel them away from the parchment paper one by one and transfer to a wire rack.

PULVERIZE THE RASPBERRIES: Place the freeze-dried raspberries in a resealable bag, press out the air, and seal. Use a rolling pin, mallet, or heavy-bottomed saucepan to crush the raspberries to a fine powder. Add the remaining ⅓ cup (1.3 oz / 36g) confectioners' sugar to the bag and seal again, then shake well to combine. Transfer the mixture to a fine-mesh sieve and shake it over the cookies to coat them completely in the pink sugar (sift any remaining sugar into a container and save for another use; discard any larger pieces trapped in the sieve).

FILL THE THUMBPRINTS: In a small saucepan, warm the remaining ½ cup (5.6 oz / 160g) jam over medium-low heat, whisking occasionally, just until it's fluid (or microwave it in a small bowl in 15-second bursts). Remove the saucepan from the heat and use a teaspoon to fill the impressions with the warm jam. Let the thumbprints sit uncovered until the jam is mostly set, 15 to 20 minutes.

Phyllo Cardamom Pinwheels

To make these pinwheel cookies, phyllo dough is brushed with melted butter, sprinkled with cardamom sugar, rolled into a spiraled log, and sliced and baked. In the oven, the melted butter and cardamom sugar mingle and caramelize on the sheet pan, forming a glassy surface, while the phyllo bakes up flaky and golden all the way through. The cookies are so shatteringly tender that they give palmiers, a buttery French cookie made from puff pastry (and one of my favorite cookies), a run for their money.

MAKES ABOUT 20 COOKIES

DIFFICULTY: 1 (Very Easy)

ACTIVE TIME: 25 minutes

TOTAL TIME: 1 hour 25 minutes

¾ cup demerara sugar (5.3 oz / 150g)

½ teaspoon ground cardamom

Pinch of kosher salt

9 sheets frozen phyllo dough measuring 18 × 13 inches (8 oz / 226g), thawed overnight in the refrigerator

10 tablespoons unsalted butter (5 oz / 142g), melted

MAKE THE CARDAMOM SUGAR: In a small bowl, toss together the demerara sugar, cardamom, and salt to combine. Set aside.

BUTTER AND SUGAR THE PHYLLO: Place a piece of parchment paper about the size of the phyllo sheets on the work surface and set a single sheet of phyllo on top. Place the remaining sheets of phyllo on the work surface next to the parchment and cover with a damp towel to prevent them from drying out. Use a pastry brush to gently brush the sheet of phyllo with a thin layer of the melted butter, working the butter all across the surface of the dough and trying not to tear it (you don't need to cover every square inch). Sprinkle 1½ tablespoons of the cardamom sugar evenly across the buttered phyllo. Place another sheet of phyllo on top of the first, aligning them, and butter and sugar as you did the first (be sure to keep the remaining phyllo covered with the damp towel as you work).

ROLL UP THE FIRST STACK OF PHYLLO: Starting at one of the short sides and using the parchment paper to help you, tightly roll up the stack of two sheets into a spiraled log, then gently lift the log off the parchment and set aside.

STACK AND ROLL TWO MORE SHEETS OF PHYLLO: Working on top of the same parchment paper, repeat the buttering, sugaring, and stacking process using 2 more sheets of phyllo, but don't roll them up (yet). Lift up the log you already rolled and place it along one of the short sides of the new stack, then roll up the stack of phyllo around the log as snugly as possible, again using the parchment to help you. Set the log aside.

REPEAT THE STACKING AND ROLLING TWO MORE TIMES: Repeat the stacking process two more times, each time using 2 more sheets of phyllo, and buttering each layer and sprinkling with 1½ tablespoons cardamom sugar. Roll each stack snugly around the log, building up the layers and thickening the log each time.

COVER THE LOG IN THE FINAL PHYLLO LAYER: Place the final sheet of phyllo on the parchment paper and brush with more butter (you may or may not use all the butter, depending on how generously you coated each layer), then roll up the log in the final sheet just as you did before, taking care not to tear it.

CHILL THE LOG: Gently place the log on a cutting board seam-side down, cover loosely with reusable food wrap or plastic wrap, and transfer to the freezer. Freeze until the log is very firm but not frozen solid, 15 to 20 minutes.

Make them ahead? Yes. The cookies, stored airtight at room temperature, will keep for up to 3 days, or they can be frozen for up to 1 month.

Use a different spice? Yes. Instead of cardamom, use 1 teaspoon ground cinnamon, 1 teaspoon ground coriander, or any warm spice of your choice (amount to taste).

PREHEAT THE OVEN AND PREPARE THE SHEET PAN: Arrange an oven rack in the center position and preheat the oven to 350°F. Line a large sheet pan with a silicone baking mat or parchment paper and set aside.

SLICE THE COOKIES: Remove the log from the freezer and uncover. Use a serrated knife to shave off just the loose and raggedy ends of the log, creating clean, cut sides, then slice the log crosswise into ½-inch-thick slices. If the delicate phyllo tears or starts to unravel, just do your best to press it back in place. Place the slices cut-side down on the prepared sheet pan, spacing them evenly (they will not spread).

BAKE: Bake the cookies until they're deep golden brown and the bottoms are caramelized, 15 to 20 minutes, rotating the sheet pan front to back after 10 minutes. Remove the cookies from the oven and let them cool for 10 minutes on the pan, then transfer them to a wire rack to cool completely.

BE A COOKIE HERO

A cookie hero is someone who shows up to any event, get-together, party, or gathering with a plate full of freshly baked cookies. I am a repeat cookie hero because I plan ahead and use my freezer to store dough so it's always available for baking off at any moment. While you can freeze baked cookies (make sure they're well wrapped or sealed airtight) for a month or two, freezing dough and baking it as needed is preferable because the cookies always taste fresh and flavorful. Here are my storage tips and strategies for using your freezer so you, too, can be a cookie hero on any occasion.

For portioned dough, practice IQF: If a recipe calls for cookie dough to be rolled into balls or scooped onto a sheet pan, go ahead and portion the dough and place the pieces on a lined sheet pan or dinner plate (no need to space them out—the pieces can touch). Freeze the dough uncovered, then when the pieces are frozen solid, transfer them to a food storage bag, seal well, and keep frozen until you're ready to bake them. This is called IQF, or "Individual Quick Freeze," and it maintains the shape of the pieces and prevents them from sticking together in the freezer.

For slice-and-bake, freeze logs whole: Follow the steps in Forming Logs of Cookie Dough (page 352) to make the dough logs. Make sure they're tightly wrapped, then freeze. Plan when you're going to bake the cookies and transfer the logs to the refrigerator about 12 hours prior. You want the dough to be cold but not frozen solid when slicing the logs, otherwise the slices will break apart.

Add sugar just before baking: If the recipe calls for the dough to be rolled or coated in sugar before baking, do this after you take the dough out of the freezer, not before (otherwise the sugar could potentially draw moisture out of the dough and then dissolve in the oven). You may need to let the dough sit at room temperature for several minutes so the very outer layer thaws and softens, giving the sugar a surface it can adhere to.

Extend the bake time slightly: You do not need to thaw frozen dough before baking, but note that the cookies will take an extra minute or two in the oven (follow the baking instructions in the recipe). If, however, you're only baking a few cookies at a time—a great bonus of keeping frozen cookie dough!—they won't take quite as long.

Seedy Whole Wheat
Chocolate Chip Skillet Cookie

Early in the pandemic, my husband, Harris, and I, like many people, did a LOT of cooking. One of Harris's projects during that time was creating a wholesome chocolate chip cookie made with whole wheat flour and packed with things like hemp hearts and flaxseeds. This skillet cookie is inspired by that flurry of baking. Here I've adapted the chocolate chip cookie recipe in *Dessert Person* and streamlined it so the batter is both assembled and baked directly in a skillet. The first two steps are toasting the seeds and browning the butter, which warms the batter and partially melts some of the chocolate, resulting in a chewy texture. While the cookies in *Dessert Person* require you to chill the dough for several hours before baking, this can be made from start to finish in under an hour, delivering almost-instant gratification. It's chocolaty, multitextured, and wholesome without feeling virtuous. For best results, use a well-seasoned cast-iron skillet.

MAKES ONE 12-INCH COOKIE THAT CAN BE SLICED INTO MANY WEDGES

DIFFICULTY: 1 (Very Easy)

ACTIVE TIME: 25 minutes

TOTAL TIME: 45 minutes, plus time to cool

SPECIAL EQUIPMENT: 12-inch ovenproof skillet (preferably cast-iron)

2 tablespoons pumpkin seeds

2 tablespoons sunflower seeds

1 tablespoon sesame seeds

2 tablespoons chia and/or poppy seeds, preferably a mix

1 stick plus ½ tablespoon unsalted butter (4.2 oz / 120g)

1 cup whole wheat flour (4.8 oz / 135g)

1 teaspoon Diamond Crystal kosher salt or ½ teaspoon Morton kosher salt

¼ teaspoon baking soda

½ cup packed light brown sugar (3.9 oz / 110g)

¼ cup granulated sugar (1.8 oz / 50g)

1 large egg (1.8 oz / 50g), beaten, at room temperature

1½ teaspoons vanilla extract

5 ounces (142g) semisweet chocolate, (64%-70% cacao) chopped

Flaky sea salt, for sprinkling (optional)

PREHEAT THE OVEN: Arrange an oven rack in the center position and preheat the oven to 350°F.

TOAST THE SEEDS: In a 12-inch skillet, preferably cast-iron, toast the pumpkin, sunflower, and sesame seeds over medium heat, stirring constantly with a heatproof flexible spatula, until they're golden and fragrant, about 5 minutes. Transfer the seeds to a medium bowl and set the skillet aside. Add the chia and/or poppy seeds to the bowl and toss to combine. Set the seeds aside to cool.

BROWN THE BUTTER: Add 1 stick (4 oz / 113g) of the butter to the skillet and melt over medium heat, stirring with the spatula, until it comes to a boil and starts to sputter. Cook, stirring constantly and scraping the bottom and sides of the skillet, until the sputtering subsides and you see tiny golden brown specks floating in the butter, about 5 minutes (see Browning Butter, page 353). Remove the skillet from the heat and continue to stir until the specks turn a deep coppery brown, about 30 seconds. Add an ice cube and stir vigorously until the ice is melted (it will sputter). Set the skillet aside, stirring the browned butter occasionally, until the bottom of the skillet is warm to the touch but not hot, 10 to 15 minutes.

MEANWHILE, MIX THE DRY INGREDIENTS: To the bowl with the seed mixture, add the whole wheat flour, kosher salt, and baking soda and whisk to combine. Set aside.

MAKE THE BATTER: To the skillet with the browned butter, add the brown sugar and granulated sugar and stir with the spatula until the mixture is well blended and smooth, about 1 minute. Add the beaten egg and vanilla and mix vigorously with the spatula until the mixture is smooth, very evenly mixed, and slightly thickened, about 1 minute. Add the dry ingredients (reserve the bowl) and stir with the spatula, scraping the bottom and sides thoroughly, until the batter is evenly mixed. Add the chocolate and stir until the pieces are distributed and some of it has melted and streaked through the batter.

→

FORM THE COOKIE: Scrape the batter into the reserved bowl you used for the dry ingredients and set aside. Rinse and dry the skillet, then set over low heat and add the remaining ½ tablespoon butter and swirl until the butter is melted. Remove the skillet from the heat. Scrape the batter back into the skillet and press it into an even layer with the spatula, working it all the way to the sides. Lightly sprinkle flaky salt (if using) across the surface.

BAKE AND COOL: Transfer the skillet to the oven and bake until the cookie is golden brown across the surface and firm to the touch around the edge, 16 to 22 minutes. Transfer the skillet to a wire rack and let cool. Use a sharp knife or wheel cutter to slice the cookie into wedges, then use a small offset spatula to lift the wedges out of the skillet one at a time.

Can I . . .

Make it ahead? Yes. The wedges, stored in an airtight container at room temperature, will keep for up to 3 days, or they can be frozen for up to 1 month.

Make it gluten-free? Yes. Replace the whole wheat flour with an equal amount of your preferred gluten-free flour blend and bake as directed.

Bake this in a different pan? Yes. Use any 10- or 12-inch ovenproof skillet to assemble the batter, then scrape it into a parchment-lined 10-inch cake pan, 10-inch springform pan, or 9 × 9-inch baking pan and proceed as written. The bake time will be about the same.

Cocoa-Chestnut Brownies

The combination of earthy chestnuts and rich chocolate—which I love—is well-recognized in French baking, but I have found, after lots of tinkering, that the best expression of the duo is the great American brownie. This is a cocoa brownie, a style I appreciate for its pure chocolatiness and its high proportion of butter, since there's no added fat from the cocoa butter that's present in bar chocolate. Cocoa brownies tend to have a matte, non-crackly surface, making them a little homely, so I cover them in a simple but luxurious ganache. Look for peeled and roasted chestnuts in bags or jars on grocery store shelves around the winter holidays.

MAKES 16 BROWNIES

DIFFICULTY: 1 (Very Easy)

ACTIVE TIME: 45 minutes

TOTAL TIME: 2 hours 15 minutes

SPECIAL EQUIPMENT: 8 × 8-inch baking pan (preferably metal), potato masher

1½ sticks unsalted butter (6 oz / 170g), cut into pieces

7 ounces (198g) peeled roasted chestnuts, from a bag or jar (about 1¼ cups), rinsed and patted dry

⅔ cup unsweetened cocoa powder (1.8 oz / 50g), sifted if lumpy

2 large eggs (3.5 oz / 100g), cold from the refrigerator

1 cup granulated sugar (7 oz / 200g)

¼ cup packed light brown sugar (1.9 oz / 55g)

2 teaspoons vanilla extract

¾ cup all-purpose flour (3.5 oz / 100g)

1 teaspoon Diamond Crystal kosher salt or ½ teaspoon Morton kosher salt

6 ounces (170g) semisweet chocolate (64%–70% cacao), chopped

⅔ cup heavy cream (5.6 oz / 160g)

Can I . . .

Make them ahead? Yes. The brownies, stored airtight in the refrigerator, will keep for up to 4 days.

Double the recipe? Yes. Line a 13 × 9-inch pan, preferably metal, with foil. Double all of the ingredient quantities and proceed with the recipe as written, but use a large saucepan to melt the butter and cook the chestnuts. Note that you'll have to extend the bake time, so watch for the given indicators.

Make them gluten-free? Yes. Replace the all-purpose flour with an equal amount of chestnut flour or your preferred gluten-free flour blend and bake as directed.

Bake this in a different pan? Yes. Bake the brownies in a foil-lined, buttered 9-inch cake pan. The bake time will be about the same.

PREHEAT THE OVEN AND PREPARE THE PAN: Arrange an oven rack in the center position and preheat the oven to 350°F. Line an 8 × 8-inch baking pan, preferably metal, with foil, pressing it into the corners and smoothing it up the sides. Melt the butter in a small saucepan over medium-low heat, then remove it from the heat. Use a pastry brush to coat the bottom and sides of the foil with a thin layer of the melted butter, then set the pan aside.

COOK THE CHESTNUTS: Set the saucepan of melted butter over medium heat and add the chestnuts. Bring the mixture to a simmer and sizzle the chestnuts in the butter, mashing them occasionally with a potato masher, until the chestnuts are fragrant and have broken down into a coarse paste with the biggest pieces about the size of a lentil. Remove the saucepan from the heat and add ¼ cup (2 oz / 57g) water and the cocoa powder and whisk until smooth. Set the saucepan aside and let cool slightly.

WHISK THE EGGS, SUGAR, AND VANILLA: In a medium bowl, whisk the eggs until they're streak-free, then add the granulated sugar, brown sugar, and vanilla and whisk vigorously until the mixture is slightly pale, about 1 minute.

MAKE THE BATTER: Scrape the chestnut mixture into the bowl with the egg mixture and whisk to combine, then whisk in the flour and salt. Switch to a flexible spatula and fold the mixture several times, scraping the bottom and sides of the bowl, until the batter is smooth.

BAKE: Scrape the batter into the prepared pan, working it to the sides and corners with the spatula in an even layer. Bake until the surface of the brownies is puffed, dry, and firm to the touch, 22 to 28 minutes. Let the brownies cool completely in the pan.

MEANWHILE, MAKE THE GANACHE: Place the chopped chocolate in a medium heatproof bowl. In a small saucepan, heat the cream over medium heat just until you see gentle bubbling around the sides. Remove the saucepan from the heat and set it aside for about 30 seconds to cool slightly, then pour it over the chocolate. Let the chocolate sit for about a minute, then whisk the ganache gently, starting in the center of the bowl and working outward, until the mixture is completely smooth. Let the ganache cool, whisking occasionally, until it's thickened and spreadable, 35 to 45 minutes.

SPREAD THE GANACHE OVER THE BROWNIES: Use the foil to lift the cooled brownies out of the pan and transfer to a cutting board. Scrape the ganache onto the brownies and smooth across the surface with the back of a spoon or a small offset spatula. Let the brownies sit until the ganache is set, then slice with a serrated knife into a 4-by-4 grid to make 16 brownies.

Honey & Tahini Toffee Matzo

In the pantheon of Passover desserts, the champion (at least in my eyes) is toffee-covered matzo. As good as any flourless chocolate cake or coconut macaroon can be, I usually think that the combination of crunchy-salty matzo and buttery, toasty toffee is better. It's typically made by tiling a sheet pan with matzo, pouring a liquid toffee mixture on top, and baking it until the toffee is crunchy and brittle. Then it's covered in melted chocolate and often sprinkled with nuts or coconut. Here I lean into a different flavor profile inspired by sesame and honey candies common in the Mediterranean, Middle East, and other parts of the world (my family loves them—we buy them at the Russian supermarket near my parents' house). I forgo the chocolate and toppings and coat the matzo in a tahini and honey toffee mixture stirred through with a copious quantity of toasted sesame seeds. The toffee maintains a pleasing chew even after baking, thanks to the tahini, making this a unique Passover treat both in flavor and in texture.

MAKES SEVERAL DOZEN PIECES

DIFFICULTY: 2 (Easy)

ACTIVE TIME: 30 minutes

TOTAL TIME: 55 minutes, plus time to cool

SPECIAL EQUIPMENT: 18 × 13-inch sheet pan

4 to 5 sheets plain salted matzo

¾ cup sesame seeds (3.8 oz / 107g)

1 teaspoon Diamond Crystal kosher salt or ½ teaspoon Morton kosher salt

¼ teaspoon baking soda

1 cup packed light brown sugar (7.8 oz / 220g)

6 tablespooons unsalted butter (3 oz / 85g)

⅓ cup honey (4 oz / 113g)

⅓ cup tahini (3 oz / 85g)

PREPARE THE MATZO LAYER: Line an 18 × 13-inch sheet pan with a silicone baking mat or cover it entirely with foil, ensuring that the foil extends up and over all four sides of the pan to contain the toffee mixture. Arrange the matzo sheets on the prepared pan so they cover the entire area with no gaps, breaking the sheets to fit as needed. Set aside.

PREHEAT THE OVEN: Arrange an oven rack in the center position and preheat the oven to 300°F.

TOAST THE SESAME SEEDS: Scatter the sesame seeds across a second sheet pan and toast until they're golden brown and fragrant, 7 to 10 minutes, tossing halfway through. Let the sesame seeds cool completely on the pan. Leave the oven on. Transfer the seeds to a small bowl, toss with the salt and baking soda, and set aside.

MAKE THE SESAME TOFFEE: In a large saucepan, combine the brown sugar, butter, honey, tahini, and ¼ cup (2 oz / 57g) water. Bring the mixture to a boil over medium-high heat, stirring constantly with a heatproof flexible spatula to dissolve the sugar and melt the butter. Once it's boiling, continue to cook, stirring the mixture often and scraping the sides and bottom of the saucepan with the spatula, until it's reduced by about half, teeming with large, slow bubbles, and slightly darkened in color, about 5 minutes. Remove the saucepan from the heat, add the sesame seed mixture, and stir quickly to combine (it will foam a bit from the baking soda). Immediately scrape the toffee mixture onto the matzo on the sheet pan, distributing it as evenly as possible. Then, working quickly, use a small offset spatula to spread it over any bare spots of matzo.

BAKE AND BREAK: Transfer the sheet pan to the oven and bake until the toffee is deep golden brown and the bubbling has mostly subsided, 30 to 35 minutes, rotating the pan front to back after 20 minutes. Let the toffee matzo cool completely on the pan, then peel it away from the baking mat or foil and break into pieces.

Can I . . .

Make it ahead? Yes. The toffee will become sticky over time if exposed to the air, so be sure to store the pieces in an airtight container. They will keep for up to 5 days at room temperature.

Salty Cashew Blondies

Raw cashews are pretty boring, but when thoroughly salted and roasted, they turn into a totally addictive snack. It's the richness and savoriness of salted roasted cashews that makes them a great addition to blondies, a type of bar cookie that's typically quite sweet. I double-roast the cashews and coat them in toffee to add a salty crunch to my straightforward blondie base. The variety of textures and nutty-butterscotch-y flavors made these a fan favorite during the testing phase.

MAKES 16 BLONDIES

DIFFICULTY: 2 (Easy)

ACTIVE TIME: 30 minutes

TOTAL TIME: 1 hour 15 minutes, plus time to cool

SPECIAL EQUIPMENT: 8 × 8-inch baking pan (preferably metal)

Melted butter for the pan

1½ cups salted roasted cashews (6 oz / 170g)

14 tablespoons unsalted butter (7 oz / 198g), divided

1¼ cups packed light brown sugar (9.7 oz / 275g), divided

2 large eggs (3.5 oz / 100g), cold from the refrigerator

1 tablespoon vanilla extract

1 cup all-purpose flour (4.8 oz / 135g)

1 teaspoon Diamond Crystal kosher salt or ½ teaspoon Morton kosher salt

Flaky sea salt (optional)

PREHEAT THE OVEN AND PREPARE THE PAN: Arrange an oven rack in the center position and preheat the oven to 350°F. Line an 8 × 8-inch baking pan, preferably metal, with foil, pressing it into the corners and smoothing it across the bottom and up the sides. Brush the bottom and sides of the foil with a thin layer of melted butter and set the pan aside.

Optional Upgrade: If your salted roasted cashews are on the paler side, toast them to further develop the flavor. Place the nuts on a sheet pan and toast until they're deep golden brown and fragrant, 7 to 10 minutes, tossing halfway through. Let them cool completely.

CHOP THE CASHEWS: Place the cashews on a cutting board and chop until the largest pieces are about the size of a pea. Set aside.

MAKE THE TOFFEE-COVERED CASHEWS: Line a small sheet pan with a silicone baking mat or parchment and set it next to the stove. Combine 4 tablespoons (2 oz / 57g) of the butter, ¼ cup (1.9 oz / 55g) of the brown sugar, and 2 tablespoons (1 oz / 28g) water in a medium saucepan. Set the saucepan over medium heat and bring to a boil, stirring with a heatproof flexible spatula to melt the butter and dissolve the sugar. Once the mixture is boiling, stir in the chopped cashews and cook, stirring constantly, until the nuts are completely coated and there's no liquid toffee oozing across the bottom of the saucepan, about 5 minutes.

Potential Pitfall: If the toffee mixture heats too quickly or isn't stirred constantly, the butter may separate out and pool in the saucepan. If this happens, remove the saucepan from the heat, add a tablespoon of water, and stir vigorously to dissolve some of the toffee and bring the mixture back together. Return the saucepan to the heat and continue to cook.

COOL THE TOFFEE CASHEWS: Scrape the cashew mixture out onto the prepared sheet pan and spread it into a thin slab with the spatula, then set aside to cool. Return the saucepan to the stove (no need to wash it).

MAKE THE BATTER: Add the remaining 10 tablespoons (5 oz / 142g) butter to the reserved saucepan and melt it over low heat. Scrape the melted butter into a large bowl. Add the remaining 1 cup (7.8 oz / 220g) brown sugar and whisk vigorously until the mixture is smooth, thick, and satiny, about 30 seconds. Add the eggs one at a time, whisking thoroughly after each addition, then continue to whisk until the mixture is completely smooth and slightly pale, about 30 seconds. Whisk in the vanilla, then add the flour and kosher salt and whisk vigorously until the batter is very smooth and thick, about 30 seconds.

→

Can I...

Make them ahead? Yes. The blondies, stored airtight at room temperature, will keep for up to 4 days. They can also be frozen for up to 1 month.

Double the recipe? Yes. Line a 13 × 9-inch pan, preferably metal, with foil and butter as directed. Double all of the ingredient quantities and proceed with the recipe as written, but use a large saucepan for making the toffee-covered cashews. Note that you will have to extend the bake time due to the larger volume of batter, so keep an eye out for the given indicators.

Make them gluten-free? Yes. Replace the all-purpose flour with an equal amount of your preferred gluten-free flour blend and bake as directed.

Bake this in a different pan? Yes. Bake the blondies in a 9-inch cake pan that has been lined with foil and buttered. The bake time will be about the same.

ASSEMBLE: Scrape half of the batter into the prepared pan and smooth it into an even layer with the spatula, working it all the way to the sides and corners. Break about half of the cooled slab of toffee-covered cashews into small clusters with your fingertips, then scatter the clusters evenly over the surface of the batter. (Depending on how thoroughly you cooked the mixture, the slab may be brittle or pliable—either way is fine.) Dollop the remaining batter on top, then smooth it into an even layer with the spatula. Break the remaining slab into clusters and scatter across the surface, then sprinkle with flaky salt (if using).

BAKE: Bake until the surface of the blondies is deep golden brown and firm to the touch, 30 to 35 minutes. Let the blondies cool completely in the pan, then use the foil to lift them out of the pan and transfer to a cutting board. Slice with a serrated knife into a 4-by-4 grid to make 16 blondies.

Glazed Spelt Graham Crackers

Graham crackers get their distinctive flavor from graham flour, a type of coarsely ground whole wheat flour, but for something a little more interesting, I use spelt flour here instead. Spelt is an ancient breed of wheat that's naturally lower in protein than modern, conventional wheat, so baked goods made with spelt flour come out softer and lighter than those made with regular whole wheat flour. It adds a nutty, savory flavor to these crispy "crackers" (they're cookies), which are spiced with just a hint of cinnamon and lightly sweetened with honey. You can keep them plain and use them for s'mores or graham cracker crusts, but on their own I like them coated with a simple confectioners' sugar glaze for a little extra sweetness.

MAKES A COUPLE DOZEN COOKIES (DEPENDING ON HOW YOU CUT THEM)

DIFFICULTY: 2 (Easy)

ACTIVE TIME: 1 hour

TOTAL TIME: 2 hours

SPECIAL EQUIPMENT: Hand mixer, 18 × 13-inch sheet pan, wheel cutter (fluted or straight) or cookie cutter

DOUGH

1½ cups spelt flour (6.2 oz / 175g)

¾ cup all-purpose flour (3.5 oz / 100g), plus more for rolling

1 teaspoon Diamond Crystal kosher salt or ½ teaspoon Morton kosher salt

¾ teaspoon baking powder

½ teaspoon baking soda

¼ teaspoon ground cinnamon

1½ sticks unsalted butter (6 oz / 170g), at room temperature

6 tablespoons packed dark brown sugar (2.9 oz / 83g)

2 tablespoons honey

1 teaspoon vanilla extract

GLAZE

2 cups confectioners' sugar (7.8 oz / 220g), sifted if lumpy

3 tablespoons whole milk, at room temperature, plus more to thin the glaze

1 tablespoon unsalted butter, melted

1 teaspoon vanilla extract

Pinch of kosher salt

MIX THE DRY INGREDIENTS: In a medium bowl, whisk together the spelt flour, all-purpose flour, salt, baking powder, baking soda, and cinnamon. Set aside.

MAKE THE DOUGH: In a large bowl, with a hand mixer, combine the butter, brown sugar, honey, and vanilla and beat on medium speed until combined, then increase the speed to high and continue to beat, pausing occasionally to scrape down the sides of the bowl with a flexible spatula, until the mixture is light and fluffy, about 3 minutes. Reduce the mixer speed to low and gradually add the dry ingredients, beating just until the last trace of flour disappears. Switch to a flexible spatula and fold the dough several times, scraping the bottom and sides of the bowl to ensure everything is evenly mixed.

CHILL THE DOUGH: Scrape the dough onto a piece of reusable food wrap or plastic and pat it into a ¾-inch-thick square. Wrap up the dough and press down on top of the square with your palms to further flatten it into an even layer. Refrigerate the dough until it's firm, at least 1 hour.

PREHEAT THE OVEN: Arrange an oven rack in the center position and preheat the oven to 325°F.

ROLL OUT THE DOUGH: Let the dough sit at room temperature for several minutes to soften slightly. Cut two sheets of parchment paper to fit inside an 18 × 13-inch sheet pan. Place one of the pieces of parchment on the work surface and dust it with all-purpose flour. Unwrap the dough and place it in the center of the floured parchment, then dust the dough with more flour and place the second piece of parchment on top. With a rolling pin, roll out the dough between the parchment, periodically peeling off and repositioning both pieces of parchment (to prevent wrinkling) and dusting with more flour as needed to prevent sticking, until you have a thin slab measuring just under ¼ inch thick that fills most of the area of the parchment.

BAKE AND CUT THE COOKIES: Peel away the top sheet of parchment, then slide the bottom piece of parchment paper (and the dough along with it) onto the sheet pan. Use the tines of a fork or the blunt end of a skewer to press decorative holes across the surface. Bake until the dough is puffed and matte across the surface and browned around the edges, 22 to 27 minutes, rotating the pan front to back after 15 minutes. While the slab

Can I . . .

Make them ahead? Yes. Once they're set, the glazed cookies can be stored in an airtight container (stack them in layers separated by sheets of parchment paper) at room temperature for up to 3 days. The dough can be refrigerated for up to 2 days or frozen for up to 1 month. Let the dough thaw overnight in the refrigerator before rolling and baking.

Use a stand mixer instead of a hand mixer? Yes. Combine the butter, brown sugar, honey, and vanilla in a stand mixer fitted with the paddle attachment and proceed with the recipe as written.

Use another whole-grain flour instead of spelt? Yes. Feel free to substitute an equal quantity of whole wheat or rye flour for the spelt.

Make them gluten-free? No. Graham crackers are a wheat-based cookie, so adapting them to be gluten-free would change the identity of the cookie.

Bake these on a jelly roll pan or cookie sheet instead of a sheet pan? Yes, but . . . in two smaller batches. Jelly roll pans and most cookie sheets are smaller than an 18 × 13-inch sheet pan, so if using one of the former, divide the chilled dough in half and roll out the two portions one at a time as directed into a rectangular slab that's just under ¼ inch thick. Bake one slab at a time as directed, but check for doneness sooner, since the smaller slabs of dough will bake a little faster.

is hot from the oven, use a fluted or straight wheel cutter to slice cleanly through the dough lengthwise and crosswise, pressing down firmly, to cut it into squares or rectangles of any size. Alternatively, use any cookie cutter to punch out shapes.

COOL: Let the cookies cool on the sheet pan for 10 minutes, then use an offset spatula to gently lift the cookies and transfer them one at a time to wire racks to cool completely. They will seem soft at first but will crisp as they cool. Reserve any scrap pieces for making graham cracker crusts.

GLAZE THE COOKIES: Place the confectioners' sugar in a medium bowl and make a well in the center. Add the milk, melted butter, vanilla, and salt and whisk, starting in the center and gradually working your way outward, until combined, then whisk vigorously until the glaze is completely smooth. You want a fluid glaze that will coat the cookies in a thin, translucent layer, so whisk in more milk by the teaspoon until it's the consistency of maple syrup. Gently grasp a cookie around the sides and dip it upside down into the glaze (don't dunk it, you just want to coat the surface). Wiggle it gently, then lift up the cookie and use a butter knife or small offset spatula to wipe away any excess glaze and let it drip back into the bowl. Transfer the cookie back to the wire rack glazed-side up. Repeat until all of the cookies are glazed. Let them sit uncovered on the wire rack until the glaze has set, about 20 minutes.

Toasted Rice Sablés

The word *sablé* means "sandy" in French. It's not a word you'd think would be positively ascribed to food, but sablé cookies, a style of shortbread known for its crumbly texture, are my favorite kind of cookie. This particular sablé earns its title, as it's made with rice flour, which is gluten-free and contributes a very sandy (there's no other way to describe it) texture to the cookie. They're also incredibly light, thanks to crispy rice cereal that's crushed and added to the dough and pressed onto the cookies' exteriors. Toasting the rice flour is an extra step I take to develop the flavor of the cookies and give them a nutty edge.

MAKES ABOUT 20 COOKIES

DIFFICULTY: 2 (Easy)

GLUTEN-FREE

ACTIVE TIME: 30 minutes

TOTAL TIME: 1 hour 20 minutes, plus time to cool

SPECIAL EQUIPMENT: Hand mixer, 1-ounce scoop (optional)

1½ cups white rice flour (7.9 oz / 225g), not glutinous rice flour

3 cups crispy rice cereal (3.5 oz / 100g), like Rice Krispies, divided

¼ cup cornstarch (1.1 oz / 32g)

1½ teaspoons baking powder

1 teaspoon Diamond Crystal kosher salt or ½ teaspoon Morton kosher salt

1½ sticks unsalted butter (6 oz / 170g), at room temperature

1 cup confectioners' sugar (3.9 oz / 110g)

1 large egg (1.8 oz / 50g), at room temperature

Can I . . .

Make them ahead? Yes. The cookies, stored in an airtight container at room temperature, will keep for up to 3 days, but they're best eaten on the day they're baked while the rice is crispy.

Use a stand mixer instead of a hand mixer? Yes. Combine the butter and confectioners' sugar in a stand mixer fitted with the paddle attachment and proceed with the recipe as written.

PREHEAT THE OVEN: Arrange an oven rack in the upper third of the oven and another in the lower third and preheat the oven to 350°F.

TOAST THE RICE FLOUR: Sprinkle the rice flour across a sheet pan and shake to work the flour into a flat, even layer. Transfer the pan to the upper rack and bake until the flour is lightly browned and smells like popcorn, 15 to 20 minutes, stirring it halfway through. Set the pan aside and let the flour cool completely. Leave the oven on.

MIX THE DRY INGREDIENTS: Place 1 cup (1.1 oz / 32g) of the rice cereal in a medium bowl and crush it with your hands or the bottom of a glass until it's broken down into fine bits. Add the cornstarch, baking powder, salt, and cooled toasted rice flour and whisk to combine. Set aside.

MAKE THE DOUGH: In a large bowl, with a hand mixer, beat the butter and confectioners' sugar on medium speed until the mixture is light and smooth, about 1 minute. Add the egg and beat on medium speed to combine, then reduce the mixer speed to low and add the dry ingredients, beating just until you have a smooth dough. Switch to a flexible spatula and fold the dough several times, scraping the bottom and sides, to make sure it's thoroughly mixed. If the dough is too soft to handle, refrigerate it for a few minutes so it can firm up.

PREPARE THE SHEET PANS: Line two sheet pans with parchment paper and set aside.

ROLL AND COAT THE COOKIES: Place the remaining 2 cups (2.3 oz / 66g) rice cereal in a small bowl and have at the ready. Using a 1-ounce cookie scoop, portion a level scoop of dough and roll it between your palms to form it into a smooth sphere. (Alternatively, roll 2 level tablespoons of the dough into a sphere.) Toss the sphere gently in the rice cereal until it's completely coated, then place it on one of the prepared sheet pans. Repeat with the remaining dough, dividing the coated spheres between the two prepared pans and spacing them evenly (you should end up with about 20 pieces total). Use the bottom of a glass or dry measuring cup to flatten the coated spheres one at a time into ½-inch-thick rounds.

BAKE: Transfer the pans to the oven, placing one on each rack, and bake until the cookies are golden across the surface and golden brown around the edges, 15 to 18 minutes, switching racks and rotating the pans front to back after 10 minutes. Let the cookies cool completely on the pans.

Lime Squiggles

These cookies are a style of shortbread called meltaways, so named because the addition of cornstarch to the buttery dough reduces gluten development and makes them melt-in-your-mouth tender. Aside from the cornstarch, though, these are not typical meltaways. I supplement the butter with cream cheese, which adds extra tang on top of the lime juice and zest, and I coat the finished cookies in a lime glaze rather than the usual confectioners' sugar. Piping them spritz-style through a star tip creates more surface area for the glaze and gives the cookies an extra-fun look.

MAKES 15 TO 20 COOKIES
(depending on how you pipe them)

DIFFICULTY: 2 (Easy)

ACTIVE TIME: 30 minutes

TOTAL TIME: 1 hour 25 minutes

SPECIAL EQUIPMENT: Hand mixer, pastry bag (or resealable plastic bag), ½-inch open star pastry tip

DOUGH

1½ cups all-purpose flour (7 oz / 200g)

¼ cup cornstarch (1.1 oz / 32g)

¾ teaspoon Diamond Crystal kosher salt or ½ teaspoon Morton kosher salt

1 stick unsalted butter (4 oz / 113g), at room temperature

4 ounces (113g) cream cheese, at room temperature

¾ cup confectioners' sugar (2.9 oz / 83g)

2 teaspoons finely grated lime zest

2 tablespoons fresh lime juice

2 teaspoons vanilla extract

GLAZE

1 cup confectioners' sugar (3.9 oz / 110g), sifted if lumpy

2 tablespoons fresh lime juice

1 tablespoon unsalted butter, melted

1 lime, for zesting

Can I . . .

Make them ahead? Yes. Once the glaze is set, the squiggles can be stored in an airtight container (stack them in layers separated by sheets of parchment paper) at room temperature for up to 3 days. The piped, unbaked squiggles can be frozen solid on the sheet pan, transferred to a freezer bag, and frozen for up to 2 months. Bake as directed (no need to thaw first).

Use a stand mixer instead of a hand mixer? Yes. Combine the butter, cream cheese, confectioners' sugar, and lime zest in a stand mixer fitted with the paddle attachment and proceed with the recipe as written.

PREHEAT THE OVEN AND PREPARE THE SHEET PAN: Arrange an oven rack in the center position and preheat the oven to 350°F. Line a large sheet pan with parchment paper and set aside.

MIX THE DRY INGREDIENTS: In a medium bowl, whisk together the flour, cornstarch, and salt to combine. Set aside.

MAKE THE DOUGH: In a large bowl, with a hand mixer, beat the butter, cream cheese, confectioners' sugar, and lime zest on medium speed until combined, then increase the speed to high and continue to beat, pausing occasionally to scrape down the sides of the bowl with a flexible spatula, until the mixture is completely smooth and slightly fluffy, about 1 minute. Add the lime juice and vanilla and beat on medium speed just until combined, then reduce the speed to low, add the dry ingredients, and mix just until combined. Switch to a flexible spatula and fold the dough several times, scraping the bottom and sides, to make sure it's thoroughly mixed.

PIPE THE SQUIGGLES: Fit a pastry bag or resealable plastic bag with the star tip and transfer the dough to the bag, doing your best not to create any air pockets (see Filling a Pastry Bag, page 342). Push the dough to the bottom of the bag, press out the air, and twist the bag to seal. Applying constant, even pressure to the bag, pipe the dough onto the prepared sheet pan in tight squiggle shapes measuring about 3 inches long. Continue to pipe the cookies, spacing them about 1 inch apart (they won't spread much), until you've used all the dough. Transfer the sheet pan to the refrigerator and chill uncovered until the dough is firm to the touch, 15 to 20 minutes.

Potential Pitfall: If it's cold in your kitchen, the butter in the batter could firm up and make it difficult to pipe. If this happens, place the bag in a warm spot (near the preheating oven, for example) and let it sit until the dough is softened.

BAKE: Bake the cookies until they're golden along the ridges and pale across the surface, 18 to 22 minutes. Let them cool completely on the sheet pan.

GLAZE THE COOKIES: In a medium bowl, whisk together the confectioners' sugar, lime juice, and melted butter until completely smooth. Lift a cookie off the sheet pan and, holding it around the sides, dip it upside down into the glaze so the entire cookie is submerged except the bottom, then wiggle it gently for a few seconds to encourage the ridged surfaces to pick up the glaze. Lift up the cookie and let any excess glaze drip back into the bowl for a moment, then transfer it to a wire rack glazed-side up. Using a rasp-style grater and the whole lime, grate a bit of lime zest over the freshly glazed cookie. Repeat the dipping process with the remaining cookies and top with lime zest while the glaze is still wet. Let the squiggles sit uncovered at room temperature until the glaze is set, 25 to 30 minutes.

Make them gluten-free? Yes. Replace the all-purpose flour with an equal amount of your preferred gluten-free flour blend and bake as directed.

Make them without a pastry bag? Yes. You can form the dough into a 10-inch-long log, refrigerate it until firm, and then slice the log crosswise into ½-inch-thick coins and bake. For step-by-step instructions, see Forming Logs of Cookie Dough, page 352.

All-In Shortbreads

Every time I test a new recipe, I hold out the somewhat delusional hope that I'll nail it on the first try. It has never happened—that is, until I made this cookie! Granted, the concept is simple, so the margin of error wasn't huge. It's a basic, buttery shortbread studded with a mix of all my most desired cookie inclusions: pretzels, pecans, chocolate, coconut, and pumpkin seeds. The very first version turned out so delicious I didn't change a thing. Judging across the board on flavor, ease, and presentation, it's my pick for top cookie in the book.

MAKES ABOUT 24 COOKIES

DIFFICULTY: 2 (Easy)

ACTIVE TIME: 40 minutes

TOTAL TIME: 1 hour 30 minutes

SPECIAL EQUIPMENT: Hand mixer

2 sticks unsalted butter (8 oz / 227g), at room temperature

⅔ cup granulated sugar (4.7 oz / 133g)

½ teaspoon Diamond Crystal kosher salt or ¼ teaspoon Morton kosher salt

1 large egg yolk (0.5 oz / 15g), at room temperature

1 teaspoon vanilla extract

2 cups all-purpose flour (9.5 oz / 270g)

1.3 ounces (38g) thin pretzel rods, broken up into small pieces (½ cup)

½ cup pecan halves or pieces (2 oz / 57g)

4 ounces (113g) semisweet chocolate (64%-70% cacao), finely chopped

¼ cup dried unsweetened coconut flakes (0.6 oz / 18g)

¼ cup pumpkin seeds (1.3 oz / 36g)

⅓ cup demerara sugar (2.4 oz / 67g), for rolling

MAKE THE DOUGH: In a large bowl, with a hand mixer, beat the butter, granulated sugar, and salt on medium speed until combined, then increase the speed to medium-high and continue to beat, pausing to scrape down the sides of the bowl with a flexible spatula, until the mixture is completely smooth and slightly fluffy, about 1 minute. Add the egg yolk and vanilla and beat on medium just until combined. Reduce the mixer speed to low and add the flour, beating just until it disappears and you have a crumbly dough.

ADD THE MIX-INS: Add the pretzel pieces, pecans, chocolate, coconut, and pumpkin seeds and fold the mixture with a flexible spatula, scraping the bottom and sides of the bowl, until the batter is evenly mixed and the pieces are thoroughly distributed.

> *Potential Pitfall:* If it's warm in your kitchen, the butter in the dough might soften, making it sticky and difficult to form into logs in the next step. If this happens, transfer the bowl to the refrigerator and chill the dough uncovered, folding it every 10 minutes with the spatula, until it's firm and moldable.

FORM THE DOUGH INTO SQUARE LOGS: Scrape half of the dough out onto a sheet of parchment paper and squeeze the dough with your hands into a rough 8-inch-long log oriented lengthwise on the parchment, taking care to squeeze out any air pockets. Pat around the log to make sure it's uniformly thick (it doesn't need to be cylindrical) and roll it up in the parchment as snugly as possible. Wrap the entire log tightly in plastic wrap, leaving a bit of overhang on both ends, then twist the ends of plastic (along with any overhanging parchment) to fully enclose the log and compress the dough inside. Press straight down along the length of the log with your palms to flatten it slightly, then give the log a 90-degree rotation and press down again along the length to flatten. Continue to rotate the log and flatten several more times until you've created four flat, equal sides (the cross section should be a square). Transfer the log to the freezer, then repeat with the remaining dough. Freeze the logs until the dough is very firm but not frozen solid, 20 to 25 minutes.

PREHEAT THE OVEN AND PREPARE THE SHEET PANS: Arrange an oven rack in the upper third and another in the lower third of the oven and preheat it to 350°F. Line two large sheet pans with parchment paper and set aside.

COAT THE FIRST LOG IN THE DEMERARA SUGAR: Gently sprinkle the demerara sugar in a thin layer across a clean work surface (it should cover an area equal in length to the logs of dough). Remove the first log from the freezer, unwrap, and place it on the sugared surface. Press down so the sugar adheres to one side of the log, then rotate and press down again to coat another side in sugar. Repeat, rotating the log several times and

$\rightarrow$

Can I . . .

Make them ahead? Yes. The cookies, stored airtight at room temperature, will keep for up to 5 days. The logs can also be frozen for up to 2 months. Let the frozen logs sit in the refrigerator for several hours before slicing, or the dough will splinter as you try to slice it.

Use a stand mixer instead of a hand mixer? Yes. Combine the butter, sugar, and salt in a stand mixer fitted with the paddle attachment and proceed with the recipe as written.

Make it gluten-free? Yes. Replace the all-purpose flour with an equal amount of your preferred gluten-free flour blend and bake as directed.

pressing, until all four sides are completely coated in the sugar (pat the sugar into any bare spots to cover, if necessary). Transfer the coated log to a cutting board and reserve the remaining sugar for the second log.

SLICE THE COOKIES AND REPEAT: Use a serrated knife to cleanly slice off about ½ inch of dough from one end of the log, exposing the square interior (discard the end). Then, starting from that end, slice the entire log crosswise into ½-inch-thick squares, periodically rotating the log so it's resting on a new side to maintain an even shape all the way around. You should end up with about 20 cookies. Place the squares on one of the prepared sheet pans, spacing evenly (they won't spread much during baking). Refrigerate the first sheet of cookies while you repeat the coating process with the second log and the reserved demerara sugar, then slice the log just as you did the first and arrange the cookies on the second prepared sheet pan.

> *Potential Pitfall:* As you slice the cookies, you might hit a larger piece of chocolate or pecan, causing the square to break apart. If that happens, just press the pieces back together.

BAKE: Transfer the pans to the oven, placing one on each rack, and bake until the cookies are golden brown across the surface, 14 to 18 minutes, switching racks and rotating the pans front to back after 10 minutes. Let the cookies cool on the pans for 5 minutes, then transfer them to a wire rack to cool completely.

Coconut Macaroon Bars

Think of these bars as a hybrid of coconut macaroons and 7-layer bars, although this recipe is all about the coconut (you could always spread a layer of melted chocolate on top of the baked bars before slicing them, if you wanted). The base is a layer of shortbread made with almond flour and shredded coconut, so it's gluten-free, and the filling is a straightforward mixture of beaten egg whites, sweetened condensed milk, and unsweetened coconut. It keeps everything I love about coconut macaroons (the coconut flavor, the chewy texture) and fixes what I don't (the extreme sweetness). Consider them along with **Honey & Tahini Toffee Matzo** (page 195) for your Passover dessert table.

MAKES 16 BARS

DIFFICULTY: 2 (Easy)

GLUTEN-FREE

ACTIVE TIME: 45 minutes

TOTAL TIME: 1 hour 45 minutes, plus time to cool

SPECIAL EQUIPMENT: 8 × 8-inch baking pan (preferably metal), hand mixer

Melted butter for the pan

1 cup almond flour (3.4 oz / 96g)

½ cup dried unsweetened shredded coconut (1.6 oz / 46g)

¼ cup confectioners' sugar (1 oz / 28g)

¼ cup cornstarch (1.1 oz / 32g)

½ teaspoon Diamond Crystal kosher salt or ¼ teaspoon Morton kosher salt, plus a pinch

6 tablespoons unsalted butter (3 oz / 85g), cut into ½-inch pieces, chilled

3 large egg whites (3.7 oz / 105g), at room temperature

7 ounces (200g) dried unsweetened coconut flakes (about 4 cups)

1 cup sweetened condensed milk (10.5 oz / 298g)

1 teaspoon vanilla extract

PREHEAT THE OVEN AND PREPARE THE PAN: Arrange an oven rack in the center position and preheat the oven to 325°F. Brush the bottom and sides of an 8 × 8-inch baking pan, preferably metal, with a thin layer of melted butter, then line the bottom and two opposite sides with a piece of parchment paper, leaving a bit of overhang. Lightly butter the parchment paper and set the pan aside.

MAKE THE SHORTBREAD: In a medium bowl, whisk together the almond flour, shredded coconut, confectioners' sugar, cornstarch, and ½ teaspoon salt until combined. Add the butter and toss to coat. Use your fingertips to smash the butter pieces completely into the almond flour mixture, working until you have lots of moist crumbs that hold together easily when squeezed and no visible bits of butter.

BAKE THE CRUST: Scatter the crumbs evenly across the bottom of the prepared pan and use your hands to flatten them into an even layer all the way to the corners and sides. Bake the shortbread until it's lightly golden across the surface, 20 to 25 minutes.

MEANWHILE, PREPARE THE EGG WHITES: In a clean, medium, nonplastic bowl, with a hand mixer, beat the egg whites on medium-low speed just until they're broken up, liquidy, and slightly foamy, about 20 seconds. Spoon about a tablespoon of the egg white into a separate small bowl and set aside (reserve the remaining egg whites in the medium bowl for assembling the filling).

BRUSH THE CRUST WITH EGG WHITE: When the crust is golden, remove the pan from the oven and brush the tablespoon of beaten egg white across the entire surface of the hot crust. Return the pan to the oven and bake just until the egg white is set, about 2 minutes (this will prevent the crust from becoming soggy beneath the filling). Set the crust aside to cool. Leave the oven on.

MAKE THE COCONUT MIXTURE: In a medium bowl (you can use the same one you used to make the shortbread, no need to wash), combine the coconut flakes, sweetened condensed milk, and vanilla and fold with a flexible spatula until the coconut is completely coated and everything is evenly mixed. Set aside.

→

Can I . . .

Make them ahead? Yes. The bars, stored in an airtight container at room temperature, will keep for up to 3 days, but they're best eaten on the day they're baked while the shortbread is firm (it will soften over time).

Use a stand mixer instead of a hand mixer? Yes. Beat the egg whites and a pinch of salt in a stand mixer fitted with the whisk attachment on medium speed until they hold a medium peak, keeping in mind that the egg whites will whip faster and be easier to overbeat in the stand mixer.

Double the recipe? Yes. Line a 13 × 9-inch pan, preferably metal, with parchment and butter as directed. Double all of the ingredient quantities and proceed with the recipe as written, slicing the bars into an 8-by-4 grid. Note that you will have to extend the bake times due to the larger volumes of crust and filling, so keep an eye out for the given indicators.

BEAT THE EGG WHITES AND ASSEMBLE THE FILLING: Add a pinch of salt to the reserved egg whites and beat with the hand mixer on medium-high speed until the egg whites are voluminous and hold a medium peak, about 1 minute (see page 339 for what this stage looks like). Try not to overbeat, or the whites will take on a dry, grainy texture and be difficult to fold into the filling. Scrape the egg whites into the bowl with the coconut mixture and fold gently, scraping the sides and bottom of the bowl, until everything is evenly mixed (for more on the proper technique, see Folding a Mixture, page 351).

FILL THE PAN AND CUT: Scrape the filling onto the warm crust and use the spatula to spread it into an even layer all the way to the corners and sides. Use a serrated knife to cut down through the filling and crust in both directions to form a 4-by-4 grid (this makes the baked bars easier to slice; you'll trace over the cuts again after baking).

BAKE: Bake the bars until the surface is puffed and golden brown all over, 35 to 40 minutes. Let the bars cool completely in the pan. Use a paring knife to cut down between the pan and the filling along the unlined sides, then use the parchment overhang on the opposite sides to lift the bars out of the pan and transfer to a cutting board. Retrace the cuts you made before baking with a serrated knife to cut 16 bars.

Caramel Peanut Popcorn Bars

My grandma kept two very specific treats in her apartment that I only ever had when my family visited. The first was coffee-flavored Nips candies, which I liked but got stuck in my teeth, and the second was Poppycock, an extremely craveable mix of caramel popcorn and nuts that forever cemented my passion for caramel popcorn. These "bars," which are basically sliced, cube-shaped popcorn balls, are my streamlined take on homemade caramel popcorn. Baking ensures the caramel forms a crispy and not sticky coating, while pressing the mixture into a pan is an easy and quick way to give it form. Use another nut besides peanuts if you prefer, but don't omit the corn syrup—it's a relatively small amount and helps prevent the caramel from crystallizing.

MAKES 9 BARS

DIFFICULTY: 2 (Easy)

GLUTEN-FREE

ACTIVE TIME: 40 minutes

TOTAL TIME: 1 hour 40 minutes

SPECIAL EQUIPMENT: 8 × 8-inch baking pan (preferably metal), large Dutch oven

Melted butter for the pan

1⅓ cups sugar (9.4 oz / 267g)

6 tablespoons unsalted butter (3 oz / 85g), cut into pieces

¼ cup light corn syrup (3 oz / 85g)

1 teaspoon Diamond Crystal kosher salt or ½ teaspoon Morton kosher salt

¾ teaspoon baking soda

10 cups unseasoned popped popcorn (2.6 oz / 75g), from about 6 tablespoons (2.6 oz / 75g) kernels

1 cup salted roasted peanuts (4 oz / 113g)

PREPARE THE PAN: Brush the bottom and sides of an 8 × 8-inch baking pan, preferably metal, with a thin layer of melted butter, then line the bottom and two opposite sides with a piece of parchment paper, leaving a bit of overhang. Lightly butter the parchment paper and set the pan aside. Lightly butter a separate square of parchment paper, which you will use to press the mixture into the pan, and set aside.

PREHEAT THE OVEN: Arrange an oven rack in the center position and preheat the oven to 250°F.

MAKE THE CARAMEL: Fill a glass with water, place a pastry brush inside, and set it next to the stove. In a large Dutch oven, combine the sugar, butter, corn syrup, and ½ cup (4 oz / 113g) water and stir gently with a heatproof flexible spatula over medium-high heat just until the butter is melted, the sugar is dissolved, and the mixture comes to a boil, about 4 minutes. Cook the mixture to a golden caramel (like the color of medium honey), following steps 3 through 5 in Cooking a Wet Caramel (page 346), then immediately remove the Dutch oven from the heat. Thoroughly stir in the salt and baking soda (the mixture will foam).

> *Potential Pitfall:* Don't cook the caramel beyond medium golden because it will continue to cook in the oven, and a deep caramel will eventually burn.

ADD THE POPCORN AND NUTS AND BAKE: Add the popcorn and peanuts to the Dutch oven and fold, thoroughly scraping the bottom and lifting the liquid caramel up and over the popcorn and nuts, until they're evenly coated and there's no caramel pooling at the bottom. Transfer the Dutch oven to the oven and bake until the caramel has turned deep amber, 30 to 35 minutes, thoroughly folding the mixture every 10 minutes with the spatula and making sure to scrape the bottom of the Dutch oven where the caramel is darkening.

PRESS THE POPCORN MIXTURE INTO THE PAN: Remove the Dutch oven from the oven and immediately scrape half of the popcorn mixture into the prepared pan. Use a gloved hand and the piece of buttered parchment, buttered-side down, to firmly press the mixture against the sides and into the bottom and corners of the pan. Scrape the rest of the mixture into the pan and use the buttered parchment again to press it and compact it into a flat, even layer. It should fill the entire pan right to the top. Set the pan aside to cool completely (the bottom should not feel warm to the touch).

SLICE THE BARS: Use the parchment overhang to lift the block of caramel popcorn out of the pan and transfer it to a cutting board. Using a serrated knife, slice the block into a 3-by-3 grid, forming 9 squares.

Can I . . .

Make it ahead? Yes. The bars, stored in an airtight container at room temperature, will keep for up to 4 days. The caramel will attract moisture from the air and become soft and sticky over time, so make sure the container is truly airtight.

Skip pressing these into the pan? Yes. While the caramel popcorn and peanut mixture is still warm from the oven, use buttered hands to form it into freeform balls. Or, spread the warm mixture out onto a parchment-lined sheet pan in a single layer and let it cool completely, then break it up into clusters.

Free-Form Hazelnut Florentines

Florentines walk the line between cookie and candy. Magic happens in the oven when the nutty batter—which is more butter and sugar than flour—bubbles and browns to form a thin, brittle, lacy sheet of caramel. Florentines can spread unpredictably as they bake, so rather than attempt to shape them in any way, I bake the batter in large slabs and break them up into fragments. And because florentines are usually coated on one side with chocolate, mine get a swipe of melted unsweetened chocolate mixed with chocolate hazelnut spread to complement the toasted hazelnuts in the batter. They're a slightly different way to enjoy the classic combination of caramel, nuts, and chocolate.

MAKES SEVERAL DOZEN PIECES

DIFFICULTY: 2 (Easy)

ACTIVE TIME: 1 hour 15 minutes

TOTAL TIME: 1 hour 45 minutes, plus time to set

½ cup blanched hazelnuts (2 oz / 57g)

4 tablespoons unsalted butter (2 oz / 57g)

⅓ cup sugar (2.3 oz / 66g)

2 tablespoons heavy cream

2 tablespoons honey

¼ cup all-purpose flour (1.2 oz / 34g)

½ teaspoon Diamond Crystal kosher salt or ¼ teaspoon Morton kosher salt

1 teaspoon vanilla extract

5 ounces (142g) unsweetened chocolate, chopped

3 tablespoons chocolate hazelnut spread

PREHEAT THE OVEN: Arrange an oven rack in the center position and preheat the oven to 350°F.

TOAST THE HAZELNUTS: Spread the hazelnuts on a sheet pan and toast until they're golden brown and fragrant, 8 to 10 minutes, tossing halfway through. Let the nuts cool on the pan, then transfer to a cutting board and chop very finely until the largest pieces are no bigger than a lentil (some of the nuts will turn to dust, which is okay). Transfer the chopped hazelnuts to a small bowl and set aside. Leave the oven on.

MAKE THE BATTER: In a small saucepan, combine the butter, sugar, cream, and honey and bring to a boil over medium-high heat, stirring constantly with a heatproof flexible spatula to melt the butter and dissolve the sugar. Once the mixture is at a full, rolling boil, remove the saucepan from the heat and vigorously whisk in the flour and salt until the mixture is smooth and lump-free, then add the vanilla and hazelnuts and stir until combined. Scrape the batter into a medium bowl and set aside.

SPREAD THE BATTER: Line a large sheet pan with parchment paper, then cut a second piece of parchment to the same size. Scrape about half of the warm batter onto the prepared pan, then place the second piece of parchment on top. Working over the second piece of parchment, use a small offset spatula to spread the batter into as thin a layer as possible between the two sheets, pressing down firmly and pushing the mixture outward toward the margins (the overall shape isn't important). Transfer the sheet pan to the refrigerator and chill until the batter is firm and set, 8 to 10 minutes.

BAKE: Remove the sheet pan from the refrigerator and carefully peel away the top piece of parchment, leaving the layer of batter on the sheet pan. Bake until the batter has transformed into a lacy, weblike slab that's golden brown across the surface, 8 to 10 minutes, rotating the pan front to back after 6 minutes. Remove the sheet pan from the oven and let it cool completely.

BREAK INTO PIECES AND REPEAT: Break the cooled slab into large fragments on the sheet pan, then transfer the pieces to a wire rack. Repeat the spreading, chilling, and baking process with the remaining batter using the same sheet pan and parchment (the remaining batter will have cooled and firmed up, so you'll need to press even more firmly with the spatula to spread it). When the second slab of florentines is cool, break it into pieces and transfer to them to the rack. Reserve the empty lined sheet pan.

→

Can I . . .

Make them ahead? Yes. The florentines, stored in an airtight container at cool room temperature, will keep for up to 5 days (stack them in layers separated by sheets of parchment or wax paper). The florentines will attract moisture from the air and become soft and sticky over time, so make sure the container is truly airtight. If your kitchen is warm, store the florentines in the refrigerator to prevent the chocolate mixture from melting.

Halve the recipe? Yes. To bake a single slab of florentines, halve all of the ingredient quantities, except for the sugar, which does not divide easily. Instead use 2 tablespoons plus 2 teaspoons sugar. Follow the recipe as written.

Make it gluten-free? Yes. Replace the all-purpose flour with an equal amount of your preferred gluten-free flour blend and bake as directed.

MELT THE CHOCOLATE MIXTURE: Fill a small saucepan with about 1 inch of water and bring to a simmer over medium heat, then reduce the heat to maintain a gentle simmer. In a medium heatproof bowl, combine the unsweetened chocolate and chocolate hazelnut spread and set it over the saucepan, taking care that the bottom of the bowl doesn't touch the water (this is called a double boiler—for more information, see Setting Up a Double Boiler, page 341). Stir the mixture occasionally with a heatproof flexible spatula until it's melted and completely smooth, then remove the bowl from the heat and set aside. Let the chocolate mixture cool, stirring occasionally, until it's thickened.

COVER THE FLORENTINES: Use a small offset spatula to spread a very thin layer of the chocolate mixture across the flat bottoms of the florentines, then set the coated florentines chocolate-side down on the reserved sheet pan (when you run out of room, line another sheet pan with parchment and place the remaining florentines on it). When all the pieces are coated, transfer the sheet pans to the refrigerator and chill until the chocolate mixture is set, 10 to 15 minutes.

Sugar Cookies

Unlike the typical sugar cookie that you decorate with royal icing or sprinkles, this cookie uses four different kinds of sugar to create different textures, so the cookies are delicious to eat all on their own without any added decoration. Because I'm not a fan of rolling out dough and punching shapes with cutters, I make these slice-and-bake style, forming the dough into a log, coating it in sparkly sanding sugar, and slicing rounds. This is one place to splurge for high-quality butter, which adds extra richness to the cookies.

MAKES ABOUT 24 COOKIES

DIFFICULTY: 2 (Easy)

ACTIVE TIME: 45 minutes

TOTAL TIME: 3 hours

SPECIAL EQUIPMENT:
Hand mixer

2 cups all-purpose flour (9.5 oz / 270g)

1 teaspoon Diamond Crystal kosher salt or ½ teaspoon Morton kosher salt

½ teaspoon baking powder

2 sticks unsalted butter (8 oz / 227g), preferably European, European-style, or cultured, at room temperature

¾ cup confectioners' sugar (2.9 oz / 83g)

¼ cup packed light brown sugar (1.9 oz / 55g)

¼ cup demerara sugar (1.8 oz / 50g)

1 large egg (1.8 oz / 50g), at room temperature

2 teaspoons vanilla extract

¼ teaspoon almond extract

½ cup white sanding sugar or color of your choice (3.5 oz / 100g)

MIX THE DRY INGREDIENTS: In a medium bowl, whisk together the flour, salt, and baking powder until combined. Set aside.

CREAM THE BUTTER AND SUGAR: In a large bowl, with a hand mixer, beat the butter, confectioners' sugar, brown sugar, and demerara sugar on medium-low speed until combined, then increase the speed to medium-high and beat, pausing occasionally to scrape down the sides of the bowl with a flexible spatula, until the mixture is very light, pale, and fluffy, about 4 minutes (see Creaming Butter and Sugar, page 351).

MAKE THE DOUGH: Scrape down the sides of the bowl, then add the egg, vanilla, and almond extract and beat on medium speed until smooth. Reduce the mixer speed to low and add the dry ingredients, beating just until you have an evenly mixed dough. Switch to a flexible spatula and fold the dough several times, scraping the bottom and sides of the bowl to ensure everything is evenly mixed.

Potential Pitfall: If it's warm in your kitchen, the butter in the dough might soften, making it sticky and difficult to form into logs in the next step. If this happens, transfer the bowl to the refrigerator and chill the dough uncovered, folding it every 10 minutes with the flexible spatula, until it's firm and moldable.

FORM THE DOUGH INTO A LOG: Scrape the dough out onto a 12-inch-long piece of parchment paper and follow the steps in Forming Logs of Cookie Dough (page 352) to shape it into a tight, even cylinder measuring about 10 inches long and 2 inches in diameter. Refrigerate until the dough is very firm, at least 2 hours.

PREHEAT THE OVEN AND PREPARE THE SHEET PANS: Arrange an oven rack in the upper third and another in the lower third of the oven and preheat it to 350°F. Line two large sheet pans with parchment paper and set aside.

ROLL THE CYLINDER IN THE SANDING SUGAR: Gently sprinkle the sanding sugar in a thin layer across a clean work surface (it should cover about a 10-inch-long area). Remove the dough from the refrigerator, unwrap, and roll it firmly across the sugared surface so the sugar adheres. Continue to roll it over the sugar until the entire log is completely covered (pat the sugar into any bare spots to cover, if necessary). Transfer the log to a cutting board, then brush the excess sanding sugar aside and reserve it for sprinkling over the sliced cookies.

→

Can I . . .

Make them ahead? Yes. The sugar cookies, stored airtight at room temperature, will keep for up to 5 days. The log of dough will keep in the refrigerator for up to 2 days, or it can be frozen for up to 2 months. Allow the frozen dough to thaw in the refrigerator overnight before coating it in sugar, slicing, and baking.

Use a stand mixer instead of a hand mixer? Yes. Combine the butter, confectioners' sugar, brown sugar, and demerara sugar in a stand mixer fitted with the paddle attachment and proceed with the recipe as written.

Make them gluten-free? Yes. Replace the all-purpose flour with an equal amount of your preferred gluten-free flour blend and bake as directed.

SLICE THE COOKIES: Working on the cutting board, use a sharp knife to cleanly slice off about ½ inch of dough from one end of the cylinder, exposing the smooth, circular interior (discard the end). Then, starting from that end, slice the entire cylinder crosswise into generous ¼-inch-thick rounds, rotating the log gradually as you slice to maintain the round shape. You should end up with about 24 cookies. Transfer the rounds to the prepared pans, dividing them evenly and spacing about 2 inches apart (they'll spread some). Sprinkle the surface of each round with a pinch of the reserved sanding sugar.

BAKE: Transfer the sheet pans to the oven, placing one on each rack, and bake until the cookies are golden brown around the edges, 15 to 18 minutes, switching racks and rotating the pans front to back after 10 minutes. Let the cookies cool completely on the pans.

Blue & White Cookies

After roughly ten years of living in New York City, I feel like I have some claim to the black-and-white cookie, a staple of NYC Jewish bakeries. The cookie itself is actually more cake than cookie, and it's covered half in chocolate icing and half in a white icing. Often, the cookie, the white icing, or both are tinged with a bit of lemon flavor. I like the lemon but find it a somewhat discordant pairing with the chocolate, so this version, which otherwise hews pretty close to the classic, uses a blueberry icing instead of chocolate for a fruit-forward take. But, if your heart is set on a chocolate version, see Can I . . . on page 222 for how to adapt the recipe.

MAKES ABOUT 16 COOKIES

DIFFICULTY: 2 (Easy)

ACTIVE TIME: 1 hour 20 minutes

TOTAL TIME: 2 hours 20 minutes, plus time to set

SPECIAL EQUIPMENT: Hand mixer, 2-ounce scoop (optional)

COOKIES

2 cups all-purpose flour (9.5 oz / 270g), plus more for rolling

1 teaspoon Diamond Crystal kosher salt or ½ teaspoon Morton kosher salt

½ teaspoon baking powder

½ teaspoon baking soda

1 cup granulated sugar (7 oz / 200g)

2 teaspoons finely grated lemon zest

1½ sticks unsalted butter (6 oz / 170g), at room temperature

2 large eggs (3.5 oz / 100g), at room temperature

2 teaspoons vanilla extract

½ cup buttermilk (4.2 oz / 120g), at room temperature

ICING

3½ cups confectioners' sugar (13.6 oz / 385g), sifted if lumpy, plus more as needed

2 tablespoons light corn syrup

2 tablespoons fresh lemon juice

1 teaspoon vanilla extract

Pinch of kosher salt

2 tablespoons boiling water

⅓ cup blueberry jam (3.8 oz / 107g)

MIX THE DRY INGREDIENTS: In a medium bowl, whisk together the flour, salt, baking powder, and baking soda until combined. Set aside.

CREAM THE BUTTER AND SUGAR: In a large bowl, combine the granulated sugar and lemon zest and massage the mixture with your fingertips until it's fragrant and looks like wet sand. Add the butter and beat with a hand mixer on medium-low speed until combined, then increase the speed to medium-high and continue to beat, pausing occasionally to scrape down the sides of the bowl with a flexible spatula, until the mixture is pale and fluffy, about 4 minutes (see Creaming Butter and Sugar, page 351).

MAKE THE DOUGH: Add the eggs one at a time and beat on medium speed until each is thoroughly incorporated. Scrape down the sides of the bowl, then beat in the vanilla. Add about half of the dry ingredients and mix on low speed until the flour has almost disappeared. Stream in the buttermilk, mixing just until incorporated, then add the remaining dry ingredients and mix just until the last trace of flour disappears. Use a flexible spatula to scrape down the sides of the bowl and fold the dough several times to make sure it's evenly mixed. It should be thick but spreadable.

PREHEAT THE OVEN AND PREPARE THE SHEET PAN: Arrange an oven rack in the center position and preheat the oven to 350°F. Line a large sheet pan with parchment paper and set aside.

PORTION AND CHILL THE DOUGH: Use a 2-ounce scoop or a ¼-cup measure to scoop level portions of dough and place them one at a time on a dinner plate or platter (they don't need to be any shape in particular, just equal in size). You should get about 16 pieces. Cover the plate and refrigerate until the pieces are firm, 20 to 25 minutes.

ROLL THE DOUGH: Transfer 6 pieces of chilled dough to the work surface, keeping the remaining pieces covered and refrigerated. Using floured hands, roll the 6 pieces one at a time between your palms into smooth spheres, using more flour as needed to prevent sticking, and transfer to the prepared sheet pan, spacing them evenly (make sure they're several inches apart; they will spread quite a bit). Flatten the spheres slightly with your palm so they're about ¾ inch thick.

BAKE: Bake the cookies until they're golden around the edges and pale, matte, and springy to the touch in the centers, 12 to 15 minutes, rotating the pan front to back after 8 minutes. Let the cookies cool completely on the pan, then carefully peel them away from the parchment and transfer them

Can I . . .

Make them ahead? Yes. The cookies, stored in an airtight container at room temperature, will keep for up to 3 days but they're best eaten the day they're made (the cookie base stales quickly). If stacking the cookies, separate layers between sheets of parchment or wax paper.

Use a stand mixer instead of a hand mixer? Yes. Use your fingertips to massage the sugar and lemon zest in a stand mixer fitted with the paddle attachment, then add the butter and proceed with the recipe as written.

Make a chocolate version? Yes. Make the icing as written, omitting the lemon juice and instead adding 2 tablespoons milk for a plain vanilla icing. Ice half of each cookie as written, then omit the blueberry jam and instead whisk 2 tablespoons unsweetened cocoa powder into the remaining vanilla icing, thinning it as needed with tap water. It's up to you if you'd like to omit the lemon zest from the cookie dough (it's classic, but the combination of chocolate and citrus isn't my favorite).

to a wire rack. Roll and bake the remaining pieces of dough in two more batches of 5 cookies each just as you did for the first batch, using the same sheet tray and transferring the cooled cookies to the wire rack.

MAKE THE LEMON ICING: In a medium bowl, combine the confectioners' sugar, corn syrup, lemon juice, vanilla, and salt. Add the boiling water to the bowl and whisk, starting in the center and gradually working your way outward, until the ingredients are combined, then whisk vigorously until you have a smooth icing. It should be thick but also fluid enough that it settles into a flat layer in the bowl. If it seems too thick, whisk in tap water ½ teaspoon at a time until you have the right consistency.

ICE HALF OF EACH COOKIE: Use a small offset spatula to cover half of each cookie in the lemon icing, spreading it across the flat bottom (not the domed side) and working it all the way to the edges. You want a generous layer, but don't apply it too thickly or the icing may run off the side of the cookie (you'll only use a portion of the total icing; whatever remains will be made into the blueberry icing). As you finish icing each cookie, place it back on the wire rack icing-side up. When you're done, set them aside while you make the blueberry icing.

MAKE THE BLUEBERRY ICING AND FINISH THE COOKIES: In a small saucepan, warm the blueberry jam over low heat, whisking frequently, just until it's fluid. (Alternatively, microwave the jam in a small bowl in 15-second bursts.) Pass it through a mesh sieve and into the bowl with the remaining lemon icing, pressing on the solids with the back of a spoon (scrape any jam solids back into the jar). Whisk the icing until it's completely smooth, then whisk in more confectioners' sugar by the tablespoon until you achieve the same consistency as the lemon icing. Use the small offset spatula again to ice the other half of the cookies with the blueberry icing. Let the cookies sit uncovered until the icing is completely set.

Prune & Almond Rugelach

When I lived in France during culinary school, I discovered the delicacy of *pruneaux d'agen fourrés,* or "stuffed prunes from Agen" (my thanks to David Lebovitz for writing about them on his blog, which is how I first learned about them). They're made by carefully removing the prunes' soft innards and mixing them with a flavoring like Armagnac, orange, or (my favorite) almond, then stuffing this mixture back inside the skins in a way that makes them look like polished jewels. My love of all prunes, and especially the almond pruneaux d'agen fourrés, inspired these rugelach. Rugelach are a filled and rolled cookie in the Jewish baking tradition, typically made with a cream cheese pastry and nut or jam filling. This version, with a prune and port filling and almond pastry, is atypical, but tasters declared them the best rugelach they've ever had.

MAKES 32 RUGELACH

DIFFICULTY: 3 (Moderate)

ACTIVE TIME: 1 hour 30 minutes

TOTAL TIME: 4 hours 30 minutes

SPECIAL EQUIPMENT: Food processor, bench scraper, wheel cutter

PRUNE FILLING

10 ounces (283g) pitted prunes (about 2 cups), coarsely chopped

6 tablespoons port or red wine (3.2 oz / 90g)

4 tablespoons unsalted butter (2 oz / 57g), cut into ½-inch pieces

¼ cup granulated sugar (1.8 oz / 50g)

Pinch of kosher salt

DOUGH AND ASSEMBLY

7 ounces (198g) almond paste

2 cups all-purpose flour (9.5 oz / 270g), plus more for rolling

¼ cup granulated sugar (1.8 oz / 50g)

½ teaspoon Diamond Crystal kosher salt or ¼ teaspoon Morton kosher salt

4 ounces (113g) cream cheese, cut into ½-inch pieces, chilled

1 stick unsalted butter (4 oz / 113g), cut into ½-inch pieces, chilled

1 teaspoon vanilla extract

1 large egg (1.8 oz / 50g), beaten

Demerara sugar, for sprinkling

COOK THE PRUNE FILLING: In a large saucepan, combine the prunes, port, butter, granulated sugar, and salt and add just enough water to barely cover the prunes. Bring the mixture to a boil over medium-high heat, stirring once or twice to dissolve the sugar. Reduce the heat to a maintain lively simmer and cook, mashing the prunes occasionally with a potato masher or the back of a spoon, until they're broken down into a coarse puree, about 4 minutes. Continue to cook the mixture, stirring frequently with a heatproof flexible spatula, until it's very thick and jammy and all the liquid has boiled off, 20 to 25 minutes (when you drag the spatula through the mixture, you should be able to see the bottom of the saucepan for a few moments). You should have about 2 cups of filling (18 oz / 510g); if you have much more than 2 cups, return it to the saucepan and continue to cook. Remove the saucepan from the heat and set aside until the filling is warm but not hot, then transfer it to a lidded container and refrigerate until cold, at least 1 hour.

MAKE THE DOUGH: Crumble the almond paste into a food processor, then add the flour, granulated sugar, and salt. Pulse the mixture until the almond paste has been broken down into small, pebbly bits about the size of a lentil, about ten 1-second pulses. Add the cream cheese and butter and pulse until those pieces are no larger than a pea, about five pulses. In a small bowl, combine the vanilla and 2 tablespoons cold water, then uncover the food processor and drizzle the water and vanilla mixture around the bowl. Replace the lid and pulse until a smooth ball of dough is gathered around the blade, about twelve pulses.

CHILL THE DOUGH: Turn the dough out onto the work surface and divide in half. Place each half on a separate piece of reusable food wrap or plastic wrap and flatten them with the heel of your hand into ¾-inch-thick disks. Wrap the disks tightly and refrigerate until they're firm, at least 2 hours.

PREHEAT THE OVEN AND PREPARE THE SHEET PAN: Arrange an oven rack in the upper third of the oven and preheat the oven to 350°F. Line a large sheet pan with a silicone baking mat or parchment paper and set aside.

ROLL OUT THE DOUGH: Remove the filling and one disk of dough from the refrigerator. Unwrap the dough and place it on a lightly floured surface, then dust the top of the dough with more flour and roll it out to a 12-inch round, periodically lifting the dough with a bench scraper and dusting

→

underneath and on top with more flour as needed to prevent sticking. Brush any excess flour off the surface of the dough, then use a wheel cutter to cut around the dough and trim away just the ragged edge to make a clean round.

FILL AND CUT INTO WEDGES: Scrape 1 cup (9 oz / 255g) of the prune filling into the center of the round and use a small offset spatula to spread it nearly to the edges in an even layer, leaving a clean ½-inch border all the way around. Use the wheel cutter to cut the dough into 4 equal wedges. Cut each wedge in half to make 8, then cut each in half again to form 16 thin, equal wedges.

ROLL THE RUGELACH: Use the bench scraper to help you lift and separate the 16 wedges so they have a little bit of breathing room on the work surface. Working with one of the wedges, start at the end opposite the point and roll it up to form a small croissant-shaped cookie. Place the rugelach on the prepared sheet pan so it's resting on the point, then repeat the rolling process with the remaining wedges, spacing the rugelach evenly on the sheet pan. Try to work quickly, as the warmer the dough gets the more delicate it becomes.

BRUSH WITH EGG AND SPRINKLE WITH DEMERARA SUGAR: Brush a thin layer of the beaten egg over the surfaces of the rugelach, then sprinkle generously with demerara sugar. Reserve the remaining egg for the second batch.

BAKE: Transfer the sheet pan to the upper rack and bake until the rugelach are golden brown and the filling along the edges is dark and glossy, 20 to 25 minutes, rotating the pan front to back after 15 minutes. Allow the rugelach to cool on the sheet pan for 5 minutes, then transfer them one at a time to a wire rack to cool completely.

REPEAT WITH THE REMAINING DOUGH AND FILLING: Roll out the remaining disk of dough just as you did the first and cover with 1 cup (9 oz / 255g) of the prune filling (if you have any leftover filling, save it for another use). Repeat the cutting and rolling process, placing the rugelach on the same sheet pan, brushing with the remaining beaten egg, and sprinkling with more demerara sugar. Bake and cool just as you did for the first batch.

Can I . . .

Make them ahead? Yes. The rugelach, stored in an airtight container at room temperature, will keep for up to 3 days, but they're best eaten on the first or second day while the pastry is still crisp (it will soften over time). The dough can be refrigerated for up to 2 days or frozen for up to 2 months. Let the frozen disks thaw in the refrigerator overnight before rolling and assembling the rugelach. The prune filling, covered and refrigerated, will keep for up to 2 weeks.

Halve the recipe? Yes. Halve all of the ingredient quantities for both the prune filling and the dough and follow the recipe as written, but cook the prune filling in a small saucepan and form the dough into a single disk.

Make them gluten-free? No. The high proportion of almond paste in the dough makes it delicate and prone to tearing, so the gluten from all-purpose flour provides necessary structure. Using gluten-free flour would make the dough too delicate to roll out.

Use a different filling? Yes. Skip the prune filling and spread a thin layer of jam (I recommend raspberry or apricot, but any flavor works) over each round of dough and proceed with the recipe as written.

Pies, Tarts, Cobblers & Crisps

If I had to choose one dessert that embodies my love of baking, it would be a classic fruit pie. Few activities bring me greater joy than sealing fresh, in-season fruit between two layers of buttery pastry and baking the pie until the filling is thick and bubbling and the crust is deep golden brown and crisp. To me, it's a labor of love—but a labor nonetheless. First, there are the intricacies of making a tender, flaky pastry dough, then there's prepping the fruit for the filling, then there's all the rolling, cutting, pressing, tucking, crimping, chilling, and brushing required for assembly. Understandably, not all home bakers feel inclined to invest this kind of time and energy.

In this chapter, I pay special attention to fruit- and pastry-based desserts that are pie-adjacent, like cobblers, crisps, and galettes. Many are time-conscious and beginner-friendly, like **Cherry & Brown Butter Buckwheat Crisp** (page 229) and **Easy Apple Galette** (page 237). There are a few different press-in crusts for tarts like **Banana-Sesame Cream Tart** (page 245) and **Roasted Lemon Tart** (page 253), so there's no worrying about rolling out pastry and keeping it cold. Even when pastry is required, I try to streamline and simplify the assembly process and let the oven do the work of coaxing flavor from butter, flour, fruits, and nuts. The recipes still vary in terms of difficulty, and of course there are centerpiece-worthy pies like **Cinnamon-&-Sugar Apple Pie** (page 267) and **Walnut & Oat Slab Pie** (page 273) that inevitably require several steps. But for every pie with a crimped edge or a parbaked crust, just know that there are three or four dead-simple recipes to add a bit of ease to your baking repertoire.

Cherry & Brown Butter Buckwheat Crisp

I am drawn to buckwheat in baking, possibly because of my Ashkenazi heritage. Buckwheat is a common ingredient in Eastern European cuisine, and my grandmother often made kasha varnishkes, a dish of toasted buckwheat groats and bow tie pasta (which only my dad liked). Buckwheat's earthy, mineral flavor shines in this easy crisp that is filled with bright, juicy cherries and studded with crispy buckwheat groats toasted in browned butter. Because buckwheat flour is naturally gluten-free and doesn't absorb moisture the way wheat flour does, I add an egg white to bind the topping and ensure that it bakes up crunchy. Make this when you have a glut of sweet cherries in the summertime, or use frozen pitted cherries and make it whenever you want.

SERVES 8

DIFFICULTY: 1 (Very Easy)

ACTIVE TIME: 30 minutes

TOTAL TIME: 1 hour 40 minutes, plus time to cool

SPECIAL EQUIPMENT: 2-quart shallow baking dish (preferably ceramic)

6 tablespoons unsalted butter (3 oz / 85g)

¼ cup raw buckwheat groats (1.6 oz / 45g), not kasha

2½ pounds (1.1 kg) pitted fresh or frozen sweet cherries (about 7½ cups), no need to thaw if frozen

½ cup granulated sugar (3.5 oz / 100g)

3 tablespoons cornstarch

2 teaspoons finely grated lemon zest

2 tablespoons fresh lemon juice

1 teaspoon vanilla extract

A pinch plus ½ teaspoon Diamond Crystal kosher salt or ¼ teaspoon Morton kosher salt

1 large egg white (1.2 oz / 35g)

1 cup all-purpose flour (4.8 oz / 135g)

¼ cup buckwheat flour (1.1 oz / 30g)

6 tablespoons packed dark brown sugar (2.9 oz / 83g)

½ teaspoon ground cinnamon

Can I . . .

Make it ahead? Yes. The cooled crisp, covered loosely and stored at room temperature in the baking dish, will keep for up to 3 days, but it's best served on the first or second day while the topping is crisp (it will soften as it sits). To rewarm the crisp, bake it uncovered on a sheet pan in a 325°F oven until the filling is warm in the center, 25 to 30 minutes.

Make it gluten-free? Yes. Substitute 1 cup of your favorite gluten-free flour blend for the all-purpose flour.

PREHEAT THE OVEN: Arrange an oven rack in the center position and preheat the oven to 350°F.

TOAST THE BUCKWHEAT GROATS: In a small saucepan, melt the butter over medium heat. When the butter starts to foam, add the buckwheat groats and cook, stirring frequently with a heatproof flexible spatula, until the groats are toasty smelling and the foaming butter has taken on a golden brown hue, about 5 minutes. Remove the saucepan from the heat and scrape the butter and groats into a medium bowl. Set the bowl aside and stir occasionally until the mixture is warm but not hot, 15 to 20 minutes.

MEANWHILE, MAKE THE FILLING: In a large bowl, combine the cherries, granulated sugar, cornstarch, lemon zest, lemon juice, vanilla, and a pinch of salt. Use a large flexible spatula to gently fold the mixture until all the cherries are coated evenly, then scrape the filling into a 2-quart shallow baking dish, preferably ceramic, and scatter the cherries in an even layer. Set the baking dish aside.

MAKE THE TOPPING: Whisk the egg white into the bowl with the butter and groats until the mixture is smooth, then add the all-purpose flour, buckwheat flour, brown sugar, cinnamon, and ½ teaspoon salt. Stir the mixture with the flexible spatula to incorporate the dry ingredients, scraping the bottom and sides of the bowl. Switch to your fingertips and rub the mixture until no floury spots remain and the mixture is crumbly.

ASSEMBLE AND BAKE: Sprinkle the topping evenly over the cherries (it will seem like a lot of topping, but use it all). Place the baking dish on a sheet pan to catch any drips and bake until the topping is deeply browned and the cherry juices are bubbling around the sides, 1 hour to 1 hour 10 minutes for fresh cherries, or 1 hour 10 minutes to 1 hour 20 minutes for frozen. If the topping looks like it's getting a little dark in places before you see bubbling juices, place a small piece of foil loosely over the surface of the crisp to prevent burning and continue to bake. Let the crisp cool completely before serving.

Pastry Bianco
with Slow-Roasted Plums

Any time I'm walking near a location of renowned baker Jim Lahey's Sullivan Street Bakery in New York, I stop in to admire the rustic breads and pick out one to take home, plus a slice of pizza bianca. Pizza bianca is an unadorned Roman flatbread, flavored just with olive oil and salt. The last time I ate a piece, I had an idea to create a sweet analog. My pastry bianco is a slab of buttery pastry topped with a little sugar and baked until it's golden, flaky, and caramelized. Here I finish it with slow-roasted plums layered over whipped crème fraîche, but feel free to swap in a different stone fruit or use the pastry bianco as the base for any kind of tart you can dream up.

SERVES 8

DIFFICULTY: 1 (Very Easy)

ACTIVE TIME: 30 minutes (does not include making the pastry)

TOTAL TIME: 2 hours 45 minutes

SPECIAL EQUIPMENT: 13 × 9-inch baking pan

1½ pounds (680g) firm but ripe Italian or other small plums, halved and pitted, some quartered

6 tablespoons demerara sugar (2.7 oz / 76g), divided

1 rectangular portion **All-Purpose Flaky Pastry Dough** (page 331), chilled

All-purpose flour, for rolling

1 large egg (1.8 oz / 50g), beaten

½ cup crème fraîche (4.2 oz / 120g), chilled

½ cup heavy cream (4.2 oz / 120g), chilled

2 tablespoons confectioners' sugar

Can I . . .

Make it ahead? Yes, but . . . Wait to assemble the components until just before serving. The plums can be slow-roasted up to 8 hours ahead. Let them cool completely in the pan, then keep covered at room temperature. The pastry bianco can be baked up to 8 hours ahead. Let it cool completely on the sheet pan, then cover loosely and store at room temperature. The whipped crème fraîche can be prepared up to 2 hours ahead; keep it covered and refrigerated.

Top it with another fruit? Yes. In place of the plums, you can slow-roast an equal weight of apricots or small peaches or nectarines, also halved and pitted, some quartered. Or, top the pastry bianco with macerated strawberries or blackberries (see Macerating Fruit, page 355), or the poached rhubarb and raspberry mixture from **Rhubarb & Raspberry Shortcakes with Poppy Seeds** (page 251).

PREHEAT THE OVEN: Arrange an oven rack in the center position and preheat the oven to 250°F.

SLOW-ROAST THE PLUMS: Toss the plum halves with 4 tablespoons (1.8 oz / 50g) of the demerara sugar in a 13 × 9-inch baking pan, then arrange the halves cut-sides down in a single layer (you can overlap them a bit if needed). Cover the baking dish tightly with foil and roast until the plums have released their juices and the flesh is soft but not mushy, 1 to 1½ hours. Uncover the baking pan and set it aside to cool.

PREHEAT THE OVEN AGAIN AND PREPARE THE SHEET PAN: Increase the oven temperature to 400°F. Line a sheet pan with a silicone baking mat or parchment paper and set aside.

ROLL OUT THE DOUGH: Let the dough sit at room temperature for a minute or two to soften slightly, then unwrap it and place on a lightly floured surface. Use a rolling pin to beat the dough across the surface to make it more pliable. Dust underneath and on top of the dough with more flour, then roll it out, dusting with more flour as needed to prevent sticking, into a rectangle measuring about 13 × 9 inches (a little wider or longer is fine; for step-by-step visuals, see Rolling Out Chilled Pastry Dough, page 332). Transfer the slab of dough to the prepared sheet pan, then transfer the pan to the refrigerator and chill until the dough is very firm, 10 to 15 minutes.

BAKE THE PASTRY: Brush the entire surface of the pastry with a thin layer of the beaten egg and then sprinkle with the remaining 2 tablespoons demerara sugar. Prick the surface all over with the tines of a fork, then bake the pastry until the surface is puffed and deep golden brown, 15 to 20 minutes, rotating the sheet pan front to back after 12 minutes. Set the pan aside to cool completely.

WHIP THE CRÈME FRAÎCHE: In a large bowl, with a whisk or hand mixer, whip the crème fraîche, heavy cream, and confectioners' sugar on low speed to start and gradually increase the speed to medium-high as the mixture thickens, until you have medium peaks (see Whipping Cream, page 355).

ASSEMBLE: Using a serrated knife, cut the pastry in half lengthwise, then cut crosswise into quarters to make 8 equal pieces. Dollop the whipped crème fraîche onto each piece of pastry, dividing evenly. Arrange the plum halves over the cream cut-sides up and drizzle any juices that accumulated in the baking pan on top. Serve immediately.

Berry Crisp

with Seedy Granola Topping

As a rule, I never make health claims about recipes. However, I think it's safe to say that this crisp, packed with berries and seeds, probably has a better nutrition profile than most desserts (not necessarily a selling point, just saying). Although I tend not to favor sweet breakfasts, I'd feel great eating this moderately sweet crisp with a little plain yogurt in the morning. At the same time, it doesn't feel excessively wholesome as a dessert, especially if served with vanilla ice cream. The topping is inspired by my mom's granola recipe, which will always be my favorite granola, and the filling combines raspberries, blackberries, and blueberries for a variety of textures. Don't let the lengthy ingredient list put you off—this is quick and easy.

SERVES 8

DIFFICULTY: 1 (Very Easy)

ACTIVE TIME: 20 minutes

TOTAL TIME: 1 hour 20 minutes, plus time to cool

SPECIAL EQUIPMENT: 2-quart shallow baking dish (preferably ceramic)

FILLING

12 ounces (340g) fresh or frozen blueberries (about 3 cups), no need to thaw if frozen

12 ounces (340g) fresh or frozen blackberries (about 2 cups), no need to thaw if frozen

8 ounces (227g) fresh or frozen raspberries (about 1¾ cups), no need to thaw if frozen

6 tablespoons granulated sugar (2.6 oz / 75g)

2 tablespoons cornstarch

1 tablespoon fresh lemon juice

1 teaspoon vanilla extract

½ teaspoon Diamond Crystal kosher salt or ¼ teaspoon Morton kosher salt

SEEDY GRANOLA TOPPING

⅔ cup old-fashioned rolled oats (1.9 oz / 53g)

½ cup all-purpose flour (2.4 oz / 67g)

⅓ cup whole wheat flour (1.7 oz / 47g)

½ cup packed light brown sugar (3.9 oz / 110g)

2 tablespoons wheat germ

½ teaspoon ground cinnamon

½ teaspoon Diamond Crystal kosher salt or ¼ teaspoon Morton kosher salt

1 stick unsalted butter (4 oz / 113g), melted and cooled

¼ cup pumpkin seeds (1.3 oz / 36g)

¼ cup sunflower seeds (1.3 oz / 36g)

2 tablespoons sesame seeds

1 tablespoon flaxseeds

1 tablespoon chia seeds

PREHEAT THE OVEN: Arrange an oven rack in the center position and preheat the oven to 350°F.

MAKE THE FILLING: In a large bowl, combine the blueberries, blackberries, raspberries, granulated sugar, cornstarch, lemon juice, vanilla, and salt. Use a large flexible spatula to gently fold the mixture until the berries are evenly coated, then scrape the filling into a 2-quart shallow baking dish, preferably ceramic, and arrange in an even layer. Set the baking dish aside.

MAKE THE SEEDY GRANOLA TOPPING: In a medium bowl, whisk together the oats, all-purpose flour, whole wheat flour, brown sugar, wheat germ, cinnamon, and salt. Drizzle the butter into the bowl, then use a fork to toss the mixture until the butter is incorporated and the mixture is clumpy (there will be some dry spots). Switch to your fingertips and rub the mixture to further work in the butter until no dry spots remain. Add the pumpkin seeds, sunflower seeds, sesame seeds, flaxseeds, and chia seeds and toss with your hands to distribute.

ASSEMBLE AND BAKE: Sprinkle the topping evenly over the fruit (it will seem like a lot of topping, but use it all). Place the baking dish on a sheet pan to catch any drips and bake until the topping is deep golden brown and the juices are bubbling around the sides, 50 to 60 minutes for fresh berries, or 1 hour to 1 hour 10 minutes for frozen. If some of the seeds on the surface look like they're getting a little dark before you see bubbling juices, place a small piece of foil loosely over the surface to prevent burning and continue to bake. Let the crisp cool and serve warm or at room temperature.

Can I . . .

Make it ahead? Yes. The cooled crisp, covered loosely and stored at room temperature in the baking dish, will keep for up to 3 days, but it's best served on the first or second day while the topping is crisp (it will soften as it sits). To rewarm the crisp, bake it uncovered on a sheet pan in a 325°F oven until the filling is warm in the center, 25 to 30 minutes.

Make it gluten-free? Yes. Substitute 1 cup of your favorite gluten-free flour blend for both the all-purpose and whole wheat flours and omit the wheat germ.

Use a single berry in the filling? Yes. Substitute 2 pounds (907g) blueberries or blackberries in place of the mixed fruit in the recipe.

Omit some of the seeds or use a different variety? Yes. You could make the topping exclusively with pumpkin, sunflower, or sesame seeds, adding a quantity to taste. You could also add a tablespoon of poppy seeds or hemp hearts, or substitute them for the flaxseeds or chia seeds.

Easy Apple Galette

I have a hard time resisting the (flawed) logic that "if some is good, more is better," so it's a mark of my growth as a recipe developer that I can recognize when a recipe is just right and stop myself from adding unnecessary ingredients or steps. Editing oneself is hard, but this dead-simple free-form apple tart is direct evidence of how important it is. Comprising no more than a layer of pastry, a layer of bread crumbs (to absorb some of the appley juices), thinly sliced apples, and cream and sugar, it's incredible.

SERVES 8

DIFFICULTY: 1 (Very Easy)

ACTIVE TIME: 35 minutes (does not include making the pastry)

TOTAL TIME: 1 hour 50 minutes, plus time to cool

⅓ cup demerara sugar (2.3 oz / 66g)

Seeds scraped from ½ vanilla bean or 2 teaspoons vanilla extract

Pinch of kosher salt

1 round portion **All-Purpose Flaky Pastry Dough** (page 331), chilled

All-purpose flour, for rolling

2 tablespoons fine dried bread crumbs or panko

1½ pounds (680g) firm sweet-tart apples, such as Pink Lady (3 or 4 medium), peeled, cored, and thinly sliced

½ cup heavy cream (4.2 oz / 120g)

½ cup apricot jam (5.6 oz / 160g)

Can I . . .

Make it ahead? Yes. The baked galette, covered loosely and stored at room temperature, will keep for up to 3 days but is best served on the first or second day while the pastry is still crisp.

Use store-bought puff pastry? Yes, but . . . your galette will be rectangular rather than round. Two common brands of frozen store-bought puff pastry are Dufour, which comes in a 14-ounce (397g) box and contains one large sheet, and Pepperidge Farm, which comes in a 17.3-ounce (490g) box and contains two smaller sheets (I recommend Dufour or any brand labeled "all butter"). For either brand, thaw one box overnight in the refrigerator, then unfold the sheet(s) and roll out on a lightly floured surface (if using Pepperidge Farm, stack the two sheets one on top of the other and roll out as a single piece) into a rectangle measuring about 12 × 9 inches. Proceed with the recipe as written, folding in the border along all four sides and thoroughly pricking the surface with the tines of a fork. Keep in mind that the pastry will puff dramatically as it bakes, causing the border to unfold a bit.

PREHEAT THE OVEN AND PREPARE THE SHEET PAN: Arrange an oven rack in the center position and preheat the oven to 350°F. Line a sheet pan with a silicone baking mat or parchment paper and set aside.

MAKE THE VANILLA SUGAR: In a small bowl, combine the demerara sugar, vanilla seeds, and a pinch of salt and massage the mixture with your fingertips until it's fragrant and the vanilla seeds are evenly distributed (if using vanilla extract, skip to the next step). Set the vanilla sugar aside.

ROLL OUT THE DOUGH: Let the dough sit at room temperature for a minute or two to soften slightly, then unwrap it and place on a lightly floured surface. Use a rolling pin to beat the dough all across the surface to make it more pliable. Dust more flour on top and underneath the dough, then roll it out, dusting with more flour as needed to prevent sticking, into a 13-inch round (for step-by-step visuals, see Rolling Out Chilled Pastry Dough, page 332). Use a paring knife or wheel cutter to cut around the dough and trim away the ragged edge to make a clean 12-inch round.

ASSEMBLE: Transfer the dough round to the prepared sheet pan, then fold a ½-inch-wide border of dough inward toward the center to form a raised edge all the way around, pressing firmly so it stays in place. Prick the surface of the dough in several places with the tines of a fork, then spread the bread crumbs in an even layer inside the border. Arrange the apple slices on top, tightly overlapping them in any pattern you like. If using vanilla extract, combine it with the cream in a small bowl. Use a pastry brush to brush a thin layer of cream over the border, then drizzle the remaining cream evenly over the apples. Sprinkle the vanilla sugar (or, if using vanilla extract, just the demerara sugar and salt) across the surface of the galette, covering both the apples and the border. Transfer the pan to the refrigerator and chill until the dough is firm, 10 to 15 minutes.

BAKE AND GLAZE THE GALETTE: Bake the galette until the border is deep golden brown and the edges of the apples are golden, 1 hour to 1 hour 10 minutes. Remove the pan from the oven and set aside to cool. In a small saucepan, warm the jam over low heat, stirring occasionally with a heatproof flexible spatula, until it's fluid. Press the jam through a fine-mesh sieve, catching the liquid in a small bowl (you can scrape the strained solids back into the jam jar, if you wish). While the galette is still warm, brush the strained jam over the apples. Serve the galette warm or at room temperature.

Apricot & Strawberry Galette

Whenever I ask myself what I should bake with the fruit I pick up at my local farmers' market, a galette is usually the answer. It's a kind of free-form, open-faced tart, and a great vehicle for peak-season produce. For especially juicy fruit, I place a layer of bread crumbs mixed with cornstarch between the pastry and the fruit to soak up and thicken any juices, ensuring that the bottom of the galette bakes up crispy and golden. Fresh apricots are one of my favorite fruits to bake with because, interestingly, they intensify in tartness in the oven, and here I pair them with sweet strawberries. A dousing of vanilla syrup over the filling before and after baking enhances its floral fruitiness.

SERVES 8

DIFFICULTY: 1 (Very Easy)

ACTIVE TIME: 40 minutes (does not include making the pastry)

TOTAL TIME: 1 hour 50 minutes, plus time to cool

Seeds scraped from ½ vanilla bean (pod reserved)

4 strips lemon zest, removed with a vegetable peeler

Pinch of kosher salt

½ cup plus 2 tablespoons demerara sugar (4.4 oz / 125g), plus more for sprinkling

2 tablespoons fine dried bread crumbs

2 teaspoons cornstarch

1 rectangular portion **All-Purpose Flaky Pastry Dough** (page 331), chilled

All-purpose flour, for rolling

1 pound (454g) small apricots, halved and pitted (about 12)

8 ounces (227g) strawberries, hulled, halved if small, thinly sliced lengthwise if large

1 large egg (1.8 oz / 50g), beaten

Can I . . .

Make it ahead? Yes. The baked galette, covered loosely and stored at room temperature, will keep for up to 3 days but is best served on the first or second day while the pastry is still crisp.

Use different fruit? Yes. Substitute an equal weight of any stone fruit such as plums or peaches for the apricots (slice them into ½-inch wedges if large), and an equal weight of any berry, such as blackberries or raspberries, for the strawberries.

MAKE THE VANILLA SYRUP: In a small saucepan, combine the vanilla seeds and pod, zest, salt, ½ cup (3.5 oz / 100g) of the demerara sugar, and ¼ cup (2 oz / 57g) water. Bring the mixture to a simmer over medium-low heat and cook, whisking occasionally to dissolve the sugar, until the syrup is reduced and slightly thickened, about 5 minutes. Set the saucepan aside.

MAKE THE BREAD CRUMB MIXTURE: In a small bowl, toss together the bread crumbs, cornstarch, and remaining 2 tablespoons demerara sugar. Set aside.

PREHEAT THE OVEN AND PREPARE THE SHEET PAN: Arrange an oven rack in the center position and preheat the oven to 425°F. Line a large sheet pan with a silicone baking mat or parchment paper and set aside.

ROLL OUT THE DOUGH: Let the dough sit at room temperature for a minute or two to soften slightly, then unwrap it and place on a lightly floured surface. Use a rolling pin to beat the dough all across the surface to make it more pliable. Dust more flour underneath and on top of the dough, then roll it out, dusting with more flour as needed to prevent sticking, into a rectangle measuring about 13 × 9 inches (a little wider or longer is fine; for step-by-step visuals, see Rolling Out Chilled Pastry Dough, page 332).

ASSEMBLE: Transfer the slab of dough to the prepared sheet pan and prick the surface in several places with the tines of a fork. Sprinkle the bread crumb mixture across the dough and spread it in an even layer, leaving a 1½-inch border all the way around. Arrange the fruit on top of the bread crumb layer, tucking the strawberries in and around the larger pieces of apricot to fill any gaps and leaving the border uncovered. Using the parchment paper to help you, fold the 1½-inch border of dough up and over the filling along all four sides, leaving the center open and pressing on the folds at each of the four corners to help the dough adhere to itself.

BRUSH WITH THE EGG AND VANILLA SYRUP: Brush the border with the beaten egg, then sprinkle it generously with more demerara sugar. Clean the pastry brush well and use it to dab about half of the vanilla syrup over the fruit (leave the vanilla pod and zest in the saucepan). Reserve the remaining syrup for brushing over the baked galette. Transfer the sheet pan to the refrigerator and chill until the dough is firm, 15 to 20 minutes.

BAKE: Bake the galette for 15 minutes, then reduce the oven temperature to 350°F and continue to bake until the pastry is puffed and deep golden brown and the apricots are browned along the edges, another 30 to 35 minutes. Remove the galette from the oven and let it cool slightly, then brush the remaining vanilla syrup over the fruit (discard the vanilla pod and zest). Let the galette cool to room temperature before slicing and serving.

Can I . . .

Use store-bought puff pastry?
Yes. Two common brands of frozen store-bought puff pastry are Dufour, which comes in a 14-ounce (397g) box and contains one large sheet, and Pepperidge Farm, which comes in a 17.3-ounce (493g) box and contains two smaller sheets (I recommend Dufour or any brand labeled "all butter"). For either brand, thaw one box overnight in the refrigerator, then unfold the sheet(s) and roll out on a lightly floured surface (if using Pepperidge Farm, stack the two sheets one on top of the other and roll out as a single piece) to the given dimensions. Proceed with the recipe as written, thoroughly pricking the surface with the tines of a fork. Keep in mind that the pastry will puff dramatically as it bakes, causing the border to unfold a bit.

Honeyed Nut & Phyllo Pie

Frozen phyllo dough is a remarkable product: It's easy to use, works well in both sweet and savory dishes, always produces an ultraflaky result, and, unlike frozen puff pastry, does not need to be chilled before baking. The deliciousness of this pie, a large-format take on baklava, comes as much from the phyllo itself, which is layered with butter and sugar so it caramelizes in the oven, as from the honeyed nut filling. The styling of the tart, which borrows from pastis gascon, a kind of apple pie from the Gascony region of France that features wild folds of phyllo dough draped and gathered on top, looks hard to execute, but I assure you it's easy.

SERVES 8

DIFFICULTY: 2 (Easy)

ACTIVE TIME: 50 minutes

TOTAL TIME: 2 hours, plus time to cool

4 cups raw walnuts, pistachios, pecans, sliced almonds, and/or pine nuts (1 lb / 454g)

¾ teaspoon ground cardamom

½ teaspoon Diamond Crystal kosher salt or ¼ teaspoon Morton kosher salt

⅓ cup plus 2 tablespoons honey (5.5 oz / 155g)

16 tablespoons unsalted butter (8 oz / 226g), melted, divided

2 tablespoons fresh lemon juice, divided

12 sheets frozen phyllo dough measuring 18 × 13 inches (10.7 oz / 303g), thawed overnight in the refrigerator

¾ cup demerara sugar (5.3 oz / 150g), divided

½ teaspoon orange blossom water

PREHEAT THE OVEN: Arrange an oven rack in the center position and preheat the oven to 350°F.

TOAST THE NUTS: Scatter the nuts on a sheet pan and toast until they're golden brown and fragrant, 8 to 10 minutes, tossing halfway through. Let the nuts cool completely on the pan. Leave the oven on.

MAKE THE FILLING: Transfer the cooled nuts to a resealable bag, press out the air, and seal. Use a rolling pin, mallet, or heavy-bottomed saucepan to bash the nuts, breaking them into pieces of all different sizes, until the largest pieces are about the size of a pea. Transfer the nuts to a medium bowl. Add the cardamom, salt, ⅓ cup (4 oz / 113g) of the honey, 4 tablespoons (2 oz / 57g) of the melted butter, and 1 tablespoon of the lemon juice. Toss with a flexible spatula until the nuts are evenly coated. Set the filling aside.

BUTTER AND SUGAR THE PHYLLO: Line a large sheet pan with a silicone baking mat or parchment paper, then place the remaining 12 tablespoons (6 oz / 170g) melted butter in a small bowl alongside it. Place a single sheet of phyllo on the prepared sheet pan, orienting it lengthwise, then place the remaining sheets of phyllo on the work surface and cover with a damp towel to prevent them from drying out. Use a pastry brush to brush the sheet of phyllo with a thin layer of the melted butter, working the butter all across the surface of the dough and trying not to tear it (you don't need to cover every square inch). Sprinkle the buttered phyllo with 1 tablespoon of the demerara sugar, then place another sheet on top of the first (be sure to keep the remaining phyllo covered on the work surface while you work).

STACK THE PHYLLO: Brush the second sheet with a thin layer of butter, sprinkle with another tablespoon of demerara sugar, and continue the layering process with more phyllo, butter, and demerara sugar until you've stacked 8 sheets (butter and sugar the top sheet as well). Keep the remaining 4 sheets of phyllo covered (they're for draping over the top of the pie). Reserve any remaining melted butter for drizzling over the assembled pie and reserve any remaining demerara sugar for making the syrup.

ASSEMBLE: Scrape the filling into the center of the stack of phyllo and use the spatula to work it into a rectangle measuring about 12 × 8 inches running lengthwise along the sheet pan. Press gently on top of the filling to flatten it into an even layer, then fold the phyllo up and over the four sides of the filling to form a rectangular bundle with an area of exposed filling in the center. Working one at a time, gather and drape the 4 remaining sheets

→

of phyllo over the surface of the pie, creating three-dimensional folds and wrinkles like handkerchiefs. Drizzle any reserved melted butter over the top.

BAKE: Transfer the pie to the oven and bake until the phyllo is deep golden brown, 50 to 60 minutes, rotating the pan front to back after 30 minutes. Remove the pie from the oven and set aside.

MAKE THE SYRUP AND POUR OVER THE PIE: In a small saucepan, combine the remaining 2 tablespoons honey, remaining demerara sugar (you should have about 4 tablespoons—if you have less, add more to get there), and ⅓ cup (2.7 oz / 76g) water. Bring to a simmer over medium heat, stirring to dissolve the sugar and honey. Reduce the heat and simmer gently, swirling the saucepan occasionally, until the syrup is reduced and slightly thickened, about 5 minutes. Remove the saucepan from the heat and stir in the orange blossom water and remaining 1 tablespoon lemon juice. While the pie is hot, slide the tip of a paring knife down through valleys of phyllo into the filling in a dozen or so places across the surface. Slowly drizzle the hot syrup over the pie, focusing on the valleys and allowing it to be fully absorbed into the filling. Allow the pie to cool completely.

Can I . . .

Make it ahead? Yes. The pie, loosely covered and stored at room temperature, will keep for up to 3 days but is best served on the first or second day while the phyllo is at peak crispiness.

IMPROVE YOUR CRUST IQ

I am partial to using buttery, flaky pastry to make pies and tarts, but it's not always the right choice depending on the volume and style of filling that goes inside the crust. Recognizing the individual characteristics of different crusts will help you understand why, for example, apple pie is almost always made with flaky pastry, while cream pies typically have graham cracker crusts. The differences mostly come down to how the fat is incorporated and the impact this has on the final texture. Below I list the pros and cons of each style of crust so you can better understand how to use them and when you can substitute one for another.

PIE DOUGH
(**All-Purpose Flaky Pastry Dough,** page 331)

Characteristics: Cold butter is worked into the dry ingredients but left in discrete pieces, so when the pastry is rolled out, the butter flattens into sheets and results in flaky layers.

Pros: Buttery flavor and shattering, tender texture with sufficient sturdiness to support the weight of fruit and other heavy fillings.

Cons: Must be kept cold so the butter can properly melt and create steam in the oven (steam = flakiness). Overworking can make the dough tough and prone to shrinking. Parbaking for custard pies requires weighting the dough to prevent slumping and puffing.

Applications: Fruit pies, deep-dish pies, galettes, and denser custard pies

SHORTBREAD CRUST
(as in **Roasted Lemon Tart,** page 253, and **Quince & Pineapple Jam Tart,** page 265)

Characteristics: Cold or room temperature butter is worked completely into dry ingredients, resulting in a uniformly crisp, tender cookie-like texture.

Pros: Can be flavored with spices and extracts. Doesn't require a rolling pin and can be quickly pressed into tart pans. Parbaking or fully baking an unfilled crust doesn't require weights.

Cons: Lack of structure makes it unsuitable for holding fruit and other heavy fillings and can cause the dough to slump down the sides of a pie plate (or any high-sided pan) during parbaking.

Applications: Jam tarts, custard tarts, and no-bake tarts

GRAHAM CRACKER OR COOKIE CRUMB CRUST
(as in **S'mores Tart,** page 257, and **Banana-Sesame Cream Tart,** see opposite)

Characteristics: A mix of melted butter and fine graham cracker or cookie crumbs results in a crumbly, tender crust. Unlike other crusts, this style is almost always baked before it's filled.

Pros: Multiple kinds of store-bought cookies can be used. Easy to assemble. No flour means the mixture cannot be overworked. Minimal slumping and shrinking during baking.

Cons: Can be tricky to press evenly and firmly into a pie plate or tart pan. The crumbly texture means it will fall apart beneath heavier fillings or those consisting of large pieces of fruit.

Applications: Cheesecakes and other egg-based custard tarts (which contain their own structure and help hold the crust together), some no-bake fillings

Banana-Sesame Cream Tart

I have very few reference points when it comes to banana cream pie, having only tasted it once or twice. When I set out to develop my own version, this proved to be a good thing because I felt free to interpret it any way I liked. Here I make more of a tart than a pie (thereby increasing the ratio of crust to filling) and eliminate the layer of sliced bananas (which quickly take on an unappealing color and texture). Instead, I incorporate banana directly into the creamy custard filling and flavor it with toasted sesame oil for a sweet-savory balance. The topping includes a good amount of sour cream because I cannot resist the combination of bananas and sour cream (it must be familial—my grandmother used to eat bananas and sour cream sprinkled with sugar as a snack). With toasted sesame seeds on top, the combination is craveable.

SERVES 8

DIFFICULTY: 2 (Easy)

ACTIVE TIME: 1 hour

TOTAL TIME: 5 hours 15 minutes (includes 4 hours for chilling)

SPECIAL EQUIPMENT: 9-inch removable-bottom tart pan, blender (handheld or standard)

6 ounces (170g) Nilla wafers or graham crackers (about 46 wafers or 11 crackers)

5 tablespoons unsalted butter (2.5 oz / 71g), melted and cooled

1 tablespoon toasted sesame seeds, plus more for garnish

2 tablespoons plus ⅓ cup sugar (3.2 oz / 92g)

A pinch plus ½ teaspoon Diamond Crystal kosher salt or ¼ teaspoon Morton kosher salt

3 tablespoons cornstarch

4 large egg yolks (2.1 oz / 60g)

1⅔ cups plus ¾ cup heavy cream (20.5 oz / 580g), chilled

1 cup mashed overripe banana (8.5 oz / 240g), from about 2 medium

2 teaspoons toasted sesame oil

½ cup sour cream (4.2 oz / 120g), chilled

PREHEAT THE OVEN: Arrange an oven rack in the center position and preheat the oven to 350°F.

MAKE THE CRUST: Place the Nilla wafers or graham crackers in a resealable bag, press out the air, and seal. Use a rolling pin or heavy-bottomed saucepan to crush the cookies, periodically shaking the bag so the larger pieces settle to one side, and continue to crush until you have very fine, uniform crumbs (you can also pulse them in a food processor until finely ground, but it's very doable by hand). Transfer the crumbs to a medium bowl and add the melted butter, sesame seeds, 2 tablespoons sugar, and a pinch of salt. Toss with a fork to combine then rub the mixture between your fingers until it looks like wet sand.

PRESS IN THE CRUST AND BAKE: Transfer just shy of half the mixture to a 9-inch removable-bottom tart pan and scatter the crumbs evenly around the perimeter. Use a straight-sided glass or 1-cup dry measure to press the mixture firmly against the fluted sides all the way around, then scatter the remaining crumbs across the bottom of the pan and use the bottom of the glass or measuring cup to flatten the mixture in an even layer. Place the tart pan on a sheet pan and bake until the crust is fragrant, firm to the touch, and dark brown around the edges, 13 to 18 minutes. Remove from the oven and let cool on the sheet pan.

ASSEMBLE THE BANANA-SESAME CUSTARD: In a small saucepan, whisk together the cornstarch, ½ teaspoon salt, and the remaining ⅓ cup (2.4 oz / 67g) sugar to break up any lumps. Add the egg yolks and whisk slowly until combined (it will be very thick at first), then whisk more vigorously, making sure no unincorporated sugar is trapped around the bottom of the saucepan, until the mixture is pale and slightly thickened, about 1 minute. Whisking constantly, slowly stream in 1⅔ cups (14.1 oz / 400g) of the heavy cream, then whisk in the mashed banana. Use a handheld blender to blend the mixture directly in the saucepan until it's completely smooth. (Alternatively, transfer the mixture to a standard blender and blend on medium, then return to the saucepan.)

COOK THE CUSTARD: Have a clean medium bowl nearby for transferring the hot custard. Place the saucepan over medium heat and cook, whisking constantly, until the custard is thickened, the foam on the surface has subsided, and it holds the marks of the whisk, about 5 minutes. Stop whisking for a few seconds and check for slow bubbling beneath the

→

surface, indicating the mixture is at a boil, then immediately remove the saucepan from the heat and pour the custard into the reserved medium bowl.

> *Potential Pitfall:* Don't scrape the bottom of the saucepan where you might have a bit of curdling, since it will mar the smooth texture. If some curdled custard gets into the bowl, it's okay—you're going to whisk in the sesame oil, which will help to smooth it out.

FILL THE TART: Add the sesame oil to the bowl with the custard and whisk thoroughly to combine. Pour the hot custard into the cooled crust, filling it right to the top, and smooth the surface. Press a piece of plastic directly onto the custard to prevent a skin from forming and transfer the pan to the refrigerator. Chill until the custard is cold and set, at least 4 hours.

WHIP THE SOUR CREAM: In a large bowl, with a whisk or hand mixer, whip the sour cream and remaining ¾ cup (6.3 oz / 180g) heavy cream on low speed to start and gradually increase the speed to medium-high as the mixture thickens, until you have medium peaks (see Whipping Cream, page 355).

ASSEMBLE AND SERVE: Remove the tart from the refrigerator, uncover, and dollop the whipped sour cream over the custard. Spread the cream across the surface all the way to the crust and sprinkle with more toasted sesame seeds. Press up on the bottom of the tart pan to pop it out of the fluted ring and place on a serving plate. Cut into slices and serve.

Can I ...

Make it ahead? Yes. The assembled tart can be made and refrigerated uncovered up to 3 hours ahead. The custard-filled tart (without the whipped sour cream) will keep, covered and refrigerated, for up to 3 days but is best served within 24 hours while the crust is still crisp (it will soften as it sits). Top with whipped sour cream and sesame seeds just before serving.

Make it gluten-free? Yes. Use a brand of gluten-free vanilla wafers or graham-style crackers for the crust.

Make this without sesame? Yes. Omit the sesame seeds from the crust, then substitute 1 tablespoon of smooth natural peanut butter for the sesame oil in the custard and top the assembled tart with crushed roasted peanuts instead of sesame seeds. Or simply omit the sesame seeds and oil entirely for a pure banana tart.

Peach Drop Biscuit Cobbler

I don't bake with peaches often because I've always felt that nothing is better than just eating a ripe peach outright. But peach cobbler is such a revered dish that I set out to prove otherwise, and I learned that peaches resist breaking down and become silky and succulent when cooked—different than fresh, for sure, but something to be appreciated nonetheless. When it comes to peach cobbler, I also learned that the filling should be cooked on the stovetop to reduce the juices prior to baking or you'll have either a soupy cobbler or one that requires an unpalatable amount of thickener. It's a helpful step, actually, because the hot filling helps the underside of the biscuit topping to bake through. I skip the process of blanching and peeling the fresh peaches (especially since the skins add a rosy tint and texture to the filling), as it feels fussy for such a homestyle dish. I also give you permission to use frozen peaches, which are consistent and always available, unlike fresh.

SERVES 10

DIFFICULTY: 2 (Easy)

ACTIVE TIME: 1 hour (does not include making the biscuit dough)

TOTAL TIME: 2 hours, plus time to cool

SPECIAL EQUIPMENT: 12-inch skillet, 3-quart shallow baking dish or 13 × 9-inch baking dish (preferably ceramic or glass)

4 pounds (1.8kg) fresh firm but ripe peaches, halved, pitted, and cut into ½-inch wedges, or thawed frozen sliced peaches

¾ cup packed light brown sugar (5.8 oz / 165g)

1 tablespoon cornstarch

1½ teaspoons ground ginger

½ teaspoon ground cinnamon

¼ teaspoon ground nutmeg

½ teaspoon Diamond Crystal kosher salt or ¼ teaspoon Morton kosher salt

3 tablespoons fresh lemon juice

2 teaspoons vanilla extract

All-Purpose Drop Biscuit Dough (page 336), formed into biscuits and chilled

Heavy cream, for brushing and serving

Demerara sugar, for sprinkling

Can I . . .

Make it ahead? Partially. The cobbler is best served the day it's baked, but the scooped, unbaked biscuits can be frozen on a parchment-lined sheet pan and then transferred to a resealable bag and kept frozen for up to 1 month (you can bake the biscuits from frozen). Any leftover cobbler will keep, loosely covered and stored at room temperature, for up to 2 days, but the biscuits will stale quickly.

Bake this in a skillet? Not recommended. The peach filling will react with cast-iron or stainless steel, so a glass or ceramic baking dish is recommended.

PREHEAT THE OVEN AND PREPARE THE SHEET PAN: Arrange an oven rack in the center position and preheat the oven to 425°F. Line a sheet pan with a silicone baking mat or aluminum foil and set aside.

COOK THE PEACHES: In a 12-inch skillet, combine the peaches (plus any juices, if using thawed frozen), brown sugar, and 2 tablespoons (1 oz / 28g) water and cook over medium-low heat, gently stirring every now and then, until the peaches have released their juices and the sugar is dissolved, 7 to 10 minutes. Increase the heat to medium and bring the mixture to a boil, then reduce to maintain a simmer. Continue to cook, shaking the skillet occasionally, until the liquid is syrupy and reduced to the point where the fruit is no longer fully submerged, and the peach slices are translucent and tender (a cake tester or toothpick will slide into them without resistance), 25 to 30 minutes for fresh peaches, and 35 to 40 for frozen. Remove the skillet from the heat and set aside.

FINISH THE FILLING: In a small bowl, combine the cornstarch, ginger, cinnamon, nutmeg, and salt and stir with a fork until the mixture is uniform and there are no clumps of cornstarch. Sprinkle the mixture into the skillet and stir gently to combine, then place the skillet back over medium-high heat and cook the filling, stirring just until it comes up to a boil. Boil the filling for 20 seconds or so, then remove the skillet from the heat and stir in the lemon juice and vanilla. Scrape the filling into a 3-quart shallow baking dish or 13 × 9-inch baking dish, preferably ceramic or glass.

ASSEMBLE AND BAKE: Remove the drop biscuits from the refrigerator and arrange them over the hot peach filling (it might seem weird to put cold pastry on hot filling, but go with it!). Brush the tops of the biscuits with heavy cream, then sprinkle generously with demerara sugar. Place the baking dish on the lined sheet pan and bake for 15 minutes, then reduce the oven temperature to 350°F and continue to bake until the tops of the biscuits are deep golden brown and the filling is bubbling around the sides, another 35 to 45 minutes. Remove from the oven and let the cobbler cool until it's warm but not hot.

SERVE: Spoon the warm cobbler into shallow bowls and drizzle with chilled cream.

Rhubarb & Raspberry Shortcakes
with Poppy Seeds

I spent quite a bit of time making sure that my all-purpose shortcake dough bakes up into fluffy, flaky, tender shortcakes, so it was important that I give them a worthy topping. Instead of strawberries, which are the standard, I turned to strawberry's frequent partner, rhubarb, which rarely stands in the limelight but should more often. I cut the stalks into batons and poach them gently in wine and orange juice so they retain a bit of firmness, then I reduce the poaching liquid to a syrup for drizzling on top, ensuring none of the rhubarb flavor is lost. Though I add raspberries to bring some additional texture to the dish, they're more of a supporting player. For the prettiest presentation, pick the reddest stalks of rhubarb you can find, which will impart a hot pink tint to the poaching liquid.

SERVES 9

DIFFICULTY: 2 (Easy)

ACTIVE TIME: 45 minutes (does not include making the shortcake dough)

TOTAL TIME: 2 hours

SPECIAL EQUIPMENT: Hand mixer

POACHED RHUBARB AND RASPBERRIES

1 cup dry white or rosé wine (8 oz / 227g)

1 cup granulated sugar (7 oz / 200g)

½ cup orange juice (4 oz / 113g)

2 teaspoons vanilla extract

Pinch of kosher salt

12 ounces (340g) rhubarb stalks, halved lengthwise if thick, cut crosswise into 1-inch pieces (about 3 cups)

6 ounces (170g) raspberries (about 1½ cups)

SHORTCAKES AND ASSEMBLY

All-Purpose Shortcake Dough (page 336), cut into squares and chilled

1½ cups heavy cream (12.7 oz / 360g), chilled, plus more for brushing

Poppy seeds, for sprinkling

Demerara sugar, for sprinkling

8 ounces (227g) mascarpone cheese, chilled

POACH THE RHUBARB: In a large saucepan or small Dutch oven, combine the wine, granulated sugar, orange juice, vanilla, salt, and 1 cup (8 oz / 227g) water. Bring to a simmer over medium-high heat, stirring to dissolve the sugar. Once the poaching liquid is simmering, remove the saucepan from the heat and add the rhubarb. Cut a round of parchment paper the same diameter as the saucepan and place it directly on the surface of the poaching liquid, pressing out large air bubbles and allowing some of the liquid to pool on top of the parchment (this will keep the rhubarb in full contact with the poaching liquid so it cooks evenly). Set the saucepan back over medium heat just until you see gentle bubbling around the edge of the parchment, then remove from the heat immediately (see Poaching Fruit, page 357, for a step-by-step guide).

ADD THE RASPBERRIES AND LET COOL: Discard the round of parchment paper, add the raspberries to the saucepan, and stir delicately to incorporate. Set the saucepan aside to cool until lukewarm, 20 to 25 minutes—the rhubarb and raspberries will gently cook through from the residual heat.

REDUCE THE POACHING LIQUID: With a slotted spoon, gently lift out the warm rhubarb and raspberries, allowing excess liquid to drip back into the saucepan, and transfer the fruit to a bowl. Set aside. Place the saucepan with the poaching liquid over medium-high heat and bring to a boil, then continue to cook, whisking occasionally, until you have a thick, syrupy liquid that is reduced to about 1 cup, 15 to 20 minutes (pour it into a heatproof liquid measuring cup to check the volume and return to the saucepan and continue to reduce if it's not there yet). Set the syrup aside to cool.

PREHEAT THE OVEN AND PREPARE THE SHEET PAN: Arrange an oven rack in the center position and preheat the oven to 425°F. Line a large sheet pan with parchment paper and set aside.

Potential Pitfall: Do not use a silicone baking mat to line the pan, as it will cause the shortcakes to spread excessively and flatten during baking.

Can I . . .

Make them ahead? Yes, but . . . wait to assemble them. The rhubarb and raspberries can be poached 1 day ahead. Transfer the fruit to a lidded container (be gentle, it's fragile) and refrigerate, then reduce the poaching liquid to a syrup. Store the syrup in a separate airtight container in the refrigerator. Bring the fruit and syrup to room temperature before serving. The shortcakes are best served the day they're baked, but the unbaked shortcakes can be wrapped well and frozen for up to 1 month.

Use another fruit? Yes. Instead of the poached rhubarb and raspberries, top the shortcakes with macerated sliced strawberries or blackberries (see Macerating Fruit, page 355), or **Slow-Roasted Plums** (page 233).

BAKE: Place the chilled, unbaked shortcakes on the lined pan, spacing them evenly. Brush the tops with cream and sprinkle generously with poppy seeds and demerara sugar, then bake until the shortcakes have risen and the tops are deep golden brown, 18 to 22 minutes, rotating the sheet pan front to back after 12 minutes. Set the shortcakes aside to cool on the sheet pan for 10 minutes, then transfer them to a wire rack to cool completely.

WHIP THE MASCARPONE: In a large bowl, with a hand mixer, whip the mascarpone and 1½ cups (12.7 oz / 360g) cream on low speed to start and gradually increase the speed to medium-high as the mixture thickens, until you have a softly whipped cream that holds a droopy peak (see Whipping Cream, page 355). Set the cream aside.

ASSEMBLE AND SERVE: Use a serrated knife to halve the shortcakes horizontally and remove the tops. Set the bottoms on serving plates and top each with a dollop of the whipped mascarpone, dividing it evenly. Spoon the rhubarb and raspberries (and a bit of the juices that have accumulated around them) on top, also dividing evenly, then sprinkle with poppy seeds. Drizzle the fruit with the reserved syrup (no need to use it all) and place the top halves over the shortcakes. Serve immediately.

Roasted Lemon Tart

I've always loved the sour flavor of citrus fruits, but I also equally appreciate their bitterness, which is why I gravitate toward whole-citrus desserts. It's a tricky genre, though, because the bitterness from a citrus fruit's pith can become unpleasantly dominant—unless, it turns out, it's roasted first. In this tart, sugared lemon slices are caramelized in the oven, which tames their bitterness and adds a rounded, nuanced flavor to the filling. It's a riff on a Shaker lemon pie, a traditional whole-lemon pie developed by the early nineteenth-century religious group known for their thrift. Despite the economy of using the whole fruit, the final tart has a luxurious quality.

SERVES 8

DIFFICULTY: 2 (Easy)

ACTIVE TIME: 1 hour

TOTAL TIME: 2 hours 50 minutes, plus time to cool

SPECIAL EQUIPMENT: 9-inch removable-bottom tart pan

Neutral oil for the sheet pan

2 medium-large lemons (11 oz / 313g), sliced into very thin rounds, seeds and ends discarded

1 cup plus 3 tablespoons sugar (8.4 oz / 237g)

¼ cup heavy cream (2.1 oz / 60g)

2 tablespoons fresh lemon juice

1 cup all-purpose flour (4.8 oz / 135g), plus more for pressing

2 tablespoons cornstarch

½ teaspoon Diamond Crystal kosher salt or ¼ teaspoon Morton kosher salt, plus a pinch

12 tablespoons unsalted butter (6 oz / 170g), at room temperature, divided

1 large egg yolk (0.5 oz / 15g), at room temperature

4 large eggs (7 oz / 200g), beaten, at room temperature

2 tablespoons cornmeal

PREHEAT THE OVEN AND PREPARE THE SHEET PAN: Arrange an oven rack in the center position and preheat the oven to 350°F. Line a large sheet pan with a silicone baking mat or parchment paper and brush with a thin layer of oil.

ROAST THE LEMONS: Arrange the lemon slices across the prepared pan, spacing them evenly. Place 1 cup (7 oz / 200g) of the sugar in a medium bowl, then sprinkle a couple of spoonfuls of the sugar from the bowl over the lemon slices to coat them lightly. Set aside the bowl of sugar and reserve it for making the lemon filling. Transfer the sheet pan to the oven and roast the lemon slices until they're translucent all over and golden brown and caramelized in spots, 25 to 30 minutes, rotating the pan front to back after 15 minutes.

Potential Pitfall: The slices will go from golden and caramelized to blackened quickly, so keep an eye on them. Also keep in mind that thinner slices caramelize faster, so if your slices are a little uneven, you might want to remove the thinner ones from the sheet pan as they brown and return the thicker slices to the oven for another minute or two so they all bake evenly.

MACERATE THE ROASTED LEMON: Let the lemon slices cool slightly on the sheet pan, then transfer around 10 slices to a plate and set aside for decorating the top of the tart. Transfer the remaining slices to a cutting board and let cool completely, then coarsely chop them—the slices might harden or become tacky in places as they cool, so use a sturdy chef's knife. Transfer the chopped lemon to the reserved bowl of sugar, then add the cream and lemon juice and stir to combine. Set the bowl aside to allow the lemon pieces to soften while you make the crust.

MAKE THE SHORTBREAD CRUST: In a small bowl, whisk together the flour, cornstarch, and ½ teaspoon salt, then set aside. In a medium bowl, use a flexible spatula to combine 8 tablespoons (4 oz / 113g) of the butter with the remaining 3 tablespoons sugar and blend until the mixture is creamy and thoroughly combined. Continue to mix, vigorously beating it against the side of the bowl with the spatula, until the mixture is pale and just a little bit fluffy, about 1 minute. Add the egg yolk and stir to combine. Add the flour mixture to the bowl with the butter mixture and stir with the spatula, working the mixture and scraping the bottom and the sides of the bowl, until you have a firm, evenly mixed dough with no dry spots.

→

PRESS IN THE CRUST: Scrape the dough into a 9-inch removable-bottom tart pan and use a flat hand to press it across the bottom and up the sides of the pan in a thin even layer, flouring your hand as necessary to prevent sticking. Once you have the dough pressed in, use a straight-sided glass or 1-cup dry measure to flatten and smooth the dough, flouring the bottom of the glass or measuring cup as needed. Continue to press the dough evenly up the sides until it extends just above the edge of the pan, then transfer the pan to the freezer and chill until the dough is firm, 10 to 15 minutes.

TRIM AND LINE THE CRUST: Remove the pan from the freezer and place it on a sheet pan. Hold a paring knife parallel to the sheet pan and slice horizontally around the rim of the tart pan, removing the excess dough and creating a smooth edge flush with the top of the pan (save the scraps of raw dough for patching any cracks in the crust after baking). Prick the bottom all over with the tines of a fork, then press a layer of foil directly onto the surface of the dough and up the sides, carefully working it into the groove where the bottom and sides meet (this will help prevent the dough from slumping as it bakes).

PARBAKE THE CRUST: Bake the tart crust until the edge is golden (peek under the foil to check), 20 to 25 minutes. Remove the pan from the oven and carefully peel away the foil. Return the pan to the oven and bake until the crust is golden all over, another 15 to 20 minutes. Remove the pan from the oven and set aside on the sheet pan while you make the filling. Leave the oven on.

MAKE THE FILLING: Melt the remaining 4 tablespoons (2 oz / 57g) butter and set aside. To the bowl with the roasted lemon and sugar mixture, add the whole eggs and whisk until the mixture is completely smooth and streak-free, about 30 seconds. Add the cornmeal and melted butter and whisk until the mixture is completely smooth.

FILL THE TART: If any cracks formed in the crust during baking, smear a tiny pinch of the reserved raw dough into the cracks to fill (no need to bake it again before adding the filling). Pour the filling into the tart crust and spread the bits of lemon around so they're evenly distributed. Arrange the reserved lemon slices across the surface of the tart.

BAKE: Carefully transfer the sheet pan to the oven and bake the tart until the filling is puffed all across the surface and firm to the touch in the center, 20 to 25 minutes. Transfer the baked tart to a wire rack to cool completely. Press up on the bottom of the tart pan to pop it out of the fluted ring and place on a serving plate.

Can I . . .

Make it ahead? Yes. The tart, covered loosely and stored at room temperature, will keep for up to 2 days but is best served on the first day while the crust is still crisp (it will soften as it sits).

Make it gluten-free? Yes. Substitute 1 cup of your favorite gluten-free flour blend for the all-purpose flour in the crust.

S'mores Tart

S'mores desserts are typically a little maximalist for my taste. But over the past couple of years I've been lucky to spend a portion of my time in the Hudson Valley, about ninety minutes outside of New York City, where, thanks to the regular occurrence of indoor and outdoor fires, I rediscovered my childhood love of classic s'mores. It got me brainstorming ways to translate s'mores into a more refined dessert, and since nothing is more refined than a chocolate tart, that became my starting point. The filling is a basic ganache lightened with whipped cream to give it a mousse-like texture (a genius technique I learned from Dorie Greenspan, who uses it for the topping of her chocolate Lisbon Chocolate Cake). It's set inside a thick graham cracker crust and topped with my homemade marshmallow (note that you should wait to prepare the marshmallow topping until after you've filled the tart).

SERVES 8

DIFFICULTY: 2 (Easy)

ACTIVE TIME: 55 minutes (does not include making the marshmallow)

TOTAL TIME: 3 hours 30 minutes

SPECIAL EQUIPMENT: 9-inch removable-bottom tart pan, hand mixer, kitchen torch (optional)

9 tablespoons unsalted butter (4.5 oz / 128g), divided

7 ounces (198g) graham crackers (about 13 sheets)

1 large egg yolk (0.5 oz / 15g)

2 tablespoons plus ¾ cup sugar (6.2 oz / 175g)

½ teaspoon Diamond Crystal kosher salt or ¼ teaspoon Morton kosher salt, plus several pinches

6 ounces (170g) semisweet chocolate (64%-70% cacao), finely chopped

1¼ cups heavy cream (10.6 oz / 300g), chilled, divided

Easy Marshmallows (page 341)

PREHEAT THE OVEN: Arrange an oven rack in the center position and preheat the oven to 350°F.

MAKE THE CRUST: Melt 5 tablespoons (2.5 oz / 71g) of the butter and set aside to cool. Place the graham crackers in a resealable bag, press out the air, and seal. Use a rolling pin or a heavy-bottomed saucepan to crush the crackers, periodically shaking the bag so the larger pieces settle to one side, and continue to crush until you have very fine, uniform crumbs (you can also pulse the graham crackers in a food processor until finely ground, but it's very doable by hand). Transfer the crumbs to a medium bowl and add the egg yolk, 2 tablespoons sugar, ½ teaspoon salt, and the melted butter. Toss with a fork to combine then rub the mixture between your fingers until it looks like wet sand.

PRESS IN THE CRUST AND BAKE: Transfer just shy of half the mixture to a 9-inch removable-bottom tart pan and scatter the crumbs evenly around the perimeter. Use a straight-sided glass or 1-cup dry measure to press the mixture firmly against the fluted sides (it will form a thick layer), then scatter the remaining crumbs across the bottom of the pan and use the bottom of the glass or measuring cup to flatten the mixture into an even layer. Place the tart pan on a sheet pan and bake until the crust is fragrant, firm to the touch, and dark brown around the edges, 13 to 18 minutes. Remove from the oven and let cool completely.

MAKE THE GANACHE: In a large heatproof bowl, combine the chocolate and a generous pinch of salt and set aside. In a small saucepan, heat ¾ cup (6.3 oz / 180g) of the cream over medium heat just until you see gentle bubbling around the sides. Remove the saucepan from the heat and set it aside for 30 seconds to cool slightly, then pour it over the chocolate. Cut the remaining 4 tablespoons (2 oz / 57g) butter into ½-inch pieces and add them to the bowl. Let the chocolate mixture sit undisturbed for about 5 minutes to allow the chocolate to melt. Whisk the ganache gently, starting in the center of the bowl and working outward, until the mixture is completely smooth. Set the bowl aside while you whip the cream.

Potential Pitfall: Make sure you allow the cream to cool slightly before pouring it over the chocolate. Ganache is temperature-sensitive and will "break" if it gets too hot, meaning that the cocoa butter will separate from the solids and make the mixture look oily. If it does break, whisk in 2 tablespoons water to bring it back together.

→

Can I . . .

Make it ahead? Partially, yes. The filled tart, without the marshmallow topping, can be made up to 1 day ahead. Cover and refrigerate, then let it come to room temperature before topping. The assembled tart, loosely covered and stored at cool room temperature, will keep for up to 2 days, but the marshmallow topping may deflate slightly (it will also start to weep at warmer temperatures).

Use a stand mixer instead of a hand mixer? Yes. Assemble the ganache as written, then whip the remaining ½ cup cream (4.2 oz / 120g) in a stand mixer fitted with the whisk attachment. Scrape the cream into a separate bowl, then add the ganache to the stand mixer and whip, but don't exceed medium speed (the ganache is easy to overwhip, which will make it firm). Add the whipped cream to the stand mixer and fold by hand into the whipped ganache.

Make it gluten-free? Yes. Use a brand of gluten-free graham-style crackers for the crust.

Toast the marshmallow under the broiler? No. The crust and ganache filling will burn quickly if the entire tart is placed under the broiler, so only attempt to toast it with a kitchen torch.

WHIP THE REMAINING CREAM: In a medium bowl, with a hand mixer, whip the remaining ½ cup (4.2 oz / 120g) cream on low speed and gradually increase the speed to medium-high as it thickens until you have medium peaks (see Whipping Cream, page 355). Set the bowl aside.

WHIP THE GANACHE AND FILL THE TART: Beat the ganache with the hand mixer (no need to wash after whipping the cream) on low speed to start and gradually increase the speed to medium-high until the ganache thickens to the consistency of chocolate pudding and holds the marks of the whisk, about 4 minutes. Scrape in the whipped cream and fold until the mixture is streak-free (for more on the proper technique, see Folding a Mixture, page 351). Scrape the whipped ganache into the cooled tart crust and smooth the surface, working it to the sides in an even layer. Set the tart aside, uncovered at room temperature, until the filling is set, at least 15 minutes.

TOP WITH THE MARSHMALLOW: Follow the recipe for the marshmallows, but rather than transferring the mixture to a pastry bag, scrape it onto the tart and swirl with the back of a spoon across the surface. Let the tart sit uncovered at cool room temperature until the marshmallow is firm and set, at least 2 hours. If desired, brown the surface of the marshmallow with a kitchen torch. Press up on the bottom of the tart pan to pop the tart out of the fluted ring and place it on a serving plate.

Caramelized Pear Turnover

with Sage

When pears are baked for a long time, the exposed flesh turns dry and grainy, but when insulated between two layers of pastry, as in this giant turnover, they turn perfectly juicy and soft. The pears must be precooked, though, or they would release too much moisture inside the pastry, so I bathe halves in a sage-infused caramel and roast them just until they're tender (it sounds harder than it is—the oven does all the work). It's a true delight to eat the nearly-whole pears inside the flaky turnover, and I especially love how the combination of pears, caramel, and piney sage feels both modern and timeless.

SERVES 8

DIFFICULTY: 2 (Easy)

ACTIVE TIME: 1 hour 30 minutes (does not include making the pastry)

TOTAL TIME: 3 hours 35 minutes, plus time to cool

SPECIAL EQUIPMENT: 12-inch ovenproof skillet

¼ cup heavy cream (2.1 oz / 60g)

4 tablespoons unsalted butter (2 oz / 57g)

½ cup demerara sugar (3.5 oz / 100g), plus more for sprinkling

Generous pinch of kosher salt

2 large leafy sage sprigs, plus more sage leaves for topping

5 medium firm but ripe pears (2 lb / 907g), preferably Bosc

2 teaspoons finely grated lemon zest

2 rectangular portions **All-Purpose Flaky Pastry Dough** (page 331), chilled

All-purpose flour, for rolling

1 large egg (1.8 oz / 50g), beaten

PREHEAT THE OVEN AND PREPARE THE PAN: Arrange an oven rack in the center position and preheat the oven to 400°F. Line a large sheet pan with a silicone baking mat or parchment paper and set it aside.

MAKE THE SAGE CARAMEL: In a 12-inch ovenproof skillet, combine the cream, butter, demerara sugar, salt, and 2 tablespoons (1 oz / 28g) water. Cook over medium heat, stirring constantly, until the butter is melted and the sugar dissolves. Add the sage sprigs and stir to coat them, then transfer the skillet to the oven and bake until the mixture is deep golden brown and caramelized, 10 to 15 minutes, stirring once halfway through. Set the skillet aside. Leave the oven on.

> *Potential Pitfall:* If the caramel crystallizes (meaning it hardens and turns grainy), remove the skillet from the oven and stir in 2 tablespoons (1 oz / 28g) water until the sugar dissolves and the caramel is smooth again. Return it to the oven to finish caramelizing. It's easy to forget that the entire skillet is hot, so place a kitchen towel or oven mitt over the handle when you remove it from the oven so you don't grab it barehanded.

MEANWHILE, PREPARE THE PEARS: Peel and halve the pears lengthwise. Use a paring knife to slice out the narrow fibrous portions of the core at the stem end and base, then use a melon baller or a round teaspoon measure to scoop out the cores and seeds. Set the pears aside until the caramel is done.

ROAST THE PEARS: Add the pears to the skillet and turn them carefully to coat in the sage caramel. Return the skillet to the oven and roast the pears, turning them once, until they've released their juices and the tip of a paring knife slides easily into the flesh, 20 to 30 minutes. Remove the skillet from the oven and turn the oven off. (Note: If you wanted to stop here, you could serve the caramelized pears over vanilla ice cream.)

FINISH THE CARAMEL: Use a slotted spoon to carefully remove the pears from the skillet (take care, they're delicate) and transfer them to a plate. Discard the sage sprigs, which have infused the caramel with their flavor. If the butter separated from the rest of the caramel during baking and the mixture looks greasy, vigorously whisk 2 teaspoons water into the mixture to bring it back together. The caramel should be thick and reduced, but if it's runny because the pears released lots of juice, set the skillet over medium heat and cook, whisking constantly, until it's thick and bubbling all over. Whisk the lemon zest into the caramel, then scrape it over the pears and set the plate aside until the pears and caramel have cooled completely.

$\rightarrow$

ROLL OUT THE FIRST PIECE OF DOUGH: Let 1 portion of dough sit at room temperature for a minute or two to soften slightly, then unwrap it and place on a lightly floured surface. Use a rolling pin to beat the dough all across the surface to make it more pliable. Dust underneath and on top of the dough with more flour, then roll it out, dusting with more flour as needed, into a long, narrow rectangle measuring about 4 × 9 inches (for step-by-step visuals, see Rolling Out Chilled Pastry Dough, page 332).

ARRANGE THE PEARS: Fold the dough in half, transfer it to the prepared sheet pan, and unfold. Carefully transfer the cooled pear halves one at a time to the dough, arranging them in two rows down the center of the dough and leaving a border of at least 1 inch all the way around (alternate the position of the pears so the fat ends line up next to the skinny ends). Scrape any remaining caramel down the center of the pears, avoiding the border. Transfer the sheet pan to the refrigerator.

ROLL OUT THE REMAINING DOUGH AND ASSEMBLE: Roll out the second portion of dough just as you did the first, but this time roll it slightly longer and wider. Remove the sheet pan from the refrigerator and brush the border around the pears with the beaten egg (reserve the rest of the egg for later). Place the second piece of dough on top, aligning the sides and corners and allowing it to drape over the pears. Press firmly along the borders to seal the two pieces of dough together. Then, using the tines of a fork, press around the perimeter of the turnover to crimp it on all four sides, dipping the tines in flour as needed to prevent sticking. Use a knife or wheel cutter to trim away just the ragged edge to make a clean, straight rectangle. Transfer the sheet pan to the refrigerator and chill until the top layer of dough is firm and cold, 10 to 15 minutes.

COAT WITH EGG, SAGE, AND SUGAR: Brush the entire surface and crimped edge of the turnover with a thin layer of the egg. Press a few sage leaves into the dough, lightly brush the leaves with more egg to coat, then sprinkle the surface generously with demerara sugar. Use the tip of a paring knife to cut several slits in the dough to allow steam to escape.

BAKE: Bake the turnover until the pastry is puffed and deep golden brown, 40 to 50 minutes, rotating the sheet pan front to back after 20 minutes. Remove from the oven and let cool completely on the pan.

Quince & Pineapple Jam Tart

Quince, an ancient fruit that looks like a knobby, yellowish-green apple, comes into season in October and November, and when ripe, it smells so distinctly of pineapple that it felt like an epiphany when I thought to combine the two fruits (in fact, the most common variety of quince in the Northeast is called pineapple quince). The raw flesh is hard and astringent, so quince must be cooked to be edible, which gives it a deep coral tone. I cook it down into a rosy jam with pineapple and vanilla, both of which highlight the beguiling, slightly tropical flavor of quince and make a fantastic filling for a simple jam tart. At the farmers' market, look for quince that are more yellow than green and have a strong tropical perfume.

SERVES 8

DIFFICULTY: 2 (Easy)

ACTIVE TIME: 2 hours

TOTAL TIME: 6 hours, plus time to cool

SPECIAL EQUIPMENT: Potato masher, hand mixer, 9-inch removable-bottom tart pan

QUINCE PINEAPPLE JAM

1 pound (454g) ripe quince (about 2 large)

8 ounces (227g) coarsely chopped fresh pineapple (about 1¼ cups)

1 cup sugar (7 oz / 200g)

2 tablespoons fresh lemon juice

Pinch of kosher salt

Seeds scraped from ½ vanilla bean (pod reserved)

SHORTBREAD CRUST

2⅓ cups all-purpose flour (11.1 oz / 315g), plus more for pressing and rolling

1 teaspoon baking powder

¾ teaspoon ground cinnamon

¾ teaspoon Diamond Crystal kosher salt or ½ teaspoon Morton kosher salt

⅓ cup sugar (2.4 oz / 67g)

2 teaspoons finely grated lemon zest

1½ sticks unsalted butter (6 oz / 170g), at room temperature

1 large egg (1.8 oz / 50g), at room temperature

PEEL, CUT, AND CORE THE QUINCE: Peel the quince and quarter them lengthwise, then carefully slice out the cores and seeds. Reserve the peels, cores, and seeds for making the jam, as these contain lots of pectin.

POACH THE QUINCE AND PINEAPPLE: In a large saucepan, combine the quartered quince, pineapple, sugar, lemon juice, salt, and enough water to fully submerge the fruit. Cut a round of parchment paper the same diameter as the saucepan and set aside. Set the saucepan over medium-high heat and bring the liquid to a boil, stirring occasionally to dissolve the sugar, then reduce the heat to maintain a gentle simmer. Carefully place the parchment directly onto the surface of the poaching liquid, pressing out large air bubbles and allowing some of the liquid to pool on top of the parchment (this will keep the quince in full contact with the poaching liquid so it cooks evenly). Further reduce the heat if necessary to maintain gentle bubbling beneath the parchment and cook until the quince pieces are completely tender and have taken on a blush color, 40 to 45 minutes. Remove the parchment paper and use a slotted spoon to transfer the quince and pineapple to a medium heatproof bowl and set it aside, leaving the poaching liquid in the saucepan.

REDUCE THE POACHING LIQUID: Add the reserved quince peels, cores, and seeds to the saucepan and bring to a rolling boil over high heat. Continue to boil the mixture until the liquid is very syrupy, rosy, and reduced to approximately 1 cup, 15 to 20 minutes (the timing depends on how much water you added initially to cover the fruit). The exact volume is not important, you just want it very reduced. Remove the saucepan from the heat. Set a mesh sieve over the bowl with the poached fruit and pour the reduced poaching liquid, peels, cores, and seeds into the sieve. Press on the solids with a flexible spatula to extract any liquid, then discard the solids. Transfer the poached fruit and strained liquid back to the saucepan.

MAKE THE JAM: Add the vanilla seeds and pod to the saucepan and return the mixture to a boil over medium-high heat, mashing the fruit with a potato masher until the quince pieces are broken down into mush (the pineapple will not completely break down). Continue to boil the mixture over medium-high heat, stirring frequently with a heatproof flexible spatula and scraping the bottom and sides of the saucepan, until all the liquid has boiled off and you have a thick, glossy, reddish-pink jam that holds a mound on the end of a spoon (when you drag the spatula across the bottom of the saucepan, the jam should take a second to fill in the line), 10 to 15 minutes. Remove the saucepan from the heat and scrape the jam into a heatproof glass measuring cup. You should have between 2 and 2¼ cups (20–23 oz / 573–657g).

$\rightarrow$

Make it ahead? Yes. The tart,
loosely covered and stored at room
temperature, will keep for up to 3 days,
but it's best served on the first or
second day (the crust will soften over
time). The quince and pineapple jam,
refrigerated in an airtight container, will
keep for several months.

**Use a stand mixer instead of a hand
mixer? Yes.** To make the crust, use your
fingertips to massage the zest and
sugar in a stand mixer fitted with the
paddle attachment, then add the butter
and proceed with the recipe as written.

If you have more than 2¼ cups, return the jam to the saucepan and continue to cook. Let the jam cool slightly, then transfer it to a lidded container and refrigerate until it's cold (leave the vanilla pod in the jam so it can continue to infuse), at least 2 hours.

MIX THE DRY INGREDIENTS FOR THE SHORTBREAD CRUST: In a medium bowl, whisk together the flour, baking powder, cinnamon, and salt. Set aside.

MAKE AND CHILL THE DOUGH: In a separate medium bowl, combine the sugar and lemon zest and massage with your fingertips until the mixture is fragrant and looks like wet sand. Add the butter and beat with a hand mixer on medium speed, pausing occasionally to scrape down the sides of the bowl with a flexible spatula, until the mixture is completely smooth and slightly fluffy, about 1 minute. Add the egg and beat until incorporated, then reduce the speed to low, add the dry ingredients, and mix just until you have a smooth, stiff, evenly mixed dough. Scrape the dough out onto a piece of reusable food wrap or plastic wrap and press it into a ¾-inch-thick rectangle. Wrap it tightly and refrigerate until the dough is very firm, at least 2 hours.

PREHEAT THE OVEN: Arrange an oven rack in the center position and preheat the oven to 350°F.

PRESS THE CRUST INTO THE PAN: Unwrap the chilled dough and cut it in half, making one half slightly larger than the other. Wrap and return the smaller half to the refrigerator, then take the larger half and pinch off small pieces, flattening each piece slightly between your fingertips and pressing it into the bottom and up the sides of a 9-inch removable-bottom tart pan. Continue until you've used the entire portion of dough and covered just about the entire pan. Use a flat hand (floured, if necessary, to prevent sticking) to pat the dough across the bottom and up the sides, closing any gaps and evening out the thickness. Then use a straight-sided glass or 1-cup dry measure to smooth the surface of the dough and press it further up the sides until the dough extends just above the edge of the pan, flouring the glass or measuring cup as needed. Transfer the pan to the freezer and chill until the dough is firm, 10 to 15 minutes.

TRIM AND FILL THE CRUST: Remove the pan from the freezer and place on a sheet pan. Hold a paring knife parallel to the sheet pan and slice horizontally around the rim of the pan, removing the excess dough and creating a smooth edge flush with the top of the pan. Scrape 2 cups (20.2 oz / 573g) of the chilled jam into the tart pan and smooth it into an even layer all the way to the sides (if you have slightly more than 2 cups, save any remaining jam for spreading on toast or eating with yogurt). Set the sheet pan aside.

ROLL OUT AND CUT THE REMAINING DOUGH: Let the smaller portion of dough sit at room temperature for a few minutes to soften slightly, then unwrap it and place on a lightly floured surface. Dust the top with flour and roll out the dough, adding more flour as needed, to a rough rectangle measuring approximately 11 × 9½ inches. Use a knife or wheel cutter to cut the dough crosswise into 10 strips each measuring 1 inch wide and 9½ inches long (discard any scraps).

FORM THE LATTICE: Arrange the strips in a crisscrossing pattern across the surface of the tart, placing 5 in each direction and spacing them evenly. Don't attempt to weave the strips, as the dough is delicate and won't hold up to lots of manipulation. Where the strips meet the edge of the crust, gently press each strip into the edge and then pinch off and discard the excess.

BAKE: Transfer the sheet pan to the oven and bake until the crust is golden brown all over and the jam filling is darkened in color and bubbling around the sides, 45 to 55 minutes. Transfer the tart to a wire rack to cool completely. Press up on the bottom of the tart pan to pop it out of the fluted ring.

Cinnamon-&-Sugar Apple Pie

I'm a believer that not every apple recipe needs cinnamon, so I frequently use other complementary warm spices such as cardamom, clove, allspice, or nutmeg in apple desserts. That said, the combination of apples and cinnamon is pretty singular, and it does give pie that all-American feel. Proper pie assembly will always require a series of steps, not to mention peeling and slicing all the apples, but this one is as simple as it gets. I learned while testing this recipe that I actually prefer thicker slices of apples for pie, since they become translucent and soft during baking without turning mushy. With little more than some cinnamon, brown sugar, and butter to highlight it, the apple flavor shines loud and clear, making this my go-to apple pie from this point forward.

SERVES 8

DIFFICULTY: 3 (Moderate)

ACTIVE TIME: 1 hour (does not include making the pastry)

TOTAL TIME: 3 hours, plus time to cool

SPECIAL EQUIPMENT: 9-inch pie plate (preferably glass)

2½ teaspoons ground cinnamon

⅓ cup granulated sugar (2.4 oz / 67g)

⅓ cup packed dark brown sugar (2.5 oz / 70g)

3 tablespoons cornstarch

½ teaspoon finely grated orange zest

Pinch of kosher salt

3 pounds (1.4kg) firm sweet-tart apples (about 7 medium-large), such as Pink Lady, peeled, cored, and cut into ½-inch-thick wedges (about 8 cups)

2 teaspoons apple cider vinegar

2 teaspoons vanilla extract

1 tablespoon orange bitters or Angostura bitters (optional)

2 round portions **All-Purpose Flaky Pastry Dough** (page 331), chilled

All-purpose flour, for rolling

3 tablespoons unsalted butter, melted and cooled, divided

Vanilla ice cream, for serving

PREHEAT THE OVEN AND PREPARE THE SHEET PAN: Arrange an oven rack in the lower third of the oven and preheat it to 400°F. Line a sheet pan with a silicone baking mat or foil and set aside.

MAKE THE CINNAMON-SUGAR: In a large bowl, whisk together the cinnamon and granulated sugar to combine. Transfer 2 tablespoons of the cinnamon-sugar to a separate small bowl and set aside for sprinkling over the assembled pie.

MAKE THE FILLING: To the large bowl with the remaining cinnamon-sugar mixture, add the brown sugar, cornstarch, orange zest, and salt and whisk to combine. Add the apple slices, vinegar, vanilla, and bitters (if using) and toss the mixture with clean hands or a large flexible spatula until the apples are evenly coated. Set the filling aside.

ROLL OUT THE FIRST PIECE OF DOUGH: Let 1 portion of the dough sit at room temperature for a minute or two to soften slightly, then unwrap it and place on a lightly floured surface. Use a rolling pin to beat the dough all across the surface to make it more pliable. Dust more flour underneath and on top of the dough, then roll it out, dusting with more flour as needed, into a 13-inch round (for step-by-step visuals, see Rolling Out Chilled Pastry Dough, page 332).

LINE THE PIE PLATE AND ROLL OUT THE REMAINING DOUGH: Transfer the round to a 9-inch pie plate, preferably glass, centering it and letting the dough slump down the sides into the bottom. Firmly press the dough into the bottom and up the sides of the plate, ensuring contact everywhere and taking care not to stretch it. Transfer the lined pie plate to the refrigerator. Roll out the second portion of dough just as you did the first and set it aside at room temperature.

FILL THE PIE: Remove the lined pie plate from the refrigerator and scrape in about one-quarter of the apple filling. Fit the apple slices around the bottom of the plate to minimize gaps (this will help reduce shrinkage of the filling during baking). Scrape in the rest of the apples along with any juices that accumulated in the bowl and mound the filling in the pie plate, pressing down to compact. Drizzle the apples with 2 tablespoons of the melted butter.

→

ASSEMBLE THE PIE: Brush the border of dough around the filling with water. Place the second round of dough over the pie, letting it slump over the filling. Press very firmly all the way around the rim of the pie plate with your fingertips to seal the two layers of dough together, then use a paring knife to trim away the excess dough from around the rim. Using the tines of a fork, press around the border of the pie again to crimp it, dipping the tines in flour if needed to prevent sticking.

> *Optional Upgrade:* Chill the pastry scraps, sprinkle them with sugar, bake, and enjoy as a snack.

FINISH AND CHILL THE PIE: Brush the entire surface of the pie with the remaining 1 tablespoon melted butter, then sprinkle the reserved 2 tablespoons cinnamon-sugar evenly over the top. Freeze the assembled pie until the dough is cold and firm, 10 to 15 minutes, then use the paring knife to cut several slits in the lid to allow steam to escape during baking.

Can I . . .

Make it ahead? Yes. The pie, covered loosely and stored at room temperature, will keep for up to 4 days but is best served on the first or second day while the pastry is still crisp.

BAKE AND SERVE: Place the pie on the prepared sheet pan and bake for 20 minutes, then reduce the oven temperature to 350°F and continue to bake until the surface is deeply browned and the pastry is golden brown on the bottom (which you can only see if the plate is glass), another 1 hour to 1 hour 30 minutes. Remove the pie from the oven and let cool completely before slicing and serving with vanilla ice cream.

Fried Sour Cherry Pies

As frequently as cherries pop up in this book, I felt like I couldn't *not* include some variation on sour cherry pie, a dessert that's quite special to me, so I adapted my definitive recipe for Sour Cherry Pie from *Dessert Person* into these fried mini pies. I call for frozen sour cherries because unless you're making this in certain parts of the country in early July, that's what's available (I keep a year-round stash of frozen cherries that I pit and freeze in the summer when they're in season). There's an advantage to frozen, which is that they more readily release their juices, which can then be cooked down and thickened so the filling doesn't ooze out of the pastry. At first it was a toss-up whether I should file this recipe here or in the Stovetop Desserts chapter, since the oven plays no role, but I decided that these are first and foremost pies—flaky, golden, glossy pies. If, however, you'd like to bake these, see Can I . . . on page 272.

MAKES 8 MINI PIES

DIFFICULTY: 3 (Moderate)

ACTIVE TIME: 1 hour 30 minutes (does not include making the pastry)

TOTAL TIME: 3 hours 30 minutes

SPECIAL EQUIPMENT: Deep-fry thermometer, medium Dutch oven (or large heavy-bottomed saucepan)

1¾ pounds (795g) frozen pitted sour cherries, thawed (about 5⅔ cups)

⅔ cup granulated sugar (4.7 oz / 133g)

¼ teaspoon Diamond Crystal kosher salt or ⅛ teaspoon Morton kosher salt, plus a generous pinch

3 tablespoons cornstarch

1 teaspoon finely grated lemon zest

¼ teaspoon ground cinnamon

⅛ teaspoon almond extract

1½ teaspoons vanilla extract, divided

2 rectangular portions **All-Purpose Flaky Pastry Dough** (page 331), chilled

All-purpose flour, for rolling

6 cups neutral oil (2.9 lb / 1.3kg), such as peanut, for deep-frying

1¼ cups confectioners' sugar (4.9 oz / 138g)

1 tablespoon milk

2 teaspoons fresh lemon juice

COOK THE CHERRIES: Place a large mesh sieve over a medium bowl and set aside. In a large saucepan, combine the thawed cherries (plus any juices), granulated sugar, and salt and bring to a boil over medium-high heat, stirring gently to dissolve the sugar. Reduce the heat to medium-low and simmer the cherries, swirling the saucepan, just until they've softened and released their juices, 1 to 2 minutes. Remove the saucepan from the heat and pour the mixture through the sieve (reserve the saucepan). Allow the cherries to drain for several seconds, shaking the sieve to encourage the juices to fall into the bowl.

REDUCE THE CHERRY JUICES: Pour the juices back into the reserved saucepan, then place the mesh sieve back over the bowl so the cherries can continue to drain. Bring the juices to a boil over medium-high heat and cook, whisking occasionally, until the liquid is reduced to ¾ cup, 8 to 10 minutes (check the volume by pouring it into a heatproof glass measuring, then return to the saucepan and continue to reduce if it's not there yet). While the mixture is reducing, pour any extra cherry juices that accumulated in the bowl into the saucepan. Remove the saucepan from the heat.

THICKEN THE JUICES AND MAKE THE FILLING: Place the cornstarch in a small bowl and slowly add 3 tablespoons (1.5 oz / 42g) cool tap water, stirring constantly with a fork until smooth, then whisk the mixture into the saucepan. Place the saucepan back over medium-high heat and cook, whisking constantly, just until the mixture is bubbling, thick, gelatinous, and glossy, about 4 minutes. Remove the saucepan from the heat and whisk in the lemon zest, cinnamon, almond extract, and ½ teaspoon of the vanilla. Discard any additional liquid the cherries released, then place the cherries inside the medium bowl and scrape in the thickened juices. Fold the filling gently to combine, then refrigerate uncovered, stirring occasionally, until it's cold, about 1 hour (if chilling any longer, cover the bowl).

> *Potential Pitfall:* Make sure the juices are very thick and bubbling before you remove the saucepan from the heat, or the cornstarch won't fully activate, resulting in a runny filling (and pies that are difficult to form).

ROLL OUT AND CUT THE DOUGH: Let 1 portion of dough sit at room temperature for a minute or two to soften slightly, then unwrap it and place on a lightly floured surface. Use a rolling pin to beat the dough all across

→

the surface to make it more pliable. Dust more flour underneath and on top of the dough, then roll it out, dusting with more flour as needed, into a 12-inch square (for step-by-step visuals, see Rolling Out Chilled Pastry Dough, page 332). Trim away about a ½-inch-wide strip of dough from all four sides to make an even 11-inch square with straight sides and sharp corners (discard the scraps). Cut the square in half in both directions, forming 4 equal 5½-inch squares. Place the squares on a sheet pan, cover, and refrigerate. Repeat the same rolling and cutting process for the second portion of dough, placing the second batch of 4 squares on the same sheet pan (it's okay to stack or overlap them). Keep all 8 squares covered and refrigerated until the cherry filling is cold.

FORM THE PIES: Remove the filling and one of the dough squares from the refrigerator and place both on the work surface. Stir the filling gently to recombine. Orient the pastry like a diamond, then scrape ¼ cup of the filling (2.6 oz / 75g) onto one triangular half of the diamond, leaving a wide, clean border of dough along the outer edges. Brush the border of the entire diamond with water, then fold the uncovered half up and over the filling, aligning the corners and edges and doing your best to eliminate any air pockets, to make a triangular pie (if any filling oozes out of the pastry as you fold it, just wipe it away). Using your fingertips, press lightly along the two shorter sides to help the dough adhere to itself, then press the tines of a fork firmly along the same sides, making ½-inch-long tine marks to seal (dip the tines in flour if necessary to prevent sticking). Use a knife to trim away a thin strip of dough from the crimped sides to straighten them. Place the pie on a small sheet pan or platter, cover, and transfer to the freezer. Repeat the forming process with the remaining dough squares and filling, placing the pies one by one in the freezer as you form them. Keep the pies covered in the freezer while you heat the oil.

HEAT THE OIL: Clip a deep-fry thermometer to the side of a medium Dutch oven or large heavy-bottomed saucepan and add the oil until it reaches between one-third and halfway up the sides, but no higher (if you have any remaining oil, save it for another use). Heat the oil over medium-high heat until it reaches 325°F. Reduce the heat to medium and continue to heat the oil until it registers 350°F on the thermometer. While it's heating, line a large sheet pan with paper towels and set a wire rack on top, then place it next to the stovetop.

FRY THE PIES: Remove 3 of the pies from the freezer and slide them gently into the hot oil one at a time. Fry the pies, turning them delicately with a pair of tongs every few minutes (they will not float), until they're deep golden brown all over, 6 to 8 minutes. Transfer the pies to the wire rack, then repeat the frying process in two more batches with the remaining pies, transferring them to the wire rack as they're done.

Potential Pitfall: Pay attention to the oil temperature throughout the process—adding the cold pies will cause the temperature to drop, so increase the heat until it comes back to 350°F and then adjust as needed to maintain that temperature (or thereabouts).

GLAZE THE PIES: In a medium bowl, combine the confectioners' sugar, milk, lemon juice, a generous pinch of salt, and the remaining 1 teaspoon vanilla extract and whisk until you have a smooth, pourable glaze. If the glaze is too thick to fall off the whisk in a steady stream, whisk in 1 teaspoon of water at a time to thin it out. When the pies are cool, arrange them on the rack so the nicer sides are facing up, then drizzle the glaze across the surfaces, allowing the excess to drip off. Let the pies sit until the glaze is set, about 5 minutes, then serve immediately.

Can I . . .

Bake instead of fry them? Yes. Form the pies as written, but brush the borders of the pastry with beaten egg rather than water. Preheat the oven to 375°F, arranging one rack in the upper third and another in the lower third. Place the chilled pies on two parchment-lined sheet pans, spacing evenly, and brush the surfaces with beaten egg. Use a paring knife to cut a 1-inch slit in each pie, then bake until the pastry is deep golden brown, 40 to 50 minutes, switching racks and rotating the pans front to back after 25 minutes. Let the pies cool completely on the pans, then glaze as directed.

Make them ahead? Just the filling. The pies should be eaten within a few hours of frying, but the cherry filling, covered and refrigerated, will keep for up to 2 weeks.

Halve the recipe? Yes. Halve all of the ingredient quantities except the oil and use a single portion of the flaky pastry. Cook the filling in a small saucepan, reducing the juices to ⅓ cup, and fry the pies two at a time.

Walnut & Oat Slab Pie

The flavors of this pie are inspired by a bowl of hearty oatmeal—a breakfast that feels simultaneously nourishing and like a special treat. I take mine lightly sweetened with a little maple syrup, enriched with butter, and topped with walnuts and a pinch of cinnamon. For this pie filling, oats are cooked in browned butter and cream until the mixture is thick, then it's whisked into the brown sugar base. While it quite literally recalls oatmeal, the pie is also a faithful, delicious, and corn syrup-free interpretation of the classic pecan pie recipe from Karo syrup, so consider it for your Thanksgiving dessert table. This is the only pie in the book that requires weighting the crust and baking it prior to adding the filling and baking it again, a process called parbaking. It's an extra few steps, but if you follow the method below, you will have a crisp and not soggy crust, which for me makes the parbaking essential.

SERVES 12

DIFFICULTY: 3 (Moderate)

ACTIVE TIME: 1 hour 15 minutes (does not include making the pastry)

TOTAL TIME: 2 hours 25 minutes, plus time to cool

SPECIAL EQUIPMENT: 13 × 9-inch quarter-sheet pan, 4 cups dried beans or rice (for pie weights)

3 cups walnut halves and/or pieces (12 oz / 342g)

3 tablespoons plus ½ cup old-fashioned rolled oats (1.9 oz / 55g)

All-Purpose Flaky Pastry Dough (page 331), all the dough in one rectangular piece, chilled

All-purpose flour, for rolling

1½ sticks unsalted butter (6 oz / 170g)

1 cup heavy cream (8.5 oz / 240g), at room temperature

3 large eggs (5.3 oz / 150g), at room temperature

4 large egg yolks (2.1 oz / 60g), at room temperature

¾ cup packed dark brown sugar (5.8 oz / 165g)

⅓ cup maple syrup (4 oz / 113g)

2 teaspoons vanilla extract

1½ teaspoons Diamond Crystal kosher salt or ¾ teaspoon Morton kosher salt

½ teaspoon ground cinnamon

PREHEAT THE OVEN: Arrange an oven rack in the center position and preheat the oven to 400°F.

TOAST THE NUTS AND SOME OF THE OATS: Scatter the walnuts and 3 tablespoons of the oats on a sheet pan and toast until the walnuts are golden brown and fragrant, 7 to 10 minutes, tossing halfway through. Set the pan aside and let the nuts and oats cool. Leave the oven on for parbaking the crust.

PORTION THE DOUGH: Remove the dough from the refrigerator and unwrap. You will need two-thirds of the total dough for this slab pie, so use a knife or bench scraper to slice off about one-third of the dough. Wrap the smaller piece and return to the refrigerator for another use (or freeze).

ROLL OUT THE DOUGH: Let the dough sit at room temperature for a minute or two to soften slightly, then place it on a lightly floured surface. Use a rolling pin to beat the dough all across the surface to make it more pliable. Dust more flour underneath and on top of the dough, then roll it out, dusting with more flour as needed, into a rectangle measuring about 15 × 12 inches (for step-by-step visuals, see Rolling Out Chilled Pastry Dough, page 332).

LINE THE QUARTER-SHEET PAN: Roll the pastry onto the rolling pin, then unroll it onto a 13 × 9-inch quarter-sheet pan, centering it so you have equal overhang along all four sides. Firmly press the pastry into the bottom and against the sides of the pan, ensuring contact everywhere and taking care not to stretch it. Use scissors to trim the edges of the dough, leaving a ½-inch overhang all the way around (discard the scraps). Tuck the overhang underneath itself so you have a thick border of dough resting on the rim of the pan along all four sides. Using your thumb on one hand and your thumb and forefinger on the other, crimp the border, flouring your fingers as needed to prevent sticking.

PARBAKE THE CRUST: Freeze the pan until the dough is very firm, 10 to 15 minutes, then prick the dough in several places across the bottom of the pan with a fork to prevent it from puffing up as it bakes. Line the pan with a double layer of foil, pressing the pieces into the bottom and up the sides and leaving several inches of overhang on all sides. Fold the overhang down and over the crimped edge of the dough to cover. Fill the pan with dried

→

beans or rice and spread them in an even layer, then place the lined pan on a larger sheet pan. Bake until the edge of the crust is set and starting to turn golden when you peek underneath the foil, 25 to 30 minutes, then remove it from the oven. Leave the oven on and reduce the temperature to 325°F.

CONTINUE BAKING THE CRUST: Very carefully use the overhanging foil to lift the pie weights out of the crust and set them aside. Return the sheet pan to the oven and bake until the crust is golden brown across the bottom, 25 to 30 minutes longer, then remove it from the oven. While the crust is baking, prepare the filling.

COOK THE BUTTER AND REMAINING OATS: In a small saucepan, combine the butter and remaining ½ cup (1.4 oz / 40g) oats and cook over medium heat, stirring occasionally with a heatproof flexible spatula, until the butter is melted. Increase the heat to medium-high and bring the mixture to a boil, stirring constantly. Continue to cook, stirring all the while, until the oats are deep golden brown and the butter is foaming and you see tiny brown specks swimming in the foam, 10 to 15 minutes. Remove the saucepan from the heat.

ADD THE CREAM: Slowly add the cream to the saucepan, stirring constantly (be careful, it will sputter aggressively at first). Once all the cream is added, bring the mixture to a simmer over medium-low heat and cook, stirring constantly, until it's thickened to the consistency of a loose porridge, about 2 minutes. Remove the saucepan from the heat and set aside.

MAKE THE FILLING: In a large bowl, whisk together the whole eggs, egg yolks, brown sugar, maple syrup, vanilla, salt, and cinnamon until the eggs are broken up, then whisk vigorously until the mixture is completely smooth and streak-free. Whisking constantly, slowly pour in the hot cream mixture. Set the filling aside until the crust is finished parbaking.

ASSEMBLE THE PIE AND BAKE: Scatter the toasted walnuts and oats across the bottom of the hot parbaked crust in an even layer. Whisk the filling again and pour it into the crust, evenly distributing the cooked oats that have settled to the bottom of the bowl (the heat in the crust will set the bottom layer of filling quickly, preventing sogginess, and will help the pie bake faster). Transfer the sheet pan to the oven and bake until the filling is slightly puffed and the center is firm to the touch, 22 to 28 minutes. Transfer the pie to a wire rack to cool completely.

Can I . . .

Make it ahead? Yes. The pie, covered loosely and stored at room temperature, will keep for up to 4 days but is best served on the first or second day while the crust is crisp (it will soften over time).

Use a different nut? Yes! Use an equal quantity of pecans in place of the walnuts.

More Desserts from the Oven

Baked Custards & Puddings, Soufflés & Meringue Desserts

I initially thought of this chapter as a catchall for any baked dessert that didn't fall into one of the other oven-focused chapters—in other words, it was for not-cookies, not-cakes, and not-pies. But, after making all of them, I clearly see that these recipes constitute a distinct category unto themselves. While there are a few outliers, like the **Baked Frangipane Apples** (page 284) and **Spiced Pear Charlotte with Brioche** (page 287), the rest of the custards, baked puddings, soufflés, and meringue desserts in this chapter rely on the unique properties of egg whites and yolks to achieve silky, smooth, light, and/or airy ends inside the oven. This makes them largely gluten-free, as eggs are the ingredient lending structure rather than flour. The dishes as a whole contain a satisfying symmetry: If you make **Cajeta Pots de Crème** (page 279), which require egg yolks, you can use the whites to make **Black Sesame Merveilleux** (page 323) or another meringue dessert.

Because there's a specific temperature at which eggs will set or thicken a mixture, egg-based dishes are a little technical. A soufflé or custard needs to be removed from the oven right at the point of doneness or it risks being under- or overcooked. To ensure even and gentle cooking, many of the recipes are baked in a water bath, so you'll need a roasting pan or large shallow baking vessel to set this up (see Baking in a Water Bath, page 358, for more info). You might also want to invest in a set of glass custard cups or ramekins, as several recipes are baked and served individually (it's a sound investment—they're inexpensive and useful). While the cooking process requires some precision, the assembly is often quick and easy. **Baked Semolina Pudding with Clementines & Bay Leaves** (page 283) and **Inverted Affogatos** (page 294), for example, require few ingredients and little effort. Believe me when I say that these are doable desserts, even for beginners, and that a perfectly crackly **Crème Brûlée** (page 291) or lofty, light-as-a-feather **Kabocha & Ginger Soufflés** (page 317) are wholly within your reach.

Cajeta Pots de Crème

A less-than-successful attempt at making pots de crème in culinary school put me off this dessert for a while, which is regrettable because it's super luxurious. Simple custards baked gently in small cups inside a water bath until smooth and silky, pots de crème are a great example of how a little technique can transform a few ingredients into something greater than the sum of its parts. The principal flavor here is Mexican cajeta, a sauce or spread made from caramelized goat milk. You can find cajeta in Mexican grocery stores and some specialty shops (it's sometimes labeled a goat caramel "spread" or "topping"). One common brand is Coronado, which has a few added ingredients and a more fluid consistency, but some small-batch brands, which only use sugar and goat's milk and tend to be thicker, are also available. Either option works, though you'll get a more concentrated flavor from small-batch cajeta. If, however, you can't find it at all, dulce de leche is a close substitute.

SERVES 8

DIFFICULTY: 1 (Very Easy)

GLUTEN-FREE

ACTIVE TIME: 25 minutes

TOTAL TIME: 5 hours (includes 4 hours for chilling)

SPECIAL EQUIPMENT: 8-cup glass measuring cup (optional); eight 6-ounce custard cups, ramekins, or ovenproof glass bowls; roasting pan or large shallow baking dish

2 cups whole milk (16 oz / 480g)

1 cup cajeta or dulce de leche (13.2 oz / 375g)

1 teaspoon Diamond Crystal kosher salt or ½ teaspoon Morton kosher salt

Seeds scraped from ½ vanilla bean (pod reserved) or 1 teaspoon vanilla extract

2 cups heavy cream (16 oz / 480g), chilled, divided

4 large egg yolks (2.1 oz / 60g), at room temperature

2 large eggs (3.5 oz / 100g), at room temperature

3 tablespoons sugar

PREHEAT THE OVEN: Arrange an oven rack in the center position and preheat the oven to 300°F.

HEAT THE MILK MIXTURE: In a small saucepan, combine the milk, cajeta, salt, vanilla seeds and pod (if using vanilla extract, set it aside for later), and 1 cup (8.5 oz / 240g) of the cream. Place the mixture over medium heat, whisking occasionally to dissolve the cajeta and disperse the vanilla seeds, until it's steaming and just starting to ripple beneath the surface, about 5 minutes, then remove from the heat and set aside (leave the vanilla pod in the saucepan so it can continue to infuse the mixture).

BLANCH AND TEMPER THE EGGS: In a medium bowl, whisk together the egg yolks, whole eggs, and sugar until combined, then whisk vigorously until the mixture is slightly pale and thickened, about 1 minute. Whisking the egg mixture constantly, slowly pour the hot milk mixture into the bowl to temper the eggs (for more information, see Blanching and Tempering Eggs, page 348).

STRAIN THE CUSTARD: Pass the custard through a fine-mesh sieve and into an 8-cup glass measuring cup, pitcher, or separate medium bowl (a pour spout makes it easier to fill the cups). Discard the vanilla pod and any solids that were caught in the sieve. If using vanilla extract, stir it in now.

FILL AND COVER THE CUPS: Divide the custard evenly among eight 6-ounce custard cups, ramekins, or ovenproof glass bowls (they will be filled nearly to the top). Cut eight squares of foil large enough to cover each cup, then cover each with foil, making sure that the foil doesn't touch the surface of the custard (it does not need to be tightly sealed). Holding the foil taut, use a toothpick to poke a couple of small holes in each foil lid to allow steam to escape, then set the cups aside.

PREPARE THE WATER BATH: Bring 6 cups of water to a boil in a kettle or in a medium saucepan over high heat. While the water is heating, select a roasting pan or shallow baking dish large enough to hold the eight custard cups, line it with a thin kitchen towel, and smooth any wrinkles (this is optional but recommended to prevent the cups from sliding around). Place the cups inside the roasting pan, spacing them evenly and ensuring that they're level on the towel.

$\rightarrow$

Can I . . .

Make it ahead? Yes. The baked pots de crème, covered and refrigerated, will keep for up to 3 days. Top with the whipped cream right before serving.

Halve the recipe? Yes. Halve all of the ingredient quantities and follow the recipe as written, baking the custards in four cups. Note that they will fit in a smaller baking dish and bake slightly faster, so start checking them for doneness at 23 minutes.

Use a mix of different vessels for baking the pots de crème? Yes, but . . . only if they have the same volume capacity and are similar in height, otherwise the custards will not bake evenly.

Use two shallow baking dishes for the water bath if I don't have a large enough roasting pan? Yes. Any shallow baking dish with 2-inch-high sides will work for the water bath.

BAKE: Partially slide out the oven rack and transfer the roasting pan to the rack. Slowly and carefully pour the boiling water just inside the edge of the pan until it comes halfway up the sides of the cups (the amount of water needed will depend on the size of the pan). Try not to splash the water as you pour, although the foil will shield the custards. Slide the rack gently into the oven and bake until the custards set around the edges but slightly wobbly in the centers, 28 to 33 minutes. To test for doneness, use a pair of tongs to remove one of the foil lids and gently jostle the cup to look for wobbling. If the pots de crème need more time, press the foil back over the cup and continue to bake, checking them every couple of minutes. Carefully remove the pan from the oven.

COOL AND CHILL THE POTS DE CRÈME: Allow the pots de crème to rest in the hot water for 5 minutes, then carefully slide a spatula underneath the cups and transfer them one at a time—still covered with foil—to a wire rack. Let them sit at room temperature until they're cool enough to handle, then transfer to the refrigerator and chill until cold, at least 4 hours.

WHIP THE CREAM: In a medium bowl, with a whisk or hand mixer, whip the remaining 1 cup (8.5 oz / 240g) cream on low speed to start and gradually increase the speed to medium-high as it thickens, until you have a softly whipped cream that holds a droopy peak (see Whipping Cream, page 355).

SERVE: Uncover the pots de crème (save the foil squares for making future pots de crème), top with a dollop of the whipped cream, and serve.

Baked Semolina Pudding

with Clementines & Bay Leaves

This spoonable, custardy, clafoutis-like dessert is made from an egg-enriched semolina porridge and flavored with bay leaves (not typically added to sweets, but their flavor pairs so well with the citrus and honey here). I love the nuttiness of semolina, and to add a little brightness and textural variety to the warm pudding, I add simmered citrus slices and toasted pine nuts on top. Even in a chapter full of desserts that all check the comfort food box, this stands out as a supremely satisfying dish.

SERVES 8

DIFFICULTY: 1 (Very Easy)

ACTIVE TIME: 40 minutes

TOTAL TIME: 1 hour 10 minutes, plus time to cool

SPECIAL EQUIPMENT: 2-quart shallow baking dish

Butter for the baking dish

2 clementine or satsuma tangerines (about 6 oz / 170g), sliced into thin rounds, seeds and ends discarded

8 tablespoons granulated sugar (3.5 oz / 100g), divided

2 tablespoons honey, divided

4 bay leaves, divided

3 cups whole milk (25.4 oz / 720g)

1 teaspoon Diamond Crystal kosher salt or ½ teaspoon Morton kosher salt

½ cup semolina flour (2.4 oz / 68g)

4 tablespoons unsalted butter (2 oz / 57g), cut into pieces, chilled

1 teaspoon vanilla extract

1 teaspoon finely grated lemon zest

4 large eggs (7 oz / 200g), cold from the refrigerator

2 tablespoons pine nuts

Can I . . .

Make it ahead? Yes, but . . . wait to bake it. The pudding is best served warm from the oven, but you can assemble it in the prepared baking dish, top with the citrus slices, and cover and refrigerate it for up to 24 hours. Uncover and bake the pudding right from the refrigerator (it will take a few minutes longer to bake).

Make it gluten-free? No. Semolina is a type of wheat, and since it's the predominant flavor in the dish, it can't be substituted.

Bake this in a different pan? Yes. You can bake the pudding in any shallow pan with a 2-quart capacity, such as an 8 × 8-inch baking pan or a 9-inch cake pan.

PREHEAT THE OVEN AND PREPARE THE BAKING DISH: Arrange an oven rack in the upper third of the oven and preheat the oven to 425°F. Brush the bottom and sides of a 2-quart shallow baking dish with room temperature butter and set aside.

COOK THE CITRUS IN SYRUP: Place the clementine slices in a small saucepan and add water to cover them by about ½ inch. Bring to a boil over medium-high heat. Immediately drain the slices in a mesh sieve, then return the slices to the saucepan and add 2 tablespoons sugar, 1 tablespoon honey, 2 bay leaves, and enough water to barely cover the citrus. Bring the mixture to a simmer over low heat, swirling often to dissolve the sugar, and continue to cook, swirling, until the layer of white pith around each slice has turned orange and slightly translucent, 12 to 18 minutes. Gently transfer the slices and syrupy liquid to a small heatproof bowl and set aside to cool. Reserve the saucepan.

COOK THE SEMOLINA: In the reserved saucepan, combine the milk, salt, and the remaining 6 tablespoons (2.6 oz / 75g) sugar, 1 tablespoon honey, and 2 bay leaves. Bring the mixture to a simmer over medium-high heat, whisking a few times to dissolve the sugar and honey, then, whisking constantly, very slowly sprinkle in the semolina. Continue to whisk until the mixture is bubbling and thick enough to hold the marks of the whisk, about 5 minutes. Remove the saucepan from the heat and scrape the semolina mixture into a medium bowl. Whisk in the butter one piece at a time, waiting for each piece to disappear before adding the next, until all the butter is incorporated and the mixture is smooth. Whisk in the vanilla and lemon zest, then set the bowl aside to cool for about 5 minutes.

ADD THE EGGS: Whisk the eggs into the semolina mixture one at a time, thoroughly incorporating each before adding the next. Continue to whisk until the mixture is smooth, then pluck out the bay leaves and discard.

ASSEMBLE: Scrape the warm semolina mixture into the prepared baking dish and smooth the surface. Arrange the cooled clementine slices over the surface of the pudding, overlapping them as needed, and reserve the clementine syrup in the bowl for brushing over the pudding later.

BAKE AND SERVE: Bake the pudding on the upper rack until the edges are puffed and the surface is pale but set, 15 to 20 minutes. Remove the baking dish from the oven and brush the entire surface liberally with the reserved syrup (you don't need to use it all). Sprinkle the pine nuts across the surface, then return the baking dish to the upper rack and bake until the pudding is deep golden brown around the edges and the pine nuts are golden, another 15 to 20 minutes. Let the pudding cool until it's warm, then scoop into bowls and serve.

Baked Frangipane Apples

A dish of whole baked apples strikes me as one of the homiest and most comforting dishes ever. Even though apples generally do amazing things in the oven, baked apples can easily go sideways, turning mealy, mushy, and dry, so I had to do a little engineering. I bake the apples low and slow in a covered baking dish with a layer of cream in the bottom for added moisture, then let them bake uncovered until tender. Rather than the typical filling of brown sugar and nuts, frangipane, aka almond cream, is piped into the cavities, giving the dish a French makeover. As the apples bake, some of the frangipane cascades into the bottom of the baking dish, mingles with the cream, and caramelizes into its own chewy layer. A final drizzle of cream for serving provides a cold, rich contrast to the warm, soft apples.

SERVES 8

DIFFICULTY: 1 (Very Easy)

ACTIVE TIME: 50 minutes

TOTAL TIME: 2 hours 30 minutes

SPECIAL EQUIPMENT: Hand mixer, 13 × 9-inch baking dish, pastry bag (or resealable plastic bag), apple corer

1 cup almond flour (3.4 oz / 96g)

½ cup sliced almonds (2 oz / 57g)

½ cup sugar (3.5 oz / 100g)

6 tablespoons unsalted butter (3 oz / 85g), at room temperature, plus more for the foil

1 large egg (1.8 oz / 50g), at room temperature

2 tablespoons dark rum

½ teaspoon almond extract

2 tablespoons all-purpose flour

½ teaspoon Diamond Crystal kosher salt or ¼ teaspoon Morton kosher salt

8 small firm sweet-tart apples, such as Pink Lady (about 2¾ pounds / 1.25kg)

1¾ cups heavy cream (14.8 oz / 420g), chilled, divided

PREHEAT THE OVEN: Arrange an oven rack in the center position and preheat the oven to 325°F.

TOAST THE ALMONDS: Spread the almond flour across one half of a large sheet pan in an even layer, scatter the sliced almonds across the other half, and toast until both are golden brown and fragrant, 5 to 8 minutes, tossing the sliced almonds and stirring the almond flour halfway through. Let cool completely on the pan. Leave the oven on.

MAKE THE FRANGIPANE: In a medium bowl, with a hand mixer, beat the sugar and butter on medium-high speed until the mixture is light and fluffy, pausing occasionally and using a flexible spatula to scrape down the sides of the bowl, about 3 minutes. Add the egg and beat on medium until thoroughly incorporated, then beat in the rum and almond extract. Stop the mixer and scrape down the sides of the bowl. The mixture may look slightly broken (meaning the liquid is separated from the solids), but that's normal. Add the all-purpose flour, salt, and toasted almond flour and beat on medium until you have a smooth mixture. Set the toasted sliced almonds aside for serving.

TRANSFER TO A PASTRY BAG: Scrape the frangipane into a pastry bag or resealable plastic bag, squeeze out the air, and twist or seal to close (see Filling a Pastry Bag, page 342). Set it aside.

PREPARE THE APPLES: Set the apples on a cutting board and use a sharp knife to slice off a thin piece of flesh from the base and stem ends of each apple, creating two flat surfaces. Use a vegetable peeler to remove several strips of peel from around each apple, peeling from top to bottom, giving them a striped look. Working one at a time, stand the apples upright and use an apple corer to cut out the cores (discard the cores and peels). Place the cored apples upright inside a 13 × 9-inch baking dish.

FILL THE APPLES: Snip a ½-inch opening in the tip or corner of the bag, then place the opening just inside the hollow center of one of the apples and squeeze until you've filled the entire cavity. Repeat until all the apples are filled. Then, dividing the remaining frangipane evenly, pipe generous dollops on the cut surfaces at the tops of the apples.

→

Can I . . .

Make them ahead? Yes, but . . . wait to bake them. The apples are best eaten warm from the oven, but you can fill them, arrange inside the baking dish, cover, and refrigerate for up to 4 hours before baking. Bake them directly from the refrigerator, and don't forget to pour in the cream.

Halve the recipe? Yes. Halve all of the ingredient quantities, with these exceptions: Use ⅓ cup (2.8 oz / 80g) heavy cream for the bottom of the baking dish and 1 yolk in the frangipane rather than ½ egg. Proceed with the recipe as written, filling 4 apples and baking them in a 2-quart shallow baking dish or a 9-inch round cake pan.

Use a stand mixer instead of a hand mixer? Yes. To make the frangipane, combine the sugar and butter in a stand mixer fitted with the paddle attachment and proceed with the recipe as written.

Make it without a mixer? Yes. To make the frangipane by hand, use a flexible spatula to beat the sugar and butter in a medium bowl until light and fluffy, about 5 minutes. Switch to a whisk, add the egg, and whisk until thoroughly combined, then whisk in the rum and almond extract until smooth. Add the all-purpose flour, salt, and cooled toasted almond flour and whisk until the frangipane is smooth, then proceed with the recipe as written.

Make it gluten-free? Yes. Replace the all-purpose flour with an equal amount of your preferred gluten-free flour blend.

ADD THE CREAM, COVER, AND BAKE: Pour ¾ cup (6.3 oz / 180g) of the cream into the bottom of the baking dish and place the baking dish on a large sheet pan. Butter a piece of foil large enough to cover the baking dish and tent it loosely over the apples buttered-side down, then crimp it firmly around the sides of the baking dish.

BAKE: Bake the apples for 1 hour, then remove the foil (some of the frangipane will have melted onto the bottom). Continue to bake uncovered until the frangipane is golden brown and the apples are tender but not broken down and a cake tester or toothpick slides easily into the flesh with just a bit of resistance, another 30 to 45 minutes for small or medium apples (but possibly longer for larger ones).

SERVE: Let the apples cool until they're warm but not piping hot, then transfer them, along with any frangipane and cream that caramelized on the bottom of the baking dish, to shallow serving bowls. Drizzle 2 tablespoons of the remaining chilled cream over each apple and top with the toasted sliced almonds, dividing evenly. Serve immediately.

Spiced Pear Charlotte

with Brioche

A charlotte is a charmingly old-fashioned and humble-looking dessert consisting of crustless, buttered slices of bread fitted into a mold, filled with a thick fruit compote, and baked (charlotte russe and charlotte royale are similar molded and filled desserts, albeit much fancier). Apple is the typical filling, but I'm always trying to bake more with pears, so I cook them down here into a thick compote flavored with warm spices. Because I also wanted to maintain the integrity of the whole fruit, I delicately cook pear halves in the compote and tuck them into the filling. The charlotte is baked in a glass pie plate, which is shallower than a traditional charlotte mold, allowing for a higher ratio of crust to filling (and better monitoring of browning). Lastly, rather than a lean white bread, I use eggy, buttery brioche, which adds the perfect amount of richness.

SERVES 8

DIFFICULTY: 2 (Easy)

ACTIVE TIME: 1 hour

TOTAL TIME: 1 hour 30 minutes, plus time to cool

SPECIAL EQUIPMENT: Potato masher, 9-inch pie plate (preferably glass and not deep-dish)

⅓ cup sugar (2.4 oz / 67g)

¾ teaspoon ground cinnamon

¼ teaspoon ground allspice

⅛ teaspoon ground nutmeg

Pinch of ground cloves

Pinch of kosher salt

1 stick unsalted butter (4 oz / 113g), melted and completely cooled so it's resolidified

3½ pounds (1.6kg) small firm but ripe pears, such as Bartlett or Anjou (about 9), divided

1 square-shaped loaf brioche bread (about 20 oz / 566g), crusts removed, cut crosswise into ½-inch-thick slices

MAKE THE SPICED SUGAR AND THE BUTTER MIXTURE: In a small bowl, stir together the sugar, cinnamon, allspice, nutmeg, cloves, and salt. Place a tablespoon of the sugar mixture in a separate small bowl and add the butter. Stir the sugar and butter with a flexible spatula until it's smooth and combined. Set the butter mixture and the remaining spiced sugar aside.

ASSEMBLE THE PEAR COMPOTE: Peel, halve, core, and coarsely chop 2 pounds (907g) of the pears, selecting the ripest ones. In a large saucepan, combine the chopped pears, reserved spiced sugar, and 2 tablespoons (1 oz / 28g) water. Bring to a boil over medium-high heat, mashing frequently with a potato masher to break up the fruit. Reduce the heat to maintain a gentle simmer and cook, mashing occasionally, until the pears are mostly broken down and have released their juices, about 5 minutes. Remove the saucepan from the heat.

PREPARE THE REMAINING PEARS: Peel the remaining 1½ pounds (680g) pears and halve them lengthwise. Use a paring knife to slice out the narrow fibrous portions of the core at the stem and base ends, then use a melon baller or a round teaspoon measure to scoop out the cores and seeds.

POACH THE PEAR HALVES: Slide the pear halves cut-sides up into the compote and arrange them in a single layer. They should be mostly submerged. Bring the compote back to a simmer over medium-high heat, then reduce the heat to a gentle simmer, cover, and cook the pear halves until they're tender and a cake tester or the tip of a paring knife slides into the flesh without resistance, 10 to 15 minutes. Uncover the saucepan and use a slotted spoon to gently remove the pear halves from the compote and transfer to a plate. Set aside to cool.

REDUCE THE COMPOTE: Increase the heat to medium-high and continue to cook the compote, stirring with a heatproof flexible spatula and scraping the bottom and sides, until all the liquid has boiled off and the compote is very thick and holds a mound on the end of a spoon (when you drag the spatula across the bottom of the saucepan, the compote should slowly fill in the line), 10 to 15 minutes. Remove the saucepan from the heat and set aside.

PREHEAT THE OVEN: Arrange an oven rack in the lower third of the oven and preheat the oven to 375°F.

$\rightarrow$

BUTTER THE BREAD: Dividing evenly, spread a thin layer of the butter/sugar mixture across one side of each bread slice all the way to the edges, using all of the mixture.

LINE THE PIE PLATE: Use an upside-down water glass or a 2- to 3-inch cutter to punch out a round of bread from one of the buttered slices. Place the round buttered-side down in the center of a 9-inch pie plate, preferably glass. Using a serrated knife, cut several more slices of bread in half on a diagonal to form triangles, then arrange the triangles buttered-side down and slightly overlapping in the bottom of the pie plate so they're encircling the center round. Cut more triangles if necessary to cover the entire bottom. Next, cut several slices crosswise into 1-inch-wide strips and fit them, buttered-side down and overlapping slightly, around the sides of the pie plate. Trim them if necessary so the strips extend about ½ inch above the rim of the pie plate. Press the slices into the bottom and against the sides of the plate to flatten them slightly, then set the remaining slices aside.

FILL THE CHARLOTTE: Scrape the warm compote into the lined pie plate and spread in an even layer. Arrange the pear halves cut-side up over the compote in a single layer (leave behind any juices that may have collected on the plate). Press the pear halves gently into the compote and smooth the surface, working a little bit of compote into the pear cavities.

BAKE UNCOVERED: Cover the exposed border of bread with a strip of foil, leaving the filling uncovered. Place the pie plate on a sheet pan and bake until the bread is golden across the bottom of the pie plate, 25 to 30 minutes.

TOP WITH THE REMAINING BREAD AND BAKE AGAIN: Remove the sheet pan from the oven and pull off the foil. Arrange the remaining bread buttered-side up across the surface of the filling, cutting the slices as needed to fit them together without any gaps (this will be the bottom of the charlotte, so no need to make a nice pattern). Gently press down on top of the bread to flatten, then return the sheet pan to the oven and bake until the bread is deep golden brown across the top, bottom, and sides, another 15 to 20 minutes.

COOL AND SERVE: Transfer the charlotte to a wire rack and let it sit until it's cool enough to handle, about 30 minutes. Run a small offset spatula or butter knife around the sides of the pie plate to loosen the charlotte, then place a serving plate upside down over the pie plate and invert them together. Slowly lift off the pie plate. Serve the charlotte warm or at room temperature and use a serrated knife to cut wedges.

Can I . . .

Make it ahead? Partially, yes. The charlotte is best eaten the day it's baked, but the poached pear halves and compote can be prepared up to 3 days ahead. Refrigerate them separately in airtight containers.

Bake this in a different pan? Yes. You can make the charlotte in an 8-inch springform pan.

Choose-Your-Own-Ending Custards:
Crème Brûlée or Crème Caramel

This is a choose-your-own-ending dessert. Made with the same base using the same cooking method, crème brûlée and crème caramel are like funhouse-mirror images of one another. Both are rich, delicate, vanilla-scented custards, but the former is topped with a hard, crackly caramel lid, while the latter is coated in a liquid caramel sauce that forms during baking (the caramel actually starts on the bottom, but becomes the top when inverted, like a flan). Would you rather cook the sugar on the stove to a deep amber color at the beginning and pour into ramekins for crème caramel, or use a torch to caramelize it at the very end for crème brûlée? The answer comes down to preference and comfort (and, possibly, your desire to own a torch). And, if you can't pick one, see Can I . . . on page 293 to make half of one and half of the other.

SERVES 8

DIFFICULTY: 2 (Easy)

GLUTEN-FREE

ACTIVE TIME: 45 minutes

TOTAL TIME: 5 hours 30 minutes (includes 4 hours for chilling)

SPECIAL EQUIPMENT: Eight 6-ounce ramekins, 8-cup glass measuring cup (optional), roasting pan or large shallow baking dish, kitchen torch (if making crème brûlée)

¾ cup granulated sugar (5.3 oz / 150g)

4 cups half-and-half (32 oz / 960g)

Seeds scraped from 1 vanilla bean (pod reserved) or 2 teaspoons vanilla extract

Generous pinch of kosher salt

6 large egg yolks (3.2 oz / 90g), at room temperature

2 large eggs (3.5 oz / 100g), at room temperature

½ cup demerara sugar (3.5 oz / 100g)

FOR CRÈME BRÛLÉE: Set the granulated sugar aside and skip below to preheat the oven.

FOR CRÈME CARAMEL, MAKE THE CARAMEL: Fill a glass with water, place a pastry brush inside, and set it next to the stove. In a small saucepan, combine ¼ cup (2 oz / 57g) water and the granulated sugar and stir gently with a heatproof flexible spatula over medium-high heat just until the sugar dissolves to form a clear syrup and the mixture comes to a boil, about 3 minutes. Cook the mixture to a deep amber caramel following steps 3 through 5 in Cooking a Wet Caramel (page 346), then immediately remove the saucepan from the heat and proceed to the next step.

DIVIDE THE CARAMEL AMONG THE RAMEKINS: Quickly pour the caramel into eight 6-ounce ramekins, dividing it evenly and using a heatproof flexible spatula to scrape all the caramel out of the saucepan. Before the caramel sets, tilt the ramekins to fill in any gaps (be careful, it's hot!). It's okay if it doesn't cover the entire surface, as small gaps will disappear during baking (if the caramel hardens all in one spot, you can microwave the ramekins in 10-second bursts to liquefy it again). Set the ramekins aside to cool.

PREHEAT THE OVEN: Arrange an oven rack in the center position and preheat the oven to 300°F.

HEAT AND INFUSE THE HALF-AND-HALF: In a small saucepan, combine the half-and-half, vanilla seeds and pod, and salt and heat over medium heat, whisking occasionally to disperse the vanilla seeds, until the mixture is steaming and just starting to ripple beneath the surface, about 5 minutes (if using vanilla extract, set it aside to add later). Remove the saucepan from the heat and set aside (leave the vanilla pod in the saucepan to infuse the mixture).

BLANCH AND TEMPER THE EGGS: In a medium bowl, vigorously whisk the egg yolks, whole eggs, and demerara sugar until the mixture is frothy and slightly thickened, about 1 minute. Whisking the egg mixture constantly, slowly pour in the hot half-and-half mixture to temper the eggs, then switch to a flexible spatula and stir, scraping the bottom and sides of the bowl, to ensure the sugar is dissolved (for more information, see Blanching and Tempering Eggs, page 348). If using vanilla extract, whisk it in now.

→

STRAIN THE CUSTARD: Pass the custard through a fine-mesh sieve and into an 8-cup glass measuring cup, pitcher, or medium bowl (a pour spout makes it easier to fill the ramekins). Discard the vanilla pod and any solids that were caught in the sieve.

FILL AND COVER THE CUPS: Divide the custard evenly among eight 6-ounce ramekins (pouring it over the hardened caramel if making crème caramel). They will be filled nearly to the top. Cut eight squares of foil large enough to cover each ramekin, then cover each with foil, making sure that the foil doesn't touch the surface of the custard (it does not need to be tightly sealed). Holding the foil taut, use a toothpick to poke a couple of small holes in each foil lid to allow steam to escape, then set the ramekins aside.

PREPARE THE WATER BATH: Bring 6 cups of water to a boil in a kettle or in a medium saucepan over high heat. While the water is heating, select a roasting pan or shallow baking dish large enough to hold the eight ramekins, line it with a thin kitchen towel, and smooth any wrinkles (this is optional but recommended to prevent the ramekins from sliding around). Place the ramekins inside the roasting pan, spacing them evenly and ensuring that they're level on the towel.

Can I...

Make them ahead. Yes. The baked custards will keep in the refrigerator for up to 3 days. The crème brûlée custards are chilled uncovered, but cover the ramekins after 24 hours if making them ahead and wait to caramelize the sugar on top until right before serving.

Make half crème caramel and half crème brûlée? Yes. Make the caramel for crème caramel as instructed above, using 2 tablespoons water and 6 tablespoons (2.6 oz / 75g) sugar, then divide it among four ramekins. Follow the recipe for the custard as written, dividing it between the four caramel-filled ramekins and four additional ramekins. Follow the instructions for making crème brûlée with the four additional custards and more sugar.

Halve the recipe? Yes. Halve all of the ingredient quantities and follow the recipe as written, baking the custards in four ramekins. Note that you won't need as large a roasting pan for the water bath, and the custards may cook a bit more quickly, so start checking them after 25 minutes. If making crème caramel, note also that half the quantity of caramel will cook more quickly.

Caramelize the sugar for crème brûlée under the broiler? No. The heat from most broilers is too diffuse to caramelize the sugar evenly before melting the custard. A torch is your best option.

Use two shallow baking dishes for the water bath if I don't have a large enough roasting pan? Yes. Any shallow baking vessel with 2-inch-high sides will work for the water bath.

Use various sizes of ramekins? No. It's important that all the ramekins be of equal volume capacity and height, otherwise the custards will not bake evenly.

BAKE: Partially slide out the oven rack and transfer the roasting pan to the rack. Slowly and carefully pour the boiling water just inside the edge of the pan until it comes halfway up the sides of the ramekins (the volume of water needed will depend on the size of the pan). Try not to splash the water as you pour, although the foil will shield the custards. Slide the rack gently into the oven and bake until the custards are set around the edges but slightly wobbly in the centers, 30 to 35 minutes. To test for doneness, use a pair of tongs to remove one of the foil lids and gently jostle the ramekin to look for wobbling. If they need more time, press the foil back over the ramekin and continue to bake, checking them every couple of minutes. Carefully remove the pan from the oven.

> *Potential Pitfall:* If you are using shallow, wide ramekins designed specifically for crème brûlée (because of the greater surface area), you will need a very large roasting pan to fit all 8. Note that the custards will bake faster, so check them after 25 minutes.

COOL AND CHILL THE CUSTARDS: Let the custards rest in the hot water for 5 minutes, then carefully slide a spatula underneath the ramekins and transfer them one at a time to a wire rack. If making crème brûlée, remove the foil (reserve the pieces for baking future custards), but if making crème caramel, leave the ramekins covered. Let the ramekins sit at room temperature until they're cool enough to handle, then transfer to the refrigerator and chill until cold, at least 4 hours. Proceed for either crème caramel or crème brûlée as written below.

FOR CRÈME BRÛLÉE: Remove the chilled ramekins from the refrigerator. Sprinkle 1½ teaspoons of the reserved granulated sugar evenly over the surface of one of the custards (if using shallower, wider ramekins, you might need closer to 2 teaspoons). Hold a kitchen torch so the blue flame is hovering just above the sugared surface of the custard and move it around continuously until the sugar melts and forms a glassy layer of amber caramel with some nearly blackened spots. Repeat with the remaining custards and more sugar. Caramelize the custards a second time, sprinkling each with another 1½ teaspoons of sugar and torching again to build up a thick, shattering, evenly cooked layer of dark caramel. Depending on the dimensions of your ramekins, you may not use all the sugar. Serve immediately.

FOR CRÈME CARAMEL: Remove the chilled ramekins from the refrigerator and uncover. Run a paring knife or a mini offset spatula around one of the custards, keeping the blade pressed firmly against the side of the ramekin and along the bottom, to loosen it. Place a small serving plate upside down over the ramekin, then invert the plate and ramekin together and tap the plate on the countertop a couple of times to help release the custard. Remove the ramekin and allow any liquid caramel to drip onto the plate. Unmold the remaining custards and serve immediately.

Inverted Affogatos

I have to credit my husband, Harris, with coming up with the idea for an inverted affogato. Affogato is a beloved Italian dessert of hot espresso poured over cold vanilla ice cream, so an inverted affogato is some combination of a cold coffee component and a warm vanilla pour-over component (at least according to me—Harris's original vision was slightly different, but he agreed to loan me the concept). In my interpretation, it's a coffee pot de crème topped with warm crème anglaise, and in the interest of streamlining the recipe, both components are made from the same base of half-and-half and sweetened condensed milk (once coffee is added, the flavor recalls Vietnamese coffee, an extravagantly delicious drink). It's the intermingling of hot and cold, as in affogato, that makes the dessert.

SERVES 8

DIFFICULTY: 2 (Easy)

GLUTEN-FREE

ACTIVE TIME: 1 hour

TOTAL TIME: 5 hours 45 minutes (includes 4 hours for chilling)

SPECIAL EQUIPMENT: Eight 6-ounce custard cups, ramekins, or ovenproof glass bowls; 8-cup glass measuring cup (optional); roasting pan or large shallow baking dish

2¼ cups whole milk (1.2 lb / 540g)

2 cups heavy cream (16 oz / 480g)

1 (14 oz / 397g) can sweetened condensed milk

½ teaspoon Diamond Crystal kosher salt or ¼ teaspoon Morton kosher salt

2 teaspoons vanilla extract

6 tablespoons coarsely ground coffee (0.8 oz / 22g)

2 large eggs (3.5 oz / 100g), at room temperature

8 large egg yolks (4.2 oz / 120g), at room temperature, divided

PREHEAT THE OVEN: Arrange an oven rack in the center position and preheat the oven to 300°F.

HEAT THE MILK MIXTURE: In a small saucepan, combine the milk, cream, sweetened condensed milk, and salt and heat over medium heat, whisking occasionally to dissolve the sweetened condensed milk, until the mixture is steaming and just starting to ripple beneath the surface, about 5 minutes, then remove from the heat. Stir in the vanilla and set aside.

RESERVE SOME OF THE MILK MIXTURE: Pour 1½ cups (13.5 oz / 384g) of the warm milk mixture into a heatproof liquid measuring cup or measure it into a lidded container, cover, and refrigerate until just before serving. This is for making the vanilla sauce.

ADD THE COFFEE: Stir the coffee into the remaining milk mixture in the saucepan and set aside for 15 minutes to allow it to infuse.

TEMPER THE EGGS AND STRAIN THE CUSTARD: In a medium bowl, whisk together the whole eggs and 5 of the yolks (2.6 oz / 75g) until streak-free. Whisking the eggs constantly, slowly pour the hot coffee/milk mixture into the bowl to temper the eggs. Pass the custard through a fine-mesh sieve and into an 8-cup glass measuring cup, pitcher, or medium bowl (a pour spout makes it easier to fill the cups). Discard the coffee grounds and any solids that were caught in the sieve.

> *Potential Pitfall:* If the coffee was not coarsely ground, or if your mesh sieve is not very fine, you may have some coffee grounds left in the strained custard. If you want to remove them, pass the custard through the sieve again, this time lining it with a double layer of cheesecloth to catch the finer particles.

FILL AND COVER THE CUPS: Divide the custard evenly among eight 6-ounce custard cups, ramekins, or ovenproof glass bowls (they will be filled nearly to the top). Cut eight squares of foil large enough to cover the cups, then cover each with foil, making sure that the foil doesn't touch the surface of the custard (it does not need to be tightly sealed). Holding the foil taut, use a toothpick to poke a couple of small holes in each foil lid to allow steam to escape, then set the cups aside.

→

PREPARE THE WATER BATH: Bring 6 cups of water to a boil in a kettle or in a medium saucepan over high heat. While the water is heating, select a roasting pan or shallow baking dish large enough to hold the 8 cups, line it with a thin kitchen towel, and smooth any wrinkles (this is optional but recommended to prevent the cups from sliding around). Place the cups inside the roasting pan, spacing them evenly and ensuring that they're level on the towel.

BAKE: Partially slide out the oven rack and transfer the roasting pan to the rack. Slowly and carefully pour the boiling water just inside the edge of the pan until it comes halfway up the sides of the cups (the volume of water needed will depend on the size of the pan). Try not to splash the water as you pour, although the foil will shield the custards. Slide the rack gently into the oven and bake until the custards are set around the edges but slightly wobbly in the centers, 30 to 35 minutes. To test for doneness, use a pair of tongs to remove one of the foil lids and gently jostle the cup to look for wobbling. If the custards need more time, press the foil back over the cup and continue to bake, checking them every couple of minutes. Carefully remove the pan from the oven.

COOL AND CHILL THE CUSTARDS: Allow the custards to rest in the hot water for 5 minutes, then carefully slide a spatula underneath the cups and transfer them one at a time—still covered with foil—to a wire rack. Let them sit at room temperature until they're cool enough to handle, then transfer to the refrigerator and chill until cold, at least 4 hours.

MAKE THE VANILLA SAUCE: About 20 minutes before serving, in a medium bowl, whisk the remaining 3 egg yolks (1.6 oz / 45g) until smooth, then slowly stream in the reserved 1½ cups cold milk mixture. Transfer the mixture to a small saucepan and whisk constantly over medium heat until it has thickened to the consistency of cold heavy cream and coats the back of a spoon, about 5 minutes (see page 349 for a photo of custard coating a spoon—if you want a more precise endpoint, it will read 170°F on an instant-read thermometer). Immediately remove the vanilla sauce from the heat and pour it into a small pitcher or serving bowl. Let it sit, stirring occasionally, until the sauce is warm but not hot, 10 to 15 minutes.

SERVE: Remove the custards from the refrigerator and uncover. Pour some of the warm vanilla sauce over the surface of the custards and serve immediately, along with any remaining vanilla sauce on the side.

Can I . . .

Make it ahead? Yes. The baked custards, covered and refrigerated, will keep for up to 3 days. The vanilla sauce can be refrigerated in an airtight container for up to 3 days as well. Just before serving, rewarm the vanilla sauce over low heat, stirring frequently, until it's steaming, then pour it over the custards.

Halve the recipe? Not recommended. Because the recipe uses a single sweetened milk base to make both the custards and the vanilla sauce, cutting all of the ingredient quantities in half is tricky (dividing an egg yolk, for example). It's best to make the full recipe and have some custard and vanilla sauce left over.

Blood Orange Pudding Cake

I've been captivated by the idea of a pudding cake ever since I saw a recipe for one by the pastry chef Kristen Murray of Maurice luncheonette in Portland, Oregon, many years ago. Prepared more like a soufflé than a cake, it's a mixture of citrus juice, dairy, egg yolks, and flour, lightened with beaten egg whites and baked in a water bath. As it bakes, the egg whites rise to the surface and the batter miraculously separates into a light sponge on top and a curdlike layer on the bottom. The typical all-lemon version is lovely, but here I use blood oranges for their vibrant color and sweet-tart flavor. You can leave the cake in the baking dish for serving, but I prefer to turn it out so the pudding layer is on top. Serve it with fresh blood orange slices for a bright and light winter dessert.

SERVES 8

DIFFICULTY: 2 (Easy)

ACTIVE TIME: 35 minutes

TOTAL TIME: 1 hour, plus time to cool

SPECIAL EQUIPMENT: 2-quart shallow baking dish, 13 × 9-inch pan, hand mixer

Butter for the baking dish

⅔ cup fresh blood orange juice (5.3 oz / 150g), from 4 medium or 3 large blood oranges

½ cup plain whole-milk Greek yogurt (4.2 oz / 120g), at room temperature

⅓ cup fresh lemon juice (2.7 oz / 77g)

1 teaspoon finely grated blood orange zest

⅔ cup plus 2 tablespoons sugar (5.6 oz / 158g)

5 large eggs (8.8 oz / 250g), whites and yolks separated, at room temperature

4 tablespoons unsalted butter (2 oz / 57g), melted and cooled

½ cup all-purpose flour (2.4 oz / 68g)

½ teaspoon Diamond Crystal kosher salt or ¼ teaspoon Morton kosher salt

4 medium blood oranges, for serving

PREHEAT THE OVEN AND PREPARE THE BAKING DISH: Arrange an oven rack in the center position and preheat the oven to 350°F. Brush the bottom and sides of a 2-quart shallow baking dish with room temperature butter. If you're planning on turning out the cake to serve it, press a piece of parchment paper into the bottom of the baking dish and smooth to eliminate air bubbles, then press it up the sides, smoothing and flattening any folds (the parchment should extend up the sides all the way around). Use scissors to trim away any excess parchment, then set the baking dish aside.

BOIL WATER FOR THE WATER BATH: Bring 4 cups of water to a boil in a kettle or in a medium saucepan over high heat.

MIX THE WET INGREDIENTS: In a small bowl, whisk together the blood orange juice, yogurt, and lemon juice until smooth. Set the bowl aside.

MAKE THE BATTER: In a large bowl, combine the blood orange zest and ⅔ cup (4.7 oz / 133g) of the sugar and massage the mixture with your fingertips until it's very fragrant and looks like wet sand. Add the egg yolks and whisk vigorously until the mixture is smooth, pale, and mousse-y, about 1 minute. Whisking constantly, slowly stream in the melted butter and whisk until the mixture is smooth and satiny. Thoroughly whisk in the flour, then slowly stream in the wet ingredients, whisking constantly, until you have a smooth, liquidy batter.

BEAT THE EGG WHITES AND SUGAR: In a separate clean, large, nonplastic bowl, combine the egg whites and salt. With a hand mixer, beat on medium-low speed until the whites are broken up and frothy, about 20 seconds. Increase the speed to medium-high and continue to beat until the whites are foamy and opaque, about 30 seconds, then gradually add the remaining 2 tablespoons sugar in a slow, steady stream, beating constantly. Once all the sugar is added, continue to beat just until you have dense, glossy egg whites that hold a medium peak (see page 339 for what this stage looks like). Try not to overbeat, or the whites will take on a dry, grainy texture and be difficult to incorporate.

→

Can I . . .

Make it ahead? Yes. Although it's best served the day it's baked, the cake can be loosely covered and refrigerated for up to 1 day. If making it ahead, let the cake come to room temperature and top with the fresh blood orange slices just before serving.

Use a stand mixer instead of a hand mixer? Yes. Combine the egg whites and salt in a stand mixer fitted with the whisk attachment, then proceed with the recipe as written, keeping in mind that the egg whites will whip faster and are easier to overbeat in the stand mixer.

Make it gluten-free? No. The sponge needs the gluten in all-purpose flour to maintain its structure, so substituting a gluten-free blend would cause it to collapse.

Bake this in a different pan? Yes. You can bake the pudding cake in any shallow pan with a 2-quart capacity, such as an 8 × 8-inch pan or a 9-inch cake pan. Prepare the pan as directed in the recipe.

FOLD THE EGG WHITES INTO THE BATTER: Transfer about one-third of the egg whites to the bowl with the batter and fold with a flexible spatula until the egg whites are incorporated and the batter is lightened. The batter is liquidy, which makes it a bit difficult to incorporate the egg whites, but do your best (for more on the proper technique, see Folding a Mixture, page 351). Fold in the remaining egg whites in two additions, folding just until you see the last streaks disappear. Gently pour the batter into the prepared baking dish and smooth the surface.

PREPARE THE WATER BATH AND BAKE: Place the baking dish inside a 13 × 9-inch pan, then slowly and carefully pour the hot water into the larger pan, taking care not to splash any onto the surface of the batter, until it reaches about 1 inch up the sides of the baking dish. Carefully transfer the pan to the oven and bake uncovered until the batter has separated to form a top layer of sponge cake that's golden brown across the surface and springy to the touch in the center, 30 to 35 minutes. Remove the pan from the oven, carefully lift the baking dish out of the water, and transfer it to a wire rack. Let the cake sit until the bottom of the baking dish is cool to the touch, about 1 hour 30 minutes.

SLICE THE ORANGES: Just before serving, use a small, sharp knife to cut away the peel from 4 whole blood oranges (discard) and slice the oranges crosswise into ¼-inch-thick rounds, following the instructions in Cutting Citrus on page 357. Transfer the rounds to a medium bowl and set aside (save any juices for another use).

SERVE: If serving the cake right from the baking dish, scoop it into shallow bowls (make sure you get all of the pudding layer at the bottom) and serve with the blood orange slices on the side. If turning it out, place a serving platter upside down over the cake and invert the baking dish and platter together. Lift away the baking dish, then slowly peel away the parchment paper, revealing the layer of blood orange pudding. Arrange some of the blood orange slices over the surface of the cake and serve with the remaining slices on the side.

ℰGrand Marnier Soufflés

If you have something against Grand Marnier, an orange-flavored liqueur made with Cognac, you could use brandy or Cognac in this recipe, but Grand Marnier is a classic flavoring for soufflés and, in my opinion, well worth the expense of a bottle (it's also great in margaritas). In this particular recipe, you make a pastry cream thickened with flour, flavor it with Grand Marnier and orange zest, then fold in beaten egg whites. There's just enough flour to give the individual soufflés structure, while the moisture in the pastry cream facilitates their dramatic, lofty rise. There may be no more impressive, sophisticated dessert anywhere in this book.

SERVES 4

DIFFICULTY: 2 (Easy)

ACTIVE TIME: 45 minutes (does not include making the crème anglaise)

TOTAL TIME: 1 hour

SPECIAL EQUIPMENT: Four 6-ounce ramekins, hand mixer

Butter and sugar for the ramekins

3 large egg yolks (1.6 oz / 45g), divided

6 tablespoons sugar (2.6 oz / 75g), divided, plus more for topping

1 cup whole milk (8.5 oz / 240g)

¼ cup all-purpose flour (1.2 oz / 34g)

Seeds scraped from ½ vanilla bean, ½ teaspoon vanilla paste, or 1½ teaspoons vanilla extract

½ teaspoon Diamond Crystal kosher salt or ¼ teaspoon Morton kosher salt, plus a generous pinch

2 tablespoons unsalted butter, cut into ½-inch pieces, chilled

3 tablespoons Grand Marnier

½ teaspoon finely grated orange zest

4 large egg whites (4.9 oz / 140g), at room temperature

Crème Anglaise (page 348), for serving

PREHEAT THE OVEN: Arrange an oven rack in the center position and preheat the oven to 425°F.

PREPARE THE RAMEKINS: Brush the bottoms and sides of four 6-ounce ramekins with room temperature butter, using straight upward strokes around the sides and brushing all the way to the rim. Sprinkle the ramekins with sugar and shake to coat, then tap out the excess (the upward strokes and sugar give the batter something to cling to as it rises). Set the ramekins aside.

MAKE THE PASTRY CREAM: In a small saucepan, whisk together 2 of the egg yolks (1 oz / 30g) and 3 tablespoons of the sugar until combined, then whisk more vigorously until the mixture is pale, light, and thick, about 1 minute. Slowly stream in the milk, whisking constantly, then add the flour and whisk until the mixture is smooth and lump-free, making sure there are no unincorporated ingredients trapped around the sides. Whisk in the vanilla seeds or paste (if using extract, wait to add it after the mixture is cooked) and ½ teaspoon salt, then set the saucepan over medium heat. Cook the mixture, whisking constantly, until it's very thick and stiff and you see slow bubbling beneath the surface when you stop whisking for several seconds, about 4 minutes. Remove the saucepan from the heat and immediately scrape the pastry cream into a medium bowl.

FINISH AND COOL THE PASTRY CREAM BASE: Whisk the butter into the pastry cream a piece or two at a time, waiting for the pieces to disappear before adding more. Add the remaining egg yolk (0.5 oz / 15g), the Grand Marnier, and orange zest and whisk until smooth. If using vanilla extract, whisk it in now. Let the pastry cream base sit uncovered, stirring it once or twice to encourage cooling, until it's room temperature (or, to speed up this process, you can cool down the pastry cream in an ice bath—see Chilling in an Ice Bath, page 358). Set the bowl aside.

BEAT THE EGG WHITES AND SUGAR: In a clean, large, nonplastic bowl, combine the egg whites and a pinch of salt and use a hand mixer to beat on medium-low speed until the whites are broken up and frothy, about 20 seconds. Increase the speed to medium-high and continue to beat until the whites are foamy and opaque, about 30 seconds, then gradually add the remaining 3 tablespoons sugar in a slow, steady stream, beating constantly. Once all the sugar is added, continue to beat just until you have dense, glossy egg whites that hold a stiff peak (see page 339 for what this stage looks like). Try not to overbeat, or the whites will take on a dry, grainy texture and be difficult to incorporate into the pastry cream. Set the bowl aside.

FOLD IN THE EGG WHITES: Scrape about one-third of the beaten egg whites into the bowl with the pastry cream and fold gently with a large flexible spatula to combine. Making broad, decisive strokes with the spatula, fold in the remaining beaten egg whites in two additions, scraping the bottom and sides of the bowl and rotating the bowl as you work, until the mixture is uniformly mixed (for more on the proper technique, see Folding a Mixture, page 351).

FILL THE RAMEKINS: Gently scrape the batter into the prepared ramekins, dividing evenly and using all of it (the ramekins should be filled to the very top). Tap the ramekins delicately on the work surface to help settle the batter, then, working one at a time, use a small offset spatula or a butter knife to smooth the surface and scrape off any excess batter so it's flush and level with the very top of the ramekin. If necessary, transfer any excess batter from one ramekin to another to ensure they're all filled to the very top. Repeat until all the ramekins are leveled (at this point you could have a small amount of batter left over—if so, discard it).

> ***Potential Pitfall:*** If you don't have enough batter to fill all four ramekins all the way to the top, it's likely because you didn't whip the egg whites enough. That's okay, fill as many of the ramekins as you can all the way to the top and use all the batter. Your soufflés will still rise, they just won't achieve their maximum height.

SUGAR THE SOUFFLÉS AND WIPE AWAY A RING OF BATTER: Lightly sprinkle the surfaces of the batter with more sugar, then, working with one ramekin at a time, run a clean thumb around the inside of the rims to wipe away a ring of batter and expose the inner lip of the ramekins all the way around (use the natural indentation inside the ramekins as a guide for how deep to make the ring). This will ensure that your soufflés rise straight upward and maintain level tops. Wipe away any streaks of batter from the rim and outsides of the ramekins.

BAKE AND SERVE: Place the ramekins on a sheet pan, spacing them evenly. Transfer the sheet pan to the oven, immediately reduce the oven temperature to 375°F, and bake until the soufflés are risen, firm and springy to the touch across the surfaces, and have a slight wobble, 15 to 20 minutes. Remove the soufflés from the oven and serve immediately with the crème anglaise on the side. Encourage everyone to spoon down into the center of their soufflé and pour a few tablespoons of the crème anglaise into the interior.

Can I . . .

Make them ahead? No! Soufflés need to be served and eaten immediately after they emerge from the oven. However, the Grand Marnier base can be made several hours ahead and kept covered at room temperature until it's time to assemble the batter.

Double the recipe? Not recommended. The assembly process is time-sensitive, so it's not practical to assemble 8 soufflés at once, and they will not bake evenly in most home ovens.

Use a stand mixer instead of a hand mixer? Yes. Combine the egg whites and salt in a stand mixer fitted with the whisk attachment, then proceed with the recipe as written, keeping in mind that the egg whites will whip faster and be easier to overbeat in the stand mixer.

Chocolate Soufflés

I adore making soufflés and could write a whole cookbook about them. Soufflés are miraculous, fascinating creations made by folding whipped egg whites into a flavored base (in this case, chocolate), and though I think they unfairly have a reputation for being difficult, it's true that a successful soufflé requires a few techniques and special attention to timing. I use a flour-thickened base for my chocolate soufflés, and though this requires more steps than some versions that use straight-up melted chocolate, the resulting soufflés have superior structure and stability. While I know soufflés seem tricky, if you follow my careful steps (and read The Art of the Soufflé on page 305), you'll be able to create high-rising chocolate soufflés that rival anything you can order in a fancy restaurant.

SERVES 4

DIFFICULTY: 3 (Moderate)

ACTIVE TIME: 45 minutes (does not include making the crème anglaise)

TOTAL TIME: 1 hour

SPECIAL EQUIPMENT: Four 6-ounce ramekins, hand mixer

Butter and sugar for the ramekins

7 tablespoons sugar (3 oz / 87g), divided, plus more for sprinkling

3 large egg yolks (1.6 oz / 45g), divided

⅓ cup whole milk (2.8 oz / 80g)

2 tablespoons brewed coffee

2 tablespoons all-purpose flour

2 tablespoons unsweetened cocoa powder

4 ounces (113g) bittersweet chocolate (70% cacao), coarsely chopped

1 teaspoon vanilla extract

5 large egg whites (6.2 oz / 175g), at room temperature

1 teaspoon Diamond Crystal kosher salt or ½ teaspoon Morton kosher salt

Crème Anglaise (page 348), for serving

PREHEAT THE OVEN: Arrange an oven rack in the center position and preheat the oven to 425°F.

PREPARE THE RAMEKINS: Brush the bottoms and sides of four 6-ounce ramekins with room temperature butter, using straight upward strokes around the sides and brushing all the way to the rim. Sprinkle the ramekins with sugar and shake to coat, then tap out the excess (the upward strokes and sugar give the batter something to cling to as it rises). Set the ramekins aside.

COOK THE SOUFFLÉ BASE: Fill a medium saucepan with about 1 inch of water and bring to a simmer over medium heat, then reduce the heat to maintain a simmer. In a medium heatproof bowl, whisk together 3 tablespoons of the sugar and 2 of the egg yolks (1 oz / 30g) until combined, then whisk more vigorously until the mixture is pale, light, and thick, about 1 minute. Slowly stream in the milk, whisking constantly, followed by the coffee. Add the flour and cocoa powder and whisk until the mixture is smooth and lump-free, then set the bowl over the saucepan, taking care that the bottom of the bowl doesn't touch the water (this is called a double boiler—for more information, see Setting Up a Double Boiler, page 341). Cook the mixture over the double boiler, whisking constantly, until it's thickened to the consistency of thin pancake batter, the foam has subsided, and it faintly holds the marks of the whisk, 5 to 7 minutes. Remove the bowl from the saucepan (careful, it's hot).

FINISH AND COOL THE CHOCOLATE BASE: Add the chopped chocolate to the bowl and whisk briefly to incorporate it, then set the bowl aside for a few minutes to allow the chocolate to melt. Slowly whisk the mixture until smooth, then whisk in the remaining egg yolk (0.5 oz / 15g). Set the bowl aside to cool slightly.

Potential Pitfall: Don't let the base cool completely to room temperature or the chocolate will solidify (this is especially likely if your kitchen is cool). If this happens, rewarm the mixture over the double boiler, stirring constantly, just until it's smooth, spreadable, and loose enough to incorporate the egg whites.

BEAT THE EGG WHITES AND SUGAR: In a large, nonplastic bowl, combine the egg whites and salt and use a hand mixer to beat on medium-low speed until the whites are broken up and frothy, about 20 seconds. Increase the speed to medium-high and continue to beat until the whites are foamy and

→

opaque, about 30 seconds, then gradually add the remaining 4 tablespoons (1.8 oz / 50g) sugar in a slow, steady stream, beating constantly. Once all the sugar is added, continue to beat just until you have dense, glossy egg whites that hold a stiff peak (see page 339 for what this stage looks like). Try not to overbeat, or the whites will take on a dry, grainy texture and be difficult to incorporate into the chocolate base. Set the bowl aside.

FOLD IN THE EGG WHITES: Scrape about one-third of the beaten egg whites into the bowl with the chocolate mixture and whisk quickly and briefly to combine. Using a large flexible spatula and broad, decisive strokes, fold in the remaining beaten egg whites in two additions, scraping the bottom and sides of the bowl and rotating the bowl as you work, until the mixture is almost entirely streak-free (for more on the proper technique, see Folding a Mixture, page 351).

FILL THE RAMEKINS: Gently scrape the batter into the prepared ramekins, dividing it evenly and using all of it (the ramekins should be filled to the very top). Tap the ramekins delicately on the work surface to help settle the batter, then, working one at a time, use a small offset spatula or a butter knife to smooth the surface and scrape off any excess batter so it's level and flush with the very top of the ramekin. If necessary, transfer any excess batter from one ramekin to another to ensure they're all filled to the very top. Repeat until all the ramekins are leveled (at this point you could have a small amount of batter left over—if so, discard it).

> *Potential Pitfall:* If you don't have enough batter to fill all four ramekins all the way to the top, it's likely because you didn't whip the egg whites enough. That's okay, fill as many of the ramekins as you can all the way to the top and use all the batter. Your soufflés will still rise, they just won't achieve their maximum height.

Can I . . .

Make them ahead? No! Soufflés need to be served and eaten immediately after they emerge from the oven.

Double the recipe? Not recommended. The assembly process is time-sensitive, so it's not practical to assemble 8 soufflés at once, and they will not bake evenly in most home ovens.

Use a stand mixer instead of a hand mixer? Yes. Combine the egg whites and salt in a stand mixer fitted with the whisk attachment, then proceed with the recipe as written, keeping in mind that the egg whites will whip faster and be easier to overbeat in the stand mixer.

SUGAR THE SOUFFLÉS AND WIPE AWAY A RING OF BATTER: Lightly sprinkle the surfaces of the batter with more sugar, then, working with one ramekin at a time, run a clean thumb around the inside of the rims to wipe away a ring of batter and expose the inner lip of the ramekins all the way around (use the natural indentation inside the ramekins as a guide for how deep to make the ring). This will ensure that your soufflés rise straight upward and maintain level tops. Wipe away any streaks of batter from the rim and outsides of the ramekins.

BAKE AND SERVE: Place the ramekins on a sheet pan, spacing them evenly. Transfer the sheet pan to the oven, immediately reduce the oven temperature to 375°F, and bake until the soufflés are risen, firm and springy to the touch across the surfaces, and have a slight wobble, 15 to 20 minutes. Remove the soufflés from the oven and serve immediately with the crème anglaise on the side. Encourage everyone to spoon down into the center of their soufflé and pour a few tablespoons of the crème anglaise into the interior.

THE ART OF THE SOUFFLÉ

Soufflés have a reputation for being difficult, but I wouldn't characterize them that way. I would, however, say that they're sensitive, ethereal creations, so timing and technique are of the essence. Every soufflé, whether it's sweet or savory, gets its signature lightness from egg whites beaten into a foam. Egg white foam is inherently unstable (which is why soufflés start to collapse soon after they emerge from the oven), so successful soufflé making is all about understanding its properties and acting at every turn to maintain its network of trapped air bubbles. Here are the major points to keep in mind:

Butter and sugar the ramekins thoroughly. For the batter to rise into a tall, even, straight-sided soufflé, you need well-greased ramekins to prevent the batter from sticking. Room temperature butter is best because you can apply it thickly, and the granules of sugar coating the buttered interior act as grips for the batter, helping it climb. Make sure the butter and sugar extend all the way to the rim, or the batter could anchor itself there, begin to dome, and eventually split open as the center continues to rise (this is why the recipes instruct you to run your finger around the inside lip of the ramekins to wipe away any batter, as this could stick).

Understand your base. While egg whites provide lift, the soufflé base provides both flavor and structure. Generally, the base should be very thick and relatively lean, as fat will destabilize the egg foam. (Because I want a little richness in my soufflés, I add some fat from chocolate, butter, or another ingredient, plus the fat from egg yolks, but not enough to affect the structure.) I've found that cooking just a little bit of flour into the base adds support and helps to delay a soufflé's collapse without muting the flavor. Make sure the base is completely smooth and at room temperature before folding in the egg whites.

Beat the egg whites slowly and thoroughly. The soufflé recipes in this book instruct you to beat the egg whites slowly and to add the sugar gradually, which helps to produce very small air bubbles. The finer the bubbles, the more finely textured and smooth the soufflé will be. Beat the egg whites to stiff peaks (but not beyond), fold them quickly into the base, and fill the ramekins as directed in the recipe. Because the egg whites will begin to deflate as soon as they're incorporated into the base, transfer the filled ramekins to the oven immediately.

Start in a hot oven, then lower the heat. Make sure the oven has plenty of time to preheat so the soufflés get an initial blast of heat, which causes the air in the egg white foam to expand and kick-starts the rise. The temperature of the oven is then reduced for the duration of baking to ensure the soufflés cook evenly. The tiny air bubbles in the egg whites act like insulation, so the batter heats slowly. The lower temperature ensures that the batter at the center has time to cook through before the batter around the sides can dry out.

Know the signs of cooked soufflé. Baking a soufflé is like cooking a medium-rare steak—you want to remove it from the heat just at the point of doneness. When they're done, the soufflés will be nearly doubled in height and the surface will be set. When you press down in the center, it will feel soft but slightly springy beneath the surface—this is how you know the eggs are cooked and the interior will be set and supple and neither runny (a sign of undercooking) nor dry (a sign of overcooking).

Rye Bread Pudding

with Rye Whiskey Caramel Sauce

Bread is my life force, my raison d'être, so I let the dominant flavor of this bread pudding come from the bread itself. The obvious bread choice here was rye, since I've been exploring the sweet applications of earthy rye flour for several years (for example, my Thrice-Baked Rye Cookies in *Dessert Person*). If you can, make the extra effort to seek out an artisanal loaf of unseeded rye, since the flavor will be that much better (try to avoid seeded rye, as the caraway flavor is a little overpowering). To create textural variety, I bake the bread pudding in a loaf pan, then slice it and caramelize the sugared slices under the broiler. And, to bring it in line with more classic bread puddings, I serve it with a rye whiskey–spiked caramel sauce.

SERVES 8

DIFFICULTY: 2 (Easy)

ACTIVE TIME: 1 hour 15 minutes

TOTAL TIME: 7 hours 30 minutes (includes several hours for soaking and chilling)

SPECIAL EQUIPMENT: Metal loaf pan (4½ × 8½ inches, measured across the top), 13 × 9-inch pan

1 loaf unseeded, unsliced rye bread, preferably sourdough (about 1 lb / 453g), crust removed, cut into ¾-inch cubes (8 cups)

3½ cups half-and-half (1.9 lb / 840g)

4 large eggs (7 oz / 200g), at room temperature

2 large egg yolks (1 oz / 30g), at room temperature

1 teaspoon Diamond Crystal kosher salt or ½ teaspoon Morton kosher salt

⅔ cup demerara sugar (4.7 oz / 133g), plus more for sprinkling

2 teaspoons vanilla extract

Butter for the pan

3 tablespoons rye whiskey

Salted Caramel Sauce (page 346), warmed, for serving

PREHEAT THE OVEN: Arrange an oven rack in the center position and preheat the oven to 350°F.

TOAST THE BREAD: Scatter the bread cubes in an even layer across a large sheet pan and toast until they're dry and lightly golden all over, 15 to 20 minutes, tossing halfway through. Set the pan aside and let the bread cool. Turn the oven off.

BLANCH AND TEMPER THE EGGS: In a small saucepan, heat the half-and-half over medium heat until it's steaming and just starting to ripple beneath the surface, about 5 minutes. Remove from the heat and set aside. In a large bowl, vigorously whisk together the whole eggs, egg yolks, salt, and demerara sugar until the mixture is frothy and slightly thickened, about 1 minute. Whisking the egg mixture constantly, slowly pour in the hot half-and-half and continue to whisk until the sugar is completely dissolved, about 30 seconds (for more information, see Blanching and Tempering Eggs, page 348). Whisk in the vanilla.

SOAK THE BREAD: Transfer the bread to the bowl with the custard and stir thoroughly to combine. Cover the bowl and let the mixture sit, uncovering it and folding occasionally to encourage the bread to soak up the custard evenly, until nearly all the custard has been absorbed, about 2 hours. Meanwhile, prepare the pan.

PREHEAT THE OVEN AND PREPARE THE PAN: Preheat the oven to 325°F. Line a 4½ × 8½-inch metal loaf pan with foil, working it carefully into the corners without tearing it and leaving a couple of inches of overhang on the two longer sides and just a slight overhang along the other two. Brush the foil with a thin layer of room temperature butter.

FILL THE PAN: Scrape the soaked bread mixture, along with any unabsorbed custard, into the prepared loaf pan and use a spatula or the back of a spoon to press it firmly into the pan in an even layer. The mixture should come right to the top of the pan. Fold the overhanging foil up and over the pan, pressing it onto the surface of the bread mixture. If the overhang doesn't completely cover the surface, use another piece of foil to tightly cover the pan.

PREPARE THE WATER BATH: Bring 6 cups of water to a boil in a kettle or in a medium saucepan over high heat. Place the covered loaf pan inside a 13 × 9-inch pan and pour the boiling water into the larger pan so it comes about 1 inch up the sides of the loaf pan.

BAKE AND CHILL: Carefully transfer the pan to the oven and bake until the surface of the bread pudding is domed and the center is springy to the touch (it will be puffed up and pressing against the foil), 50 to 60 minutes. Carefully remove the pan from the oven, then lift the loaf pan out of the water bath and let it cool on a wire rack until it's warm but not hot. Transfer the covered loaf pan to the refrigerator and chill until cold, at least 3 hours.

MAKE THE RYE CARAMEL SAUCE: Stir the rye whiskey into the warm caramel sauce and set aside. Keep it warm while you finish the bread pudding.

PREHEAT THE BROILER: Arrange an oven rack in the topmost position (ignore this if you have a broiler drawer in the bottom of your oven) and preheat the broiler.

SLICE AND BROIL THE BREAD PUDDING: Line a sheet pan with a piece of foil. Remove the cold loaf pan from the refrigerator and uncover the bread pudding. Turn it out onto a cutting board and lift off the pan (tug on the sides of the foil to help release it, if necessary) and peel away the foil. Slice the loaf crosswise into 8 equal pieces, then arrange the pieces flat on the prepared sheet pan, spacing evenly. Sprinkle some demerara sugar over the slices so they're generously and evenly coated and broil until the sugar is golden and bubbling all over and some of the edges and surfaces are blackened, about 4 minutes, rotating the sheet pan front to back halfway through. Watch them closely, as the sugar can burn quickly.

SERVE: Let the slices cool on the sheet pan for about a minute, then transfer them to serving plates and drizzle with some of the rye caramel sauce. Serve the bread pudding with the remaining rye caramel sauce on the side.

Can I . . .

Use another spirit or omit the rye? Yes. You can substitute bourbon or another whiskey for the rye, or omit it entirely and serve the bread pudding with the plain salted caramel sauce.

Make it ahead? Yes. The baked, unsliced loaf of bread pudding will keep in the refrigerator for up to 2 days. Slice, sprinkle with sugar, and broil just before serving. The rye whiskey caramel sauce, refrigerated in a jar or airtight container, will keep for several months. To rewarm it, scrape the cold, solidified sauce into a double boiler (for more information, see Setting Up a Double Boiler, page 341) and stir until it's warm and fluid.

Cherry Pavlova

with Hibiscus

Pavlova is one of several desserts that combine crispy and marshmallow-y baked meringue with whipped cream and fruit to spectacular ends. The best versions are made with a relatively acidic fruit—the classic is passion fruit, which is *very* acidic—to balance out the sweet meringue. That's not to say you can't make pavlova with a sweet fruit like cherries, you just need a sour ingredient to accompany it. Normally I'd reach for citrus, but here I opt for hibiscus, a naturally tart edible flower that's used in the Caribbean, Mexico, and many parts of the world to make teas and other beverages. After briefly poaching the cherries, I add dried hibiscus petals and a few spices to the poaching liquid and reduce it to a syrup for drizzling over the pavlova. The petals rehydrate in the syrup and lend a wonderfully complex, floral sourness to the assemblage (because they're fully edible, I don't strain them out). Look for bulk bags of dried hibiscus flowers rather than individual tea bags, since the latter almost always contain other ingredients and flavorings.

SERVES 8

DIFFICULTY: 2 (Easy)

GLUTEN-FREE

ACTIVE TIME: 1 hour 15 minutes (does not include making the meringue)

TOTAL TIME: 4 hours 15 minutes

SPECIAL EQUIPMENT: Hand mixer

All-Purpose Meringue (page 344)

1 pound (454g) pitted fresh or thawed frozen sweet cherries (about 4 cups)

¼ cup sugar (1.8 oz / 50g)

2 teaspoons dried hibiscus petals

½-inch piece fresh ginger, peeled and smashed

3 strips lemon zest, removed with a vegetable peeler

½ cinnamon stick

1 tablespoon fresh lemon juice

1 teaspoon cornstarch

1½ cups heavy cream (12.7 oz / 360g), chilled

PREHEAT THE OVEN AND PREPARE THE SHEET PAN: Arrange an oven rack in the center position and preheat the oven to 200°F. Line a sheet pan with a silicone baking mat or parchment paper.

FORM AND BAKE THE MERINGUE: Scrape the meringue onto the prepared sheet pan and use the back of a spoon to spread it into a rectangle measuring about 12 × 7 inches, creating peaks and valleys in the meringue. Transfer the sheet pan to the oven and bake until the meringue is dry to the touch, very crisp on the outside, and soft and marshmallow-y on the inside, 2 to 2½ hours, rotating the sheet pan front to back after 1 hour. Test for doneness by carefully peeling the baking mat or parchment away from the meringue. It should release cleanly; if any meringue sticks, continue baking. Turn off the oven, prop the door open with a wooden spoon, and allow the meringue to cool in the oven for 30 minutes. Remove the meringue from the oven and let it cool completely on the sheet pan. If serving straightaway, prepare the cherry topping while the meringue is cooling.

POACH THE CHERRIES: Place a large mesh sieve over a medium bowl and set aside. In a large saucepan, combine the cherries and sugar and add just enough water to the saucepan to barely cover the cherries. Bring to a simmer over medium heat, swirling to dissolve the sugar, then reduce the heat to maintain a very gentle simmer and cook, swirling the saucepan occasionally, just until the cherries are softened and tender, about 5 minutes for fresh cherries and about 2 minutes for thawed frozen. Remove the saucepan from the heat and pour the mixture into the mesh sieve (reserve the saucepan). Allow the cherries to drain for several seconds, shaking the sieve to encourage any liquid to fall into the bowl. Pour the poaching liquid back into the saucepan, then place the mesh sieve back over the bowl so the cherries can continue to drain.

REDUCE THE POACHING LIQUID TO A SYRUP: Add the hibiscus, ginger, zest, and cinnamon stick to the poaching liquid and bring to a boil over medium-high heat. Reduce the heat to medium and continue to cook, swirling the saucepan occasionally, until the liquid is syrupy and reduced to about ⅔ cup (pour it into a heatproof liquid measuring cup to check the volume,

→

Can I...

Make it ahead? Yes, but . . . wait to assemble. The baked meringue, wrapped very well and stored at room temperature, will keep for up to 1 day (make sure it's wrapped airtight, or the meringue will absorb moisture from the air and become sticky). The whipped cream can be covered and chilled for up to 2 hours (if it deflates and looks a bit liquidy, whip it again until soft peaks form). The poached cherries and syrup can be combined and refrigerated in an airtight container for up to 2 days. Let the mixture come to room temperature before assembling. Any assembled pavlova that's leftover can be stored in an airtight container and refrigerated, but the meringue will lose its crispiness.

Halve the recipe? Yes. Halve all of the ingredient quantities, plus the ingredient quantities for the **All-Purpose Meringue** (page 344), and follow the respective recipes as written. Spread the meringue into an 8 × 8-inch square on the prepared sheet pan and start checking it for doneness after 1 hour 30 minutes, since the half quantity of meringue will bake faster. For the cherries, poach them in a small saucepan and proceed with the recipe as written.

Use a stand mixer instead of a hand mixer? Yes. Combine the heavy cream and salt in a stand mixer fitted with the whisk attachment and proceed with the recipe as written, but note that the cream will whip faster and be easier to overwhip in a stand mixer.

then return it to the saucepan and continue to reduce if it's not there yet). While the syrup is reducing, tip any cherry juices that accumulated in the bowl into the saucepan. Remove the saucepan from the heat.

ADD THE CORNSTARCH SLURRY: In a small bowl, stir together the lemon juice and cornstarch until combined, then whisk the mixture into the syrup. Whisking constantly, return the syrup to a boil over medium heat and continue to cook for 20 seconds so the cornstarch can thicken the syrup. Remove the saucepan from the heat and set aside to cool completely (to speed up the process, you can cool down the syrup in an ice bath—see Chilling in an Ice Bath, page 358). Cover the cherries and leave them in the sieve over the bowl at room temperature until it's time to assemble.

WHIP THE CREAM: In a large bowl, with a hand mixer, beat the cream on low speed to start and gradually increase the speed to medium-high as it thickens, until you have a softly whipped cream that holds a droopy peak (see Whipping Cream, page 355).

ASSEMBLE AND SERVE: Place the drained cherries in a medium bowl (discard any additional liquid they may have released). Fish the ginger, zest, and cinnamon out of the cooled syrup and discard, then pour the syrup over the cherries and stir gently to combine. Dollop the whipped cream onto the meringue and spread across the surface with the back of a spoon. Spoon the cherries and syrup over the cream and serve immediately, cutting the pavlova in half lengthwise and into quarters crosswise to make 8 portions.

Profiterole Bar

with Berry, Hot Fudge, and Salted Caramel Sauces

Profiteroles are a classic French dessert that fall dead-center in my Venn diagram of desserts, the perfect intersection of elegant, simple, and satisfying. It's a dish of crispy puffs of pâte à choux (or choux pastry, also used to make éclairs and cream puffs) filled with ice cream and topped with chocolate sauce. Profiteroles are a fantastic dessert for entertaining, as you can make everything ahead of time and let guests assemble their own. The choux pastry, adapted from *Dessert Person* to work with a hand mixer rather than a stand mixer, produces light and tall puffs, but what makes the dish is the three sauces: berry, hot fudge, and salted caramel. They're endlessly versatile and can be served alongside cakes, crepes, and bread puddings in addition to ice cream, so put them to use any way you like.

SERVES 10

DIFFICULTY: 2 (Easy)

ACTIVE TIME: 2 hours 30 minutes

TOTAL TIME: 3 hours 30 minutes

SPECIAL EQUIPMENT: Hand mixer (optional), pastry bag (or resealable plastic bag)

PÂTE À CHOUX

½ cup whole milk (4.2 oz / 120g)

1 tablespoon granulated sugar

½ teaspoon Diamond Crystal kosher salt or ¼ teaspoon Morton kosher salt

7 tablespoons unsalted butter (3.5 oz / 100g), cut into pieces

1 cup all-purpose flour (4.8 oz / 135g)

6 large eggs (10.6 oz / 300g)

Demerara sugar, for sprinkling

ASSEMBLY

Hot Fudge Sauce (recipe follows), warmed

Berry Sauce (recipe follows)

Salted Caramel Sauce (page 346), warmed

3 pints best-quality vanilla (or any flavor) ice cream

HEAT THE WET INGREDIENTS FOR THE PÂTE À CHOUX: In a small saucepan, combine the milk, granulated sugar, salt, butter, and ½ cup (4 oz / 113g) water and bring the mixture to a lively simmer over medium-low heat, stirring with a wooden spoon to melt the butter.

STIR IN THE FLOUR AND COOK THE DOUGH: Once you see active bubbling on the surface of the milk mixture, add the flour all at once and stir slowly to incorporate it into the liquid—the mixture will quickly form a soft dough. As soon as all the flour is incorporated, stir more vigorously until the dough holds together in a single mass and a film forms around the sides and across the bottom of the saucepan. Continue to cook the dough over medium heat, using the spoon to smack it aggressively against the sides of the saucepan, until the dough is shiny and holds together in a firm ball, and the film on the bottom of the saucepan has been reabsorbed into the dough, about 3 minutes. You want to make sure the dough has a chance to dry out and the flour loses its raw taste, so don't rush it.

COOL THE DOUGH SLIGHTLY: Scrape the dough into a large bowl and set aside for about a minute to cool slightly, stirring once or twice to help release steam. While the dough is cooling, crack 1 of the eggs into a small bowl, beat with a fork until smooth, and set aside for later (this will be your egg wash).

BEAT IN THE EGGS: Add 1 of the 5 remaining eggs to the bowl with the dough and mix with a hand mixer on medium speed or vigorously with a wooden spoon until the dough absorbs the egg and the mixture is thick but smooth (the dough will lose its cohesiveness when you add the egg but will come back together with a bit of mixing). Beat in 3 of the remaining eggs one at a time, waiting until the dough is smooth each time before adding the next egg. The dough will become glossier and looser after each addition. After beating in 4 eggs total, take a look at the consistency—it should be glossy, smooth, and thick enough to hold its shape but loose enough that it leaves a thin V-shaped trail as it falls off the end of a wooden spoon or spatula. If it's too thick, beat in the final egg (you'll likely need it, but not necessarily).

TRANSFER TO A PASTRY BAG: Scrape the dough into a large pastry bag or resealable plastic bag. Twist or seal the bag to close, squeezing out as much air as possible (see Filling a Pastry Bag, page 342).

$\rightarrow$

Can I . . .

Make it ahead? Yes. The choux dough can be refrigerated in the pastry bag for up to 24 hours. Let it come to room temperature before piping. The baked puffs, stored airtight at room temperature, will keep for up to 2 days, or they can be frozen for up to 1 month. The baked puffs will soften over time, so to recrisp the exteriors, space them out on a sheet pan and bake at 400°F for 5 to 7 minutes. Cool completely before serving.

Halve the recipe? No. I don't recommend making a half-recipe of pâte à choux, since the quantity of dough is optimal for most small saucepans. However, see above for how to freeze extra puffs.

Use a stand mixer instead of a hand mixer? Yes. To make the pâte à choux, transfer the cooked dough from the saucepan to a stand mixer fitted with the paddle attachment and proceed with the recipe as written.

PREHEAT THE OVEN AND PREPARE THE PANS: Arrange an oven rack in the upper third of the oven and another in the lower third and preheat the oven to 425°F. Line two large sheet pans with parchment paper.

PIPE THE PUFFS: Snip a 1-inch opening in the tip or corner of the bag. Starting in one corner of a sheet pan, hold the bag steady just above the parchment paper and squeeze to extrude about 2 tablespoons of the dough into a mound about the diameter of a golf ball (between 1½ and 2 inches). Repeat, spacing the mounds 2 inches apart and piping in staggered rows, until you've covered both sheet pans and used all the dough. You should end up with about 35 mounds.

BRUSH WITH EGG, TOP WITH SUGAR, AND BAKE: Use a pastry brush to dab the reserved beaten egg gently over the dough mounds, coating them all over, then generously sprinkle with demerara sugar. Transfer the sheet pans to the upper and lower racks and immediately reduce the oven temperature to 375°F. Bake until the puffs are risen and deep golden brown, 30 to 35 minutes, switching the sheets from top to bottom and rotating them front to back after 20 minutes.

COOL THE PUFFS: Turn off the oven, prop the door open with a wooden spoon, and allow the puffs to cool inside the oven for 15 minutes. Remove them from the oven and use the tip of a paring knife to poke a small hole in the bottom of each puff to allow steam to escape (trapped steam can sometimes cause the puffs to deflate as they cool). Let the puffs cool completely on the sheet pans, then use a serrated knife to cut off the tops of the puffs.

ASSEMBLE THE PROFITEROLE BAR: Pile the baked puffs (including the tops) on a large serving platter. Place the berry, hot fudge, and salted caramel sauces each in its own small pitcher or bowl with a serving spoon. Remove the ice cream from the freezer and uncover, then take out any scoops. Arrange all of the components in a buffet and encourage guests to fill the puffs with ice cream and top with the sauce(s) of their choice.

HOT FUDGE SAUCE

If you're somewhat of a regular baker, you probably already have the ingredients needed to make this excellent hot fudge sauce in your pantry right now. Don't be put off by the corn syrup—it's a functional ingredient that inhibits sugar crystallization and ensures a smooth sauce.

½ cup sugar (3.5 oz / 100g)

¼ cup unsweetened cocoa powder (0.70 oz / 21g)

¾ teaspoon Diamond Crystal kosher salt or ½ teaspoon Morton kosher salt

1 cup heavy cream (8.5 oz / 240g), at room temperature

2 tablespoons light corn syrup

3 ounces (85g) bittersweet chocolate, preferably 70%-72% cacao, chopped

2 tablespoons unsalted butter

2 teaspoons vanilla extract

MAKES ABOUT 2 CUPS

DIFFICULTY: 1 (Very Easy)

ACTIVE TIME: 45 minutes

TOTAL TIME: 45 minutes, plus time to cool

ℭan I . . .

Make it ahead? Yes. The hot fudge sauce, stored in a jar or airtight container and refrigerated, will keep for up to 6 months. To rewarm it, scrape the cold, solidified sauce into a double boiler (for more information, see Setting Up a Double Boiler, page 341) and stir until it's warm and fluid.

COOK THE HOT FUDGE: In a small, heavy-bottomed saucepan, whisk together the sugar, cocoa powder, and salt to break up any lumps. Add the cream and corn syrup and whisk until the mixture is smooth and well combined, making sure no unincorporated sugar is trapped around the sides. Add the chocolate and bring the mixture to a boil over medium-high, stirring with a heatproof flexible spatula to dissolve the sugar and melt the chocolate. When the mixture comes to a boil, reduce the heat to maintain a brisk simmer and continue to cook, stirring often and making sure to scrape the bottom and sides of the saucepan to prevent scorching, until the mixture is very thick and you see a layer of yellow fat pooling around the sides of the saucepan, 40 to 50 minutes.

FINISH THE SAUCE: Remove the saucepan from the heat and pour the mixture into a heatproof medium bowl (scrape down the sides of the saucepan, but not the bottom where some of the mixture may have scorched). Add the butter, vanilla, and 2 tablespoons (1 oz / 28g) water and let sit for 5 minutes, then whisk the mixture, starting from the center of the bowl and slowly working outward, until it comes back together and forms a smooth and glossy sauce.

SERVE: If serving immediately, let the sauce sit at room temperature, whisking occasionally, until it's warm and the consistency is thick but still pourable, about 5 minutes. If preparing ahead of time, pour the sauce into a 1-pint jar, cover, and chill.

BERRY SAUCE

This versatile, not-too-sweet berry sauce (made with frozen raspberries and blackberries, so it's enjoyable year-round) keeps for weeks in your fridge. Serve it over ice cream, pancakes, blintzes, yogurt, oatmeal, waffles, or anything else you like.

½ cup sugar (3.5 oz / 100g)

6 ounces (170g) frozen raspberries (about 1½ cups), thawed

6 ounces (170g) frozen blackberries (about 1½ cups), thawed

1 teaspoon vanilla extract

Pinch of kosher salt

MAKES ABOUT 1¾ CUPS

DIFFICULTY: 1 (Very Easy)

ACTIVE TIME: 15 minutes

TOTAL TIME: 15 minutes, plus time to cool

ℭan I . . .

Make it ahead? Yes. The sauce, covered and refrigerated, will keep for up to 1 month.

COOK THE SUGAR: In a medium saucepan, combine the sugar and ¼ cup (2 oz / 57g) water and bring to a boil over medium-high heat, stirring with a heatproof flexible spatula until the sugar dissolves to form a clear syrup, about 3 minutes. When it comes to a boil, stop stirring and cook the mixture, swirling the saucepan occasionally, until large, glassy, slow-moving bubbles form across the entire surface, about 2 minutes.

MAKE THE BERRY SAUCE: Remove the saucepan from the heat and carefully add the raspberries and blackberries (plus any juices). Stir the mixture to combine, which will cause the sugar to harden in some places. Return the saucepan to medium-low heat and stir, mashing the berries against the saucepan and scraping the bottom and sides with the spatula, until any hardened bits of sugar have dissolved and you have a smoothish sauce with some pieces of berries floating around, about 5 minutes. Remove the saucepan from the heat and stir in the vanilla and salt.

CHILL: Transfer the berry sauce to a lidded container and refrigerate until cold.

Kabocha & Ginger Soufflés

Kabocha is a Japanese variety of winter squash with a squat shape, dark green skin, and vivid orange interior. Pound for pound, it's my favorite squash for baking. The dense, starchy flesh adds both structure and deep flavor to these airy autumnal soufflés, which are imbued with the flavor of fresh ginger. If you can't find kabocha, you can use cooked sweet potato or red kuri squash.

SERVES 4

DIFFICULTY: 2 (Easy)

ACTIVE TIME: 2 hours 20 minutes (includes cooking the squash)

TOTAL TIME: 2 hours 40 minutes

SPECIAL EQUIPMENT: Blender (or food processor), four 6-ounce ramekins, hand mixer

1 small kabocha squash (2.5 lb / 1.1kg), halved, seeds and stringy innards scooped out

Butter and granulated sugar for the ramekins

2 tablespoons unsalted butter

¼ cup whole milk (2.1 oz / 60g)

2 tablespoons all-purpose flour

½ teaspoon Diamond Crystal kosher salt or ¼ teaspoon Morton kosher salt, plus a generous pinch

2 tablespoons dark brown sugar

3 large egg yolks (1.6 oz / 45g), divided

¾ teaspoon finely grated fresh ginger

1 teaspoon vanilla extract

4 large egg whites (4.9 oz / 140g), at room temperature

¼ cup granulated sugar (1.8 oz / 50g), plus more for topping

Crème Anglaise (page 348), for serving

PREHEAT THE OVEN: Arrange an oven rack in the center position and preheat the oven to 425°F.

ROAST AND PUREE THE SQUASH: Place the squash halves cut-side down on a small sheet pan and add water until you have a thin layer covering the sheet. Roast the squash until it's completely tender and a fork slides into the flesh with no resistance, 50 minutes to 1 hour. Let the squash sit at room temperature until it's cool enough to handle, then scoop the flesh from the skins and mash. Measure out ½ cup (4.2 oz / 120g) of the flesh, transfer to a blender or food processor, and puree until it's completely smooth. Set the pureed kabocha aside (save any remaining cooked squash for another use, like eating with a little butter and salt and pepper).

PREPARE THE RAMEKINS: Brush the bottoms and sides of four 6-ounce ramekins with room temperature butter, using straight upward strokes around the sides and brushing all the way to the rim. Sprinkle the ramekins with granulated sugar and shake to coat, then tap out the excess (the upward strokes and sugar give the batter something to cling to as it rises). Set the ramekins aside.

BROWN THE BUTTER AND MAKE THE KABOCHA MIXTURE: In a small saucepan, bring the 2 tablespoons butter to a boil over medium heat and cook, stirring constantly with a heatproof flexible spatula and scraping the bottom and sides of the saucepan, until the sputtering subsides and you see tiny golden brown specks floating in the butter, about 2 minutes (see Browning Butter, page 353). Remove the saucepan from the heat and stir the pureed kabocha into the browned butter until combined (it will sputter a bit). Add the milk, flour, and ½ teaspoon salt and whisk until the mixture is smooth.

BLANCH AND TEMPER THE YOLKS: In a large bowl, vigorously whisk the brown sugar and 2 of the egg yolks (1 oz / 30g) until the mixture is pale and thick, about 1 minute. Whisking the yolk mixture constantly, add a few tablespoons of the hot kabocha mixture, 1 tablespoon at a time, to temper the eggs, then whisk the warmed contents of the bowl into the kabocha mixture (reserve the bowl). Scrape around the bottom and sides of the saucepan with a heatproof flexible spatula to make sure everything is incorporated (for more information, see Blanching and Tempering Eggs, page 348).

COOK AND COOL THE KABOCHA BASE: Cook the mixture over medium heat, whisking constantly, until it thickens to the consistency of a stiff pudding, about 4 minutes. Remove the saucepan from the heat and immediately scrape the mixture into the reserved bowl. Let the kabocha mixture sit uncovered, whisking it occasionally to encourage cooling, until it's room temperature (or, to speed up this process, you can cool down the kabocha mixture in an ice bath—see Chilling in an Ice Bath, page 358). Whisk in the remaining egg yolk, the ginger, and vanilla. Set aside.

→

BEAT THE EGG WHITES AND SUGAR: In a separate clean, large, nonplastic bowl, combine the egg whites and a pinch of salt and beat with a hand mixer on medium-low speed until the whites are broken up and frothy, about 20 seconds. Increase the speed to medium-high and continue to beat until the whites are foamy and opaque, about 30 seconds, then gradually add the granulated sugar in a slow, steady stream, beating constantly. Once all the sugar is added, continue to beat just until you have dense, glossy egg whites that hold a stiff peak (see page 339 for what this stage looks like). Try not to overbeat, or the whites will take on a dry, grainy texture and be difficult to incorporate into the kabocha base. Set the bowl aside.

FOLD IN THE EGG WHITES: Scrape about one-third of the beaten egg whites into the bowl with the kabocha base and whisk quickly and briefly to combine. Using a large flexible spatula and broad, decisive strokes, fold in the remaining beaten egg whites in two additions, scraping the bottom and sides of the bowl and rotating the bowl as you work, until the mixture is streak-free (for more on the proper technique, see Folding a Mixture, page 351).

FILL THE RAMEKINS: Gently scrape the batter into the prepared ramekins, dividing it evenly and using all of it (the ramekins should be filled to the very top). Tap the ramekins delicately on the work surface to help settle the batter, then, working one at a time, use a small offset spatula or a butter knife to smooth the surface and scrape off any excess batter so it's level and flush with the very top of the ramekin. If necessary, transfer any excess batter from one ramekin to another to ensure they're all filled to the very top. Repeat until all the ramekins are leveled (at this point you could have a small amount of batter left over—if so, discard it).

> *Potential Pitfall:* If you don't have enough batter to fill all four ramekins all the way to the top, it's likely because you didn't whip the egg whites enough. That's okay, fill as many of the ramekins as you can all the way to the top and use all the batter. Your soufflés will still rise, they just won't achieve their maximum height.

SUGAR THE SOUFFLÉS AND WIPE AWAY A RING OF BATTER: Lightly sprinkle the surfaces of the batter with more granulated sugar, then, working one ramekin at a time, run a clean thumb around the inside of the rims to wipe away a ring of batter and expose the inner lip of the ramekins all the way around (use the natural indentation inside the ramekins as a guide for how deep to make the ring). This will ensure that your soufflés rise straight upward and maintain level tops. Wipe away any streaks of batter from the rim and outsides of the ramekins.

BAKE AND SERVE: Place the ramekins on a sheet pan, spacing them evenly. Transfer the sheet pan to the oven, immediately reduce the oven temperature to 375°F, and bake until the soufflés are risen, firm and springy to the touch across the surfaces, and have a slight wobble, 15 to 20 minutes. Remove the soufflés from the oven and serve immediately with the crème anglaise on the side. Encourage everyone to spoon down into the center of their soufflé and pour a few tablespoons of the crème anglaise into the interior.

Can I . . .

Make them ahead? No! Soufflés need to be served and eaten immediately after they emerge from the oven. However, the kabocha base can be made several hours ahead and kept covered at room temperature until it's time to assemble the batter.

Double the recipe? Not recommended. The assembly process is time-sensitive, so it's not practical to assemble 8 soufflés at once, and they will not bake evenly in most home ovens.

Use a stand mixer instead of a hand mixer? Yes. Combine the egg whites and salt in a stand mixer fitted with the whisk attachment, then proceed with the recipe as written, keeping in mind that the egg whites will whip faster and be easier to overbeat in the stand mixer.

Eton Mess Two Ways

Eton Mess, named for the English boarding school where it originated, ranks high on my list of my most favorite, best, winningest desserts of all time. It's a simple mix of crumbled crispy meringues, whipped cream, and fruit—so basically, a broken-up pavlova. Here I interpret Eton Mess two ways. The first is with macerated strawberries, which are the classic choice, and the second is with a silky passion fruit curd (passion fruit being the traditional fruit used for pavlova). This makes the strawberry version the easier of the two (for true dessert transcendence, use peak-season, ripe strawberries), but both are superlatively good. If you want to be extra ambitious, you can make both and layer the two together. The recipe calls for a half recipe of **All-Purpose Meringue**, so see Can I . . . on page 344 for instructions for scaling down.

SERVES 6

DIFFICULTY: 2 (Easy)

GLUTEN-FREE

ACTIVE TIME: 45 minutes (does not include making the meringue)

TOTAL TIME: 4 hours 15 minutes

SPECIAL EQUIPMENT: Hand mixer, 6 serving glasses

½ recipe **All-Purpose Meringue** (page 344)

PASSION FRUIT VERSION

½ cup sugar (3.5 oz / 100g)

4 large egg yolks (2.1 oz / 60g)

¾ cup fresh passion fruit pulp and seeds (6 oz / 172g), scooped from 6 to 8 medium passion fruits

2 tablespoons fresh lemon juice

½ teaspoon Diamond Crystal kosher salt or ¼ teaspoon Morton kosher salt

4 tablespoons unsalted butter (2 oz / 57g), cut into ½-inch pieces, chilled

1 teaspoon vanilla extract

STRAWBERRY VERSION

¼ cup red currant jelly (2.8 oz / 80g)

2 tablespoons fresh lemon juice

1 tablespoon elderflower liqueur or crème de cassis (optional)

1½ pounds (680g) strawberries, hulled and thinly sliced lengthwise

ASSEMBLY

2 cups heavy cream (16.9 oz / 480g), chilled

Pinch of kosher salt

1½ teaspoons vanilla extract

PREHEAT THE OVEN AND PREPARE THE SHEET PAN: Arrange an oven rack in the center position and preheat the oven to 200°F. Line a sheet pan with a silicone baking mat or parchment paper.

FORM AND BAKE THE MERINGUES: Use a spoon to form 6 equal dollops of the meringue spaced out evenly across the prepared sheet pan (use all the meringue). Flatten the dollops slightly with the back of the spoon, then bake the meringues until they are dry to the touch, very crisp on the outside, and soft and marshmallow-y on the inside, 1 hour 40 minutes to 2 hours, rotating the sheet pan front to back after 1 hour. Test for doneness by carefully peeling one of the meringues away from the baking mat or parchment. It should release cleanly; if it sticks, continue baking. Turn off the oven, prop the door open with a wooden spoon, and let the meringues cool in the oven for 30 minutes. Remove the sheet pan from the oven and set aside to cool completely.

FOR THE PASSION FRUIT VERSION, PREPARE THE CURD: In a small heavy-bottomed saucepan, combine the sugar and yolks and whisk vigorously, making sure no unincorporated sugar is trapped around the sides, until the mixture is pale, mousse-y, and slightly thickened, about 2 minutes. Whisking constantly, slowly stream in the passion fruit pulp and continue to whisk to break up the pulp and loosen the seeds. Whisk in the lemon juice and salt.

Optional Upgrade: Some recipes for passion fruit curd will have you blitz the passion fruit pulp in a food processor to loosen the seeds and break up any stringy fibers, but I usually skip this step. All of the whisking of the curd breaks up the fibers and releases the seeds, and any stringy bits usually get caught in the whisk and are removed that way. For an ultrasmooth curd, though, pulse the pulp a few times in a food processor.

COOK THE CURD: Place the saucepan over medium-low heat and cook, whisking constantly, until the foam on the surface subsides and the curd is thick, opaque, and coats the back of a spoon, 5 to 6 minutes (see A Word on Curd, page 70, for a photo of curd coating a spoon—if you want a more precise endpoint, it will read 170°F on an instant-read thermometer). Immediately remove the saucepan from the heat.

WHISK IN THE BUTTER AND VANILLA AND CHILL: Whisk in the butter one piece at a time, waiting for each piece to disappear before adding the next, until all the butter is incorporated and the mixture is smooth. Whisk in the vanilla. Fill a large bowl about a quarter of the way with ice water and

$\rightarrow$

place the saucepan inside, making sure that the water level hits below the top of the saucepan. Let it sit, whisking occasionally, until the curd is cold, about 5 minutes (see Chilling in an Ice Bath, page 358). Set the cold curd aside and proceed to whipping the cream and assembling.

FOR THE STRAWBERRY VERSION, MACERATE THE STRAWBERRIES: About 30 minutes before you want to assemble the Eton Messes, in a small saucepan, warm the red currant jelly over medium-low heat, whisking often, until it's smooth and fluid, about 2 minutes. Scrape the jelly into a large bowl and whisk in the lemon juice and elderflower liqueur (if using). Add the strawberries and toss gently with a large spoon until the berries are coated. Set the bowl aside and let the mixture sit at room temperature, gently stirring it once or twice, until the berries are softened and have given off their juices, 25 to 30 minutes (this is called maceration—see Macerating Fruit, page 355, for more on the process).

WHIP THE CREAM AND ADD IN THE MERINGUES: In a large bowl, combine the cream and a pinch of salt and whip with a hand mixer on low speed to start and gradually increase the speed to medium-high as it thickens, until you have stiff peaks (see Whipping Cream, page 355). Beat in the vanilla. Working over the bowl of cream, break the meringues one at a time into bite-sized pieces and add to the bowl. Once you've broken up all of the meringues and added them to the bowl, use a large flexible spatula to fold the mixture several times until all the pieces are coated and evenly distributed.

ASSEMBLE AND SERVE: For either the passion fruit or strawberry version, divide about half of the meringue/cream mixture evenly among six serving glasses, spooning it into the bottoms and doing your best to avoid smearing it around the sides. Spoon 2 generous tablespoons of the passion fruit curd or ⅓ cup of the strawberry mixture (making sure to include some of the syrupy juices) into each glass. Spoon the remaining meringue/cream mixture into the glasses, dividing it evenly. Top each of the glasses with another 2 tablespoons of curd (you'll have a little bit leftover; save it for another use), or, divide the remaining berries and accumulated juices evenly on top. Serve immediately.

Can I . . .

Make it ahead? Yes. The Eton Messes can be assembled, covered, and refrigerated for up to 2 hours before serving (any longer and the meringue will start to disintegrate). The baked meringues, wrapped well or stored in an airtight container at room temperature, will keep for up to 1 day (make sure they're stored absolutely airtight, or the meringue will absorb moisture from the air and become sticky). If you're making the passion fruit version, the curd can be stored in an airtight container and refrigerated for up to 1 week. Do not store it in a metal bowl, or the curd will pick up a metallic flavor.

Use a stand mixer instead of a hand mixer? Yes. Combine the heavy cream and salt in a stand mixer fitted with the whisk attachment and proceed with the recipe as written, but note that the cream will whip faster and be easier to overwhip in a stand mixer.

Black Sesame Merveilleux

Merveilleux (which means "marvelous" in French) is a dessert that originated in the French city of Lille, near the Belgian border. It's a confection made of two light, crispy meringues that are spackled together with whipped cream, then covered in more whipped cream, and coated in chocolate shavings, but here I ribbon unsweetened black sesame paste through the meringue. The bitterness and pungency of the black sesame offsets the sweetness of the meringue, plus it adds pockets of chewiness throughout. In the spirit of the traditional recipe, which has a cherry hidden in the center, I decorate the tops with a cherry set on a rosette of cream, but feel free to skip this flourish. Look in Asian markets for black sesame paste that lists black sesame as the only ingredient (Chinese or Japanese brands are the most common).

SERVES 8

DIFFICULTY: 2 (Easy)

GLUTEN-FREE

ACTIVE TIME: 1 hour 10 minutes (does not include making the meringue)

TOTAL TIME: 3 hours 40 minutes

SPECIAL EQUIPMENT: Hand mixer

All-Purpose Meringue (page 344)

6 tablespoons black sesame paste (3.4 oz / 96g), well stirred

2½ cups heavy cream (24 oz / 600g), chilled

½ cup mascarpone cheese (4.2 oz / 120g), chilled

Pinch of kosher salt

1 teaspoon vanilla extract

½ cup black sesame seeds (2.5 oz / 71g)

8 maraschino cherries with stems (optional), rinsed, drained, and patted dry

PREHEAT THE OVEN AND PREPARE THE SHEET PANS: Arrange an oven rack in the upper third of the oven and another in the lower third and preheat the oven to 200°F. Line two large sheet pans with silicone baking mats or parchment paper and set them aside.

FOLD THE BLACK SESAME PASTE INTO THE MERINGUE: Have the meringue at the ready in a large bowl. Drizzle the black sesame paste across the surface of the meringue, scraping in every last bit, then fold the meringue briefly just to marble it through with the black sesame (for more on the proper technique, see Folding a Mixture, page 351).

Potential Pitfall: Don't fold the mixture more than a few times or the black sesame will loosen the consistency of the meringue and cause it to spread too much on the sheet pans.

FORM THE MERINGUES: Using a large spoon, portion about half of the meringue onto one of the prepared sheet pans in 8 tall, equal dollops about the size of tennis balls, spacing them evenly and trying to keep the dollops as round as possible. Dollop the remaining meringue across the second sheet pan in 8 equal portions, this time making the dollops slightly wider and flatter than the first batch (keep in mind that the meringue will settle and spread some as it bakes). Once they're baked, you are going to stack the taller meringues on the flatter ones.

BAKE: Transfer the sheet pans to the oven, positioning one on the upper rack and one on the lower rack, and bake the meringues until they are dry to the touch and peel away cleanly from the baking mat or parchment paper, 2 hours to 2 hours 30 minutes, switching racks and rotating the sheet pans front to back after 1 hour. Turn off the oven, prop the door open with a wooden spoon, and allow the meringues to cool in the oven for 30 minutes. Remove the sheet pans from the oven and let cool completely.

WHIP THE CREAM: In a large bowl, with a hand mixer, whip the cream, mascarpone, and salt on low speed to start and gradually increase the speed to medium-high as it thickens, until you have stiff peaks (see Whipping Cream, page 355). Beat in the vanilla.

Potential Pitfall: If the cream isn't firmly whipped, it won't be able to hold its shape as you cover the meringues, so pay close attention to the visual indicators described and illustrated in step 3 on page 355.

→

Can I . . .

Make them ahead? For the most part, yes. The baked meringues, wrapped well or stored in an airtight container at room temperature, will keep for up to 1 day (make sure the container is absolutely airtight, or the meringues will absorb moisture from the air and become sticky). The finished merveilleux can sit at room temperature for up to 1 hour before serving. Any leftovers can be stored in an airtight container and refrigerated, but the meringues will lose their crispiness.

Use a substitute for the black sesame? Yes. Instead of the black sesame paste, use an equal amount of tahini, natural peanut butter, or almond butter. In place of the black sesame seeds, use white sesame seeds, crushed roasted peanuts, or toasted sliced almonds.

Halve the recipe? Yes. Halve all of the ingredient quantities, as well as the ingredient quantities for the **All-Purpose Meringue** (page 344), and follow the respective recipes as written, forming 8 meringues total (4 tall, 4 squat) on a single lined sheet pan. Bake the meringues in the center of the oven, and start checking them for doneness after 2 hours.

Use a stand mixer instead of a hand mixer? Yes. Combine the heavy cream, mascarpone, and salt in a stand mixer fitted with the whisk attachment and proceed with the recipe as written, but note that the cream will whip faster and be easier to overwhip in a stand mixer.

ASSEMBLE: Place the black sesame seeds in a shallow bowl and set aside. Top the 8 flatter meringues, still on the sheet pan, with a generous dollop of the cream mixture. Then, one by one lift the 8 taller meringues off the other sheet pan and place on top of the dollops, pressing down so the two meringues adhere, making 8 little stacks (reserve the empty sheet pan). Holding one of the stacks in the palm of your hand, generously top it with more cream and use a small offset spatula or a butter knife to smooth the cream down and around the sides in a generous, even layer. Working over the bowl of sesame seeds, sprinkle the stack generously with the black sesame, then place it on the reserved sheet pan and set aside. Coat the remaining stacks of meringue one at a time with the remaining cream and sprinkle with sesame seeds, placing each on the sheet pan.

> *Optional Upgrade:* Once all the stacks are coated, transfer any remaining cream to a pastry bag fitted with a star tip and pipe rosettes of cream on top of each merveilleux, then set a cherry on top.

SERVE: Transfer the merveilleux to plates and serve immediately.

Souffléed Lemon Bread Pudding

I've never been a bread pudding person, but I think it's because the versions I'd tried in the past were almost always very, very heavy. But the concept of custardy baked bread appeals to me on so many levels that I knew it was just a matter of coming up with a lighter and brighter version. The lightness here comes from beaten egg whites that are folded into the bread and custard mixture, giving it a souffléed texture, while the brightness is from lemons—lemon curd, more specifically, which is used also as a sauce for the finished bread pudding. It's so different from the typical dense, cloying bread puddings I've had that it almost feels like a different dessert. Mission accomplished.

SERVES 9

DIFFICULTY: 3 (Moderate)

ACTIVE TIME: 1 hour

TOTAL TIME: 4 hours, plus time to cool

SPECIAL EQUIPMENT: 8 × 8-inch pan (preferably metal), hand mixer, 13 × 9-inch pan

LEMON CURD

¾ cup sugar (5.3 oz / 150g)

5 large egg yolks (2.6 oz / 75g)

¾ cup fresh lemon juice (6 oz / 170g), from about 5 lemons (zest 2 of the lemons before juicing and reserve for assembly)

½ teaspoon Diamond Crystal kosher salt or ¼ teaspoon Morton kosher salt

1 stick unsalted butter (4 oz / 113g), cut into ½-inch pieces, chilled

1 teaspoon vanilla extract

ASSEMBLY

1 medium challah (10 oz / 283g), crust removed, cut into ¾-inch cubes (about 8 cups)

2 tablespoons finely grated lemon zest, from about 2 lemons

½ cup sugar (3.5 oz / 100g), divided, plus more for sprinkling

2 large eggs (3.5 oz / 100g), at room temperature

2 cups buttermilk (16 oz / 480g), at room temperature

1 cup heavy cream (8.5 oz / 240g), at room temperature

Butter for the pan

3 large egg whites (3.7 oz / 105g), at room temperature

Pinch of kosher salt

BEAT THE SUGAR AND EGGS FOR THE CURD: In a small heavy-bottomed saucepan, vigorously whisk together the sugar and egg yolks, making sure no unincorporated sugar is trapped around the sides, until the mixture is very pale, light in texture, and thick, about 2 minutes.

ADD THE LEMON JUICE AND COOK THE CURD: Slowly stream in the lemon juice, whisking constantly and scraping around the sides, until the mixture is smooth. Whisk in the salt. Place the saucepan over medium-low heat and cook, whisking constantly, until the curd turns opaque yellow, barely holds the marks of the whisk, and is thick enough to coat the back of a spoon, 7 to 10 minutes (see A Word on Curd, page 70, for a photo of curd coating a spoon—if you want a more precise endpoint, it will read 170°F on an instant-read thermometer). Immediately remove the saucepan from the heat.

WHISK IN THE BUTTER AND VANILLA: Whisk the butter into the curd a couple of pieces at a time, waiting for the pieces to disappear before adding more, until all the butter is incorporated and the mixture is smooth. Whisk in the vanilla. Transfer the curd to an airtight container, press a piece of plastic directly onto the surface of the curd to prevent a skin from forming, and refrigerate until you're ready to assemble the bread pudding.

PREHEAT THE OVEN: Arrange an oven rack in the center position and preheat the oven to 350°F.

TOAST THE BREAD: Scatter the bread cubes across a large sheet pan in an even layer and toast until the pieces are dry and very light golden brown all over, 12 to 18 minutes, tossing halfway through. Set the pan aside and allow the bread to cool. Turn off the oven.

MAKE THE CUSTARD BASE: In a large bowl, combine the lemon zest and ¼ cup (1.8 oz / 50g) of the sugar and massage the mixture with your fingertips until it's very fragrant and the zest is distributed throughout the sugar. Add the eggs and whisk vigorously until the mixture is pale and slightly thickened, about 1 minute. Whisking constantly, slowly pour in the buttermilk, followed by the heavy cream. Remove the curd from the refrigerator, measure out 1 cup, and whisk it into the custard base until smooth. Keep the remaining curd covered and refrigerated until it's time to serve.

ADD THE BREAD AND SOAK: Add the toasted bread to the bowl with the custard and use a large flexible spatula to fold the mixture gently but thoroughly until combined. Cover the bowl and set it aside at room

→

temperature until the bread has absorbed most of the custard and the pieces are completely soaked through, about 2 hours, gently folding the mixture once or twice.

PREHEAT THE OVEN AND PREPARE THE PAN: Arrange one oven rack in the center position and one in the uppermost position (ignore this if you have a broiler drawer in the bottom of your oven) and preheat the oven to 325°F. Brush the bottom and sides of an 8 × 8-inch baking pan, preferably metal, with room temperature butter, then line the bottom and two opposite sides with a piece of parchment paper, leaving a slight overhang. Lightly butter the parchment paper and set the pan aside.

BOIL WATER FOR THE WATER BATH: Bring 6 cups of water to a boil in a kettle or in a medium saucepan over high heat.

MEANWHILE, BEAT THE EGG WHITES AND SUGAR: In a separate clean, medium, nonplastic bowl, combine the egg whites and salt and beat with a hand mixer on medium-low speed until the whites are broken up and frothy, about 20 seconds. Increase the speed to medium-high and continue to beat until the whites are foamy and opaque, about 30 seconds, then gradually add the remaining ¼ cup (1.8 oz / 50g) sugar in a slow, steady stream, beating constantly. Once all the sugar is added, continue to beat just until you have dense, glossy egg whites that hold a medium peak (see page 339 for what this stage looks like). Try not to overbeat, or the whites will take on a dry, grainy texture and be difficult to incorporate.

FOLD IN THE EGG WHITES: Uncover the bread mixture and fold it a couple of times with the flexible spatula to loosen. Scrape about one-third of the egg whites into the bread mixture and fold gently to combine (for more on the proper technique, see Folding a Mixture, page 351). Fold in the remaining egg whites in two additions, using broad, decisive strokes and scraping the bottom and sides of the bowl.

BAKE THE BREAD PUDDING IN A WATER BATH: Scrape the bread mixture into the prepared pan and work it to the sides and into the corners in an even layer, then smooth the top. Place the pan inside a 13 × 9-inch pan and carefully pour the boiling water into the bottom of the larger pan, avoiding any splashing, until it reaches about 1 inch up the sides of the smaller pan. Cover the entire 13 × 9-inch pan with a piece of foil, crimping it tightly to seal, and carefully transfer the pan to the center oven rack. Bake until the entire surface of the bread pudding is puffed and the center springs back when pressed (it will be pushing up against the foil), 55 to 65 minutes. Carefully remove the pan from the oven and uncover. Leave the bread pudding in the water bath.

BROIL THE TOP: Preheat the broiler. Lightly sprinkle the surface of the bread pudding with more sugar, then place under the broiler, still inside the water bath, and broil until the sugar on the surface is caramelized in leopard-like spots, keeping a close watch and rotating carefully as needed to promote even caramelization, about 3 minutes. Remove the bread pudding from the oven, carefully lift it out of the water bath, and set aside to cool to room temperature.

SERVE: Remove the remaining lemon curd from the refrigerator and stir to loosen its consistency. Slice the bread pudding into a 3-by-3 grid, forming 9 squares. Serve the squares topped with dollops of the lemon curd.

Can I . . .

Make it ahead? Yes. The bread pudding, tightly wrapped and refrigerated, will keep for up to 3 days, but it's best served on the day it's made. Before serving, let the cold bread pudding come to room temperature or cover it with foil and heat in a 325°F oven just until it's warm. The reserved lemon curd, refrigerated in an airtight nonmetal container, will keep for 1 week.

Use a stand mixer instead of a hand mixer? Yes. Combine the egg whites and salt in a stand mixer fitted with the whisk attachment, then proceed with the recipe as written, keeping in mind that the egg whites will whip faster and be easier to overbeat in the stand mixer.

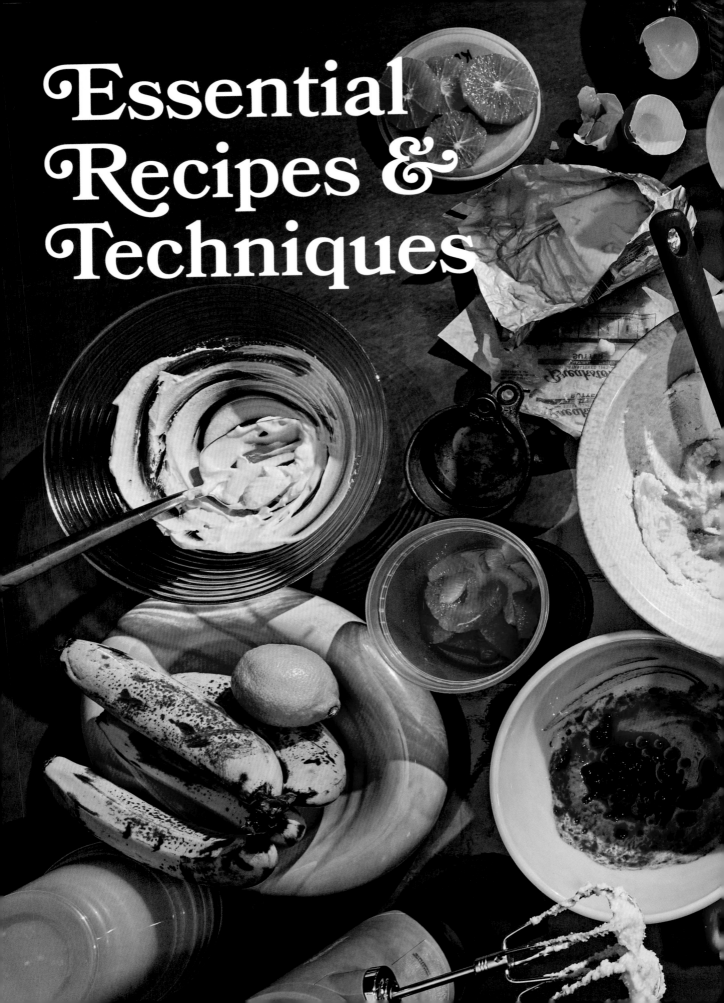

Essential
Recipes &
Techniques

QUINCE PINEAPPL

One of my favorite pastimes is reading old cookbooks. When I read an especially old one, written a century ago or more, I'm always struck and somewhat entertained by the lack of detail in the recipes. Instructions like "prepare a stiff meringue," "make a good crust," or "cook in a moderate oven" are given without further elaboration. This is because as a genre, cookbooks were originally written by professionals to teach other professionals, and authors could therefore assume a shared level of knowledge and experience among their readers. Now, fortunately, cookbooks find a wide audience, and the knowledge contained in them is available to all. I approached the recipes here knowing that this book could just as easily find its way into the hands of a novice as it could an experienced baker, so I'm careful to make as few assumptions about my readers' experience and knowledge as possible.

This chapter takes an in-depth look at the essential recipes and techniques that underpin many of the desserts in this book. The six essential recipes, which include **All-Purpose Flaky Pastry Dough** (page 331) and **All-Purpose Meringue** (page 344), are used several times throughout the chapters, and each features at least one essential technique that itself is referenced many more times throughout. Additionally, you'll find step-by-step guides to stand-alone techniques and processes such as whipping cream to stiff peaks, browning butter, and forming cookie dough into logs. More experienced bakers might think some of the techniques are no-brainers, like creaming butter and sugar, but since even a seemingly simple step can determine the outcome of a recipe, I gloss over nothing. What's obvious or routine for one reader might not be to another, but with practice—and by using these steps and photos as a reference and guide—anyone can develop instincts for those make-or-break moments when, for example, eggs cook to thicken a custard, or sugar starts to caramelize in a saucepan.

All-Purpose Flaky Pastry Dough

Pastry dough is one of those things that trips people up, so I'm perpetually tweaking and modifying my technique to make it more foolproof. While the proportion of ingredients never changes much, this method is my most forgiving yet. It relies on a bench or bowl scraper to bring the dough together directly on the work surface (if you don't have a bench scraper, get one—they're inexpensive and multipurpose). Using a bench scraper instead of your hands keeps the butter cold and limits gluten development while you distribute the water throughout the flour, producing an evenly hydrated dough can be rolled out without cracking once it's chilled. This is key, because keeping the dough as cold as possible leads to a more tender and flaky crust. The rolling process, an essential technique, is detailed step by step in Rolling Out Chilled Pastry Dough (page 332). This recipe yields two portions, but even if you only need one, I recommend making the full quantity and freezing the other portion since it's a handy thing to have around. That said, I've included instructions in Can I . . . , below, to scale it down, if that's what you prefer.

MAKES 2 PORTIONS (ENOUGH FOR 2 SINGLE-CRUST PIES, 1 DOUBLE-CRUST PIE, OR 2 GALETTES)

DIFFICULTY: 1 (Very Easy)

ACTIVE TIME: 25 minutes

TOTAL TIME: 2 hours 25 minutes

SPECIAL EQUIPMENT: Bench scraper

3 cups all-purpose flour (14.2 oz / 405g), plus more for rolling

2 tablespoons sugar

2 teaspoons Diamond Crystal kosher salt or 1 teaspoon Morton kosher salt

2½ sticks unsalted butter (10 oz / 283g), thinly sliced crosswise, chilled

1. COMBINE THE DRY INGREDIENTS: In a large bowl, whisk together the flour, sugar, and salt.

2. ADD THE BUTTER AND ICE WATER: Prepare about 1 cup (8 oz / 227g) of ice water and set it aside. Add the butter to the bowl with the dry ingredients and toss, separating the pieces and coating them in the flour mixture. Use your fingertips to quickly break and smash the pieces of butter into smaller bits (it's okay if some of the butter is left in large pieces; you'll break it up more in the next step). Make a well in the center of the bowl and add ⅔ cup (5.6 oz / 158g) of the ice water. Toss with a fork to distribute the water until you have a clumpy mixture with lots of dry spots **[see photo A, page 333]**.

3. WORK THE MIXTURE DIRECTLY ON THE SURFACE: Tip the contents of the bowl out onto a clean work surface **[B, page 333]**. Use the straight edge of a bench or bowl scraper to chop up the mixture directly on the surface, breaking up the clumps and pieces of butter and periodically using the scraper to toss and push the mixture back into a pile. Continue to chop and toss the mixture until it's broken down into small, uniform pieces with very few floury spots and the butter pieces are no larger than a pea **[C, D, page 333]**. This process helps you bring the dough together without working it excessively, increasing tenderness.

4. BRING THE DOUGH TOGETHER: Push the mixture into a pile and squeeze it with your hands all over so it holds together in large pieces **[E, page 333]**. Depending on the butter and flour you're using, the entire mixture might hold together without any dry spots—if that's the case, skip to the next step. If you still have some floury areas, move any large pieces to one side, leaving the dry bits in the pile. Drizzle ½ tablespoon of ice water over the floury area, then use the bench scraper in the same chopping motion to evenly distribute the water **[F, page 333]**. Squeeze to bring it together, moving the pieces to the side, then repeat with more ice water as needed until no dry flour remains on the surface.

Can I . . .

Make it ahead? Yes. The dough, tightly wrapped and refrigerated, will keep for up to 2 days (after that it will start to oxidize). The dough can also be frozen for up to 3 months (make sure it's thoroughly wrapped). Let frozen dough thaw overnight in the refrigerator before using.

Halve the recipe? Yes. To make just a single portion of dough, halve the quantities of all ingredients, including the ice water, and proceed with the recipe as written, forming the dough into a single round or rectangle.

5. STACK THE DOUGH (SEE PHOTOS J THROUGH M, FOR STACKING SHORTCAKE DOUGH ON PAGE 338): Use your hands to pat the dough firmly into a square, then use a floured rolling pin to flatten the square until it's ¾ inch thick. Pat around the four sides with your hands or the scraper to square off and compact the dough, then use the flat edge of the scraper or a knife to cut the dough in half. Lift one half up (again, using the scraper to help) and place it directly on top of the other. Use the scraper to lift the stack of dough and dust underneath with more flour, then roll over it with the pin to flatten it slightly, dusting the top with flour if needed to prevent sticking. Cut the dough in half again, this time crosswise, and stack the halves again. The stacking and flattening increases the flakiness of the dough and further distributes the moisture, making it easier to roll out.

> **Potential Pitfall:** If you're working in a hot kitchen, the butter might soften and make the dough sticky and difficult to handle. If this happens, transfer the dough to the refrigerator or freezer and chill until it's firm, 10 to 15 minutes, before proceeding. Don't skip the stacking process, as it's needed to give the dough structure. Bringing the dough together with the bench scraper is such a gentle method that it might not develop sufficient gluten, so without stacking, the dough could crack during baking.

6. PORTION AND SHAPE THE DOUGH: Working quickly, use the scraper to loosen the dough from the surface and dust underneath and on top with more flour, then flatten it with the rolling pin into a long rectangle measuring ¾ inch thick. Cut the rectangle in half crosswise to make 2 equal portions (if making the **Walnut & Oat Slab Pie,** page 273, leave the rectangle whole—do not cut in half—and proceed to wrapping and chilling). Whatever form the dough takes when it's chilled is the form it will most easily assume when being rolled out, so if it's destined to be round, as for a pie, use the heel of your hand to round off any corners and press the portion(s) into more of a disk shape. If it's destined to be rectangular, pat around the sides to straighten and square off the corners.

7. WRAP AND CHILL: Wrap each piece in plastic or reusable food wrap, maintaining the round or rectangular shape. Roll over the wrapped pieces with the rolling pin to flatten the dough and force it to fill out the plastic or food wrap (applying this pressure will help prevent cracking later). Transfer the pieces to the refrigerator and chill until they're very cold and firm, at least 2 hours. If a recipe requires a single portion of dough, freeze the other portion and save it for another use.

Essential Technique

ROLLING OUT CHILLED PASTRY DOUGH

8. SOFTEN THE DOUGH SLIGHTLY: Remove the cold pastry dough from the refrigerator and let it sit at room temperature for a minute or two to soften slightly. Unwrap the dough and place it on a lightly floured surface.

9. BEAT THE DOUGH TO MAKE IT PLIABLE: Use a rolling pin to beat the dough evenly across the surface, applying enough force to leave an imprint but not enough to crack or splinter it. If rolling it into a round, lift and rotate the dough every couple of whacks to keep the round shape. If rolling it into a square or rectangle, beat the dough lengthwise across the entire surface, then rotate it 90 degrees and beat crosswise, repeating several times in both directions. Continue to beat the dough, lifting it frequently and adding more flour if needed to prevent sticking, until it's just under ½ inch thick **[G, H]**. This will make the dough pliable and easier to roll out while cold.

10. ROLL OUT THE DOUGH: Dust underneath and on top of the dough with more flour, then roll it out, frequently lifting and rotating the dough to work it into a round, or turning it 90 degrees every so often and rolling it lengthwise and crosswise for a square or rectangle. Continue to roll, keeping the dough moving on the work surface and dusting it with more flour as needed to prevent sticking, until you have the size and/or thickness specified in the recipe **[I, J]**. If it starts to feel soft or sticky, transfer the dough to a sheet pan and refrigerate until it's cold and firm, about 10 minutes, then proceed.

> **Potential Pitfall:** If your dough is slightly underhydrated, meaning it doesn't have enough moisture to bind the flour (unlikely given the above method, but not impossible), it might crack in places. If this happens, stop rolling and trim off a piece of dough from along the edge large enough to cover the entire cracked area. Press the piece of dough firmly over the area and proceed with rolling **[K, L]**.

↑ ALL-PURPOSE FLAKY PASTRY DOUGH → ALL-PURPOSE DROP BISCUIT OR SHORTCAKE DOUGH

All-Purpose Drop Biscuit or Shortcake Dough

If you've made any kind of pastry before, you've probably heard the following conventional wisdom: Handle the dough very little, add a Goldilocks level of moisture, and keep everything as cold as possible. All of that applies to this basic cream biscuit dough, which I use for biscuit-topped cobblers and shortcakes, but what makes this pastry especially rich and tender is grating frozen butter into the dry ingredients on a box grater, then using cold cream to bring the mixture together. Grating the butter creates uniform shreds, and as the dough is rolled and stacked several times during assembly, the shreds flatten into sheets. In the oven, the water in the butter turns to steam and puffs to form flaky layers. That rolling and stacking process is an essential technique (also used to make the **All-Purpose Flaky Pastry Dough** on page 331) and can be applied to other kinds of pastry where flakiness is desired. While all of the butter and cream could weigh down the dough, a generous amount of baking powder helps to lift it up high.

MAKES ENOUGH FOR
9 SHORTCAKES OR
ONE 13 × 9-INCH COBBLER

DIFFICULTY: 2 (Easy)

ACTIVE TIME: 30 minutes

TOTAL TIME: 50 minutes

SPECIAL EQUIPMENT: Box grater, 1½-ounce scoop (optional), for drop biscuits

⅓ cup sugar (2.3 oz / 66g)

1 teaspoon finely grated orange or lemon zest

3 cups all-purpose flour (13.8 oz / 390g), plus more for the surface

4 teaspoons baking powder

1½ teaspoons Diamond Crystal kosher salt or ¾ teaspoon Morton kosher salt

1½ sticks unsalted butter (6 oz / 170g), frozen

1½ cups heavy cream (12.7 oz / 360g), plus ½ cup (4.2 oz / 120g) if making drop biscuits, chilled

Can I . . .

Make it ahead? Yes. The scooped, unbaked biscuits, covered and refrigerated, will keep for up to 12 hours (after that, the baking powder will start to lose some of its oomph), or they can be frozen for up to 1 month (make sure they're well wrapped). The unbaked shortcakes can be wrapped tightly on the plate or transferred to an airtight container and frozen for up to 1 month. Do not thaw before baking.

Add other flavorings to the dough? Yes. Before grating the frozen butter into the bowl, you can add finely chopped fresh herbs such as thyme, ground spices such as cinnamon, toasted seeds, or finely chopped nuts to the dry ingredients.

1. MIX THE DRY INGREDIENTS: In a large bowl, combine the sugar and zest and use your fingertips to massage the mixture until it's fragrant and looks like wet sand. Add the flour, baking powder, and salt and whisk to combine.

2. GRATE IN THE BUTTER: Toss the frozen sticks of butter in the flour mixture to coat, then, working quickly before your hands can warm them, grate the sticks on the large holes of a box grater directly into the bowl with the flour mixture **[see photo A, page 337]**. Toss the mixture with your hands, separating the butter shreds and coating them completely in the flour **[B, page 337]**.

3. BRING THE DOUGH TOGETHER: Make a well in the center of the bowl, add 1½ cups (12.7 oz / 360g) cream, and toss the mixture with a fork until you have a mix of shaggy pieces and loose floury bits **[C, page 337]**. Use your fingertips to break up any large, wet clumps of dough into smaller pieces, then toss the mixture loosely with your hands by lifting it up gently from the bottom of the bowl and letting it fall through your fingers (this helps to distribute the cream more evenly) **[D, E, page 337]**. Follow instructions below for making either drop biscuits or shortcakes.

4. FOR DROP BISCUITS, ADD MORE CREAM, MIX, AND PORTION: Drizzle the additional ½ cup (4.2 oz / 120g) cream into the bowl, tossing constantly with the fork to incorporate the drier areas, then switch to a flexible spatula and fold the mixture just until you have a firm, evenly mixed dough with no dry spots. Use a 1½-ounce scoop to portion the dough into pieces the size of golf balls, transferring the pieces to a dinner plate and arranging them in a single layer **[F, page 337]**. (Alternatively, use two spoons to form the drop biscuits—either eyeball the size or weigh the pieces with a kitchen scale.) You should end up with about 25 pieces. Cover the plate, transfer to the refrigerator, and chill for at least 20 minutes before using as directed for **Peach Drop Biscuit Cobbler** on page 248 or as the topping for any cobbler recipe.

5. FOR SHORTCAKES, PAT DOWN THE DOUGH: Scrape the shaggy mixture out onto a clean work surface and gather it into a pile **[G, page 337]**. Use your hands to pat the dough firmly into a square, then use a floured rolling pin to flatten the square until it's 1 inch thick **[H, I, page 337]**. Pat around the four sides with your hands to square off and compact the dough.

Essential Technique

STACKING SHORTCAKE DOUGH

6. CUT THE DOUGH IN HALF AND STACK: Use the flat edge of a bench or bowl scraper to cut the square of dough in half **[J]**, then use the bench scraper to carefully lift up one half and place it directly on top of the other (the dough will be crumbly at this point, so do your best to keep it in one piece—if it breaks apart anywhere, just press it back together). This doubles the number of layers of dough separated by shreds of butter **[K]**.

7. FLATTEN THE STACK: Use the scraper to loosen and lift the stack and dust a bit of flour underneath. Roll over the dough with the pin to lengthen it into a 1-inch-thick rectangle, dusting with more flour as needed to prevent sticking. This flattens the sheets of dough, which will turn into flaky layers in the oven.

8. CUT, STACK, AND ROLL OUT AGAIN: Cut the dough in half again, this time crosswise, and stack the halves

(doubling the layers again) as you did before **[L, M]**. Roll out the dough, dusting with more flour as needed, into a 7-inch square that's 1¼ inches thick.

> *Potential Pitfall:* For flaky shortcakes, the butter must remain cold. If it has softened, making the dough sticky, freeze it until it's firm, 10 to 15 minutes, then proceed.

9. CUT THE SHORTCAKES: Use a knife to slice off a thin strip of dough from all four sides, straightening and squaring them off (discard the strips). Cut the square into a 3-by-3 grid, making 9 square shortcakes **[N, O]**. Transfer the shortcakes to a plate, cover, and freeze until they're very firm, 15 to 20 minutes.

10. BAKE: For **Rhubarb & Raspberry Shortcakes with Poppy Seeds** on page 251, bake the shortcakes as in directed in the recipe. For plain shortcakes, space the pieces out on a parchment-lined sheet pan. Brush the tops with heavy cream and sprinkle with sugar. Bake in a 425°F oven on the middle rack until the shortcakes are risen and deep golden brown, 18 to 22 minutes. Let them cool completely on a wire rack.

EGG WHITES AND SUGAR BEATEN TO VARIOUS STAGES

Beaten egg whites are used to lighten all sorts of preparations in this book, from the filling of **Coconut Macaroon Bars** (page 209) to the batter of **Blood Orange Pudding Cake** (page 297) to the custard in **Souffléed Lemon Bread Pudding** (page 325). The proportion of sugar varies depending on the desired sweetness of the finished recipe, while the texture depends on the consistency of the base into which the egg whites are folded. Below are examples of egg whites and sugar beaten to soft, medium, and stiff peaks (and an example of overbeaten whites), which you can use as a visual reference for recipes throughout the book.

SOFT PEAKS

MEDIUM PEAKS

STIFF PEAKS

OVERBEATEN

Easy Marshmallows

Here is an easy method for making marshmallows that does not require a candy thermometer. You melt gelatin in a double boiler, add egg whites and sugar, warm the mixture until the sugar is dissolved, then whip it until it's thick and voluminous and glossy—in other words, it's a Swiss meringue set with gelatin. The recipe is less technical than the usual way of making marshmallows, which requires cooking a sugar solution to a precise temperature. This streamlining comes at a slight cost to the marshmallows' stability, as they have a tendency to weep at warmer temperatures, so store them in a cool place and plan to use them the day they're made. There are a few essential techniques to call out here: The first is softening unflavored gelatin powder, a necessary step before melting it into any mixture, be it these marshmallows, **Persimmon Panna Cotta** (page 51), or **Mango-Yogurt Mousse** (page 83), so it can set evenly and to its full potency. The second is setting up a double boiler, which provides a means of gently warming a sensitive mixture, and third is filling a pastry bag. All easy, all essential.

MAKES ABOUT 25 MARSHMALLOWS

DIFFICULTY RATING:
2 (Easy)

ACTIVE TIME: 30 minutes

TOTAL TIME: 2 hours 30 minutes

SPECIAL EQUIPMENT:
Hand mixer, pastry bag (or resealable plastic bag), kitchen torch (optional)

2½ teaspoons unflavored gelatin powder

⅔ cup granulated sugar (4.7 oz / 133g)

2 tablespoons light corn syrup

3 large egg whites (3.7 oz / 105g)

⅛ teaspoon cream of tartar or ½ teaspoon white distilled vinegar

Generous pinch of kosher salt

1 teaspoon vanilla extract

Confectioners' sugar, for dusting

Can I . . .

Make them ahead? Yes, but . . . only up to 12 hours. These marshmallows are not as stable as ones made with a cooked sugar syrup, so plan to use them the day they're made. Once they're set, keep them on the sheet pan and cover without touching any of the marshmallows (an upside-down bowl or pan works well for this). Store at cool room temperature to prevent weeping.

Use a stand mixer instead of a hand mixer? Yes. Follow the recipe through the step of dissolving the sugar in the egg white and gelatin mixture over the double boiler, then pour it into a stand mixer fitted with the whisk attachment and proceed as written.

Essential Technique

SOFTENING GELATIN

1. SPRINKLE THE GELATIN OVER COLD WATER: Fill a small, shallow bowl with ¼ cup (2 oz / 57g) of cold tap water and slowly sprinkle the gelatin across the surface so the granules separate as they fall into the bowl **[see photo A, page 343]**. Do not stir the mixture. Using cold water ensures that the granules hydrate slowly and evenly.

2. LET THE GELATIN HYDRATE: Let the gelatin sit until the granules have absorbed the water, look swollen and translucent, and the mixture is solid and bouncy to the touch, 5 to 10 minutes. Hydrating the gelatin, also known as "blooming," is required so it can melt fully and evenly into the recipe.

Essential Technique

SETTING UP A DOUBLE BOILER

3. SIMMER WATER IN A SAUCEPAN: Fill a medium saucepan with about 1 inch of water and bring to a simmer over medium-low heat, then reduce the heat to low. You want the water to be steaming and barely bubbling, if at all.

4. PLACE A BOWL OVER TOP: Rest a medium heatproof bowl, preferably metal, on top of the saucepan **[B, page 343]**. The bottom of the bowl should sit stably inside without touching the water, while the sides should extend several inches beyond the rim of the saucepan so you can lift it off easily (be careful, the bowl will quickly heat up). This setup, which mimics a piece of cookware called a double boiler, uses the steam inside the saucepan to gently warm the contents of the bowl.

5. MELT THE GELATIN: Scrape the softened gelatin into the bowl of the double boiler **[C, page 343]** and stir with a flexible spatula until it's completely melted and translucent with no sign of any granules, 1 to 2 minutes **[D, page 343]**.

→

Potential Pitfall: If the gelatin isn't completely melted, the marshmallow mixture won't fully set and will deflate as it sits. Make sure you examine the melted gelatin closely to confirm it's granule-free.

6. ADD THE SUGAR AND EGG WHITES AND HEAT UNTIL DISSOLVED: Carefully remove the bowl from the saucepan, place it on the work surface, and let it cool for a minute. Add the sugar, corn syrup, egg whites, cream of tartar, and a generous pinch of salt and whisk to combine. Place the bowl back over the saucepan and whisk continuously until the sugar is dissolved and the egg white mixture has a sticky, syrupy consistency **[E]**, about 5 minutes (rub a dab between your fingers—it should feel grit-free). If you are concerned about consuming unpasteurized egg whites, continue to whisk the mixture constantly over the double boiler until it registers 160°F on an instant-read thermometer, which will take several minutes longer.

7. BEAT THE MARSHMALLOW MIXTURE: Carefully remove the bowl from the saucepan. Use a hand mixer to beat the mixture, starting on medium-low and gradually increasing to high, until you have a very thick, dense, and glossy meringue-like mixture that holds a stiff peak, 7 to 9 minutes **[F]**. Beat in the vanilla. If making the **S'mores Tart** (page 257), proceed to the recipe. If making individual marshmallows, set the bowl aside and proceed to step 8.

Essential Technique

FILLING A PASTRY BAG

8. FOLD OVER THE BAG: Place a pastry bag or resealable plastic bag inside a tall and narrow 1-quart container or large, tall glass and fold down the top of the bag around the outside of the container or glass (this will help keep the sides of the bag clean).

9. FILL THE BAG: Use a flexible spatula to scrape about one-third of the mixture into the bag and push it down toward the bottom. Scrape in the remaining mixture, taking care not to form big air pockets, which would make it more difficult to pipe **[G]**.

10. SEAL: Lift up the sides of the bag to unfold them and pull the bag out of the container **[H]**. Then, pinning the top of the bag to the work surface and starting at that end, drag the edge of a bench scraper or other straightedge firmly down the length of the bag to force the mixture toward the point or corner **[I]**. Gather the ends of the bag and twist to seal. Set the bag aside.

11. PIPE THE MARSHMALLOWS AND LET SET: Line a sheet pan with a silicone baking mat or parchment paper and use a fine-mesh sieve to dust the entire surface generously and evenly with a layer of confectioners' sugar. Snip a 1-inch opening in the tip or corner of the bag and pipe ping-pong-sized dollops of the marshmallow mixture onto the prepared sheet pan, piping until you've used the entire mixture. If you prefer a looser look, you could spoon free-form blobs of marshmallow onto the sheet pan. Set the pan in a cool spot and let the marshmallows sit uncovered until they are set, about 4 hours.

All-Purpose Meringue

Meringue is one of those pastry preparations that, by definition, is sweet. For egg whites to transform into a billowy and glossy meringue that bakes into a light and crispy shell with a perfectly marshmallow-y center, they're beaten with an even greater weight of sugar (all that sweetness just means that meringue pairs best with unsweetened ingredients like tart fruit and toasted nuts). To achieve maximum volume and stability, the whites are beaten on their own until foamy before any sugar is added. Then, to prevent weeping (when meringue releases a syrupy liquid), the sugar is added gradually so it has time to dissolve. The process requires some patience and attention, but it's an essential technique that's called upon repeatedly and to varying degrees throughout the book so egg whites can lift and lighten preparations such as mousses, cake batters, and soufflés. For a visual guide to beaten egg whites at different stages, see page 339.

MAKES ENOUGH MERINGUE FOR 1 PAVLOVA OR 16 LARGE MERINGUE COOKIES

DIFFICULTY: 2 (Easy)

DAIRY-FREE, GLUTEN-FREE

ACTIVE TIME: 10 minutes (does not include baking)

TOTAL TIME: 10 minutes

SPECIAL EQUIPMENT: Hand mixer

6 large egg whites (7.4 oz / 210g), at room temperature

½ teaspoon Diamond Crystal kosher salt or ¼ teaspoon Morton kosher salt

⅛ teaspoon cream of tartar or ½ teaspoon distilled white vinegar

1 cup granulated sugar (7 oz / 200g)

1 teaspoon vanilla extract

1 cup confectioners' sugar (3 oz / 110g)

Can I . . .

Halve the recipe? Yes. Halve all of the above ingredient quantities and follow the recipe as written, beating the meringue in a clean medium bowl. Keep in mind that the smaller quantity of egg whites will whip faster.

Use a stand mixer instead of a hand mixer? Yes. Combine the egg whites, salt, and cream of tartar in a stand mixer fitted with the whisk attachment and proceed with the recipe as written, but note that the mixing times will be shorter because of the stand mixer's superior power.

Make it without an electric mixer? Not recommended. While it's possible to whip meringue by hand (it's what they did before electric mixers, after all), it's only practical to do so with a very large whisk and a copper bowl. Unless you have these items—or superhuman arm strength and stamina—I recommend using a hand or stand mixer.

Essential Technique

BEATING EGG WHITES AND SUGAR

1. START WITH A CLEAN NONPLASTIC BOWL: Ensure you have a large, clean bowl that's completely grease-free, as any fat residue will inhibit whipping (to be extra sure, you can rub the inside of the bowl with the cut side of a lemon wedge or a paper towel dipped in vinegar). Don't use a plastic bowl, because even clean plastic retains fat residue **[see photo A, page 345]**.

2. BREAK UP THE WHITES: In the bowl, combine the egg whites, salt, and cream of tartar or vinegar (cream of tartar and vinegar make the egg whites more acidic, which helps to stabilize them). Beat the mixture using a hand mixer on medium-low speed until the egg whites are broken up and fluid, about 30 seconds **[B]**, then increase the speed to medium and beat until the mixture goes from yellow and translucent to white and foamy, about 45 seconds **[C]**.

3. ADD THE SUGAR GRADUALLY: Beating constantly on medium-high, very gradually add the granulated sugar, allowing a thin, steady stream of granules to cascade into the bowl. Incorporating the sugar will take several minutes, so be patient, as you want the egg whites to whip slowly and the sugar to dissolve **[D]**.

4. WHIP THE MERINGUE: Once you've added all the granulated sugar, increase the mixer speed to high and beat until the sugar is dissolved (rub a dab between your fingers to check for any grit) and the meringue is thick, glossy, and holds a stiff peak, about 2 minutes **[E, F]**.

5. ADD THE VANILLA AND CONFECTIONERS' SUGAR AND BAKE: Beat in the vanilla, then turn off the mixer and set it aside. Holding a fine-mesh sieve over the bowl of meringue, add the confectioners' sugar to the sieve and sift it over the meringue **[G]**. Use a large flexible spatula to gently fold the confectioners' sugar into the meringue just until it's incorporated **[H]** (for more on the proper technique, see Folding a Mixture, page 351). Form and bake the meringue as directed in the recipe.

Salted Caramel Sauce

This salted caramel sauce is a good place to start for any beginner looking to get more comfortable with caramel cookery. The essential technique here is cooking a "wet" caramel, which starts by dissolving the sugar in water and then bringing it to a boil (in contrast to a "dry" caramel, which starts by melting sugar directly in a dry pan with no liquid). The sugar will only start to caramelize once all the water has boiled off, which takes several minutes, but once it starts to color, the process happens quickly, so pay close attention to avoid burning and have all your other ingredients ready. The lighter the color, the sweeter and less intense the caramel flavor. Because I prefer the intensity of a very bittersweet caramel in most applications, I cook mine to a dark amber and halt the cooking when I see wisps of smoke, just shy of the burning point.

MAKES ABOUT 2 CUPS

DIFFICULTY: 2 (Easy)

GLUTEN-FREE

ACTIVE TIME: 20 minutes

TOTAL TIME: 20 minutes, plus time to cool

1 cup sugar (7 oz / 200g)

1 cup heavy cream (8.5 oz / 240g), at room temperature

6 tablespoons unsalted butter (3 oz / 85g), cut into ½-inch pieces, chilled

Seeds scraped from ½ vanilla bean or 2 teaspoons vanilla extract

1 teaspoon Diamond Crystal kosher salt or ½ teaspoon Morton kosher salt

Essential Technique

COOKING A WET CARAMEL

1. GET YOUR BRUSH READY: Fill a glass with water, place a pastry brush inside, and set it next to the stove. You will use this brush to wash down the sides of the saucepan, dissolving any sugar crystals that form during cooking, since any undissolved crystals could cause the entire sugar mixture to crystallize and turn grainy.

2. STIR TO DISSOLVE THE SUGAR AND BRING TO A BOIL: Pour ¼ cup (2 oz / 57g) water into a heavy-bottomed medium saucepan, then add the sugar (adding the water first encourages the sugar to dissolve). Avoid using a flimsy saucepan, as the caramel will more readily burn around the sides. Stir the mixture gently with a heatproof flexible spatula over medium-high heat just until the sugar dissolves to form a clear syrup and the mixture comes to a boil, about 3 minutes.

3. STOP STIRRING AND WASH DOWN THE SIDES: When the syrup boils, stop stirring and instead swirl the saucepan to equalize the temperature and promote even cooking (stirring at this phase encourages crystallization, which you want to avoid). Using the wet pastry brush, occasionally wash down the sides of the saucepan where you see stuck-on sugar crystals **[see photo A, page 347]**.

4. COOK THE SYRUP, SWIRLING: As the water boils off and the syrup becomes more viscous, the bubbles will become larger and slower to pop, a sign that caramelization is near. Continue to cook, swirling the saucepan and brushing down the sides as needed, until the syrup has taken on a faint golden color, about 4 minutes **[B]**.

5. COOK UNTIL THE CARAMEL IS DEEP AMBER: Turn the heat down to medium and continue to cook, keeping a close watch and swirling the saucepan frequently, until the mixture turns medium golden **[C]**, then amber (it will also become progressively more fluid and less bubbly). When the mixture reaches a deep amber, is very fluid, and just starting to release wisps of smoke **[D]**, remove the saucepan from the heat and proceed immediately to the next step, which will halt the cooking (otherwise the hot caramel will continue to cook and quickly burn).

A

B

C

D

E

F

Make it ahead? Yes. The salted caramel sauce, refrigerated in a 1-pint jar or lidded container, will keep for up to 6 months. To rewarm it, scrape the cold, solidified sauce into a double boiler (for more information, see Setting Up a Double Boiler, page 341) and stir until it's warm and fluid.

Get stuck-on caramel out of my saucepan? Yes. Caramel, like sugar, will dissolve, so simply flush the saucepan with warm water and eventually it will disappear.

6. ADD THE CREAM AND BUTTER AND FINISH THE SAUCE: Add the cream in a slow, steady stream and stir until the sauce is completely smooth **[E]** (it will sputter, so watch out—because this is a liquid caramel, we're not worried about crystallization at this point, so stirring is okay). Add the butter a piece or two at a time, stirring until the pieces are melted and incorporated before adding more **[F]**. Stir in the vanilla and salt. Let the sauce cool at room temperature, stirring occasionally, until it's warm but not hot. It will thicken as it cools.

Crème Anglaise

Crème anglaise may sound fancy but it's a very basic custard—a stirred custard, more specifically, made entirely on the stovetop. If you've made pastry cream or pudding, it's the same series of steps but without added starch, which keeps the consistency thin and pourable. Crème anglaise is used as the base for vanilla ice cream and as an all-purpose sauce for topping other desserts such as soufflés, but, poured over ripe berries, it constitutes a dessert unto itself. The essential technique highlighted in this recipe, blanching and tempering eggs, applies to almost every custard or curd recipe you'll ever make. "Blanching," a term that comes from the French verb *blanchir*, which means "to whiten," is a process in which egg yolks and/or whole eggs and sugar are beaten until the mixture is pale, thick, and ribbony, while tempering gradually raises the temperature of the eggs by streaming in a portion of the hot custard base so they don't scramble in the custard.

MAKES ABOUT 3 CUPS

DIFFICULTY: 2 (Easy)

GLUTEN-FREE

ACTIVE TIME: 20 minutes

TOTAL TIME: 4 hours 20 minutes (includes 4 hours for chilling)

2 cups half-and-half (16 oz / 480g)

Seeds scraped from ½ vanilla bean (pod reserved) or 2 teaspoons vanilla extract

Generous pinch of kosher salt

5 large egg yolks (2.6 oz / 75g), at room temperature

⅓ cup sugar (2.3 oz / 66g)

1. HEAT THE CUSTARD BASE: In a small saucepan, whisk together the half-and-half, vanilla seeds and reserved pod, and salt. (If using vanilla extract, set it aside to add at the end.) Heat the mixture over medium heat, whisking occasionally, until it's steaming and just starting to ripple beneath the surface, about 5 minutes. Remove the saucepan from the heat.

Essential Technique

BLANCHING AND TEMPERING EGGS

2. WHISK THE EGG YOLKS AND SUGAR: In a medium bowl, whisk the egg yolks and sugar until combined. Continue to whisk, this time vigorously, until the mixture is very pale, thick, and voluminous, and forms a "ribbon" as it falls off the whisk back into the bowl, about 2 minutes **[see photo A, page 349]** (a "ribbon" means that the mixture will layer onto itself in a ribbon-like shape and sit above the surface for a few seconds before it settles into the bowl).

> *Potential Pitfall:* Proceed with this step only once the half-and-half is hot, as prolonged contact between the sugar and yolks leads to the formation of hardened bits of yolk that won't dissolve in the custard.

3. STREAM SOME OF THE HOT BASE INTO THE YOLKS: Whisking the yolk mixture constantly, slowly pour about two-thirds of the hot base into the bowl. This will gradually raise the temperature of the yolks so they don't curdle when you add them to the saucepan. Whisk the contents of the bowl into the saucepan with the remaining base **[B]**.

4. COOK THE CUSTARD: Set the saucepan over medium-low heat and cook the custard, stirring constantly with a heatproof flexible spatula and continuously scraping all around the sides and across the bottom, until the foam on the surface disappears and the mixture is thickened to the consistency of smooth tomato soup, about 4 minutes, then remove the saucepan from the heat. Do not let the mixture boil.

5. CHECK THE CONSISTENCY: Dip a wooden or metal spoon into the custard and run your finger across the back—it should leave a sharp, clean line with an opaque coating of custard on either side **[C]**. This means your custard is cooked. If you want to be absolutely sure, take the temperature with an instant-read thermometer—it should register 170°F.

Can I . . .

Make it ahead? Yes, recommended. The chilled crème anglaise will keep, covered and refrigerated, for up to 1 week. Serve it cold.

Add a flavoring? Yes. Stir 2 tablespoons Grand Marnier (or another spirit), 2 tablespoons brewed espresso, or 1.8 oz (50g) chopped bittersweet chocolate into the hot custard (if chocolate, until melted) to flavor it.

6. COVER AND CHILL: If using vanilla extract, stir it into the custard, then transfer the mixture to a 1-quart lidded container, cover, and refrigerate until the crème anglaise is cold, at least 4 hours. If, for any reason, you have lumps in the custard (a result of the eggs overcooking in places), strain it first through a fine-mesh sieve.

Other Essential Techniques

FOLDING A MIXTURE

Folding is a gentle mixing method typically employed to preserve the volume of an airy component like beaten egg whites or whipped cream while incorporating it into another preparation, like a soufflé base or mousse, in order to lighten it. It works best when the components are similar in texture, but if they're not—for example, melted chocolate and beaten egg whites for chocolate mousse—the denser component is quickly mixed with a portion of the lighter one to lighten it before the two are folded together. Folding can also be used to incorporate flour when you want to minimize gluten development.

1. COMBINE, SCRAPE, AND LIFT: Working in a wide bowl with plenty of room to maneuver, combine the two components and, holding the bowl with one hand, use the other hand to draw a large flexible spatula down the side of the bowl and along the bottom so it's underneath the mixture, then bring it upward through the mixture while simultaneously turning the spatula over. The idea is to mix the components gently by lifting what's sitting on the bottom of the bowl and bringing it to the top.

2. ROTATE AND REPEAT: Rotate the bowl slightly and repeat the motion, this time drawing the spatula down through the center of the mixture, along the bottom, then back up again, turning it over with a flick of the wrist as you reach the surface. Continue to fold, using this motion and rotating the bowl each time, until the end point noted in the recipe.

CREAMING BUTTER AND SUGAR

While it's possible to cream butter and sugar to a moderate degree by hand with a wooden spoon or flexible spatula (and lots of persistence and elbow grease), it's so much easier to achieve thorough creaming with an electric mixer. The mixture should be pale, fluffy, and voluminous. The beating action forces sharp-edged sugar crystals to cut into the soft butter, which creates tons of tiny air pockets and dissolves some of the sugar. Those tiny air pockets carry over into batters and doughs and expand in the hot oven during baking, which is why creaming lends lift to cakes and cookies (called "mechanical leavening").

1. COMBINE THE SUGAR AND BUTTER: Make sure the butter is at room temperature but not warm. It should have a waxy, malleable texture and not look shiny or greasy. In a large bowl, combine the butter and sugar and beat with a hand mixer on low speed just until the mixture is smooth. (You can also combine the butter and sugar in a stand mixer fitted with the paddle attachment and mix on low.)

2. BEAT THE MIXTURE, SCRAPING DOWN THE SIDES, UNTIL LIGHT AND FLUFFY: Increase the mixer speed to medium-high and continue to beat, pausing often to thoroughly scrape down the sides of the bowl, until the mixture is very pale, voluminous, and fluffy. Depending on the quantities of butter and sugar, this could take upwards of 5 minutes with a hand mixer (and a minute or two less with a stand mixer). It is possible to overbeat the butter and sugar, which would cause the mixture to deflate, so no need to go beyond the point of light and fluffy.

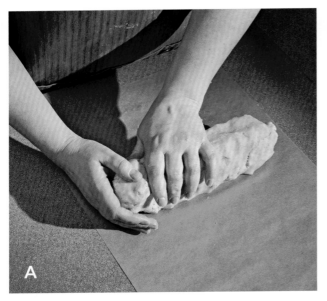

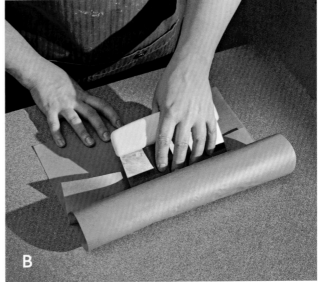

FORMING LOGS
OF COOKIE DOUGH

Shaping cookie dough into tight, compact cylinders allows you to slice and bake dozens of uniform coin-shaped cookies efficiently and with very few scraps.

1. SQUEEZE THE DOUGH INTO A ROUGH LOG: Place a rectangular piece of parchment paper on the work surface and place all (or a portion, depending on the recipe) of the dough on top. Squeeze the cookie dough with your hands to form it into a rough log running across the center of the parchment, taking care to squeeze out any air pockets **[A]**.

2. PRESS THE DOUGH INTO THE PARCHMENT: Fold the edge of parchment paper that's farthest from you over the dough. Hold the parchment paper in place with one hand, then, with your other, rest the flat edge of a bench scraper on top of the parchment and push it toward the dough at a downward angle **[B]**. This will compress the

dough inside the parchment into a round shape. Repeat this motion across the length of the dough, trying not to tear the parchment, until you have a tight, even cylinder.

3. WRAP THE LOG IN PLASTIC AND COMPACT AGAIN: Roll up the log in the parchment paper as snugly as possible, then wrap the entire log tightly in plastic, leaving a bit of overhang on both ends. Firmly twist the ends of the plastic wrap (along with any overhanging parchment), further compressing the dough into a cylinder and flattening the ends **[C, D]**. Refrigerate the dough until it's firm and sliceable.

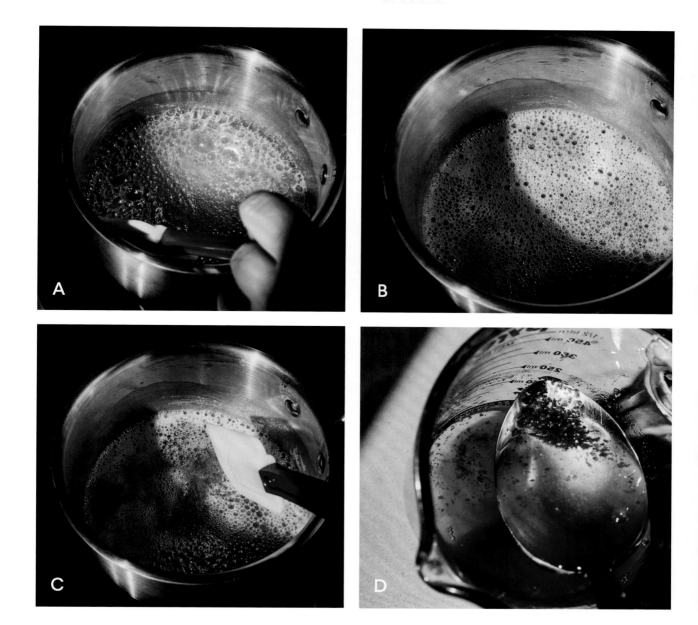

BROWNING BUTTER

Brown butter has an intensely buttery and toasty caramel-like flavor and can be used in place of regular butter in many recipes. It's made by cooking butter until the water content boils off completely and the milk solids (made of proteins and sugars) turn golden brown. The lack of water means browned butter won't contribute to gluten development, so cakes and cookies made with it will have a tender, at times crumbly texture (as well as, sometimes, a subtle greasiness). If substituting browned butter for regular butter, let it come to the temperature specified in the recipe.

1. BRING THE BUTTER TO A BOIL: In a saucepan (whatever size specified in the recipe), melt the butter over medium heat, then bring it to boil, stirring constantly and scraping the bottom and sides with a heatproof flexible spatula to prevent the milk solids from sticking as well as to prevent hot butter from splattering as the water boils off **[A]**.

2. COOK UNTIL THE WATER HAS EVAPORATED: Continue to cook the butter, scraping the bottom and sides of the saucepan, until the sputtering subsides and a foam forms on the surface, a sign that the water is nearly gone and browning will soon occur **[B]**. Continue to stir until you see tiny golden brown specks floating throughout the butter and the mixture smells like caramel **[C]**.

3. REMOVE FROM THE HEAT: Remove the saucepan from the heat and continue to stir until the foam subsides and the specks of milk solids turn a deep shade of coppery brown, then scrape it into a heatproof bowl, making sure you get every last speck **[D]**. Don't leave the butter in the hot saucepan as the milk solids will continue to cook and quickly burn.

WHIPPING CREAM (AND RESCUING OVERWHIPPED CREAM)

Cream with a fat content over 30% (heavy cream is around 36%) can be whipped until it's light and voluminous. Whipped cream is a common garnish but can also be used to lighten mixtures such as mousses and semifreddos. The consistency can range anywhere from loose and droopy to firm and stiff-peaked. Another high-fat dairy product such as sour cream, mascarpone, or crème fraîche can also be combined with heavy cream and whipped.

1. WHIP TO SOFT PEAKS: In a large bowl, with a hand mixer or whisk, beat chilled heavy cream (make sure it's very cold or it will not whip) and a pinch of salt, starting on low speed to avoid splatters. Gradually increase the speed to medium-high as the cream thickens and beat just until it's thick, barely pourable, and forms a flat, droopy mound when you lift up the beaters or whisk. This is softly whipped **[see photo A, page 354]**. (You can also beat the cream in a stand mixer fitted with the whisk attachment, but keep in mind it's harder to judge the consistency and easier to overbeat.)

2. WHIP TO MEDIUM PEAKS: For a medium whipped cream, continue to beat the cream on medium-high just until it forms a mound that holds its shape but does not stand straight upright **[B]**.

3. WHIP TO STIFF PEAKS: For a firmly whipped cream, continue to beat just until the cream forms a straight, upright peak off the end of the beaters or whisk (aka a "stiff" peak) and holds the clear, sharp trail of the beaters or whisk **[C]**. Do not beat beyond this stage, or the particles of fat will start to clump together and separate from the liquid and make the whipped cream grainy (at this point, you're on your way to making butter). If this happens, see step 5.

4. SWEETEN AND FLAVOR THE WHIPPED CREAM (IF DESIRED): To sweeten the whipped cream, beat in confectioners' sugar (sifted first, if lumpy) a tablespoon at a time until combined and you're satisfied with the sweetness. You can also sweeten the whipped cream with a tablespoon or two of maple syrup. To add a flavoring, beat in 1 teaspoon vanilla extract, 1 tablespoon bourbon, or a pinch of cinnamon or nutmeg for every cup of liquid cream you started with.

5. RESCUE OVERWHIPPED CREAM: If your whipped cream has gone grainy from overbeating, fear not. For every 1 cup of liquid cream that you started with, heat 4 additional tablespoons of cream in a small saucepan over medium-low heat (or in a small bowl in the microwave), just until it's warm. Pour the warm cream into the bowl of overwhipped cream **[D]** and fold with a flexible spatula until thoroughly combined **[E]** (for more on the proper technique, see Folding a Mixture, page 351). This will loosen and smooth out the texture of the overwhipped cream **[F]**.

MACERATING FRUIT

Sugar is hygroscopic, meaning it will pull water from its environment. When sugar is mixed with fruit, it draws out the juices in a process called maceration. Often, a bit of liquid such as citrus juice or alcohol is added to the mixture, which is left at room temperature until the fruit is softened and the sugar has dissolved into the juices to form a syrup. Macerating intensifies flavor and removes the raw texture of fruits like berries and stone fruit, and the syrup it produces can be used as a sauce in desserts (strawberry shortcake, for example).

1. PREPARE THE FRUIT: Wash the fruit in cold water and remove any stems, hulls, and/or pits. Whole fruit must be cut or broken up in some way, otherwise the sugar will not be able to penetrate the skin, so slice or lightly crush the fruit to expose the interior. Place it in a bowl.

2. MIX WITH SUGAR AND LET SIT: Sprinkle sugar over the fruit (either the amount specified in the recipe or to taste). If desired, add a tablespoon or more of lemon, lime, or orange juice, or a splash of wine or liqueur, and very gently stir the mixture just to coat the pieces of fruit. Cover the bowl and let it sit at room temperature, swirling the bowl a few times to encourage the sugar to dissolve, until you see pooling, syrupy juices and the fruit is soft, at least 30 minutes.

CUTTING CITRUS

Separating juicy citrus segments from the tough, bitter portions of the fruit allows you to fully enjoy the flavor and texture of oranges, grapefruits, and other citrus fruits. It's done by cutting away the peel and pith with a sharp knife and then cutting between the membranes to free individual segments.

1. SLICE OFF THE ENDS OF THE FRUIT: Using a small, sharp knife and cutting crosswise, slice off the stem and opposite ends of the citrus fruit (the north and south poles), cutting just enough to create two flat surfaces and expose the fruit inside **[see photo A, page 356]**.

2. REMOVE THE PEEL AND PITH: Stand the fruit upright on one of the cut ends and use the knife to slice lengthwise down along one side, following the contour of the fruit and removing all of the peel and white pith, as well as the membrane covering the outer portion of the segments **[B]**. Rotate the fruit and continue cutting lengthwise all the way around until you've removed the entire exterior, exposing the segments.

3. SLICE CROSSWISE INTO ROUNDS OR CUT INTO SEGMENTS: For rounds of citrus, slice the fruit crosswise into rounds of any thickness **[C]**. For segments, also called suprêmes, hold the citrus in the palm of your nondominant hand over a bowl. Use the knife to cut down along either side of each membrane to release the segments one at a time, allowing them and any juices to fall into the bowl below **[D]**. Continue until you've worked your way around the entire fruit. Squeeze the membranes to extract any remaining juices, then discard it along with any seeds.

POACHING FRUIT

Poaching is the technique of gently cooking fruit—particularly firmer fruits such as pears, cherries, and pineapple—in a sweetened liquid until the flesh is tender but not falling apart. The sugar in the poaching liquid sweetens the fruit and draws out some of its juices, reducing the water content of poached fruit so it keeps for a long time refrigerated in its poaching liquid. Some fruits such as quince shouldn't be eaten raw (raw quince is hard and astringent), so poaching is a common method of preparing them. Dried fruit such as prunes and apricots can also be poached to plump and tenderize them.

1. PREPARE THE FRUIT: Peel, core, pit, and/or cut the fruit as necessary. Set it aside.

2. ASSEMBLE THE POACHING LIQUID: Select a saucepan, high-sided skillet, or Dutch oven large enough to hold the fruit in a single layer. Combine the liquid ingredients (water, wine, fruit juice, etc.), sugar and/or other sweetener (such as honey), and a pinch of salt in the poaching vessel. Add other flavorings if desired, such as whole spices or citrus zest. There should be sufficient poaching liquid to submerge the fruit.

3. BRING THE POACHING LIQUID TO A SIMMER: Bring the mixture to a simmer over medium-low heat, stirring occasionally to dissolve the sugar. It should be bubbling gently, not aggressively. Meanwhile, cut a round of parchment paper the same diameter as the poaching vessel.

4. ADD THE FRUIT AND COVER: Add the fruit and arrange the pieces in a single layer, then place the parchment round directly onto the surface of the poaching liquid so it's covering the fruit. Press out any air bubbles and allow some of the liquid to pool on top of the parchment. This will keep the fruit submerged so it cooks evenly.

5. POACH: Heat the mixture over medium-low heat just until you see tiny bubbles forming around the edges of the parchment. Adjust the heat to maintain a bare simmer and cook the fruit until it's tender but not falling apart and the tip of a paring knife slides into the flesh with no resistance, then remove from the heat. The poaching time will vary depending on the fruit, the size of the pieces, and ripeness. For some fruits that are prone to breaking down, such as rhubarb (not technically a fruit, but you know what I mean), you'll want to remove the saucepan from the heat as soon as it comes back to a simmer to allow the residual heat to slowly cook the pieces. Refer to specific recipes for cooking times.

2. BRING THE WATER TO A BOIL: The amount of water you'll need depends on the size of your roasting pan and the baking vessel(s), but it probably won't exceed 8 cups. Bring the water to a boil in a kettle or in a medium saucepan over high heat (a kettle is handy because the spout will make it easier to pour), then remove from the heat.

3. POUR THE WATER CAREFULLY INTO THE PAN: Line the bottom of the roasting pan with a thin kitchen towel to create a nonslip surface, then place the baking vessel(s) in the center (some recipes will first have you cover it/them). If you're baking multiple ramekins, space them out evenly. Slide out the oven rack and carefully transfer the roasting pan to the rack, then slowly pour the hot water into the roasting pan until it reaches halfway up the sides of the inner vessel(s), trying not to splash any water (filling the roasting pan with water directly on the rack is safer and more spill-proof than transferring it to the oven already filled). Cover the entire roasting pan if directed in the recipe, then gently slide in the rack and bake as directed.

CHILLING IN AN ICE BATH

A quick way to cool down a hot mixture or liquid is to stir it in a metal bowl partially submerged in ice water, called an ice bath. Because of the direct heat transfer that takes place, an ice bath is much more efficient at cooling a mixture than the air inside a refrigerator or freezer.

1. FILL A BOWL PARTIALLY WITH ICE WATER: Fill a large, wide bowl about one-quarter full with ice, then add cold water just until the ice is barely submerged.

2. SET A METAL BOWL INSIDE THE ICE WATER: Place a medium metal bowl inside the large bowl (metal works best because it's a good conductor and will help cool the mixture quickly, unlike glass or plastic). Press down on the metal bowl to displace the water and make sure the water level does not reach the top of either bowl or overflow. If it does, pour out some of the ice water.

3. STIR THE MIXTURE UNTIL COLD: Pour any hot mixture such as a custard, curd, or compote into the smaller metal bowl and use a flexible spatula to stir it continuously, scraping the bottom and sides of the bowl where the mixture cools down and thickens fastest, in order to equalize the temperature. Continue to stir until the entire mixture is room temperature, cool, or cold to the touch, depending on the recipe, then remove the bowl from the ice water.

BAKING IN A WATER BATH (BAIN-MARIE)

Custards, custard-based desserts such as cheesecake and bread pudding, and some sponge cakes require gentle and even cooking, so they're baked inside a shallow baking dish or roasting pan partially filled with hot water (called a water bath or bain-marie). Because the temperature of the surrounding water never exceeds 212°F (boiling), the baking vessel is insulated from higher temperatures, ensuring that the eggs in custard and sponge cake don't overcook around the sides before the center is done, producing an even, consistent texture.

1. PREHEAT THE OVEN AND SELECT A PAN OR BAKING DISH FOR THE WATER BATH: Make sure your oven is preheated to the temperature specified in the recipe and that your oven rack is in the correct position. Select a roasting pan or large shallow baking dish that's at least 2 inches deep and can comfortably hold the baking vessel(s) called for in the recipe (whether it's individual ramekins, a springform pan, or something else). You want the baking vessel(s) to have an inch or two of clearance all the way around.

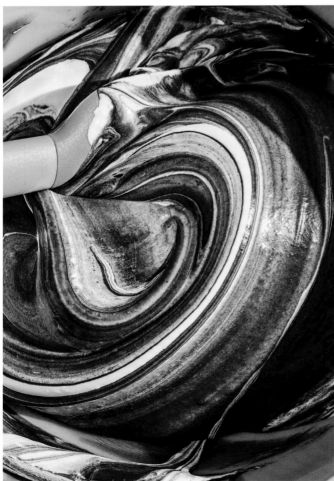

Acknowledgments

First and foremost, I want to thank my husband, Harris, for providing unwavering and impassioned support, inspiration, and encouragement—always, but especially throughout the process of writing this book and *Dessert Person* as well. I could not have done either without you. I also want to thank my family: Mom, Dad, Emily, Jane, Don, Nick, my niece and nephew, and my in-laws, Ross and Morisa. You have all nurtured me, bolstered me, and provided much-needed (and much-appreciated) perspective.

My heartfelt thanks also goes out to:

My literary agent, David Black, a great friend and most trusted resource, for his guidance and reassurance, as well as Ayla Zuraw-Friedland and Rachel Ludwig at the David Black Agency, for their hard work and assistance.

The team at Clarkson Potter: My editor, Raquel Pelzel, for her patience, understanding, and guidance; Stephanie Huntwork, for her artistic input and support; Mia Johnson, for designing such a beautiful book and sharing in my vision; Francis Lam, for his thoughtful encouragement; Joyce Wong, for her incredible attention to detail and commitment throughout the editing process; and Bianca Cruz, for her superb assistance with practically every aspect of this project.

My creative team: Photographer Jenny Huang for the extraordinary talent and dedication she brought to conceiving and executing the exceptional images in this book, with assistance from Shri Prasham Parameshwaran; food stylist Tyna Hoang, along with Alyssa Kondracki and Veronica Martinez, for their superlative food styling and tireless work throughout our shoot; and prop stylist Nicole Louie, with assistance from Camila Guerrero, for bringing boundless creativity and supreme organization to building the world of *What's for Dessert*.

My video crew: Vincent Cross, Cal Robertson, and Michael Guggino. You all supported me through this process with humor, understanding, and encouragement. I am so appreciative of your friendship and the work you've put into helping me build the *Dessert Person* YouTube channel.

My friends, especially Emily Graff, for her compassionate advice and patient listening, and Sue Li, for always inspiring me. Albert Husmillo, for assisting me with the utmost attention and care, and for being such a joy to work with. My neighbors, Brant and Anne Marie Janeway, for their enthusiastic feedback. My recipe testers, for volunteering their time and energies and helping me to make the recipes as good as they could be.

All the Dessert People out there who bake from *Dessert Person,* watch my videos on YouTube, and support my work: This book is for you, too.

Lastly: Maya, Felix, and Archie—what would I do without you!

A special acknowledgment to the following brands for loaning us props to help make the photography in *What's for Dessert* beautiful and unique.

- Lily Juliet: Tapas Bowls in Celadon (page 34, 334, 356), pink (pages 28 to 29, 356), and blue (page 28, 34, 268, 345, 356); Violet Cake Stand with Celadon Base (page 226)

- Caspari: Dress Stewart Tartan Die-Cut Placemat (page 155); Dessin Passementerie Paper Linen Cocktail Napkins (page 36, 37, 78, 205, 226); Color Theory Paper Cocktail Napkins (page 177); Garden Gate Paper Linen Cocktail Napkins (page 21, 131, 139, 313, 314)

- Areaware: Steven Bukowski Terrace Candle Holder (page 21, 131), Dusen Dusen Taper Candles (page 21, 131), Hex Vase (page 130, 168)

Index

Published in the United States by Clarkson Potter/
Publishers, an imprint of Random House, a division of
Penguin Random House LLC, New York.
ClarksonPotter.com
RandomHouseBooks.com

CLARKSON POTTER is a trademark and POTTER
with colophon is a registered trademark of Penguin
Random House LLC.

Library of Congress Cataloging-in-Publication Data
has been applied for.

ISBN 978-1-9848-2698-5
Ebook ISBN 978-1-9848-2699-2

Photographer: Jenny Huang
Food Stylist: Tyna Hoang
Prop Stylist: Nicole Louie
Editor: Raquel Pelzel
Editorial Assistant: Bianca Cruz
Designer: Mia Johnson
Production Editor: Joyce Wong
Production Manager: Jessica Heim
Compositors: Merri Ann Morrell and Hannah Hunt
Copy Editor: Kate Slate
Indexer: Elizabeth Parson
Marketer: Allison Renzulli
Publicist: Erica Gelbard

Printed in China

10 9 8 7 6 5 4 3 2 1

First Edition

Claire Saffitz is the *New York Times* bestselling author of *Dessert Person* and host of the cookbook companion YouTube series *Dessert Person*. She lives in and out of New York City with her husband, cats, and chickens.